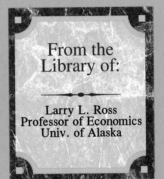

D1053436

Macroeconomics
**EQUILIBRIUM AND
DISEQUILIBRIUM ANALYSIS**

James Rolph Edwards

NORTHERN MONTANA COLLEGE

Macroeconomics

EQUILIBRIUM AND
DISEQUILIBRIUM ANALYSIS

Macmillan Publishing Company
NEW YORK

Collier Macmillan, Inc.
TORONTO

Maxwell Macmillan International
NEW YORK   OXFORD   SINGAPORE   SYDNEY

Editor: Caroline Carney
Production Supervisor: Elaine W. Wetterau
Production Manager: Sandra Moore
Cover Designer: Natasha Sylvester
Cover Photograph: Marjory Dressler
Illustrations: Academy Artworks, Inc.

This book was set in Times Roman by Polyglot Pte Ltd.,
printed by Book Press, Inc., and bound by Book Press, Inc.
The cover was printed by Phoenix Color Corp.

Macmillan Publishing Company
866 Third Avenue, New York, New York 10022

Collier Macmillan Canada, Inc.
1200 Eglinton Avenue, E.
Suite 200
Don Mills, Ontario, M3C 3N1

Library of Congress Cataloging in Publication Data

Edwards, James Rolph.
    Macroeconomics : equilibrium and disequilibrium analysis / James
Rolph Edwards.
        p.   cm.
    Includes bibliographical references.
    ISBN 0-02-331555-5
    1. Macroeconomics. 2. Equilibrium (Economics) 3. Quantity theory
of money. 4. Keynesian economics. I. Title.
HB172.5.E38   1991
339.5—dc20   90-32982
                                                                  CIP

Printing: 1 2 3 4 5 6 7 8   Year: 1 2 3 4 5 6 7 8 9 0

This is for my teachers, and for all those economists who have had both the ability to perceive the orderly patterns in people's voluntary interactions, and the courage to state publically that freedom works better than any of the feasible alternatives.

Preface

The essential flaw in the Keynesian interpretation of macroeconomic phenomenon was the absence of a consistent foundation based on a choice theoretic framework of microeconomics. Two important papers, one by Milton Friedman (1968) and the other by Robert Lucas (1976), forcefully demonstrated examples of this flaw in critical aspects of Keynesian reasoning and set the stage for modern macroeconomics.

Charles I. Plosser
Journal of Economic Perspectives
Summer 1989

Macroeconomics is simultaneously one of the most important and frustrating of studies. For good or ill, macroeconomic *policy* exists. Every government has one. Theoretical guidance for such policy is diverse and seems confusing, however. Since the collapse of the Keynesian consensus around 1970, several schools of thought, including neo-Keynesianism, monetarism, new classical economics, and supply-side economics, have competed with partial success for acceptance among economists and policy makers.

Partly as a consequence of this lack of theoretical consensus, and partly from marketing considerations, some textbook authors have structured their books to give equal play to all viewpoints, however contradictory. The intent seems to be to arrive at as few conclusions as possible, to please everyone and to offend no one. As a marketing tool this strategy is probably successful. As an educational tool it probably is not. The impression left with the bulk of students by such textbooks is that everything is confused, that nothing is or can be known with any assurance on the subject, and that the study of macroeconomics is futile.

A far better strategy is to develop the study of macroeconomics from a single coherent theoretical viewpoint, giving clear and fair treatment (but less emphasis) to alternate perspectives at appropriate points. This strategy is in fact employed by some authors. In the vast majority of such textbooks, however, the primary perspective employed is the Keynesian (or neo-Keynesian, as they now prefer to be called). Alternate approaches have been underrepresented among such textbooks.

The central theoretical perspective employed in this book is that of the modern quantity theory of money. There are several reasons for this approach. First, the quantity theory has stood the test of time. In its older version it was the pre-World War II orthodoxy. Eclipsed for a time by the Keynesian revolution, the quantity theory emerged with renewed vigor to the forefront of theoretical and empirical research. Second, in its modern version the quantity theory is rooted very firmly in orthodox neoclassical microeconomics. This yields not only a coherent macroeconomics, but also a coherent economics, essentially reuniting what was split assunder in the "Keynesian synthesis." Third, the quantity theory is a central element of at least two of the major schools of thought, the monetarist and new classical schools. Indeed, it is also central to another school with a long history, known as the Austrian School, which has recently reemerged with renewed vigor.

Even supply-side economics (which has a chapter of its own in this book) seems actually more complementary to, rather than competitive with, quantity theory views, and many of its less radical proponents are also quantity theorists. There are meaningful differences among all these schools, but recognizing what they have in common (and in contrast with the Keynesian school) sharpens awareness of the central issues.

The structure of the book is as follows: Part I deals primarily with the microfoundations of the labor and financial markets necessary to understand macroeconomic phenomena, and also with the particular techniques employed to measure macroeconomic variables. Part II begins by employing Say's principle and Walras's law to derive macro phenomena from micro behavior in a monetary model. The following chapters deal in depth with the supply of and demand for money, monetary policy, and the aggregate demand and supply model. The placement of the *AD–AS* model at the end of this section (before the Keynesian material) will seem odd to some instructors, until it is understood that the interpretation given to the *AD–AS* model here is derived from, and based on, the monetary model developed in Chapters 5 to 8.

Part III develops and discusses the Keynesian model, both in its simple "Keynesian Cross" form and the more sophisticated *IS–LM* model. It also includes discussions of the origins, historical employment, and recent critiques of that model. Many of the issues separating Keynesians from their opponents are illustrated by employment of a flexible-price version of the *IS–LM* model in Chapter 13.

Part IV deals with recent developments in macroeconomic theory and the macroeconomy, such as the Phillips curve, rational expectations, inflation, and supply-side economics. Chapters 17 and 18 treat international macromonetary economics and events in depth, although discussions of such matters occur throughout the book. The last two sections of Chapter 5, for example, anticipate, in an extremely lucid and simple form, many of the crucial arguments of Chapters 17 and 18.

An important feature of this book, which distinguishes it somewhat from most others at the intermediate level, is that policy actions and economic events are intermittently analyzed in terms of their political economy. This is as it should be. As James Buchanan has taught us, political and bureaucratic decision makers are economic actors too, and hence are capable of being analyzed by economic models. Indeed, this is not just a possibility, but a necessity. To avoid doing so, on the wishful presumption that public servants act only in the "public interest" is to abrogate our responsibility as economic analysts.

Several purely pedagogical features have been incorporated into the book to make it as lucid as possible. As is fitting in an intermediate level textbook, this one (to a greater degree than some others) is more literary and graphic than mathematical. The diligent student who did reasonably well in economic principles and college algebra should have no problem understanding the material presented.

Graphs can be an excellent tool in aiding textual exposition, and I have endeavored to employ them in this manner throughout the book. Initial functional magnitudes in the graphs are represented by solid lines, while subsequent magnitudes (following shifts) are shown as dashed lines. Where I have not used actual numbers, initial equilibrium magnitudes of the variables on the axes are indicated by letters or symbols, and subsequent equilibrium magnitudes are distinguished by the addition of a prime on the right-hand side, such as G'. Where I have employed a graph to illustrate a sequence of events explained in the text, the sequence is shown as clearly as possible through the use of numbered circles and arrows.

Many of the expository graphs I have employed are, by the way, original to this book, including the following:

1. Three-quadrant Figure 4.2, although the separate graphs composing the quadrants are standard.
2. The "money multiplier diagram," first shown as Figure 7.1.
3. Two-quadrant Figure 7.4, the top quadrant of which is, of course, borrowed from Don Patinkin.

4. The Federal Reserve "balance sheet equality diagram," first shown as Figure 8.1 (which is so simple that no one else ever seems to have thought such a thing could be useful).
5. The three-quadrant "monetary policy diagram" first shown as Figure 8.2.
6. The variation of the monetary policy diagram first shown as Figure 8.6.
7. All of the three- and four-quadrant graphs employed in Chapters 12 and 13, although, of course, the graphs composing the separate quadrants are standard.
8. The two-quadrant expectations-adjusted Phillips curve diagram, Figure 14.5, although I did not invent the graphs composing the quadrants.
9. The "short-run gold coin standard graph" first shown as Figure 17.3.

The classical gold standard Figure 17.5 is my version of a graph developed and employed by Don Roper in lectures at the University of Utah during 1977 to 1981 in exposition of his and Lance Girton's well-known model of the gold standard. Dr. Roper's original version of the graph has never, to my knowledge, been published (any mistakes of interpretation here are my own).

One characteristic of previous textbooks that has bothered this author is that their footnote references seem designed more to impress the teacher than to help educate the student. In many cases, of course, it is impossible to avoid reference to difficult theoretical and empirical literatures. In this book, however, I have made as many citations as possible to sources that were written specifically for the intelligent layman with an intermediate level (or better) background in the subject. As an aid to understanding the material in the book, the student should peruse as many such references as available study time permits.

The student should also take the time to answer the questions in the **student self-test** at the end of each chapter. Indeed, the instructor may wish to insure this by assigning students to do so. The answers to most questions are contained in an instructor's manual (only suggested points of focus are given for essay questions). Although I have made an effort to provide numerical illustrations in the body of the text whenever mathematical formulas have been employed in the exposition of economic relationships, too many such examples break the flow of the prose and may reduce conceptual understanding. In this book the strategy employed has been to give *primary* (although not total) emphasis to literary and graphic exposition in the body of the chapters, and then focus on arithmetic and algebraic understanding in the completion problem sections of the problem sets at the end of each chapter.

I would like to thank several reviewers, including William N. Butos, Trinity College; Abdur R. Chowdhury, Marquette University; John B. Egger, Towson State University; Scott E. Hein, Texas Tech University; Fred N. Hendon, Stanford University; Braxton Patterson, University of Wisconsin—Oshkosh; Joseph T. Salerno, Pace University; and Barry N. Siegel, University of Oregon. Their comments beneficially affected both content and organization, and helped me to avoid embarassing errors. I should also apologize to (and thank) those of my students who, from 1985 to 1989, had versions of various chapters (knocked out on a pair of faithful Macintosh computers) inflicted upon them. Their comments, both critical and complementary, also helped.

J. R. E.

Contents

Part II

Monetary Theory and the Aggregate Economy

Part III

Keynesian Macroeconomics

Part IV

Modern Macroeconomics: Revolutions and Evolution

PART I

Macroeconomic Measurement and Microfoundations

CHAPTER 1

Introduction: Macroeconomics and the Macroeconomy

This is a book about macroeconomics. The purpose of this chapter is to introduce some primary facts and issues in the performance of Western market economies, particularly the U. S. economy, from an historical perspective. The nature and content of macroeconomics as a study is defined by contrast with microeconomics, and the nature of and some problems with the type of models necessarily employed in macromonetary analysis are discussed in order to show both the potential benefits and limits of such analysis.

Economic Growth and the Business Cycle

Sustained economic growth is a modern phenomenon. Indeed, the very idea of growth was born in the 18th and 19th centuries, together with the phenomenon itself, in that immense social, economic, philosophic, and political transformation that is mistermed the *industrial revolution*. For hundreds of years prior to the industrial revolution the Western world had been essentially stagnant. In the latter part of that period Western nations were politically monarchic. Economically, they were characterized by agrarian feudalism and a mercantilist system of pervasive state-granted monopoly, international trade restrictions, and detailed government regulation.

With the industrial revolution, pressures that had been building for centuries reached their culmination and many changes occurred. The power of monarchs was reduced or eliminated and many Western nations became constitutional democracies, characterized by the rule of law rather than of men. Private property replaced the semicommunal property rights structure of the feudal system. State monopoly, trade restrictions, and regulation were drastically curtailed, and the market price system based on voluntary transactions emerged as the primary mechanism of resource allocation. These institutional innovations reached their purest expressions in the new republic of the United States of America. It is difficult to believe that the appearance of sustained economic growth in the Western world simultaneously with these institutional innovations was coincidental.

This lesson is being learned anew in our time. The rest of the world has also experienced some growth, particularly in the 20th century, due to the spread of information on the purely technological advances associated with and resulting from these Western economic and political innovations and to foreign investment by Western nations. This is true even of some states that have had socialist institutions imposed upon them by political cadres in explicit rejection of free markets and limited government.[1] Nevertheless, most such countries and others in the third world have lagged behind Western living standards, with some experiencing very low growth.

Recently, however, several formerly underdeveloped nations have experienced extremely rapid and sustained growth, sufficient to lose their third world status. This is particularly true of certain Pacific rim states such as South Korea, Taiwan, Hong Kong, and Singapore. Although some have not yet become constitutional democracies— South Korea made the transition in 1987—all such spectacularly successful states have adopted the free market as their primary form of economic organization, and this appears to be the central factor differentiating them from less successful third world countries.

More than 200 years of accumulated experience with sustained economic growth that has regularly exceeded population growth and raised output and income per person, makes it difficult to deny that limited-government free-market economies deliver the goods. From the first, however this growth appeared variable and uneven, subject to spurts, stalls, and even temporary reversals, with significant attendant distress. Critics such as Thomas Malthus, the pessimistic British economist, were quick to point out the existence of this **business cycle** and to claim that it was inherent in the market form of economic organization.[2]

Although the phrase *business cycle* implies more about the regularity, and the predictability, of the phenomenon than is justified by the reality, intermittent expansions and contractions of business activity around the positive trend line of growth have been and still are a part of the historical experience of Western economies. Figure 1.1 shows the growth of manufacturing output in the United States from 1948 to 1987, measured in billions of dollars. The shaded bars show periods of

Figure 1.1 U.S. Manufacturing Output and Employment.

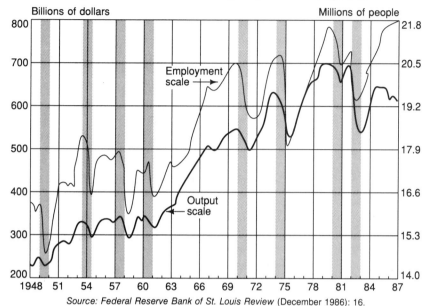

Source: Federal Reserve Bank of St. Louis Review (December 1986): 16.

business contraction, of which there have been eight, averaging one every five years. Output usually drops between 4 and 6 percent at such times, although it sometimes declines more and sometimes less. The graph also shows manufacturing employment, measured in millions of people, which falls during contractions. Contraction phases are followed by expansion phases in which output and employment grow at above-normal rates.

It should be pointed out that the existence of business cycles is not a fatal critique of market economies, particularly in comparison to other forms of socioeconomic organization. The distress associated with such cycles pales in comparison with that of the famines and plagues that repeatedly afflicted the preceding medieval economy.[3] As for Marxist economies, there is more than a little truth to the critic's observation that they have no boom-and-bust cycles only because they have no booms. Indeed, their manifest failure in this regard has apparently motivated the market-oriented reforms that have recently begun to take place in Red China and elsewhere.[4]

Moreover, to admit that intermittent expansions and contractions have always been a part of Western industrial economies, is *not* to admit that such economic instability is necessarily inherent in market processes. Although thinkers such as Malthus attributed recessions to a natural tendency toward underconsumption in market economies—an explanation revived by John Maynard Keynes in the 20th century (see Chapters 10 to 13)—others have suspected a different cause. The victory of laissez faire over mercantilism was never complete—Western economies retain many mercantilist elements, including central banks, that control national money stocks and epitomize the mercantilist policy of state monopoly and regulation. Some economists see much of the source of cyclic instability in such holdovers of the *ancien regime* (see Chapter 8). Indeed, in some respects, professional opinion seems to have swung in this direction in recent years.

Inflation As a Macroeconomic Issue

Although the debate over the causes and cures of the business cycle is a prominent element of modern macroeconomic theory, and of this book, another related problem has become important in recent decades, the problem of price-level stability. For the past several decades, prices in general have moved in one direction: upward. Yet chronic inflation is a recent historical phenomenon. Past inflations were temporary and generally significant only during wartime, such as during the War of 1812, the Civil War, and World War I. Such wartime inflations were always followed by a period of deflation, sometimes lengthy, in which falling prices restored the value of money. As Figure 1.2 shows, as recently as 1940 the price level and the value of money were essentially the same as they were in 1800, 140 years earlier.

At the bottom of the Great Depression this long period of price stability seems to have ended. The World War II inflation was not followed by post-war deflation or even by a cessation of inflation. Indeed, the problem worsened in the 1960s and 1970s and only eased, but not ended, in the 1980s. One key factor in this series of events concerns a change in the monetary system. Before 1930 money in America and in most other countries was convertible into gold or silver, which were costly to produce. After 1930, monetary notes and deposits were inconvertible.

It also turns out that convertibility was usually suspended during wartime in the gold-standard period, so the use of inconvertible currency and deposits has something to do with inflation, but what is the connection between the supply of money and its value? What incentives exist under the present monetary regime for those who control the money stock to cause prices to rise, and what motives prompt them to take actions having this effect? Is inflation purely the fault of the public at large? These and related questions are dealt with extensively in Chapters 5, 8, 14, and 15.

Figure 1.2 Wholesale Prices Since 1800.

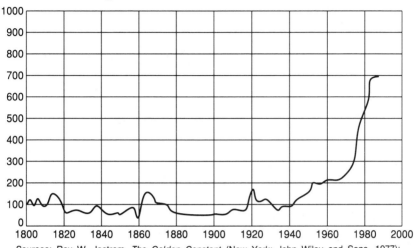

Sources: Roy W. Jastrom, *The Golden Constant* (New York: John Wiley and Sons, 1977): 145–146, and *Economic Report of The President, 1987*: 313.

Microeconomics and Macroeconomics _____

The science of economics has two branches, *microeconomics* and *macroeconomics*. *Micro* is a Greek root meaning small. Accordingly, microeconomics focuses on individual decision makers in their roles as consumers who supply inputs and demand outputs and on producers who demand inputs and supply outputs. Microeconomics essentially deals with the consequences of human choices and activities motivated by pervasively felt individual scarcity. This focus on *individual* decision makers is not myopic, however. Once the individual's responses to alterations in relative prices have been derived in the form of individual supply and demand functions, these are aggregated by horizontal summation up to the market level, at which price determination is explained. This process is termed **methodological individualism**.

The last step is to consider resource shifts between markets. At this level the economy is seen as an essentially self-regulating system due to the transmission of information and motivation through the price system and to the maximizing behavior of decision makers. It should be noted, however, that once the systematic interaction among markets, often termed the *general equilibrium*, is considered and one begins to speak of the operation of the market system, *micro*economics has blended into *macro*economics.

The Greek root *macro* means large, hence macroeconomics is intended to focus on the operation of the *whole* economic system. A formal general-equilibrium model, with a separate excess-demand equation for each economic good, is a macroeconomic model. Modern macroeconomists simplify by constructing models that aggregate micro markets into one or more macro markets having specific theorized relationships. The use of such models is to cast light on and provide solutions for such problems as chronic inflation and/or widespread, enduring unemployment.

An example of such a macroeconomic model, termed the *Aggregate Demand and Supply* or *AD–AS* model, is illustrated in Figure 1.3. This model shows the demand for and supply of final output in the economy as a whole as functions of the absolute price level. The reader may have seen this model before and seen how certain factors cause shifts in the *AD* and *AS* curves, and how such shifts can be used to illustrate and explain problems of inflation and recession. A sophisticated version of this model is developed in Chapter 9, which focuses on how and whether microeconomic supplies and demands, which are functions of *relative* prices, can logically aggregate into functions of the *absolute* price level. Applications of this and other models to macroeconomic issues appear throughout this book.

Before the *AD–AS* model or other macroeconomic models can be developed, however, it is necessary to develop the proper microeconomic background, which is the purpose of Chapters 3 and 4. Chapter 3 develops the concept of the market for credit and financial capital, beginning with the intertemporal choice constraints of the individual demanders and suppliers. This market determines the interest rate, which allocates resources intertemporally and is a crucial determinant of the rate of economic growth. Chapter 4 develops the microeconomics of labor markets and deals with issues of employment, unemployment, and wage adjustment in preparation for construction of the *AD–AS* and other macroeconomic models. In Chapter 5 macro-

Figure 1.3 Aggregate Demand and Supply Model.

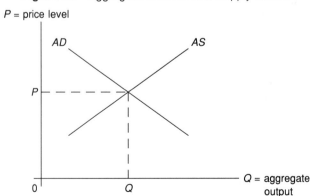

economics and microeconomics meet. Through methodological individualism and a simple theory of cash holding, individuals' budget constraints are employed to develop a supply-and-demand theory of the value of money. This simple macromonetary model provides a clear explanation of the sources of recessionary and expansionary phenomena and of the nature of the market equilibration mechanisms. Chapter 5 is, in fact, the key to the entire book.

Macroeconomic Models and the Role of Theory _____

Macroeconomic modeling is frequently criticized. It is often said, for example, that such models are too abstract. This criticism is seldom justified. All economic, and other, models are abstract. To *abstract* means to take away from. An economic model is like a model airplane. The hull of a model plane is plastic instead of titanium and it lacks a real jet engine, but it shows in miniature the essential relationships of interest.

Another example of a model is a road map. A map is abstract. It deletes unessential details. It is a good map, however, if it shows the essential relationships correctly. Considering maps also makes it clear that the most abstract model is often the best. One who stops at a gas station for directions to a house in the neighborhood might prefer a simple line drawing to a detailed city map if the relationships shown on the line drawing were both relevant and correct. A valid criticism of a macroeconomic or any other, model would be not whether it is too abstract but whether the information it deletes is truly unessential and whether the relationships it shows are both relevant and correct.

A related criticism is that the variables employed in macroeconomic models are excessively aggregative. This criticism is harder to refute. Microeconomic aggregation through horizontal summation up to the market level is justified because it involves adding units of the same or similar entities. That is, if we add the quantities of nonretractable ballpoint pens produced by all of their manufacturers at a particular price, we obtain a particular market quantity, q_b. Changes in this quantity over time tell us something meaningful. But suppose we aggregate across markets, letting Q = production in the whole economy in a given year. Given the variety of goods and services included, there are special problems involved in deriving a single number to accurately represent this quantity, and it is at best a less meaningful concept than market quantity.

The same problem emerges for other macroeconomic variables. The market price of the ith good, p_i, is a fairly meaningful concept with a concrete, observable referent, although what may actually be observed is a dispersion or distribution of prices, and p_i may be only a fiction representing the mean. But what if $P =$ the **price level** in the whole economy? This is a more aggregative and less meaningful concept, without, concrete referent, having special problems of measurement. The same is true of other macroeconomic variables such as unemployment, national income, and the money stock.

How economists have tried to provide accurate and meaningful numerical measurements of these variables is the major focus of Chapter 2. Here it is important only to point out that practical analysis of the operation of the macroeconomy and testing of the models derived from such analysis requires the use of such variables and attempts to measure them. A proper criticism would concern not the *degree* of aggregation of such variables, but the *method*. None of our measurements are perfect and much room for improvement in their construction exists.

A final criticism of macro models, although the list is not inclusive, is that they are too mechanical in nature. The variables often seem divorced from any root in human choice or action and may interact directly in a precise, mechanical fashion. Even if human propensities are considered in explaining the behavior of some variables, the view of individuals presented is much like dominoes in a row, which fall over in predictable sequence when the first is pushed. This criticism is often justified, at least for many early macro models. The classical quantity theory and the orthodox formulation of the Keynesian model, both of which are discussed in later chapters, had such defects. Macroeconomics has made progress in recent decades, however, and human choice and action have begun to return to center stage. In this book strenuous efforts are made to develop and maintain the microeconomic roots of the primary models employed.

Note that the most that can be asked of any macroeconomic model is that it be **heuristic**, which means *ultimately indefensible but useful.* Even the best macroeconomic and monetary theories, when pushed far enough, lost explanatory power. This is no less true, however, of existing cosmological theories, including classical mechanics. The question is whether we understand more with such theories than without them. If an affirmative answer can be provisionally accepted, macro-monetary economics becomes a useful pursuit.

Stocks and Flows

As a last word before leaving the subject of the essential nature of macroeconomic models, it should be pointed out that it is important to distinguish between **stock variables** and **flow variables** in such models. A flow variable is measured as a quantity *per unit* of time, whereas a stock variable is measured as a quantity existing at a given *point* in time. The two are related, because a given stock of a durable item usually has two flows associated with it, an inflow and an outflow, and, in the short run, the magnitudes of these flows interact to determine the magnitude of the stock. For example, at any given time there is an existing stock of housing in the economy. There is a flow into this stock in the form of new home construction and a flow out from it in the form of old houses being torn down. When new home construction in a given period exceeds old home destruction, the housing stock grows and vice versa.

As another example, consider business inventories of durable goods. Production of such goods constitutes the inflow into such stocks, and sales constitute the outflow. The relative magnitudes of production and sales determine whether inventories are rising or declining. The nation's stock of physical capital (tools and equipment), to which investment is the inflow and depreciation the outflow, is another good example.

A subtle yet important point is that stocks often act as buffers, allowing adjustment of rates of flow to one another. The magnitudes of stocks, and changes in such magnitudes, are not simply incidental outcomes of the relative magnitudes of the associated flows, except in the short run. In the long run, causality more likely runs in the opposite direction. The housing stock may grow because the rate of new production exceeds the rate of decay and removal of old houses, but there is an optimal stock of housing at any given time, which is determined by supply and demand factors. If the housing stock grows too large relative to demand, housing values will fall, old homes will be torn down faster, and the rate of production will fall.

Another example of stock-flow relationships may make their nature more easily grasped. There was a woman who kept a very messy house. She had a husband and two young daughters and there was always a waist-high pile of laundry on the living room floor. Also, the kitchen table was always piled high with dirty dishes. Yet this lady washed as much laundry every week and as many dishes every day as any other wife in any other four-member family, which frustrated her a great deal. This was because, in the limit given by the total amount of clothes and dishes owned, or by her desired levels of the stocks, clothes and dishes had to be washed in order for her family to have clean clothes to wear and clean utensils to eat with. By a one-time reduction of these stocks to zero, obtained by causing the flows out (through washing) to exceed the flows in (through dirtying of clothes and eating utensils) over a given period, the house could have been kept clean thereafter with no more work than before. Indeed, this woman reduced these stocks to zero twice in two years but she let them build up again both times. This demonstrates the basic point that the level of these stocks was a choice variable, although the choice may have been based on the misconception that she was saving labor.

This example demonstrates again that stocks act as buffers and adjust upward and downward in the short run as an incidental outcome of the difference between the rates of inflow and outflow. The levels of such stocks are economic choice variables, however, and in the long run the rates of flow will be purposely adjusted in order to keep a stock at or adjust it to the level desired by transactors. Throughout this book, an important part of the discussion of macroeconomic and monetary phenomena will center on such stock-flow relationships.

Summary _____

The major points of this chapter can be summarized as follows.

1. Sustained economic growth in per-capita real income is a modern phenomenon that emerged as Western nations transformed themselves into constitutional democracies with free market economies.

2. Although sustained economic growth is the norm in Western nations, intermittent fluctuations in economic activity and employment around these positive growth trends have also been pervasive. Such business cycles are a prime concern of macroeconomics.

3. Inflation is the second primary concern of macroeconomics.

4. Macroeconomic analysis involves the construction of abstract models designed to explain and illustrate key features of the aggregate economy.

5. Some macroeconomic variables are *'flow'* variables, measured as a quantity per unit of time, and others are *'stock'* variables, measured as a quantity at a given point in time.

6. Stocks often have inflows and outflows associated with them.

7. In the short run, the incidental relative magnitudes of inflow and outflow frequently determine the magnitude of a stock. In the long run, where economic actors have desired magnitudes for stocks, those intentions may often determine the relative magnitudes of the flows.

Notes _____

1. Anthony Sutton has massively documented the dependence of the Soviet economy on transfers of Western technology and capital. See, for example, Sutton, *Western Technology and Soviet Economic Development: 1930–1945* (Stanford: The Hoover Institution, 1968), or either of the two succeeding volumes. Even with such transfers,

however, Marxist economies have been unable to close the productivity gap with the West. See Abraham Bergson, "Comparative Productivity: The USSR, Eastern Europe, and the West," *American Economic Review* 77 (June 1987): 342–357.

2. Thomas R. Malthus, *Principles of Political Economy*, original publication 1820 (New York: Augustes M. Kelley, 1951): Book II.

3. As pointed out by Rushdoony, in the 13th century alone, England experienced famines in 1203, 1209, 1224, 1235, 1239, 1243, 1257, 1271, and 1286. The famine beginning in 1286 lasted for 23 years, with the worst years being 1294 to 1295 and 1298. See Rousas J. Rushdoony, *The Myth of Overpopulation* (Nutley, N.J.: The Craig Press, 1971): 3–4.

4. For an excellent discussion of the Chinese reforms and the economic improvements that have resulted, see Dwight Harold Perkins, "Reforming China's Economic System," *Journal of Economic Literature* 26 (June 1988): 601–645.

Student Self-Test _____

I. True-False

T   F   1. That Western democratic market economies have been subject to business cycles historically is proof that private-sector economic activity is unstable in the aggregate.

T   F   2. All economic models abstract from many elements of the economic phenomena they attempt to represent.

T   F   3. The process of deriving individual supply-and-demand curves from reasoning about individual choice under scarcity and aggregating up to the market level through horizontal summation is termed *methodological collectivism.*

T   F   4. Microeconomic aggregation up to the market level is more justifiable and meaningful than macroeconomic aggregation across markets.

T   F   5. Due to the measurability problems inherent in macroeconomic variables, macroeconomic models have little heuristic value.

II. Short Answer (150 words or less each)

1. Why might governments on the gold standard have suspended convertibility during wartime? What has the relative costs of producing gold and paper currency to do with this?

2. List and briefly describe at least four separate dimensions of the socioeconomic transformation referred to as the *industrial revolution.* Why might these factors have produced a positive growth trend?

3. Briefly list and explain at least three problems inherent in macroeconomic models and modeling.

4. Explain the role of theory and the nature of abstraction in economic modeling.

CHAPTER 2

Measurement of Macroeconomic Variables

To speak of the operation of an economy is to imply some form of macroeconomic model. The elements of such a model are macroeconomic variables and they are related by theory. It is impossible to say anything about the operation of an economy—about employment, unemployment, output, income, price level, and so on—without clear definitions and reasonably accurate measurements of such macroeconomic variables. The purpose of this chapter is to introduce macroeconomic variable concepts and measurement methods that economists have developed.

Measuring Gross National Product

Since Adam and Eve left the Garden of Eden, people have always had to produce—employing scarce resources as inputs—in order to consume. What is more, in a monetary market economy with extensive specialization and division of labor, individuals seldom consume more than a small portion of their *personal* production. Typically, each individual sells a particular good or service and uses the income obtained to purchase goods and services produced by others. In the *aggregate*, however, our physical output is essentially the same as our real (i.e., physical) income, since what we produce as a nation is what is available to consume.[1] Because incomes earned in production are used to purchase output, there must be a close connection between the value of income and the value of output in the aggregate.

The concept of the market value of aggregate output is critical because aggregate physical output consists of a mass of heterogeneous goods and because intangible services are also an important part of national output. That is, where $i = 1, \ldots, n$ types of goods and services exist and q_i is the quantity of the ith one produced per year.

$$\sum_{i=1}^{n} q_i = Q.$$

This is a conceptually meaningful notion, and the symbol Q will be used generically to mean **real national output and income** throughout this book. Simply adding physical units of automobiles, pins, and hamburgers, however, will not do for practical measurement. A rise in Q resulting from a four-unit fall in automobile output and a six-unit rise in hamburger output would be misleading. Heterogeneous economic goods must be expressed in some common unit of measurement, by which they can be compared and summed. The standard solution has been to use their monetary market values. That is, if p_i = the price of the ith good, then the nominal or dollar value of national output and income is

$$\sum_{i=1}^{n} p_i q_i = Y.$$

Economists and statisticians charged with measuring national output and income have developed a set of accounts termed the National Income and Product Accounts (NIPA) in which the value of income and output are conceptually equal. The NIPA do not simply sum the prices times the quantities of all goods and services sold per year as does the generic definition of nominal income. This is because many items, known as **intermediate products**, are sold to businesses, where they become part of products eventually resold either to other businesses for further transformation or to their ultimate consumers. If all such transactions were included, the value of aggregate production and income would be overestimated due to **double counting.**

The problem and its solution can be illustrated with a circular flow diagram (Figure 2.1) representing a simplified two-sector (i.e., business and household) economy in which no saving or investment occurs and no government or foreign trade exists. The reader may have seen similar diagrams in economic principles courses. In the version employed here, three groups or levels of firms, A, B, C, are shown. Households provide a flow of inputs to firms at all three levels and receive incomes totalling one trillion dollars, all of which they use to purchase consumer goods from firms at level A.

Firms at level C can be assumed to be raw materials producers, selling iron ore, for example, to firms at level B for $200 billion, all of

Figure 2.1   Circular Flow with a Vertical Production Structure.

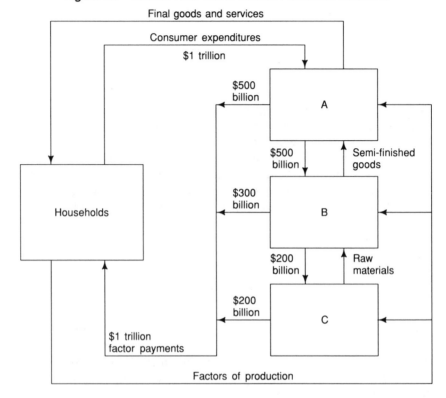

which is used to pay input suppliers and owners. Firms at level B are purchasing the raw materials for $200 billion and employing labor and other inputs worth $300 billion to produce semifinished goods such as steel, which they sell to firms at level A for $500 billion, thus covering their costs.

Firms at level A are purchasing steel and other semifinished goods worth $500 billion and employing household-sector inputs worth another $500 billion to produce consumer goods that sell for $1000 billion (i.e., one trillion), thus covering their costs. Note that if we try to add the values of all transactions up to final sales in order to estimate the value of final output, we would obtain $500 + $500 + $200 + $200 = $1700 billion. This exceeds the value of final sales and total household income by $700 billion.

The problem is that the raw materials and semifinished goods are counted twice. By deleting the intermediate transactions, the $200 billion raw materials sale and the $500 billion semifinished goods sale, leaving only the factor payments (i.e., the **values added**) at each stage of production to be summed, we obtain $500 + $300 + $200 = $1000 billion, the value of expenditure on final goods and services. This is known as **Gross National Product** (GNP).

In order to get an accurate statement of GNP, however, some oversimplifications must be removed from the model, such as the assumption that all expenditures on final goods and services are for consumption. Typically, both households and firms save and invest part of their income. In an average year about 63 percent of all income is spent on consumption and about 15 percent is invested in new housing, durable producer goods, and inventories, as shown in Table 2.1. This is also expenditure on final goods. The dollar value of such investment is termed **Gross Private Domestic Investment** and is added to consumption expenditures in measuring GNP hereafter.

Another glaring oversimplification is the absence of a government from the model. In reality, both households and firms pay taxes to support federal, state, and local governments, which use part of the revenue to purchase final goods and services, part to employ members of the household sector, and part to make **transfer payments** in the form of welfare, social security and so on. Although taxes reduce

TABLE 2.1 Nominal Gross National Product, 1970 to 1987 (billions of dollars)

Year	Gross national product	Personal consumption expenditures	Gross private domestic investment	Government purchases	Net exports
1970	1015.5	640.0	148.8	218.1	8.5
1971	1102.7	691.6	172.5	232.4	6.3
1972	1212.8	757.6	202.0	250.0	3.2
1973	1359.3	837.2	238.8	266.5	16.8
1974	1472.8	916.5	240.8	299.1	16.3
1975	1598.4	1012.8	219.6	335.0	31.1
1976	1782.8	1129.3	277.7	356.9	18.8
1977	1990.5	1257.2	344.1	387.3	1.9
1978	2249.7	1403.5	416.8	425.2	4.1
1979	2508.2	1566.8	454.8	467.8	18.8
1980	2732.0	1732.6	437.0	530.3	32.1
1981	3052.6	1915.1	515.5	588.1	33.9
1982	3166.0	2050.7	447.3	641.7	26.3
1983	3405.7	2234.5	502.3	675.0	−6.1
1984	3772.2	2430.5	664.8	735.9	−58.9
1985	4014.9	2629.0	643.1	820.8	−70.0
1986	4240.3	2807.5	665.9	871.2	−104.4
1987	4526.7	3012.1	712.9	924.7	−123.0

Source: Economic Report of the President, 1989: 308–309.

household net income, they are not deducted from GNP, probably on the theory that they are essentially a payment for governmental services provided. Governmental purchases *are* added in, however, although transfer payments are *not*, since such payments are not for goods or services provided. Symbolically, G = the dollar value of government expenditure on final goods and services.

The last major oversimplification is the absence of foreign trade from the model, because Americans both purchase goods and services from foreigners and sell part of U.S. output to foreigners. If the dollar value of sales of physical merchandise and services to foreigners is designated EX = exports and the dollar value of purchases of such items from foreigners is IM = imports, then the net impact of foreign trade on measured domestic GNP is given by $EX - IM$, known as **net exports.** Adding this completes the definition of Gross National Product, so

$$GNP = Co + I + G + (EX - IM).$$

Table 2.1 shows nominal GNP from 1970 to 1987 with its component measurements.

Additional Income and Production Concepts _____

The NIPA adjust GNP in several ways in order to arrive at other useful accounting concepts. GNP is gross, because it includes gross private domestic investment. Much investment replaces equipment used up in production, however, and does not add to capital stock. Where D = the estimated value of depreciation, adjustment for wear and tear, called the capital consumption allowance, yields a measure known as **Net National Product** (NNP), so

$$NNP = GNP - D.$$

Neither GNP nor NNP, as expression of the value of final output, is equivalent to the value of income earned in production, however, since the price of many goods includes sales taxes and excise taxes, termed **Indirect Business Taxes** (IBT). Removing the value of IBT revenue from NNP yields national income (Y^n), which is the conceptual counterpart of GNP. That is,

$$Y^n = NNP - IBT.$$

One problem with the national income measurement is that it includes corporation profits, Π, as income. Corporations are considered legal entities that are separate and distinct from their owners under U.S. law. An income measurement is needed, however, to measure the income of real, rather than artificial,people. Another problem with the national income measurement is that the income of many people, obtained from transfer payments, is not included, because it was not included in GNP deliberately, as pointed out earlier. Accordingly, the NIPA adjust national income by adding in transfer payments (Tr) and subtracting corporate profits, net interest earned (ni), and social insurance payments (si) of corporations. Because corporate bondholders earn interest income and profits are the source of investor income, stock dividends (sd) and personal interest income (pi) must be added in. These adjustments yield **personal income** (Y^p), where

$$Y^p = Y^n - \Pi - ni - si + Tr + pi + sd.$$

By subtracting personal taxes (T^p), a final income concept known as **disposable income** (Y^d) is obtained. Therefore,

$$Y^d = Y^p - T^p.$$

Where N = population, it is often highly useful to adjust these income and product measures by expressing them as a ratio to that variable. Thus **per-capita GNP** = GNP/N, and so on. This process is important because it is not apparent from a rise in GNP, Y^p, or Y^d from one year to the next whether individual production or income has grown, because population might have risen by a larger percentage. To know whether individuals really are better or worse off on average, one must compare either the ratios or growth rates of these variables, which will be discussed later in this chapter. Figure 2.2 shows per-capita GNP, which has clearly been rising over time. Even measures such as this can be misleading, however.

Figure 2.2 Per Capita Nominal Gross National Product (*GNP/Population*).

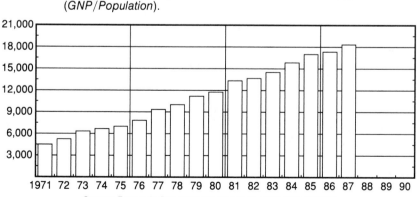

Source: Economic Report of the President, 1989: 308 and 343.

Price Indices _____

The use of monetary market values solves many problems in the measurement of aggregate output and income. It provides a common unit, the dollar, in which heterogeneous goods and services can be measured and given their appropriate relative weight in the sum, which is much better, for example, than adding one diamond and one lug wrench. It is also appropriate that the dollar is a unit of monetary value, because we wish to know how well we are doing collectively.

Measurement of value in terms of money, however, is not the same as measuring physical dimensions in terms of an objectively defined and unchanging inch. Imagine the problems resulting if the length of the inch, and of all other units of length, changed over time relative to other things.[2] The relative lengths of different items could always be accurately determined by using the inch existing at the moment of comparison. It would be difficult to know the *absolute* length of anything, however, unless the amount by which the inch had changed over a specific time period could be measured. That would require comparison with something known to have remained unchanged in length over the period and would amount to the establishment of an objectively defined and unvarying base-period inch.

The use of money as a measure of value induces a similar but worse problem, because money is not an objectively defined and unchanging unit of value. It is itself an economic good, the value of which is established by and changes with its conditions of supply and demand (see Chapter 5). A fall in the relative value of money, however, shows up as a general rise in the nominal (i.e., money) prices of other goods and services and vice versa for a rise in the value of money.

The problem resulting for the measurement of national output and income is easily illustrated. Because any useful definition involves adding the products of prices and quantities, a rise in such a measure over time might not mean that the quantity of actual goods and services available has increased, but that prices have risen. It is necessary to know what has happened to prices, then, in order to know what has happened to quantities or vice versa. For this purpose economists invented price indices.

The most widely reported index is the **Consumer Price Index** (CPI). It is based on the idea of comparing the market values of a representative set of 1000 commonly purchased consumer goods at different points in time. The set contains items from several categories such as food, housing, transportation, medical care, clothing, and entertainment. Also, the number of items of each type in the set is weighted by the relative importance of that item in consumers' expenditure pattern in a base year.

The **Bureau of Labor Statistics** (BLS) uses collected data to compute the cost of the whole basket (B_b) in the base year, then it does the same for another year, such as the current year, for example (B_c). The CPI is then expressed as the ratio of the two, multiplied by 100 to obtain a percentage expression. That is,

$$\text{CPI}_c = \frac{\$B_c}{\$B_b} \times 100.$$

Note that if $c = b$ the value of the CPI is

$$\text{CPI}_b = \frac{\$B_b}{\$B_b} \times 100 = 100.$$

Until 1987 the base year for the CPI was 1967, so the 1967 value of the CPI was set at 100. The CPI was updated, however, and the index value was set at 100 early in 1984 (the 1983 value is 99.6). By the old index, the CPI reached 331.1 in December, 1986, which means that the price level had more than tripled in 20 years and the purchasing power of the dollar had fallen to less than one third of its 1967 value.

The government computes other similar indices for different sets of goods. The **Producer Price Index** (PPI), for example, contains raw materials and semifinished goods. The process of weighting in such indices can be illustrated by example. Imagine that the leaders of a Communist nation wish to construct a **Bolshevik Price Index** (BPI) for items the government commonly purchases. For simplicity, only four items are included in the set and dollar equivalents of local monetary values are employed. Table 2.2 shows the items, the quantities in the set, and their prices in both the base year and the current year. From this information, calculation of the BPI is straightforward:

$$\text{BPI} = \frac{(4 \times \$12) + (10 \times \$6) + (2 \times \$50) + (8 \times \$275)}{(4 \times \$10) + (10 \times \$5) + (2 \times \$40) + (8 \times \$250)} \times 100$$

$$= \frac{\$2408}{\$2170} \times 100$$

$$\approx 110.97.$$

There are several problems associated with constructing an index in this fashion. First, such indices are affected by *relative* price changes,

TABLE 2.2

Item	Quantity	Price b	Price c
Whip	4	$10	$12
Chain	10	$5	$6
Barbed wire roll	2	$40	$50
Machine gun	8	$250	$275

particularly for items that weigh heavily in the index. Second, by employing the base year weight in all years, such indices ignore systematic changes in people's relative expenditures that result from relative price changes. The CPI probably overestimates inflation, for example, by implicitly assuming that people do not switch purchases from items whose prices have risen more to items whose prices have risen less. Last, all price indices suffer from quality changes. What does it mean if the price of a 1987 Ford is higher than that of a 1967 Ford when, by and large, they are not the same car? Problems like these increase with time, which is why such indices must be updated at intervals.

Although the CPI is the most widely reported U.S. price index, the BLS computes another index of a different type, termed the **GNP deflator**, which is probably more accurate. This index is constructed by taking nominal GNP in the current or other year and then pricing the same set of goods and services in the prices they had in the base year, given that $b = 1982$.[3] The sum resulting from the multiplication of year c quantities by 1982 prices is termed **real** or **constant-dollar** GNP. The GNP deflator, P, is then calculated as the ratio of nominal GNP to real GNP and is multiplied by 100. That is,

$$P = \frac{\text{nominal GNP}}{\text{real GNP}} \times 100 = \frac{Y}{Q} \times 100.$$

Ignoring the multiplication by 100 as a mere convenience, we have

$$P = \frac{Y}{Q}.$$

The symbol P was defined as representing the price level and is used as the GNP deflator here because measuring the price level at a particular point in time, relative to its base year value, is precisely what such an index is about.

Note that the previous equation implies

$$P \cdot Q = Y,$$

which means that multiplying the value of real GNP in a particular year by that year's GNP deflator yields nominal or **current-Dollar** GNP. It also follows that

$$Q = \frac{Y}{P}.$$

That is, dividing nominal GNP by the price index yields real GNP. Figure 2.3 plots real and nominal GNP from 1970 to 1987. Notice that $Q > Y$ before 1982, $Q = Y$ in 1982, and $Q < Y$ since 1982. This is because 1982 is the base year for the deflator and prices have been rising throughout this period. Where $P \cdot Q = Y$, $P = 1$ in 1982 (again, ignoring the multiplication by 100) makes $Q = Y$ that year. $P < 1$ before 1982 makes $Q > Y$, and $P > 1$ after 1982 makes $Q < Y$.

The process of dividing a nominal magnitude by a price index is termed **deflating** by a price index, and it can be performed by using any appropriate index, not just the GNP deflator, on any nominal magnitude. It is an extremely important process. Throughout this book nominal magnitudes such as income, hourly wage rates, and product

Figure 2.3 Real GNP (in Billions of 1982 Dollars) and Nominal GNP (in Billions of Current Dollars).

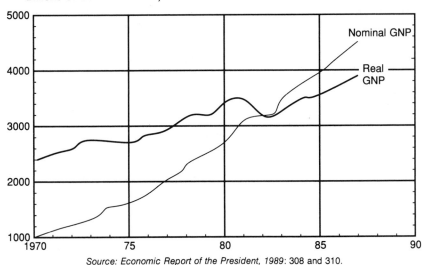

Source: Economic Report of the President, 1989: 308 and 310.

Figure 2.4   Real Per Capita GNP (Q/N) in 1982 Dollars.

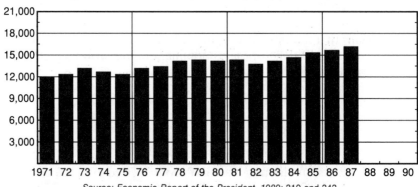

Source: *Economic Report of the President, 1989*: 310 and 343.

prices are distinguished from and transformed into real constant-dollar magnitudes by expressing them as a ratio to the price level.

Deflating by a price index allows avoidance of the frequent confusion that results from comparing nominal magnitudes from different periods in which the value of money was not the same. This is the problem with the per-capita GNP graph shown in Figure 2.2. Figure 2.4 corrects for changes in the value of money by showing per capita real GNP over the same period. Improvements clearly occurred, but more slowly than indicated in Figure 2.2.

Another example may illustrate the hazards of comparing purely nominal magnitudes over time. In December, 1982, a *Des Moines Register* editorial castigated President Reagan for creating a huge deficit (i.e., excess of expenditure over revenue; see Chapter 11) in the federal budget. The editor claimed that the Reagan deficit dwarfed President Carter's 1976 deficit, which had been the largest nominal deficit in previous history. In so doing, the editor forgot that 1976 dollars and 1982 dollars did not have the same value. Deflating each nominal deficit by that year's CPI allows a more accurate comparison, as shown in Table 2.3.

The figure of $44.24 billion for the real deficit in 1982 is found by dividing the nominal deficit of $127.9 billion for that year by the 1982

TABLE 2.3

Year	Nominal deficit	CPI	Real deficit
1976	$73.7 billion	170.5	$43.23 billion
1982	$127.9 billion	289.1	$44.24 billion

Source: *Economic Report of the President (1987)*: 307 and 331.

CPI value of 289.1, then multiplying the number obtained by 100. The real deficit for 1976 is found by the same procedure. A somewhat simpler method involves moving the decimal point in the CPI two places to the left before dividing. This eliminates the necessity for multiplying the result by 100 to obtain the real magnitude.

Whichever calculation method is employed, expressing both deficits in 1967 dollars makes it clear that the 1982 deficit was not significantly larger than the 1976 deficit, as Table 2.3 shows. An alternate procedure would be to express both deficits in 1982 dollars by deflating the 1976 deficit, than multiplying the result by the 1982 index number. That is, $43.23 billion × 2.891 = $124.97 billion, and again the two deficits are virtually the same. Indeed, expressed as a ratio to GNP, which is an appropriate measure of the magnitude of a deficit, the 1982 deficit is slightly smaller than the 1976 deficit.[4]

Definition and Measurement of the Money Stock ⎯⎯⎯

Because aggregate output and income can be measured sensibly only in monetary terms, given our present state of knowledge, and adjustments must be made for changes in the value of money, macroeconomics must be highly concerned with the economic factors determining that value. On the provisional assumption that money is an economic good, the value of which is determined by supply and demand conditions, it becomes important for the testing of theory and the design of policy to be able to define and measure the supply of money.

Money can be defined at least partly with regard to its functions. Historically, money originated to solve a problem that appeared as primitive economies developed markets. This transformation involved the appearance of an increasing division of labor as people began to specialize in different productive activities in which they had comparative advantages and to trade among themselves for the other things they needed. As the division of labor extended on a barter basis, transactions became more and more costly because it became increasingly difficult for an individual to find someone who not only had what he wanted but also wanted what he had.

This phenomenon is called the **double coincidence of wants problem**. It was solved when people noted that there were some commodities that almost everyone wanted and began acquiring such commodities, whether needed for their direct use or not, in order to use them in exchange. The emergence of such goods as mediums of exchange drastically lowered transaction costs and allowed full extension of the division of labor with its productive advantages. Over time the set of such mediums employed narrowed as some were found to make better money than others.

Serving as a medium of exchange is the first and most crucial function of money, but it is not its only function. Any durable money commodity acquired by sale need not be spent immediately. It can be held for later expenditure and thus act as a **store of purchasing power**. Also, the emergence of money increasingly meant that everything was priced in terms of one thing, or of a small set of things, which thus served as a **unit of account**. This made rational calculation of revenues and costs much easier, again increasing the efficiency of the economic system.

Here we have at least a partial definition: Things that perform all three of these functions are money. Special emphasis should be laid on the medium of exchange property because the others are both historically and economically derivative and because it yields a fairly sharp criterion. There are various financial assets and durable goods that store value and are liquid in the sense that they can be quickly exchanged for assets that can be spent directly, but as such they are not themselves mediums of exchange and are not money. Also, they are not the unit of account but are denominated in terms of money.

In the present-day United States the Federal Reserve system is charged with defining and measuring the money supply and it has developed several definitions. Each week the Fed obtains reports from financial deposit institutions and uses the information obtained to construct the monetary aggregates. In accordance with the sort of arguments employed here, its primary aggregate (M1) is termed **transactions funds** and consists of the sum of currency and coin in circulation plus checkable deposits in all domestic financial institutions. This includes certain recently developed types of deposits such as NOW and ATS accounts (see Chapter 7), and credit union share drafts. Travelers' checks are also included in M1.

Figure 2.5 shows the dollar magnitudes and growth of M1 from 1970 to 1987. It also shows values of and changes in the price level over that period as measured by the GNP deflator. Values of the money stock are to be read on the left-hand vertical scale, and values of the price level are to be read on the right-hand scale. In this period the M1 money stock and the price level have clearly moved up together.

Many economists argue that an expanded list of assets should be included in the money stock, because they store value, are highly liquid, and affect the level of expenditure even if they are not themselves mediums of exchange. As such the Fed computes a measure known as M2 that adds small uncheckable savings deposits, overnight repurchase agreements (overnight loans of corporate funds to banks), and money-market mutual funds to M1.

There is also an M3, which adds to M2 certain other liquid assets, such as large-denomination time deposits and dollar-denominated de-

Figure 2.5 Money Stock and Price Level.

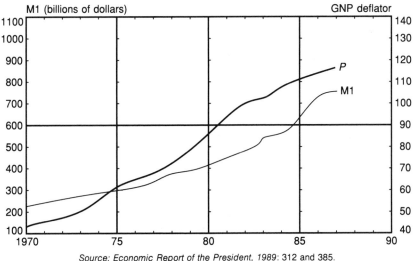

Source: *Economic Report of the President, 1989*: 312 and 385.

posits in foreign banks. The problem with all such measures is that once one begins using the liquidity of assets, which are not mediums of exchange, as a criterion for inclusion in the money stock, there is no logical stopping point before an M96 that includes used cars, old clothes, and houses. Long before that point all distinction between that which is money and that which is not is lost. Accordingly, the term money stock as used in this book always refers to transactions funds.[5]

Measures of Employment and Unemployment _____

Since the Great Depression, employment and unemployment have been primary social and political concerns. Accordingly, government economists have made efforts to define and measure these phenomena. This is not nearly as easy as one might think, because there are degrees of unemployment and numerous reasons why given individuals are not employed.

Each month the Census Bureau conducts a survey of 100,000 adults, the results of which are tabulated by the Bureau of Labor Statistics. Everyone questioned is placed into one of three categories. The category **employed** includes everyone who is a self-employed professional, works in a family business, or works for pay, even if only part time. The category **unemployed** includes all who claim to be willing to work, able, and currently active in searching for a job, but not currently employed.

The third category, termed **not in the labor force**, includes the remainder who are not employed but are *not* unemployed by the definition above because they do not *wish* to be employed. This distinction is necessary, because *voluntary* unemployment is clearly not a social problem in the sense that *involuntary* unemployment is.

Having obtained sample data on these categories, the BLS extrapolates to the general population in order to obtain its estimates, which are then expressed both in raw numbers and as ratios or percentages. The **labor force** (F) is defined as the sum of the number employed (e) and the number unemployed (u). The **unemployment rate** (Ω) can then be expressed as the ratio $\Omega = u/F$. Figure 2.6 plots the unemployment rate from 1970 to 1988. It has been rising for most of that period (see Chapter 4).

The construction and interpretation of the unemployment rate statistic is subject to much debate. Some observers claim that it underestimates actual unemployment because many long-term unemployed people become discouraged and stop looking for work, with the result that they are counted in the third category, reducing the numerator of the ratio. This is termed the **discouraged worker phenomenon** and certainly has some validity. Another reason the statistic as reported may underestimate actual unemployment is that many people who are working part-time may wish they were working longer hours at their present employment or be looking for full-time work elsewhere. Because present practice is to categorize anyone with a job as employed, the statistic does not reflect such partial unemployment.

Figure 2.6   Percentage of Labor Force Unemployed $(u/F = \Omega)$.

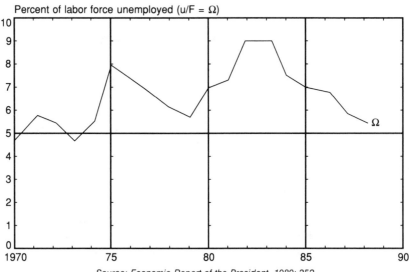

Source: Economic Report of the President, 1989: 352.

On the other hand, it can be claimed that there are several factors causing the statistic as presently measured to overestimate the actual unemployment rate. Some people who are nominally unemployed are actually employed in what is termed the **underground economy**.[6] That is, they are employed at illegal activities or are not reporting legal employment and income. The underground economy grew rather significantly during the 1970s (see Chapter 16). Such illegal employment may particularly swell during recession periods.

Unemployment compensation also seems to distort the unemployment statistic, because such payments reduce the cost of job search and increase the average time spent looking for work (see Chapter 4). As a consequence, some measured unemployment is actually voluntary, because unemployed persons reject available options with the hope of finding better ones. Some people may report that they are looking for work when they are not, in order to remain eligible for the compensation payments. Last, the observation that some people work fewer hours than they desire must be tempered by the observation that in periods of tight labor markets many workers are required to work *more* hours than they desire. The net effect of these contrasting distortions of the unemployment statistic is unknown.

If N = population, another important statistic is the ratio F/N, which is termed the **labor force participation rate**. This rate changes over time as people's values and constraints change. It has a tendency to vary positively with the business cycle, falling during the later stages of a recession due to the discouraged worker phenomenon and rising during the early phases of an expansion as word spreads that employment opportunities are emerging.

Sometimes the labor force participation rate will fall so much during the contraction phase that the unemployment rate actually *falls* for a period, *even though employment is also falling*. Similarly, F/N will sometimes rise so quickly during an expansion that Ω will rise, although employment is rising. For this reason a statistic termed the **employment rate**, calculated as the ratio of total employment to population, e/N, may be a better general indicator of economic conditions.

Figure 2.7 plots F/N and e/N from 1970 to 1987. Comparison with Figure 2.6 shows that even the secular trends of the employment and unemployment rates can tell different stories, because both are generally rising over this period. Looking at the unemployment rate alone, as network news reporters and journalists often do, might lead to the conclusion that conditions in the economy have been worsening over time, a conclusion clearly tempered by the trend in the employment rate. Just as clearly, the secular rise in F/N lies behind the secular increases in both the employment and unemployment rates.

Table 2.4 shows data on the civilian population, labor force, and employment from 1965 to 1987. The labor-force participation rates and

Figure 2.7 Civilian Labor Force Participation Rate (F/N) and Civilian Employment Rate (e/N).

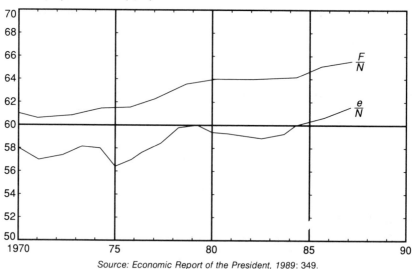

Source: Economic Report of the President, 1989: 349.

employment rates shown can be derived by calculation from the numbers in the three left-hand columns by employing the definitions given in this chapter. The data for Figures 2.6 and 2.7 are from the same source used to construct Table 2.4 and can be found in the table.

Growth Rates and Percentage Changes _____

There are two mathematical rules that are employed in the exposition of many concepts in this book. They express the growth rates of products and ratios of variables that are functions of time. The rules are derived by calculus. If $a = f(t)$, the instantaneous rate of growth of a is $(1/a)(da/dt)$. If

$$a = b \cdot c,$$

then

$$\frac{1}{a}\frac{da}{dt} = \frac{1}{b}\frac{db}{dt} + \frac{1}{c}\frac{dc}{dt},$$

which means that the instantaneous growth rate of a product of variables that are functions of time is the sum of the growth rates of its

TABLE 2.4

Date	Civilian noninstitutional population (thousands)	Civilian labor force (thousands)	Civilian employment (thousands)	Civilian labor force participation rate	Civilian unemployment rate	Civilian employment rate
1965	126,515	74,455	71,088	58.9	4.5	56.2
1966	128,058	75,770	72,895	59.2	3.8	56.9
1967	129,874	77,374	74,372	59.6	3.8	57.3
1968	132,028	78,737	75,920	59.6	3.6	57.5
1969	134,335	80,734	77,902	60.1	3.5	58.0
1970	137,085	82,771	78,678	60.4	4.9	57.4
1971	140,216	84,382	79,367	60.2	5.9	56.6
1972	144,126	87,034	82,153	60.4	5.6	57.5
1973	147,096	89,429	85,064	60.8	4.9	57.8
1974	150,120	91,949	86,794	61.3	5.6	57.8
1975	153,153	93,775	85,846	61.2	8.5	56.1
1976	156,150	96,158	88,752	61.6	7.7	56.8
1977	159,033	99,009	92,017	62.3	7.1	57.9
1978	161,910	102,251	96,048	63.2	6.1	59.3
1979	164,863	104,962	98,824	63.7	5.8	59.9
1980	167,745	106,940	99,303	63.8	7.1	59.2
1981	170,130	108,670	100,397	63.9	7.6	59.0
1982	172,271	110,204	99,526	64.0	9.7	57.8
1983	174,215	111,550	100,834	64.0	9.6	57.9
1984	176,383	113,544	105,005	64.4	7.5	59.5
1985	178,206	115,461	107,150	64.8	7.2	60.5
1986	180,587	117,834	109,597	65.3	7.0	61.1
1987	182,753	119,865	112,440	65.6	6.2	61.9

independent variables. However, if

$$a = \frac{b}{c},$$

then

$$\frac{1}{a}\frac{da}{dt} = \frac{1}{b}\frac{db}{dt} + \frac{1}{c}\frac{dc}{dt},$$

which means that the growth rate of a ratio of such variables is the difference between the growth rates of its numerator and denominator.

Because many students of intermediate macroeconomics have taken algebra but not calculus, it will be useful to employ algebraic substitutes for these rules. Over a relatively small interval, $\Delta a / a \approx (1/a)(da/dt)$. Therefore, we can substitute percentage change approximations for the growth rate rules: If $a = b \cdot c$,

$$\frac{\Delta a}{a} \approx \frac{\Delta b}{b} + \frac{\Delta c}{c} \quad (\text{or } \% \, \Delta a \approx \% \, \Delta b + \% \, \Delta c).$$

If $a = b/c$, however,

$$\frac{\Delta a}{a} \approx \frac{\Delta b}{b} - \frac{\Delta c}{c} \quad \text{or} \quad \% \, \Delta a \approx \% \, \Delta b - \% \, \Delta c.$$

These are the forms in which the rules will be employed in subsequent chapters. They have obvious implications for and applications to such concepts as per-capita GNP (i.e., GNP/N), and real income (Y/P). Note, however, that in the form employed these rules are only algebraic approximations of the correct calculus expressions, accurate for relatively small numbers only.

Summary

The major points of this chapter include the following.

1. With minor qualifications, our aggregate real production and income are the same. What we produce is what is available to consume.

2. The only sensible common unit in which aggregate output and income can be measured is monetary market value.

3. Gross National Product (GNP) is the value of final goods and services, where intermediate products are excluded to avoid double counting. Other measures of aggregate output and income are derived from this.

4. Since, unlike physical units of measurement, the value of the dollar varies, prices indices must be constructed and employed to allow measurement of real constant-dollar production and income over time.

5. The uses of money as a medium of exchange, store of value, and unit of account make exchange and production more efficient and less costly.

6. Employment and unemployment are not easier to measure than other macroeconomic variables, and our official statistics may be inaccurate to some degree; nevertheless, the direction and magnitude of movement in these statistics provide useful information.

Notes

1. There are qualifications to this statement due to the holding of inventories and to international trade.

2. This is not a totally absurd postulate. The length of the Egyptian cubit in antiquity was defined as the distance from the pharaoh's elbow to his fingertip and varied from pharaoh to pharaoh.

3. This index was recently updated. Until 1985 the base year for the GNP deflator was 1972.

4. From 1983 on, Reagan period deficits exceeded those of previous administrations, although this growth was part of an ongoing secular trend dating back to the early 1960s (see Chapter 11). The point is not to apologize for the Reagan administration, but to illustrate the inaccuracy of intertemporal comparisons of purely nominal magnitudes when the value of money is changing.

5. This does not mean that attempts should not be made to define and measure a better transactions aggregate than M1. A possible start in this direction has been made by Paul Spindt, "Money is What Money Does: Monetary Aggregation and the Equation of Exchange," *Journal of Political Economy* 93 (February 1985): 175–204.

6. See Peter Gutman, "The Subterranean Economy," *Financial Analysts Journal* 33 (November/December 1977): 26–27 and 34, and "The Grand Unemployment Illusion," *Journal of the Institute for Socioeconomic Studies* 4 (Summer 1979): 20–29.

Student Self-Test

I. True–False

T F **1.** Government expenditures for welfare and social security are deleted from the measurement of personal income.

T F **2.** Foreign trade may cause the value of domestic final production and consumption to differ.

T F **3.** The real value of money rises when the price level rises.
T F **4.** The unemployment rate and the employment rate may rise at the same time.
T F **5.** All assets that store value over time are money.

II. *Short Answer* (150 words or less each)

1. Briefly explain:(a) the connection between income and production, and (b) why it is the common practice to use monetary values to measure aggregate income, particularly what problem is solved by doing so.
2. Briefly explain the problem provided for national income accounting by the fact that many firms sell products to each other for use as inputs in furher production.
3. Why are transfer payments excluded from the government expenditures that are added as a component in GNP?
4. Briefly explain the central problem with the use of money as a measure of the value of goods and services.
5. Does the official method of calculating the U.S. unemployment rate result in an overestimate or an underestimate? Explain briefly, listing and discussing the important factors.

III. *Completion Problems*

1. Assuming that the U.S. population grew from 239,283,000 to 241,489,000 in one year, and that nominal GNP grew from $3998.1 billion to $4208.5 billion, and the implicit price deflator rose from 111.5 to 114.5 in the same year, fill in the blanks.
   A. Population grew _____ percent and nominal GNP grew _____ percent that year.
   B. Applying the appropriate percentage change rule, real per-capita income grew about _____ percent that year.
   C. Comparing the actual ratios in the two years, per capita real GNP grew _____ percent, so the percentage change rule was off by _____ percent.
2. Imagine yourself to be the official in charge of computing the Bolshevik Price Index (BPI) for this year (year *t*), using the price and quantity data in the following table. Employ the same procedures used in constructing the U.S. Consumer Price Index.

Goods	Quantity	Base-year price	*t* price
Chains	8	$ 6.00	$ 4.00
Microphones	20	10.00	11.00
Thumbscrews	30	1.50	1.20

3. In the table are columns for nominal disposable income, the GNP deflator, and real disposable income from 1982 (the base year of the deflator) to 1986.

Year	Nominal Y^d (billions)	GNP deflator	Real Y^d (billions)
1982	$2261.4	100.0	$ _____
1983	2428.1	103.9	_____
1984	2670.6	107.9	_____
1985	2828.0	111.5	_____
1986	2973.7	114.5	_____

A. Fill in the blanks with the correct values of real Y^d to within two decimal places.
B. The nominal Y^d figures are all _____ (higher/lower) than the real Y^d figures because _____ .
C. Real Y^d for any given year is definitionally nominal Y^d calculated in base-year prices. Algebraically, real disposable income is _____ .
D. Use of the base-year index number and value of money for expressing real magnitudes is arbitrary, and non-base-year index numbers and money values can be used. Real Y^d for 1986 calculated in 1985 dollars is $_____ . Real Y^d for 1984 expressed in 1985 dollars is $_____ .
E. If nominal income were rising by 5 percent per year and the inflation rate (the rate at which the price level was rising) was 7 percent per year, real output would be _____ (rising/falling) by about _____ percent per year.

CHAPTER 3

Interest Rate: Time, Income, and Financial Markets

Interest rates are some of the most important relative prices in the economic system. They are *intertemporal* prices which, under the appropriate competitive conditions, will act to allocate resources efficiently through time. This chapter explains the major factors behind the phenomenon of interest. The explanation will rely heavily on the work of Irving Fisher and will involve a certain amount of oversimplification. There are in fact many interest rates established in many markets. They tend to move together, however, and on the reasonable assumption that these submarkets are highly integrated, it will be assumed that there is essentially one market for credit and financial capital determining a single rate of interest.

Income, Capital, and Capital Value

Irving Fisher pointed out that income is really a series of psychic events, essentially a flow of utility experienced as one applies *means* toward the attainment of ultimate *ends*.[1] Note that it is the utility generated by final goods and services that constitute ultimate income. Intermediate production processes and money transactions are of significance only because they are necessary preliminaries to the generation of this ultimate, psychic income. The purely *subjective* nature of ultimate income presents a very large problem in macroeconomics, however, because no *objectively* defined unit exists by which utility can be measured. The closest we can come is to use the money value of people's expenditures on final goods and services, preferably deflated by a price index to a *real* value. This, of course, is the real GNP concept developed in Chapter 2.

The final goods and services that provide utility to consumers, and the values of which have been defined here as income, are nearly all *outputs* of production processes in which *inputs* in the form of raw materials, tools, labor, and intermediate products were applied over time. The inputs generate the output, so to speak. It might be said that the inputs used, and the way they are used, determine the output. Indeed, such a **production function** will be specifically introduced later. When it comes to the values of inputs and outputs, however, the causality is completely reversed: Inputs are valued only for their ability to produce outputs capable of satisfying consumers. As Fisher put it, the orchard may produce the apples, but the value of the orchard depends upon the value of the apples.[2] The basic methods of calculating such present and future values are easily explained.

Computing Future Values _____

Suppose that i = the annual rate of interest, P_v = a sum of money of current value, and F_n = the value of P_v after some number of periods, n, given i. If i = .05, P_v = \$100 and is loaned out for one year (so n = 1), then

$$F_1 = \$100 + (\$100 \times .05) = \$105,$$

so

$$F_1 = P_v + P_v i,$$

or

$$F_1 = P_v(1 + i).$$

If the principle and interest were left untouched for a second year, then

$$F_2 = \$105(1 + .05) = \$110.25,$$

but because \$105 = \$100(1.05),

$$F_2 = \$100(1.05)(1.05),$$
$$= \$100(1.05)^2.$$

So in general, the formula for the future value of a present sum, or **future value formula**, after any number of annual compounding periods, n, is

$$F_n = P_v(1 + i)^n.$$

A complication arises whenever interest is compounded more frequently than once per year. This can be dealt with rather simply, however, by dividing the annual interest rate, i, by the number of times interest is to be compounded per year and using as the exponent the total number of such compounding periods for which P_v is to be invested. For example, if $i = .06$, compounding is semiannual, and P_v is to be invested for a year and a half, then

$$F_3 = P_v\left(1 + \frac{.06}{2}\right)^3,$$

which reduces to

$$F_3 = P_v(1.03)^3.$$

For simplicity, however, annual compounding will be assumed in this book.

Present Value Formula

If $F_n = P_v(1 + i)^n$, then it follows that

$$\frac{F_n}{(1 + i)^n} = P_v,$$

so a sum of money due or expected to accrue at any particular time in the future can be discounted to a present market value using the known market rate of interest. Also, if any sum to be available in any future period can be discounted to a present value, then any set or series of such sums available at different times can be discounted to their present values and added into a single present value. Suppose that a lottery prize is to be paid at $1000 per year for the next five years. Suppose also that $i = .05$. The present value of the payment is

$$P_v = \frac{\$1000}{(1.05)} + \frac{\$1000}{(1.05)^2} + \frac{\$1000}{(1.05)^3} + \frac{\$1000}{(1.05)^4} + \frac{\$1000}{(1.05)^5}$$

$$= \$952.38 + \$907 + \$863.84 + \$822.70 + \$783.53$$

$$= \$4329.45.$$

In general, then,

$$P_v = \frac{F_1}{1 + i} + \frac{F_2}{(1 + i)^2} + \cdots + \frac{F_n}{(1 + i)^n}$$

Mathematicians have discovered that, for any identical set of payments expected to go on forever, such that n approaches infinity, the formula simplifies to

$$P_v = \frac{F}{i}.$$

Note that P_v varies *directly* with the magnitude of the future values. Obviously, the larger they are, the larger P_v is, and vice versa. The P_v varies *inversely* with the interest rate, however. The larger the market rate of interest is, the smaller P_v is, and the smaller the interest rate is, the larger P_v is.

Time Preference

Unfortunately, an important misconception may be gained from the previous exercises. In all of these formulas, the value of money at different times is calculated using the market interest rate. The impression gained may be that a given sum of money has different values at different times because there is an interest rate. Actually, the economic causation is precisely the reverse. One of the prime reasons there is an interest rate is that the same goods, sums of money, or satisfactions available at different times do not have the same value *now*. In particular, it almost always takes more than a dollar's worth of goods or satisfaction available a year from now to have the same value now as a dollar's worth that is available now. This is termed **positive time preference**.

Although it is a mystery why people's time preferences are generally positive, perhaps Ludwig von Mises gave the best answer:

> Time for man is not a homogeneous substance of which only length counts. It is not a *more* or a *less* in dimension. It is an irreversible flux, the fractions of which appear in different perspective according to whether they are nearer or remoter from the instant of valuation and decision. Satisfaction of a want in the nearer future is, other things being equal, preferred to that in the further distant future. Present goods are more valuable than future goods.[3]

Irving Fisher termed time preference *impatience* and expressed it as the *percentage excess of the present marginal want for one more unit of present goods over the present marginal want for one more unit of future goods.*[4] He further noted that an individual's rate of time preference depends on and varies with the relative magnitudes of that individual's present and future income.

To illustrate and clarify these points, consider a two-period model in which the individual's utility can be written as a function of both present (i.e., the current year's) income and future (i.e., the next year's) income; $U = U(Y_p, Y_f)$. It can be argued that each level of satisfaction or utility can be provided by many different combinations of present and future income. A line connecting all such different combinations that yield the same utility is termed an **indifference curve**. Two such curves, yielding different levels of satisfaction, U_0 and U_1, are shown in Figure 3.1. Two different combinations of present and future

Figure 3.1   Indifference Curves for Present and Future Income.

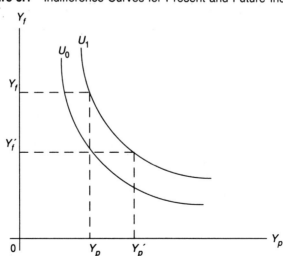

income that provide satisfaction level U_1, (Y_p, Y_f) and (Y_p', Y_f'), are marked.

The slope of such an indifference curve at any point is known as the **marginal rate of substitution** (MRS) between present and future income and shows the individual's relative valuation of one in terms of the other at that point. If MU_p = the marginal utility of present income and MU_f = that of future income, then

$$MRS = - \left(\frac{MU_p}{MU_f} \right).$$

This expression allows simple explanation of the convexity of the indifference curves, because as one moves down such a curve to the right, obtaining more present income and less future income, MU_p falls and MU_f rises, reducing the marginal rate of substitution. For numerical illustration, suppose that an objectively defined unit of utility does exist, and that $MU_p = 8$ and $MU_f = 1$, such that $MU_p/MU_f = 8$ at Cartesian coordinate (Y_p, Y_f). A movement to coordinate (Y_p', Y_f') might reduce the marginal utility of present income to $MU_p' = 6$ and raise that of future income to $MU_f' = 4$, such that $MU_p'/MU_f' = 1.5$. The MRS thus varies systematically with the relative provision of present and future income. This is not yet quite what Fisher meant in referring to the percentage of excess marginal want for a unit of present goods over one of future goods, however.

Saving, Consumer Credit, and the Interest Rate ⎯⎯⎯⎯

For purposes of simplicity, the initial model of the credit market developed here incorporates the following assumptions: First, both demanders and suppliers are price takers who view the interest rate as a parameter beyond their control. Second, borrowing occurs for consumption purposes only and not for investment. Third, credit contracts have a duration of one year. Fourth, little uncertainty about the magnitudes of present and future income exists. Fifth, the value of money is constant. Sixth, the transactor's initial present and future incomes are given.

Consider Figure 3.2(a), which shows a person's initial present and future incomes, Y_p and Y_f, and assumes for simplicity that $Y_p = Y_f$. A zero rate of interest in the credit market involving a dollar-for-dollar tradeoff between present and future income could be represented by a straight line with a slope of -1 passing through point $A = (Y_p, Y_f)$. Such a line (i.e., the "feasibility set" or "budget line") would describe

Figure 3.2 An Individual's Intertemporal Budget Constraint and Choice.

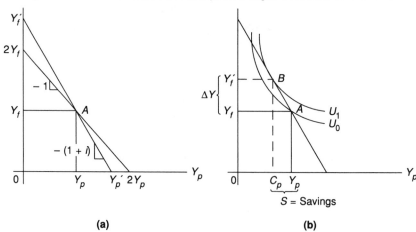

(a)   (b)

the two-year consumption possibilities faced by the individual. That is, it would be arithmetically possible for the individual to consume as much as $2Y_p$ in the present year by borrowing an amount equal to the next year's income and consuming nothing in the second year as the loan is repaid. Alternatively, the person could arithmetically consume as much as $2Y_f$ in the second year by saving all of Y_p and consuming nothing in the first year.

The existence of a positive interest rate can be illustrated in Figure 3.2(a) by a steeper line passing through point A, having a slope of $-(1 + i)$. It has a horizontal intercept at $Y_p' < 2Y_p$ because, with a positive interest rate, the most the individual can borrow is the discounted *present* value of Y_f. Also, the vertical intercept is at $Y_f' > 2Y_f$, because the individual could (arithmetically) add as much as $Y_p(1 + i)$ to next year's income by saving all of Y_p. In essence, a positive interest rate rotates the individual's intertemporal budget constraint through the initial two-period income point.

The budget constraint and the indifference map can be combined to explain how the individual with a given two-period income stream shown by point $A = (Y_p, Y_f)$ can alter that income stream through credit transactions in order to maximize satisfaction. Consider an individual at point A in Figure 3.2(b) facing positive interest rate i, who has not engaged yet in borrowing or lending. Note that point A is on indifference curve U_0, which cuts the budget line from below at that point. Given the absolute values of the slopes, this means that the marginal rate of substitution is less than one plus the interest rate.

Whereas $MU_p/MU_f < 1 + i$ at point A and there is a point on some higher indifference curve U_1 (point B), which is just tangent to the budget line, this person can increase his or her satisfaction by saving until current income available for present consumption is reduced to C_p and future income is raised to Y'_f. Where S = the amount saved, the increase in future income is $\Delta Y_f = S(1 + i)$.

At point B the individual's utility is maximized and $MU_p/MU_f = 1 + i$, because saving out of current income *raised* the marginal utility of remaining present income and *reduced* that of future income until the marginal rate of substitution reached on the highest indifference curve equaled the slope of the budget line. But if

$$\frac{MU_p}{MU_f} = 1 + i,$$

then

$$\frac{MU_p}{MU_f} - 1 = i.$$

For $i > 0$, this implies $MU_p > MU_f$ by a percentage equal to the rate of interest, which is a condition of positive time preference. Accordingly, the term on the left, $(MU_p/MU_f) - 1$, can be termed the **marginal rate of time preference**. This is exactly what Fisher meant by the percentage excess marginal want for a unit of present goods over one of future goods.

The conditions at point A and the nature of the readjustment can be easily described in verbal terms. Individuals who find that their marginal rate of time preference is less than the market rate of interest would find it profitable to save up to the point that the difference disappears and the marginal rate of time discount is equated to the social rate. It seems to follow that increases in the rate of interest should result in increased saving out of current income, although at a decreasing rate.

For an individual with given earnings Y_p and Y_f, an increase in the rate of interest rotates the budget line through point A, as shown in Figure 3.3(a), reducing its horizontal intercept and raising its vertical intercept. This graph essentially duplicates Figure 3.2(b), except that another indifference curve labeled U_2 has been added, which is just tangent to the new budget line. As expected, the individual's saving increases to $S' = S + \Delta S$ and the incremental addition is smaller than the initial value.

Figure 3.3   Deriving the Market Saving Function.

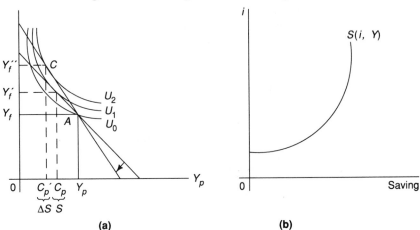

(a)   (b)

Hypothetically, by rotating the budget line continuously through the indifference map an infinite number of utility-maximizing tangencies could be found. By plotting these interest rates and the associated values of saving, a curve could be derived showing this individual's saving out of present income as a positive function of the interest rate. Indeed, because this experiment could be performed for all individuals, the resulting personal saving functions could be summed horizontally to derive the saving function or credit supply curve for the whole economy, as shown in Figure 3.3(b).

Note that aggregate nominal income is shown as a **shift variable** in this graph. Because the curve is drawn for a given level of national income, the ratio of savings to income, S/Y, which expresses the percentage saved, varies directly with the market rate of interest. Both logically and empirically, saving is a positive function of income, increasing (i.e., shifting toward the right in the graph) as aggregate income rises and falling as aggregate income falls.[5]

Demand for Consumer Credit _____

Oddly enough, the same logic that was just applied in deriving the credit supply curve can be applied in deriving the demand curve for consumer credit. Consider an individual with given present and next year earnings who has not yet engaged in borrowing or lending, and hence is at point A, as before. This individual's preferences, however, as shown by indifference curves U_0, U_1, and U_2 in Figure 3.4(a), are different. The U_0 curve cuts the solid budget line passing through point A from above, and point $B = (Y'_p, Y'_f)$ (at which the initial budget line is tangent to U_1, the highest indifference curve reached) is below and to the right of point A.

By comparing the slopes of U_0 and the budget line at point A, it is obvious that the individual's marginal rate of time preference exceeds the rate of interest and that an opportunity to increase satisfaction exists. Credit is a bargain to this individual, who will therefore borrow against future income, reducing the remainder available next year to Y'_f (raising MU_f) and increasing present income and consumption to Y'_p (reducing MU_p), until point B is reached. At that point $(MU_p/MU_f) - 1 = i$ and satisfaction is maximized.

If the interest rate were lower, however, as shown by the flatter budget constraint, the individual's final equilibrium would not be at point B, but at point C, at which a larger amount is borrowed for current consumption. Upon rotating the budget line through point A and noting the amounts borrowed at the equilibrium associated with each interest rate, a schedule could be plotted showing credit demanded by this person as an inverse function of the interest rate. Summing horizontally across all such individuals would yield the market demand curve for consumer credit, as shown in Figure 3.4(b). If this were the total demand for credit, the excess demand mechanism would clear the market at interest rate i, which would then become the parameter to which each individual's marginal rate of time preference would be adjusted.

Figure 3.4   Deriving the Demand for Consumer Credit.

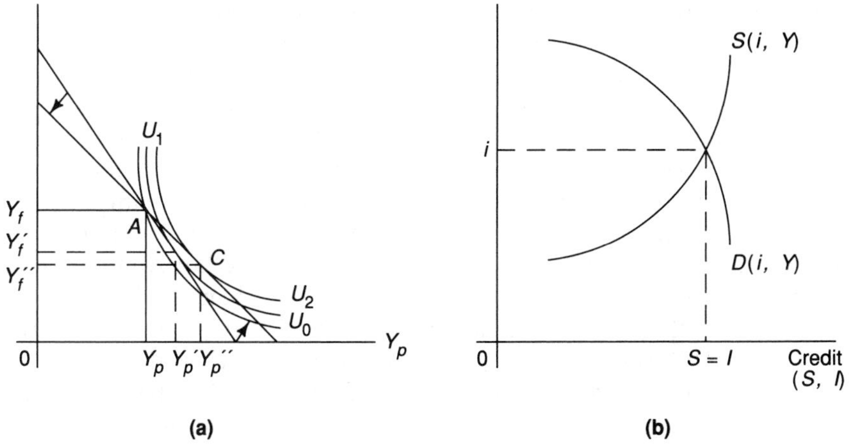

(a)   (b)

Investment Decision _____

The discussion of the credit market so far has been framed solely in terms of saving and borrowing by individuals for consumption purposes alone. A large portion of total saving is undertaken by firms, however, and much of the demand for credit is by firms and individuals who wish to invest in durable capital goods or structures to be used in production. Such a building or item of equipment, by adding to the production of valuable goods or services, generates a stream of revenues extending over its usable life.

There are also fixed costs associated with such an investment, including depreciation and interest foregone over the life of the equipment. In deciding whether to invest or not, the entrepreneur must estimate the additional **Net Benefits** (NB) resulting in each year or additional revenue in excess of operating expenses, which is available to cover such fixed costs and provide economic profits. These estimated net benefits must then be discounted to a present value using the market rate of interest. That is,

$$P_v = \frac{NB_1}{1 + i} + \frac{NB_2}{(1 + i)^2} + \cdots + \frac{NB_n}{(1 + i)^n}.$$

The present value of the expected net benefit stream can then be compared with the investment outlay, I_0. If $P_v - I_0$ is defined as the **Net Present Value** (NPV) of the investment and if $P_v > I_0$, such that NPV > 0, then the investment should be made, even if the firm must borrow the money.

Note that for a given stream of future net benefits, the present value of a potential investment varies inversely with the market rate of interest. The higher the interest rate is, the lower the present value of the investment becomes. For a given investment outlay, I_0, a higher interest rate also reduces the NPV, as shown in Figure 3.5(a). A high enough rate of interest will make the NPV of a given investment negative, at which point it becomes an unprofitable investment.

Figure 3.5(b) shows the NPV curves of a set of investment options faced by a firm. Because the investments have different streams of future net benefits and initial outlays, they cross the horizontal axis at different points and may even cross each other, changing NPV rankings. Given the investment decision rule (i.e., invest if NPV > 0), however, the level of investment can be predicted. Consider points d, e, and f on the horizontal axis of Figure 3.5(b). If the market interest rate is greater than that represented by point d, no investment will take

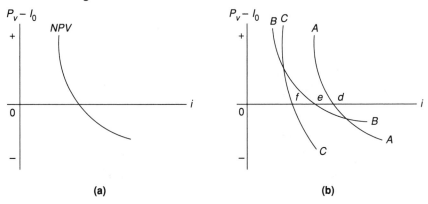

Figure 3.5 Net Present Value and Investment Choice.

place, because all projects have negative net present values. At any $e < i < d$, however, the firm will invest in project A, because its net present value is positive.

For $f < i < e$ the firm will invest in projects A and B, but not in C, because its net present value is still negative. At any $i < f$, all three investments will be made, and since investment pays whenever NPV > 0 even if the money must be borrowed, the demand for producer credit will clearly be an inverse function of the interest rate. Adding such producer demand to consumer demand yields the total demand for credit in the economy.

A graph such as that shown in Figure 3.4(b) could now be assumed to represent the complete market for credit and financial capital—sometimes inaccurately termed the **loanable funds market**—in which both producer and consumer saving and demand are included. Figure 3.6 shows real gross private domestic investment for the aggregate U.S. economy for the period 1970 to 1987 expressed in 1982 dollars; that is, the nominal dollar magnitudes have been deflated by the GNP deflator, which has 1982 as its base year. It also shows real net private domestic investment (in excess of depreciation), over the same period. The figures include not only business investment in structures, equipment, and inventory, but also residential investment.

There were recessions in the U.S. economy in 1974, 1980, and 1982, and there were significant declines in both gross and net investment during those periods. Economists of the Keynesian school of thought believe declines in investment to be a primary causal factor in such recessions, and investment certainly is a factor, although the direction of causation is somewhat controversial. All of these recessions will be discussed in later chapters.

Figure 3.6 Private Domestic Investment, Billions of 1982 Dollars □
Net Private Domestic Investment, Also Deflated ■.

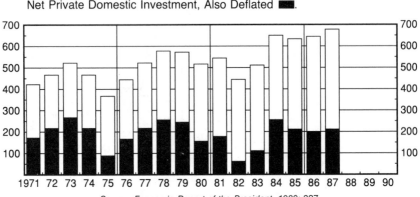

Source: *Economic Report of the President, 1989*: 327.

Uncertainty and Multiperiod Consumption _____

It is important to relax two assumptions of the model developed previously. First, looking at intertemporal consumption over only two periods is somewhat constraining, so the time horizon needs to be extended. Think of aggregate income as a pie of a certain size, all of which gets eaten except a single piece. The portion eaten represents consumption and the remainder is the portion saved. For a given level of aggregate output and income (i.e., given size of the pie), the primary determinant of the relative proportions consumed and saved is, of course, the interest rate. The higher i is, *ceteris paribus*, the smaller the portion consumed and the larger the portion saved. That is, $\Delta Co/\Delta i < 0$ and $\Delta S/\Delta i > 0$, as previously argued.

In terms of real output, the portion saved consists of capital goods and raw materials to be invested as inputs with labor in order to produce, hopefully, a slightly larger pie in the next period. On average, real output and income in the United States have grown historically at just under 3.5 percent per year. The measured growth rates for the period 1950 to 1987 are shown in Figure 3.7, and for this period the average is 3.43 percent. This ongoing real growth tendency is not all attributable to capital stock growth, of course, but to growth in all factors of production as well as in technological advance.

The proportion of income consumed seems to be fairly stable. Figure 3.8, which is computed from Table 2.1, shows that consumption averaged between 62 and 63 percent of GNP from 1970 to 1986 with relatively little variation; investment, which is also shown as a proportion of GNP, varies somewhat more. Clearly, as real output and

Figure 3.7 Real GNP, Annual Percentage Changes.

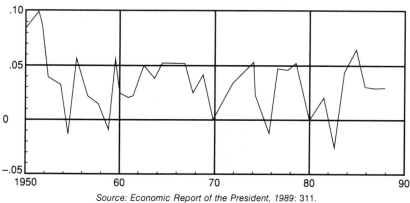

Source: Economic Report of the President, 1989: 311.

income grow, so do consumption expenditures, *ceteris paribus* (particularly, holding the interest rate constant). Algebraically,

$$Co = f(Y, i)$$

and more specifically,

$$Co = \delta Y,$$

where $0 < \delta < 1$, $\delta = \delta(i)$, and $\Delta\delta/\Delta i < 0$. This is usually termed the **long-run consumption function**.

The second assumption of the analysis that needs to be relaxed is that present and future income are known with certainty. In fact, both the

Figure 3.8 Consumption/GNP and Gross Private Domestic Investment/GNP.

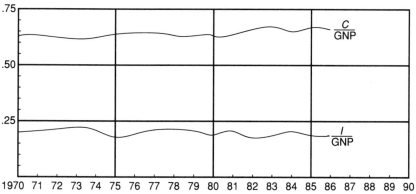

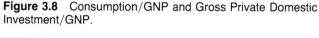

magnitude and future growth of income are subject to variability and we can never be completely sure what they are going to be. People must therefore make decisions about such things as present consumption based on *estimates* (i.e., **expectations**) of those magnitudes.

The nature of such expectations, and the ways in which they may be formed, constitutes one of the most important topics of this book and is dealt with in several chapters. Regarding income and consumption, however, Milton Friedman has developed an important theory known as the **permanent income hypothesis**.[6] **Permanent income** is people's current expectation of the average magnitude of income. This expectation is assumed to be formed by observing past values of income. It is a weighted average of such observations, with higher weights attached to the more recent observations, although Friedman specifically assumed that the sum of the weights on the prior observations exceeds that on the current observation.

Throughout this book expected values of variables will be designated with asterisk superscripts, so that Y^* = the current expectation of income (i.e., permanent income), $'Y^*$ = the previous expectation, and Y = actual current income as defined earlier. By Friedman's argument

$$Y^* = \beta Y + (1 - \beta)'Y^*$$

where $\beta < .5$. Note that this seems to be a simple two-period model of expectations formation, until it is realized that $'Y^*$ was formed during the preceding period by the same process.

By placing higher weights on more recent observations, the model allows expectations to adjust as new information becomes available. The adjustment is in the direction of the deviation between current income and the previous expectation, and its magnitude will be some fraction of the difference. To illustrate, suppose that $\beta = .4$ and an individual's previous expectation was correct. That is,

$$
\begin{aligned}
Y^* &= .4(\$40,000) + .6(\$40,000) \\
&= \$16,000 + \$24,000 \\
&= \$40,000.
\end{aligned}
$$

In this case the expectation will not change.

Now suppose that the individual is surprised in the present by a positive difference between current income and the previous expectation, such that

$$
\begin{aligned}
Y^* &= .4(\$50,000) + .6(\$40,000) \\
&= \$20,000 + \$24,000 \\
&= \$44,000.
\end{aligned}
$$

Note that the expectation rises, *although by less than the rise in income.* If the higher income level persists, however, the expectation will approach it over time. The same would occur for negative differences between current income and the prior expectation, causing the current expectation to adjust downward.

Because current income can deviate from the prior expectation, current income has two components. One is permanent income and Friedman labeled the other **transitory income**. That is, $Y = Y^* + Yt$, such that $Y - Y^* = Yt$, where Yt can be positive, negative, or zero. Friedman then theorized that people ignore the essentially random deviations of income from its expected value, basing their consumption plans solely on permanent income. That is, what may be termed **permanent consumption** is a function of *permanent* income. Symbolically,

$$Co^* = \delta Y^*$$
$$= \delta \beta Y + \delta (1 - \beta)' Y^*.$$

This is sometimes termed the **short-run consumption function**.

Of course, Friedman realized that plans often go astray. Just as there are random deviations of income from its expected value, there are also random deviations of consumption from its intended value. A person may find unintended medical expenditures necessary, for example, or an unexpected decline in such expenditures may occur. Telephone and utility bills may be higher or lower than expected, or an unusually good bargain on a desired item may be discovered and generate an unplanned expenditure. Such random **transitory consumption**, positive or negative, is also a component in total consumption, such that

$$Co = Co^* + Ct$$
$$= \delta \beta Y + \delta (1 - \beta)' Y^* + Ct.$$

Among the strong assumptions Friedman made was that there is no relationship between transitory income and transitory consumption. This implies that either $Yt > 0$ or $Ct < 0$ will simply cause saving to rise by that amount and, perhaps, cause borrowing to fall for those who are net debtors. Similarly, $Yt < 0$ or $Ct > 0$ will result in saving's being reduced in order to maintain permanent consumption or to finance the unintended consumption, increased borrowing may also be employed where past accumulated savings are inadequate.[7] In Chapter 5 it is argued, in consonance with the broader sweep of Friedman's theoretical contributions, that most nonzero Yt and Ct simply cause transitory changes in people's cash balances.

Perhaps the most important implication of the permanent income hypothesis, however, is that by planning their permanent consumption on the basis of permanent, rather than on current, income, people act to smooth their consumption out over time, so that it has less variability than current income. People's incomes vary systematically over their lifespans, being low during their youth, relatively high during their peak earning years, and low again after retirement. By Friedman's theory, they should be net borrowers early and also net dissavers late in their lives, in order to raise consumption when $Y < Y^*$ and $Yt < 0$, and they should be net savers in their high earning years, paying off past debt and shifting income forward while $Y > Y^*$ and $Yt > 0$, so that consumption can be raised in their retirement years.[8]

The theory also implies the smoothing of aggregate consumption expenditures over the business cycle. Near the peak of the cycle, $Y > Y^*$ and $Yt > 0$. Consumption rises as income rises, but not by as much as income because, from the consumption function above, $\Delta Co/\Delta Y = \delta\beta$—hence $\Delta Co = \delta\beta \cdot \Delta Y$—and $0 < \delta\beta < 1$. Consumption rises less than income; therefore, saving increases, shifting purchasing power forward, so that people can increase their consumption in the contraction phase of the cycle.

As the economy approaches the trough (i.e., bottom) of the cycle, $Y < Y^*$ and $Yt < 0$, causing consumption to fall. Consumption does not fall as much as income, however, and savings are drawn down in order to help maintain permanent consumption. Theoretically, this smaller variability of consumption than of income, and greater variability of saving than of income, should act to moderate—but not to eliminate–the business cycle itself.

Friedman's permanent income theory of consumption is a key to understanding many such matters, vital for its recognition of the expectational element in the human actions behind microeconomic and macroeconomic phenomena. An earlier and less sophisticated theory of consumption, known as the **absolute income hypothesis** and which simply relates consumption to current income, provided the basis for Keynesian economics, which will be discussed in later chapters.

Financial Instruments

All saving, investment, and credit market transactions involve the exchange of either a physical asset or a financial asset. Examples of the latter include entries in savings account passbooks, stocks, bonds, and other financial securities. Such financial assets are really titles (i.e. certificates of ownership) establishing a property right to an income stream. There are two broad categories of financial assets, **debt instruments** and **equity instruments.** Debt instruments may be referred to broadly as **bonds.**

The issuance (i.e., sale) of bonds is the primary means by which corporations incur debt, that is, borrow money for investment purposes. It is also the way governments at all levels incur debt. Purchasers of bonds from their primary (i.e., original) issuers are therefore lenders. The credit nature of these transactions can be seen from the fact that most bonds have a **term to maturity** of 10, 20, or 30 years and a contracted annual interest payment. A $1000 bond, for example, may have a 20-year term to maturity—after which the purchase price is returned to the holder—and an annual interest payment of $80.

The basic rate of return, that is, interest, on a bond is termed the **dividend yield** and can be approximated by the ratio of the annual interest payment to the purchase price of the bond. That is,

$$i = \frac{d}{p_b},$$

where i = the dividend yield or interest rate, d = the fixed interest payment, and p_b = the initial price of the bond. In the case just described the dividend yield would be

$$i = \frac{\$80}{\$1000} = .08.$$

That the dividend yield thus expressed is only an approximation of the true rate of interest on a normal bond can be seen from the present value formula. For such a 20-year bond under competitive conditions,

$$P_b = \frac{\$80}{1 + i} + \frac{\$80}{(1 + i)^2} + \cdots + \frac{\$80}{(1 + i)^{20}} + \frac{\$1000}{(1 + i)^{20}}.$$

Now if the bond had no term to maturity, such that $n \to \infty$, the formula would simplify to

$$P_b = \frac{d}{i},$$

from which it would follow that

$$\frac{1}{P_b} = \frac{i}{d}$$

and

$$\frac{d}{p_b} = i.$$

So for a bond with a term to maturity, the interest rate expressed this way would not be exactly correct, although it would be closer the longer the remaining term to maturity is.

Often an individual who has purchased a bond experiences a change in circumstances and wishes to regain the invested funds prior to the maturity of the asset. Therefore, a **secondary** (i.e., resale) **market** for bonds has emerged. To the extent that this market is efficient, the current price of a bond should always equal the discounted present value of its remaining interest payments and initial price, and it should approach the initial price more closely the shorter the remaining period is to maturity. But because the market rate of discount (i.e., interest) can change with time preferences, estimations of future states of the economy, and so on, the price of a bond in the secondary market can deviate upward or downward from its initial price. This possibility is known as **market risk**.

A bondholder experiences a **capital gain** if the value of a bond appreciates on this market and a capital loss (i.e., negative capital gain) if it falls. That is, where g = the capital gain and p_b' = the subsequent price of the bond,

$$g = \frac{P_b' - P_b}{P_b}$$

$$= \frac{\Delta P_b}{P_b}.$$

This effect can be captured in what is termed the **total return**, expressed as the sum of the dividend yield and capital gain. That is,

$$i_t = \frac{d}{p_b} + \frac{\Delta p_b}{p_b}$$

$$= i + g.$$

In the case of the $1000 bond with an $80 interest payment, a rise in the price in the secondary market to $1050 would make the total return

$$i_t = \frac{\$80}{\$1000} + \frac{\$50}{\$1000}$$

$$= .08 + .05$$

$$= .13.$$

There is one more important factor that must be considered in accurately determining the return on a security. Both the dividend yield and total return are nominal (i.e., dollar value) expressions, and the value of the dollar may itself change. That is, the dollar prices of goods may rise over time, termed **inflation**, such that the purchasing power of each dollar falls, or prices may fall over time, termed **deflation**, such that the value of each dollar rises. If we want to know what is happening to our real wealth as a result of an investment, it is important to distinguish the **real rate of return** from these purely nominal returns. If P = the price level—or an index, such as the GNP deflator—α = $\Delta P/P$ on an annual basis, and r = the real rate of return, then for a security such as those under discussion,

$$r = i + g - \alpha.$$

For passbook accounts, or credit transactions in which no active secondary market exists for the assets involved, this simplifies to

$$r = i - \alpha.$$

If the inflation rate were 7 percent, then the bond above would earn

$$r = .08 + .05 - .07$$
$$= .06.$$

Generally speaking, as the capitalized present values of future income flow, financial asset prices should adjust enough to compensate for inflation, leaving the underlying real rate of interest undisturbed. This depends on accurate expectations, however. More will be said about such market reactions in future chapters.

In contrast to bonds, which are debt instruments, the primary equity instrument is the **stock**, although mortgages are also an important equity instrument. A stock is a share of ownership in a corporation. Like bonds, stock issues have credit, or at least investment, aspects. The firm issues stock to obtain financial capital when it goes into business and may also issue more shares to obtain additional capital later. Purchasers are restricting present consumption to obtain future income and consumption (i.e., they are investing).

There are three important differences between stocks and bonds. First, stocks have no term to maturity and hence are not a loan. Second, bonds confer no right to vote for corporate management. Third, and most important, bondholders are *contractual* claimants on the value of the firm's output. Annual interest payments on bonds are contractually set at a fixed amount. The bondholder only bears the market risk discussed above and some default risk from the possibility of the firm's going broke. Stockholders, in contrast, have *no* contractually set interest payment and are the *residual* claimants on the value of the firm's output. Bondholders get paid first, as do workers, who are also contractual claimants. Stockholders get paid only if a residual still exists. They thus bear additional risk, but risk bearing is a major function of ownership.

The issuance of stock actually provides the firm with another method of raising capital. If a residual exists, the firm can decide not to pay all of it out to its owners as stock dividends. The **retained earnings** can then be invested. It turns out that investors generally do not mind if the firm retains earnings. Stocks, like bonds, are also traded in an active secondary market. The stock market is highly competitive and efficient and acts with rapidity to capitalize all available information on a firm's future prospects into the current value of its shares. Because current investment raises the prospects of future earnings, the price of a firm's stock will generally rise by the amount of undistributed profits per share. Thus investors not paid a portion of dividends are happy because they receive equivalent capital gains.

"Flow" and "Stock" Markets

There is an important distinction between the primary (i.e., new issue) and secondary (i.e., resale) markets for both stocks and bonds that should be highlighted. The primary markets are described best, both in terms of supply and demand, as consisting of regular flows per unit of time, just as supply and demand in most other markets are interpreted. The ongoing flow supply of new stocks and bonds, however, both from corporations and governmental units, really constitutes part of the demand. Another part is the demand by corporations for retained earnings, and the demand for purely consumer credit rounds out the total flow demand for credit.

The supply of credit also consists of a set of distinct elements. Certainly, the demand for new issues of stocks and bonds is part of it, as are people's savings deposits. The nature of the supply of retained earnings matching the demand raises a minor issue: Should funds invested directly be considered part of the credit market? Actually, retained earnings are an instance of credit rather than direct investment. Investors really supply the funds, or concur in their appropriation by the firm, and simply obtain their interest on the loan in the form of capital gains.

The question asked is still relevant, however, and the answer is *yes and no*. Irving Fisher pointed out that even if everyone invested only their own funds, as long as markets were integrated, a common rate of return on investment, or interest rate, would emerge. The credit market is simply a part of this larger time market. Graphically, this can be handled by including in the credit supply-and-demand curves the amounts directly invested, so that despite the credit market label, the graph really refers to the overall time market.

The crucial difference between the primary and secondary markets for debt and equity refers to the fact that, while the former are best described in flow supply and demand terms, the latter are "stock" markets in a distinct sense of the term. Because both debt and equity instruments are durable, and because they are often traded, the supply of either is interpreted best as consisting of the entire existing "stock" (i.e., quantity), drawn as a vertical line in Figure 3.9, and the demand is best interpreted as the demand to own and hold these claims on income streams.

In this interpretation, if more people decided to sell than to buy—at the initial price—this would show up as a decline in the demand to hold. Dashed line D' indicates such a reduced demand in Figure 3.9. The price of bonds, which might here be interpreted as a form of weighted average of such debt instruments, would fall from p_b to p'_b, causing capital losses to sellers since $g = \Delta p_b/p_b < 0$, but raising the yield since $d/p'_b > d/p_b$. This rise in the yield would increase the quantity demanded until people were willing to hold the entire existing stock, clearing the market at p'_b.

In this analysis the stock of bonds shifts outward overtime as long as the flow supply of new issues exceeds the rate of bond retirement. If we apply the same reasoning to the equity shares of corporations, the flow of new issues would accrete to the existing "stock," making it shift outward over time unless, in a recession, bankruptcies caused shares

Figure 3.9   Stock Supply and Demand in a Security Market.

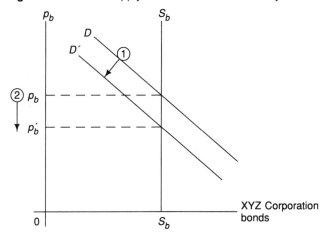

Figure 3.10 Yields on Corporate Aaa Bonds and Thirty-Day Treasury Bills.

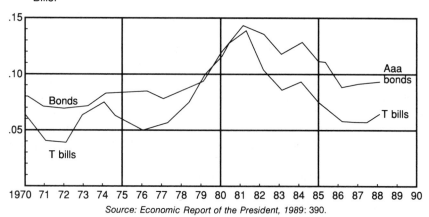

Source: Economic Report of the President, 1989: 390.

removed to be larger than new issues. It is primarily by shifts in the demand to hold, however, that these secondary markets capitalize new information on firm prospects and future market conditions into the present value of debt and equity at the rate of interest established in the time market, and equate the yield on financial instruments to that on real capital. For this reason the demand for such financial claims can be written as

$$D = f(p_b, i, Y^*),$$

with negative signs on the first two independent variables and a positive sign on the third.

Figure 3.10 shows percentage yields over nearly two decades on two types of securities: Treasury bills issued by the U.S. government, with a term to maturity of only 30 days, and Aaa corporate bonds, with maturities of ten years or longer. The most interesting feature of the graph is the persistent rise in these interest rates from the mid-1970s through 1981 and their slow decline until 1986. This was the result of certain macroeconomic policies and events that will be discussed in later chapters, particularly Chapter 15.

International Financial Market Integration

An important qualification to the analysis of this chapter has to do with international trade in financial assets. Individuals with significant savings to invest usually learn rather quickly not to put all of their eggs in one basket. Financial asset prices have some market price variability, and therefore it is rather risky for a transactor to invest all available funds in a single asset. Because in normal times the prices of different assets are moving in different directions and their price movements tend to cancel in the aggregate, risk can be reduced by investing in a **portfolio** (i.e., diversified set) of such assets.

Of course, there are times when financial asset prices tend to move upward or downward together, such as when financial transactors anticipate a coming recession or expansion, beneficial or adverse changes in the tax law and so on. Domestic portfolio investment cannot eliminate this risk. One way of reducing it, however, and of further diversifying the portfolio, is to invest part of available funds in foreign financial assets.[9] Many U.S. investors do this and, also, many foreigners purchase U.S. corporate or governmental securities.

Modern communications technologies combined with severe reductions in governmental barriers to such transactions during the post-World War II period have greatly reduced the cost to transactors of such international investments. As a consequence, national financial markets—particularly, those of Western nations—have become increasingly integrated into a single, global, financial capital market. In this market interest rate differentials between countries will tend to be rapidly eliminated as profit-seeking investors switch investments by shifting funds internationally, selling assets in low-yield nations and raising demand for assets in high-yield nations.

The effect this has on the model is illustrated in Figure 3.11. If we remember that the flow supply of credit and financial capital represents

Figure 3.11 International Capital Market Integration and Domestic Supply Elasticity.

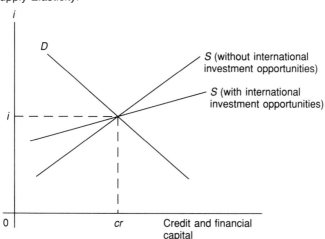

demand for new issues of financial assets, and that financial capital is demanded through the supply of such assets, the presence of actual and potential foreign investment in the domestic market is best modeled as increasing the elasticity of the supply curve as shown. This is because any change in domestic demand that tends to alter the domestic interest rate will quickly cause both foreign and domestic investors either to shift investments here, in the case of rising demand and i, or overseas, in the case of falling demand and i.

Such shifts clearly limit the potential domestic interest rate movements from a given demand shift. In the extreme case of zero transactions and information costs resulting in perfect capital market integration in which the United States represented a small part of the world economy, the supply curve would be perfectly elastic or horizontal. In that case, no change in domestic demand would alter the domestic interest rate. The United States cannot be modeled in that way, however, although many other nations could be, because our economy is so large that demand changes in our capital market will often be large even relative to the world economy, so the supply curve for our market must be modeled with a positive slope, as shown.

The same reasoning can be applied to the secondary or resale markets for U.S. financial assets. Neither Americans nor foreigners need purchase new issues of securities either at home or abroad. In these markets, the opportunity for U.S. and foreign citizens to shift investments internationally must be modeled as making the demand curve for domestic securities more elastic, as shown in Figure 3.12. In the case of perfect international capital market integration and a small

Figure 3.12 International Financial Integration and Domestic Security Demand.

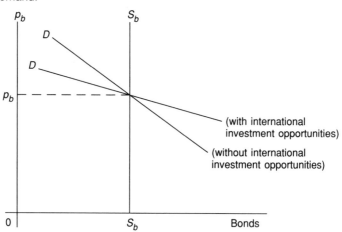

country, the demand curve would be horizontal. In the U.S. case it must be modeled as elastic, but still sloping downward.

International investment, in various forms, has a very long history. In the 20th century the dollar value of U.S. purchases of foreign securities (i.e., imports, or overseas investment) has usually exceeded our sales of domestic securities (i.e., securities exports or foreign investment) to foreigners. In recent years many observers of the U.S. scene have been worried by the fact that foreign investment in the United States has come to exceed our overseas investment. This is claimed to reduce our growth and economic welfare.

As explained in Chapter 18, these fears are not well-founded either in theory or by empirical evidence. As the result of the operation of certain equilibrating mechanisms, our financial capital export surplus is simply offsetting a deficit ($EX > IM$) that we are running in our transactions in goods and services with foreigners. It should be remembered anyway that for many decades after the Revolutionary War the United States experienced a net inflow of investment funds. Indeed, British investors provided much of the financial capital for investment in our basic infrastructure (e.g., canals and railroads in this country) and these investments hardly stunted our growth.

Summary

Here, appropriately simplified, are the major points of this chapter.

1. Whereas inputs employed (and the way they are employed) determine the output obtained, the expected value of the output determines the value of the inputs.

2. The same goods or sums of money available to a person later, rather than now, have a lower present value to that person now. Such positive time preferences are a prime determinant of the interest rate.

3. A person's rate of time preference varies at the margin through diminishing marginal utility as that person's present and likely future income change.

4. People with given present and future income streams adjust their marginal rates of time preference to equality with the market rate of interest through borrowing or lending.

5. Corporate investment, which has less to do with time preference than consumer borrowing does (because future income generated by the productive capital is expected to cover interest payments on funds acquired for the investment), is an important component of the demand for credit and financial capital.

6. The interest rate, which equilibrates the supply of and demand for credit and financial capital, determines the proportions of aggregate income that are consumed and saved. Consumption is therefore a function of both the magnitude of income and the interest rate. The same is also true of saving.

7. Given normal uncertainty about the magnitudes of their present and future incomes, people may base their consumption plans on an expectation about the magnitude and growth of their income.

8. Such expectations are more stable than actual income and income growth; hence the time path of people's consumption is more stable.

9. Financial assets are certificates of ownership establishing property rights to income streams generated by physical assets.

10. The "primary" markets for new issues of debt and equity are part of the "flow" supply of and demand for credit and financial capital that interact to determine the interest rate.

11. The "secondary" markets in which previously issued debt and equity instruments are held and traded are "stock" markets in a special sense. In these markets the demands to hold (i.e., own) such assets interact with existing quantities to establish their prices at the discounted present values of the income streams to which they are claims.

12. The opportunity for Americans to invest abroad as well as at home and for foreigners to do the same, makes supply more elastic in our primary (financial capital) market and demands more elastic in our secondary (i.e., financial asset) markets.

Notes

1. Irving Fisher, *The Theory of Interest* (reprint, New York: Porcupine Press, 1977): 1–3.

2. *The Theory of Interest*: 55.

3. Ludwig von Mises, *Human Action* (3rd ed., Chicago: Henry Regnery, 1963): 483. Some economists, including Fisher, have argued that time preference may not be positive. However, Mancur Olson and Martin J. Bailey, "Positive Times Preference," *Journal of Political Economy* 88 (February 1981): 1–25, demonstrate that the case for positive time preference is compelling.

4. *The Theory Interest*: 62.

5. Theoretically, saving will be a positive function of the interest rate as long as the substitution effect of an interest rate change is larger than the income effect. For a survey of studies on the empirical relationship between saving and the interest rate, see Thorvaldur Gylfason, "Interest Rate, Inflation, and the Aggregate Consumption Function," *Review of Economics and Statistics* 63 (May 1981): 233–245.

6. See Milton Friedman, *A Theory of the Consumption Function* (Princeton, N.J.: Princeton University Press, 1957).

7. This does not mean, as superficial critics have claimed, that positive or negative Y_t does not affect consumption at all. It does so, of course, by changing Y^*.

8. Note that this argument introduces a different element into the formation of the expectation. As modeled, the expectation is formed only by observing past values of income. Such an expectation formation process would not allow young people whose incomes are rising over time to have an expectation larger than their current income. The argument here implies that they form Y^* by observing a cross section of individuals and their incomes by age distribution. This is important because, as Chapter 14 discusses, the modern view is that people use sources of information other than mere observation of past values of the variable about which the expectation is being formed.

9. Despite some perceptions to the contrary, stock price movements in different countries do not seem to be highly correlated. See Gerald P. Dwyer, Jr., and R. W. Hafer, "Are National Stock Markets Linked?" *Federal Reserve Bank of St. Louis Review* (November/December 1988): 3–23.

Student Self-Test _____

I. True–False

T F **1.** The value of outputs is determined by the value of inputs used in their production.

T F **2.** It generally takes less than a dollar available to a person now to have the same value to that person now as a dollar available in the future.

T F **3.** A bond is understood best as a debt instrument.

T F **4.** Positive transitory income ($Yt > 0$) would initially tend to raise an individual's marginal rate of time preference.

T F **5.** The current price of a bond should closely approximate the discounted present value of its remaining interest payments and initial price.

II. Short Answer *(150 words or less each)*

1. Briefly describe both the production and value relationships between income (interpreted as the value of final goods and services) and the factors of production, including the role of time preference.
2. Briefly explain the preferred method of modeling the demand for and supply of financial assets in their secondary market, and why that method is preferred.
3. Is it contradictory to claim that individuals adjust their intertemporal income stream through borrowing or saving until their marginal rate of time preference equals the market rate of interest and then to claim that the interaction of such borrowers and savers *determines* the interest rate to which each is adjusting? Explain.
4. Explain why stockholders often are not bothered when management retains a portion of net earnings for investment purposes instead of paying all such earnings out in dividends.
5. What is the ultimate nature of income, and what problems does this provide for macroeconomics?

III. Completion Problems

1. Mrs. Lotta Luchre borrowed $1000 from her husband to purchase a bond for $1000 on which the annual interest payment was $d = \$85$ and eventually sold it for $1050. The rate of inflation over the period during which she owned the bond was $\alpha = 6$ percent per year.
   A. Mrs. Luchre's dividend yield was _____ percent.
   B. In dollars her capital gain was $_____.
   C. In percentage terms the gain was _____ percent.
   D. The total return on her investment was _____ percent.
   F. The real return she earned was _____ percent.
   G. Her husband's first name is probably _____.

2. Consider an individual with a prior permanent income expectation $'Y^* = \$30,000$ per year who is surprised to find that his income this year is only $Y = \$24,000$. Assume that the parameter in the individual's permanent income equation is $\beta = .49$.
   A. After assimilating the new information, the individual's current income expectation (permanent income) is $Y^* =$ _____ .
   B. Assuming that $Co^* = \delta Y^*$ where $\delta = .9$, and that transitory consumption of $Ct = -\$500$ in the form of reduced automotive repair bills occurs, the family's actual consumption that year will be $Co =$ $_____ .
   C. If the annual income of $24,000 endures for three more years, then this person's permanent income reaches $_____ and permanent consumption reaches $_____ .

3. In 1982 you loaned your cousin $5000 at 8 percent annual interest to aid his ailing business.
   A. When he paid you off in 1988, you collected $_____ .
   B. If you had specified that the interest was to be compounded quarterly, you would have collected $_____ .

4. Northern South-Pole Enterprises is considering the purchase of a teleportation machine to transport polar ice to the Sahara Desert, where it can be sold to a consortium that has the lemonade concession at the local Camel-race track. The machine is expected to last three years and yield $500,000 net benefits over operating expenses each year. It will cost $1 million, however, and the interest rate is 6 percent.
   A. The expected present value of the machine is $_____ .
   B. The net present value is $_____ .
   C. Should the firm invest in the machine? _____ (yes/no)

5. Consider an individual who experiences utility in the present from both present and expected future income. The individual has a job with a salary that is expected to stay constant in real terms. The market rate of interest is 8 percent. If MU_p is the marginal utility of present income to the individual before any saving or borrowing is undertaken, and MU_f is the marginal utility of future income, suppose that $MU_p = 106$ and $MU_f = 100$.
   A. This individual's marginal rate of time preference is _____ percent.
   B. Will this individual borrow or save? _____ .
   C. The formula for the equilibrium condition is _____ .
   D. Based upon your answers to (A) and (B), briefly explain how this equilibrium is brought about by the individual's actions.

CHAPTER 4

Labor Markets and Unemployment

Unemployment is one of the two prime concerns of macroeconomic analysis. It is impossible to treat the subject exhaustively in a single chapter, and aspects of the problem are dealt with throughout this book. Chapter 2 discusses the way the U.S. government attempts to measure various employment and unemployment categories. In this chapter the basic microeconomics of labor markets are developed and certain causes and aspects of macroeconomic unemployment are analyzed. The first step, however, is to derive the demand and supply curves for a representative type of labor.

The Firm's Demand for Labor

Consider a firm that employs inputs to produce the ith good or service. Assume that the firm is operating in the **Marshallian short run:** its technology is given, its capital and plant are in place, and any changes in the rate of production are made by altering the remaining variable input (i.e., the number of man-hours of labor employed in each production period) designated here by the letter L. Assume also the following definitions, most of which may already be familiar.

TR = the **total revenue** of the firm, where TR $= p_i q_i$

K = the **capital stock**, or plant and equipment, of the firm

W = the **hourly** *nominal* **wage rate** for the type of labor employed

TVC = the **total variable costs** of the firm, where TVC $= W \cdot L$ in the simplest case

TFC = the **total fixed costs** of the firm

TC = **total cost**, where TC = TVC + TFC

MC = **marginal cost**, or the change in total cost, resulting when the firm alters its rate of production; that is, MC = $\Delta TC/\Delta q_i$

Te = the **technology of production**, where $q_i = q_i(L, K, Te)$ is the **production function** of the firm

mpl = the **marginal product of labor**, or change in output resulting from a change in the firm's labor employment; that is, mpl = $\Delta q_i/\Delta L$

vmp = the market **value of the marginal product**, where vmp = $p_i \cdot$ mpl

The firm deciding whether or not to employ an additional man-hour of labor is concerned with three things. The first is the additional output it expects, or the marginal product of labor (mpl). The second is the value of that additional output on the market (i.e., the price it can be sold for). Assuming for simplicity that the firm is a price *taker* in its output market, so that the market price does not change as it alters its output, we obtain the value vmp = p_i mpl. The firm's third concern is the change in its costs resulting from the additional employment. If we assume that the firm is also a price taker in its input market, so that the wage rate does not change as it hires additional units, the firm's total costs will simply rise by the amount of the wage rate. Symbolically, $\Delta TC = W$ if $\Delta L = 1$.

Put in these terms, and assuming that the firm wishes to maximize its **net revenues** (TR-TC, often termed *profits*), the nature of the decision is easily seen from Figure 4.1(a) and 4.1(b). Figure 4.1(a) shows the marginal addition to total product first rising, then falling as additional labor is applied in production along with the firm's fixed inputs. Figure 4.1(c), which has the same horizontal axis as Figure 4.1(a), shows the firm's total production per time period rising at an increasing rate as long as marginal product is rising (to the quantity of labor L), then rising at a decreasing rate as long as the marginal product of additional labor is falling, but still positive. Output stops rising at labor unit L_0, where mpl = 0.

Figure 4.1(b) shows the market value of the marginal products shown in Figure 4.1(a), but only for the declining portion of the *mpl* curve because the firm will never find its optimal employment in the rising portions of the curves. Both curves peak at the same quantity of employment, L. Placing the fixed wage on this graph as a horizontal line allows comparison of both the marginal benefits, vmp, and the marginal costs, W, associated with the employment of any given unit of

Figure 4.1 Short-Run Marginal Product, Total Product, and the Value of the Marginal Product of Labor.

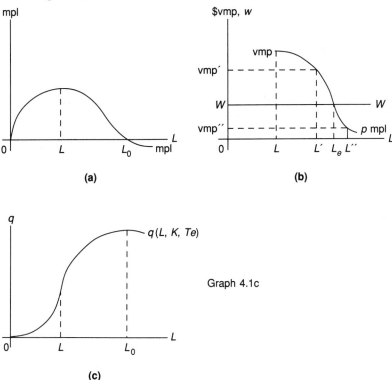

labor on the horizontal axis. As long as the value of the marginal product exceeds the wage rate (at L', where vmp$'$ > W, for example), it pays the firm to employ an additional unit of labor, because the difference either adds to profits or reduces losses.

For marginal units such as L'', where the value of the marginal product (vmp$''$) is less than the wage rate, the firm could do better by reducing employment. The firm's optimal employment is therefore quantity L_e, at which the wage rate just equals the value of the marginal product. Note also that because the vmp curve slopes downward toward the right, if the wage rate increased, then the firm's optimal employment would decrease and if the wage rate decreased, then the firm's employment would increase. The *vmp* curve therefore shows the quantities the firm will employ at each wage rate and constitutes the firm's labor demand curve.

Firm Demand Shifts

Like any other demand curve defined with respect to the variable on the vertical axis, there are other factors that can cause a firm's labor demand curve to shift inward or outward. Any change in the market price of the firm's product, p_i, will shift the firm's demand for labor in the same direction. This can be seen from the three-quadrant graph in Figure 4.2, which rearranges Figures 4.2(b) and 4.2(c) so that their common axes (L = man-hours of employment) are joined, and then connects Figure 4.1(c) to a graph showing the firm's marginal cost, average total cost, and the market price.

Since the firm is a price taker in its output market, the firm maximizes net revenue by producing and selling some output, q_i, at which price equals marginal cost. Definitionally,

$$MC = \frac{\Delta TC}{\Delta q_i},$$

Figure 4.2 Equivalence of Input-Side and Output-Side Profit Maximization Rules.

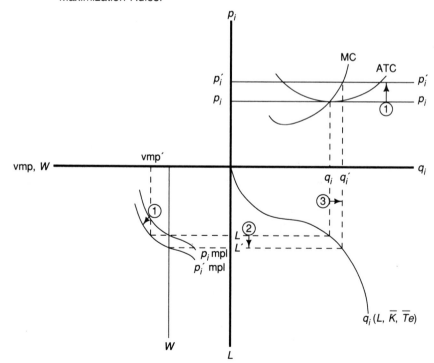

and since fixed costs are constant and the firm is also a price taker in its labor market, for each additional man-hour of labor $\Delta TC = \Delta TVC = W$. Also, as long as $\Delta L = 1$, the marginal product of labor is

$$\text{mpl} = \frac{\Delta q_i}{\Delta L} = \Delta q_i.$$

By substitution, therefore, the firm's marginal cost can be expressed as

$$MC = \frac{W}{\text{mpl}}.$$

Now in its short-run decision to employ labor, the firm maximizes net revenue by adding labor until $W = \text{vmp}$, as argued above. But $\text{vmp} = p_i \cdot \text{mpl}$, so the rule really says to add man-hours of employment until

$$W = p_i \cdot \text{mpl}$$

or

$$\frac{W}{\text{mpl}} = p_i,$$

which is

$$MC = p_i.$$

The two rules are therefore the same and are satisfied simultaneously, as shown in Figure 4.2 for the initial equilibrium values of p_i, q_i, and L.[1]

Now suppose that the market price of the firm's product rises to p_i'. This not only raises the (horizontal) demand curve for the firm's output, such that $p_i' > MC$, but simultaneously increases the value of the marginal product to $\text{vmp}' > W$, shifting the labor demand curve upward and outward. This is shown in the first and third quadrants of Figure 4.2. The firm then increases employment to L', where the wage equals the value of the marginal product again. This raises the firm's output rate to q_i', where $p_i' = MC$, satisfying both rules. This is the sequence of events shown by the numbered arrows.

Since the value of the marginal product is $p_i \cdot \text{mpl}$, anything that raises the productivity of labor, *ceteris paribus*, such as a technical innovation in production (an increase in the quality of capital), acquisition of additional tools and equipment, or an increase in the education and skills of employees (human capital) will shift the firm's labor demand curve outward. Such productivity changes involve shifts in the production function (the total product curve), and are discussed and illustrated in Chapter 9.

Market Demand Curve

Having derived the firm's demand curve for a particular type of labor (e.g., machinists, welders, etc.), it would seem to be a simple matter to derive the market demand curve by horizontal summation; that is, by adding, at each possible wage rate, all the quantities associated with the *vmp* curves of all the firms employing that type of labor. That would give us a curve such as the one shown in Figure 4.3 and labeled $D_L = \Sigma$ vmp. Unfortunately, it is not that simple. Any increase in labor supply that caused the wage rate to fall and the quantity employed to rise would cause the output prices to fall by increasing output on the product markets in all the industries employing such labor. The fall in output prices would reduce the values of the marginal products, shifting D_L back to some D'_L as shown.

Connecting the equilibrium points yields the market-demand curve, L_d, which is slightly less elastic than D_L. The curve L_d is a function of the same variables as D_L, however, and can be expressed as follows.

$$L_d = f(W, p_i, K, Te, \ldots).$$

Figure 4.3   Market Demand for Labor.

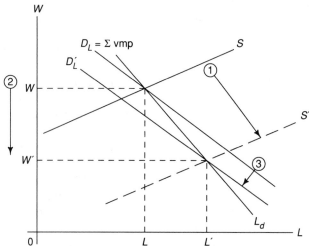

If the firm's net-revenue maximizing rule is to set

$$W = \text{vmp} = p_i \cdot \text{mpl},$$

then it can also be expressed as

$$\frac{W}{p_i} = \text{mpl}.$$

The ratio W/p_i is termed the **product wage**, because it expresses the value of the worker's wage in units of the firm's output. In this form the rule says that the firm maximizes profits by paying each worker what that individual adds to output. The labor-demand function can then be written

$$L_d = f\left(\frac{W}{p_i}, K, Te, \ldots\right).$$

The ellipsis indicates that variables not yet mentioned also may enter the function. One such omitted variable will be discussed in Chapter 9.

Labor Supply: The Choice Between Leisure and Income

The most elementary fact about people's labor-supply decisions is that they enjoy both leisure time and the things they can buy with income and that they must often give up some of one to obtain more of the other. That is, increasing our income requires that most of us work more, which means giving up some potential leisure time. Economists often express this in what is termed a **utility function**.

$$U = U(Y, L)$$

The symbol Y here stands for the income of the individual, the L stands for the number of hours the individual works during some time period (e.g., day, week, etc.), which means an equal amount of leisure foregone, and the U stands for the level of satisfaction or utility resulting from a given combination of Y and L. It is assumed also that $\Delta U/\Delta Y > 0$ and $\Delta U/\Delta L < 0$.

The relationships theorized here can be expressed graphically as in Figure 4.4, where income is measured on the vertical axis and the

Figure 4.4 Individual's Indifference Map for Labor and Income.

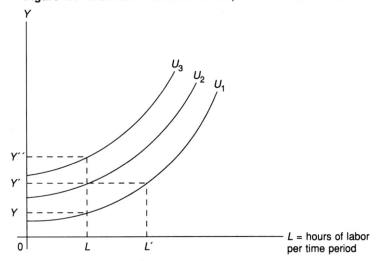

number of hours available for the individual to work per day, week, and so on, is measured on the horizontal axis. The curves marked U_1, U_2, and U_3 are **indifference curves**, connecting combinations of Y and L and yielding the same level of satisfaction to the individual.

These indifference curves appear somewhat different from those employed in analyzing the credit market in Chapter 3, in that they slope upward toward the right. This is easy to justify. Consider an individual who works L hours for income Y. If this person were required to work L' hours for the same income, the leisure lost would mean reduced utility. It seems likely, however, that there exists some increase in income (say, $\Delta Y = Y' - Y$) sufficient to compensate the individual for the lost leisure and restore the original level of satisfaction. This accounts for the positive slope of the curves.

Now consider point (L, Y) again. Clearly, the individual who could earn income Y' by working L hours would gain more utility than if only Y were earned, and income Y'' would yield more satisfaction yet. This strengthens another point learned from the first argument: Higher indifference curves represent higher levels of satisfaction. That is, $U_3 > U_2 > U_1 \ldots$ and so on. The increasing slope of the curves can be explained by diminishing marginal utility. The more hours worked, the more important the remaining leisure is to the individual because less important leisure activities are given up first, and the less important additional income is, because the most important goods are purchased first. It therefore takes increasing increments of income to motivate the sacrifice of an additional unit of leisure.

With only an indifference map, of course, it is impossible to explain individual choice. The individual's scarcity constraint can be added by pointing out, for the individual dependent on labor income,

$$Y = W \cdot L.$$

It follows that

$$\Delta Y = W \cdot \Delta L$$

and therefore

$$\frac{\Delta Y}{\Delta L} = W,$$

which means that the wage rate obtainable by an individual with marketable abilities or skills describes the rate at which that individual can trade leisure for income. Because $\Delta Y / \Delta L$ can be interpreted as the slope parameter of a linear function with an intercept of zero, a ray from the origin with slope $\Delta Y / \Delta L = W$ can be used to describe the individual's options. Steeper lines would represent higher wage rates, and vice versa.

Such a wage rate line is added in Figure 4.5. All that is then required is the standard economic assumption that the individual chooses what is considered the best of the available options. If that is true, then the

Figure 4.5 Individual's Constrained Utility Maximizing Labor Supply.

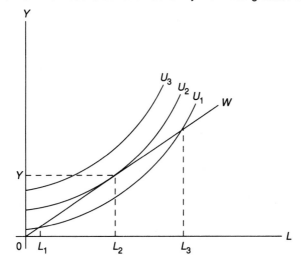

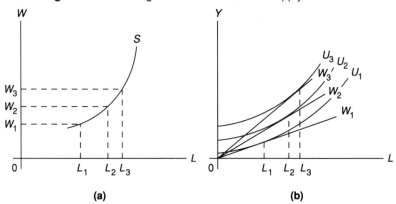

Figure 4.6   Deriving an Individual's Labor Supply Function.

person with the preferences shown, facing the objective constraint given by wage rate W, would not choose to work L_1 or L_3 hours per time period, because a higher level of satisfaction could be obtained by working L_2 hours and obtaining income Y. This is the person's desired work time.

A single tangency between a budget line and the highest indifference curve reached provides us with only one optimum point. By rotating the wage line through the indifference map, *ceteris paribus*, however, as illustrated in Figure 4.6(b), it is possible to find the person's optimal labor supply quantities at all imaginable relative wage rates. These points can be connected with a dashed line, which will generally rise steeply toward the right. The Cartesian coordinates can be read off and listed in a table and/or plotted on a graph such as the one in Figure 4.6(a), which clearly shows the individual's labor supply curve. Horizontal summation of all such curves of persons offering labor of a particular type yields the market supply curve for that type of labor.

Income and Substitution Effects _____

One result of Figure 4.6 is that the slope of the individual's labor supply curve increases at higher wage rates. Conceivably, it could even have a perverse backward-bending range in which wage rate increases were associated with decreasing quantities of employment offered. This is a consequence of a relative price change having both an **income effect** and a **substitution effect** on the quantities involved, and the two may work in opposite directions. What happens then depends on which effect dominates.

The income and substitution effects in labor supply will be analyzed in detail in Chapter 16, but here it can be briefly pointed out that the substitution effect of a wage rate increase motivates people to offer more labor by making leisure more costly. By increasing income, however, a wage rate increase motivates people to offer less employment, because leisure is a normal good of which people would like to have more as their income rises. If the income effect dominates the substitution effect at high wage rates, then individual and market labor supply curves could bend backward.

Since the early days of the industrial revolution, productivity increases have been raising wage rates and income by shifting labor demand outward relative to supply. One might expect an income effect to show up, and it does appear in the reduction of the average number of hours people work on a daily or weekly basis. That is, the 8-hour day and the 40-hour week are consequences of this productivity increase, quite to the contrary of the belief that these were legislative creations.

Within the period of available data, however, this income effect seems to have been never strong enough to cause an aggregate reduction in man-hours of labor supplied. This can be seen in Table 4.1, which lists inflation adjusted wage rates and man-hours of employment in nonagricultural industries from 1950 to 1984. Table 4.1 also shows the labor force participation rates and employment rates for those years. No inverse relationship between the real wage and employment is apparent in Table 4.1. Although individually, people have worked fewer hours per time period, the rise in wage rates over time has caused increases in the labor force participation rate, increasing the percentage of the population employed.

It seems that it is justifiable for practical purposes to draw labor supply curves as upward sloping throughout their length. Algebraically, such a functional relationship can be denoted

$$L_s = g(W, P, \ldots)$$

or

$$L_s = g\left(\frac{W}{P}, \cdots\right).$$

Note that the independent variable is written as a ratio of the nominal wage to the price level. As discussed in Chapter 1, this ratio form distinguishes real variables from nominal variables. W/P is the product

TABLE 4.1

Year	W/P (1977 = 100)	Man-hours of civilian non-agricultural employment (billions)	Labor force participation rate	Percentage of population employed
1950	64.0	2.06	59.2	56.1
1951	63.6	2.12	59.2	57.3
1952	65.5	2.14	59.0	57.3
1953	68.7	2.17	58.9	57.1
1954	70.5	2.10	58.8	55.5
1955	73.3	2.20	59.3	56.7
1956	75.9	2.26	60.0	57.5
1957	76.9	2.25	59.6	57.1
1958	78.0	2.21	59.5	55.4
1959	80.0	2.30	59.3	56.0
1960	81.4	2.32	59.4	56.1
1961	83.0	2.33	59.3	55.4
1962	85.0	2.39	58.8	55.5
1963	86.3	2.45	58.7	55.4
1964	87.5	2.50	58.7	55.7
1965	89.0	2.59	58.9	56.2
1966	90.3	2.66	59.2	59.6
1967	92.2	2.68	59.6	57.3
1968	94.0	2.72	59.6	57.5
1969	95.0	2.80	60.1	58.0
1970	95.7	2.79	60.4	57.4
1971	98.3	2.80	60.2	56.6
1972	101.2	2.91	60.4	57.0
1973	101.1	3.01	60.8	57.8
1974	98.3	3.03	61.3	57.8
1975	97.6	2.98	61.2	56.1
1976	99.0	3.08	61.6	56.8
1977	100.0	3.19	62.3	57.9
1978	100.5	3.32	63.2	59.3
1979	97.4	3.41	63.7	59.9
1980	93.5	3.38	63.8	59.2
1981	92.6	3.42	63.9	59.0
1982	93.4	3.35	64.0	57.8
1983	94.8	3.41	64.0	57.9
1984	94.4	3.58	64.4	59.5

Source: Economic Report of the President, 1985: Various tables.

wage in a more general sense than that discussed previously. It shows the purchasing power of the nominal wage in terms of goods and services in general.

The discussion here has been carried on in nominal terms for simplicity. The price level was held constant by the normal *ceteris paribus* assumption, so that the nominal wage and income changes were, in fact, real wage and income changes. The fact that economic decisions, including labor supply, are based on such relative prices will be stressed in Chapter 9, along with certain implications of the possibility that this might sometimes not be true.

Equilibrium, Market Intervention, and Unemployment ____

Having derived the market supply and demand curves for a particular type of labor, we do not require an extensive analysis to explain how the equilibrium price and quantity are determined. Although labor markets have characteristics distinguishing them from others, as long as no governmental or private monopoly power intrudes, the normal excess demand mechanism operates. At any wage rate below equilibrium (say, $W' < W_e$ as in Figure 4.7), an excess demand or labor shortage would exist as shown. Competition among employers would bid up the wage rate in this market relative to the price level and other wage rates, eventually eliminating the shortage.

The opposite occurs when the wage rate is above equilibrium, such as $W'' > W_e$. This means that an excess labor supply, known more commonly as unemployment, exists. In this case competition for the available jobs would result in the wage rate falling relative to the price level and to other wage rates, increasing the quantity demanded and motivating some workers to switch occupations or to take more leisure until the unemployment was essentially eliminated.

Figure 4.7 Equilibrium and Disequilibrium in a Typical Labor Market.

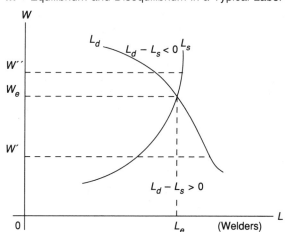

It should be pointed out that no real-world labor market would clear instantly, even if it were competitive. The mechanism would take time to operate, and real markets seem to display significant wage "stickiness," particularly downward. Some of this is a natural consequence of output demand, and hence input demand, always displaying some normal variability, and firms targeting prices, output, and employment on the estimated means of these distributions. Time is therefore required to distinguish actual shifts in the mean of output, (and hence input), demand from mere observation runs in the tails of the initial distribution.

Some downward wage rigidity may also result from a normal reluctance of workers to accept wage rate reductions and of managers to incur the ill will of workers through such reductions, even when they are justified by declining demand for products and hence for inputs. Workers in any given micro market may be highly concerned with maintaining their relative wage, interpreted as the relationship between their nominal wage and other wage rates, W_i/Wa, where $Wa =$ the weighted average of nominal wage rates generally or some index of wage rates. Hence they may resist wage rate reductions as a threat to their relative status.

This phenomenon may be particularly important under deflationary conditions (say, an enduring monetary contraction) when demands for outputs (and hence labor) are declining generally, requiring both wage rates and prices to fall to restore equilibrium; see Chapter 5. Whether particular workers are seen as being primarily concerned with their wage differential, W_i/Wa, or their real purchasing power wage, W_i/P, there may emerge a you-go-first problem, in which each resists a reduction in their nominal wage and waits for other wages and prices to fall in order to avoid the relative loss associated with going first in such reductions.[2] This also partly explains slow downward output price adjustment and the appearance of layoffs as firms try to reduce costs and pressure workers to accept the required wage reductions.

Some economists believe that the major source of downward wage and price stickiness is the existence of **long-term contracts** in labor markets, which fix the nominal wage rate and other working conditions for the duration of the contract. One reason workers are contractual claimants on the value of output while investors are residual claimants is that workers are more risk-averse than investors are and wish to have insurance against wage fluctuations in the form of a contractually set wage.[3] In the unionized sector of the labor force, where collective bargaining occurs, the typical contract length is three years. In the nonunion sector, where both formal and informal or "implicit" contracts occur, wage and working condition adjustments are typically, although not in all cases, made once a year.

Given the prevalence of such long-term contracts with recontracting occurring only at contract termination rather than on a continuous basis, both downward wage rigidity and layoffs as a response to deflationary macroeconomic shocks seem easily explained. So also is the apparently slow and painful downward adjustment of wage rates and prices as contracts terminate and are renegotiated under such deflationary aggregate-demand conditions.

Although this view is appealing and may have some validity, there is room for doubts. For one thing, only about 25 percent of the labor force is subject to formal contracts, so at least the potential for continuous recontracting and flexible adjustment seems larger than contracting theorists admit. Second, it is logically their real wage and income that workers wish to have insured. Protecting them under a deflationary aggregate demand shock requires nominal wage flexibility, so that wages and prices can fall together and restore equilibrium; see Chapter 9. It is certainly possible to write clauses in contracts allowing for such adjustments, and when contracts do not exist such adjustments cannot be prevented. Here again, explaining why recontracting occurs slowly seems to require something like the you-go-first problem.

It is useful to distinguish natural from artificial reasons for wage rigidity. If long-term contracting in the unionized sector is an important source of downward nominal wage flexibility, it is worth recognizing that much of the extent of union membership in the labor force and the power of labor unions is a consequence of favorable legislation passed in the 1930s. Unions often use their monopoly power not only to fix nominal wage rates, but also to fix them above equilibrium, preventing many labor markets from clearing, even under normal conditions.

Most Western governments also have passed **minimum wage laws**, deliberately fixing wage rates above equilibrium in many markets for unskilled and semiskilled workers. This may be particularly harmful under general deflationary conditions, because the wage rates in all such markets are prevented by law from adjusting downward as needed. Indeed, if semiskilled workers who normally earn just over the minimum wage are highly concerned with maintaining their differential over the unskilled, and skilled workers are highly concerned with maintaining their differential over the semiskilled, the minimum wage law may be a powerful source of general downward wage rigidity.

Whether these and other artificial interventions, such as unemployment compensation, or the more natural factors are more responsible for observable downward wage rigidity is a matter of debate. It is noteworthy, however, that in Hong Kong, where labor legislation is almost entirely absent, and in Japan, where it is minimal, labor markets clear much more rapidly than they do in the United States or in other Western industrial nations, and unemployment rates are very low.[4]

Job Shifting and Frictional Unemployment _____

Suppose that a labor market exists that can be analytically decomposed into few major submarkets. We might imagine, for example, that welders are hired either by firms in the aircraft industry or by the construction industry. The industry as a whole is shown in Figure 4.8(c), and the two major submarkets composing it in Figure 4.8(a) and 4.8(b). The industry-demand curve is the horizontal summation of the submarket demand curves. Also, the submarket supply curves sum horizontally into the market supply curve.

Suppose that the whole industry, including both submarkets, is initially in equilibrium at $W_1 = W_2 = W_e$. Then suppose that symmetric shifts in the demand for labor occur in the submarkets, decreasing in construction and increasing by the same amount in the aircraft sector, such that the whole industry-demand curve does not change, which allows abstraction from movements up or down the industry-supply curve. There are two ways of explaining what will now occur. In the first, information is perfect and movement costs are zero. In this case workers released in construction shift immediately to the nearest hiring aircraft firm. The leftward shift of D_1 is matched by a simultaneous leftward shift in S_1, and both D_2 and S_2 shift rightward simultaneously. Labor is reallocated between the submarkets without any change in wage rates.

In the second version, information is costly and so is moving. In this case, given a competitive market, the wage rate falls to W_1' in the construction industry, and in the aircraft sector the wage rate rises to W_2'. Workers observing the wage differential begin to shift from construction firms to the aircraft industry and the information spreads. As

Figure 4.8 Labor Reallocation Between Subcomponents of a Labor Market.

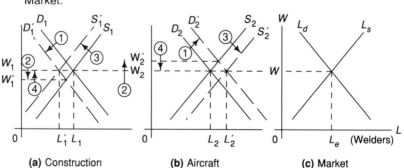

(a) Construction   (b) Aircraft   (c) Market

the labor force reallocates an excess *demand* for labor appears in construction, raising the wage rate back toward W_1, and an excess *supply* appears in the aircraft industry, causing the wage rate to fall back toward W_2, at which point all shifting ceases, *ceteris paribus*. This sequence of events is shown by the numbered arrows in the graphs.

There are several lessons here. First, what actually happens seems more like the latter story than the former, although both are extremes. Information is not free, but the labor market itself is the most vital source of both the information and the motivation causing labor resources to shift from less productive and lower-valued uses to more productive and higher-valued uses. As such it is an extremely important and beneficial institution. Anything that impedes such shifting when it is necessary acts to prevent efficient resource use and reduces the real output and income of society.

Second, markets are inherently dynamic and such resource shifting is always occurring between firms in the same industry, between industries, and across occupations. Hence, even in well-functioning markets that are basically in equilibrium (neither demand nor supply shifted in Figure 4.8(c) some unemployment exists simply because there is always some labor in transition between jobs. Such unemployment is termed **frictional unemployment**. We never would want to entirely eliminate such unemployment because it is beneficial and could only be banished by destroying the dynamism of the economy. This is not to say it could not be minimized, however, as will be shown.

Job Search

There are usually numerous firms and at least several industries employing a given type of labor, and at any time there is a distribution (in the statistical sense) of wage rates and employment conditions. A worker who has been released or who wishes to obtain a better job must search for the best offers. The costs of obtaining information on job openings, wage rates offered, and employment conditions are often termed **search costs**.

The major costs of search involve the foregone alternative uses of time spent in the search. Such time could be spent in leisure or, if alternative employments are available, in work. The major cost of time spent in search is then the value to the individual of the income and leisure foregone. Such costs tend to rise at the margin. Initially, an individual can give up the least important uses of such income or leisure. As more income is foregone, however, it may become difficult to pay the rent or mortgage.

There are benefits to time spent searching out the distribution of employment opportunities, wage offers, and working conditions. The total benefits increase as more time is spent because, until all possible employments have been found and considered, some possibility exists that a better opportunity will be found. Past some point the *marginal* benefits of time spent in search begin to fall, however, because most feasible alternatives have been checked and the probability of finding a better offer than those already discovered falls.

These basic ideas can be expressed graphically as in Figure 4.9, which shows the **marginal search costs** (MSC) rising as search time increases, and the **marginal benefits of search** (MBS) falling. Both MBS and MSC are assumed to be expressed in utility terms, and the net benefits for the individual are maximized by spending additional time in search until the marginal benefits are equal to the marginal cost at point *ST*.

There is an important distinction between search costs and **information costs** embodied in the two curves. The search costs are, as stated, the value to the individual of alternatives foregone by spending time in search. Various factors can affect such costs. Unemployment insurance, for example, whether privately or publicly provided, reduces people's search costs (thus shifting the MSC curves toward the right) and raises the average length of search, increasing the frictional unemployment rate.[5] There is also some increase in efficiency as some people find better jobs. The marginal benefits of publicly funded unemployment insurance are probably less than its cost, however, as indicated by the fact that people must be compelled to pay for it, and by the external costs imposed on a large part of the labor force for the benefit of a small part.

Figure 4.9 Optimal Employment Search Time.

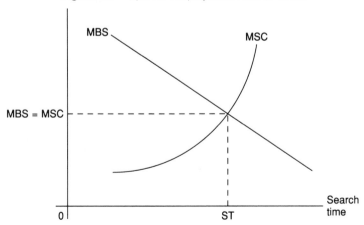

Information costs affect the MBS curve and might best be explained in terms of the productivity of a unit of time spent in search. If all of the relevant information could be obtained instantly (i.e., search was infinitely productive), so that the best option was immediately known, then the marginal benefit to additional search would be zero. Therefore, for any finite amount of required information, the higher the productivity of search is (hence the lower information costs are), the lower the marginal benefits of additional search will be.

This idea is relevant because there are market and nonmarket institutions, such as newspaper want-ad sections, employment agencies, and job data banks, that can raise the productivity of search and reduce information costs. Such institutions logically reduce average search time and hence reduce the frictional unemployment rate, *ceteris paribus*. These institutions exist because such information is valuable, and some people are willing to pay for and others to supply it.

Shifts Between Occupations

The discussion so far has focused on frictional unemployment resulting from workers shifting between jobs of the same type. Workers also shift between occupations, although less frequently, as wage and working conditions seem to warrant. For many workers this is a relatively simple matter, because most individuals manage to obtain more than one marketable skill. Everyone tends to settle in the occupation yielding the highest return (including, admittedly, both pecuniary and non-pecuniary forms of remuneration), but if the rate of pay earnable in an alternate field is not much smaller, it is easy to shift when the advantage in one's present employment disappears.

Some people's skills are highly specialized, however, and the return earned in their primary occupation may be much greater than that in any feasible alternative open to them. For such individuals a decline in demand and pay rate in their primary occupation may have to be large and prolonged in order to motivate them to switch to an alternate occupation employing their next most remunerative skill or to undertake retraining. Such declines in the demand for certain skills often occur as a systematic consequence of technological advance.

Technological advance is probably the single most important source of rising living standards over time. It has the effect, however, of constantly altering the composition of skills demanded, decreasing the demand for some and increasing the demand for others.[6] The emergence of the automobile, for example, decreased the demand for horseshoes and buggy whips and hence for those whose skills were employed in their construction. Many economists argue that the effect of technical change in making some skills obsolete gives rise, for reasons discussed previously, to a form of employment termed **structural unemployment**, which is qualitatively distinct from frictional unemployment in being more persistent and burdensome, and hence constitutes a social problem in a sense that frictional unemployment does not.

Such analysis may be seriously deficient. Consider Figure 4.10, which shows the market for a particular type of labor. Beginning from equilibrium at wage rate W_1, suppose that a technical change occurs, either in product or in process of production, which reduces demand for employees of this type, as shown. The central observation is elementary: The technical change accounts only for the decline in the demand curve. If the resulting excess supply causes the wage rate to decline to W_2, the market will be equilibrated. Quantity demanded will increase. Quantity supplied will decrease as workers either shift to alternate occupations or indulge in leisure rather than accept a wage rate considered too low. In neither case would they (nor should they) be counted as unemployed.

Any persistent unemployment in such a case must result from failure of the wage rate to equilibrate the market and be explained in terms of the market structure factors, whether minimum wage law, labor monopoly, or natural rigidities, preventing the required adjustment. Adding the number of people who are unemployed for such structural reasons to those who are frictionally unemployed and expressing this total as a percentage of the labor force yields what is termed the **natural rate of unemployment**.[7]

Figure 4.10 Structural Unemployment.

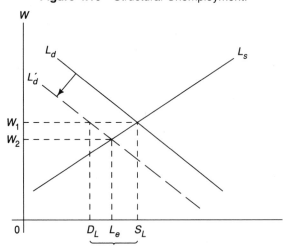

One more aspect of occupational shift should be mentioned. Much of the change in occupational composition in the economy over time results from choices made by individuals prior to entering the labor market rather than through the shifting of individuals already in the market across occupations. Young people faced with the necessity of labor-market entry make human-capital investment decisions based on the relative costs and expected rates of return associated with alternative occupations. Changes in the composition of skills demanded and the rates of return associated due to technical change greatly affect such decisions.

An example may help. In 1981 new economics Ph.D.s were lucky to find an offer at $22,000 per year, whereas new finance Ph.D.s were getting two and three offers at $30,000 per year. Some graduate economics students, observing this, shifted into finance. The result of such shifts is a tendency to eliminate the differentials motivating them. Consider Figure 4.10. The reduced remuneration in this field as the wage falls to W_2 will decrease entry into this field by new workers. Over time the supply curve will shift leftward, raising the wage rate, *ceteris paribus*.

On the other hand, the new and more highly paid fields associated with the technical change or demand shift will experience increased entry, shifting the supply curves outward and decreasing pay rates in those fields, *ceteris paribus*. For occupations requiring the same human-capital investment, the differential should tend to disappear.

Social and Demographic Factors

There are many social and demographic factors that affect the unemployment rate, and it may pay to mention briefly a few of the more important of these. Female members of the labor force are distributed across occupations in a different pattern than male workers and they earn less, on average. This often is attributed to male discrimination, although much of it is attributable to physical, physiological, and psychological factors resulting in different comparative advantages.

It is less well-known that women have higher turnover rates than men do. This has physical and social roots. Many women get pregnant and leave the labor force, often returning later to compete with male workers who have had more job experience and education. Women also tend to change jobs not only for the normal reasons, but also when their husbands change jobs and move to another area. These factors causing higher female turnover rates mean that women, on average, spend more of their careers than men do in training, where their productivity is less than it will be when they are experienced. This accounts for much of the observed differential, which has been declining in recent years. Women have tended to stay in the labor force, postponing childbearing, and the male/female skill and experience differentials have declined.

The significantly higher turnover rates of female workers affects the unemployment rate when the female labor force participation rate changes. In the 1970s, perhaps partly due to women's liberation, large-scale entry of women into the labor force significantly raised frictional unemployment and hence the natural rate of unemployment. The same was true, however, of teenagers, who also entered the labor force on a large scale in this period.[8] Teenagers have high turnover rates, because they tend to try different types of employment in a process of searching out the best and most remunerative uses of their skills before settling into a more permanent job. This brings us to the matter of job duration.

Although most new jobs (i.e., employment contracts formed in the current period, in contrast with previously existing employment) are of short duration, Robert Hall has shown that most workers are in jobs of significant duration. In fact, at any given time, one-half of all workers are in jobs that will last 15 years. Of workers aged 30 to 34, 54 percent have been employed at the same job for at least three years. Of workers aged 50 to 54, 78 percent have been employed at the same job for at least three years, and 70 percent of all workers over age 50 have been employed on the same job for at least five years.[9]

A significant point here is that, while turnover is an important feature of the labor market, it affects a relatively small number of workers. Most of these are somewhat younger and less-skilled workers who have not settled into more permanent employment. Mature workers who have found their niche in life experience infrequent turnover. This is true of all demographic categories (e.g., men, women, whites, blacks, etc.) with relatively minor variations.

Table 4.2 shows the percentages of total unemployment by duration categories over the period from 1964 to 1987 in three-year intervals. In each row the numbers in the first four left-hand columns combine to equal one, exhausting total unemployment. Since the percentages are three-year averages, they abstract somewhat from cyclic swings. The average number of weeks people are unemployed in each three-year interval are shown in the far right-hand column, and the means of the percentages in each category are shown at the bottom of the columns.

Surprisingly, over 45 percent of all spells of unemployment have a duration of less than five weeks, and over 75 percent have a duration of less than 15 weeks, although these percentages fall during recessions and rise during cyclic expansions. Similarly, less than 12 percent of

TABLE 4.2 Percentages of Total Unemployment by Duration

Period	Less than 5 weeks	5 to 14 weeks	15 to 26 weeks	27 weeks and over	Average number of weeks
1964 to 1966	.493	.286	.117	.104	11.8
1967 to 1969	.562	.292	.095	.052	8.3
1970 to 1972	.477	.309	.121	.093	10.3
1973 to 1975	.464	.308	.126	.102	11.3
1976 to 1978	.424	.303	.130	.143	14.0
1979 to 1981	.443	.316	.130	.111	12.1
1982 to 1984	.363	.290	.148	.199	17.9
1985 to 1987	.426	.303	.126	.146	15.0
Averages	.456	.301	.124	.119	12.6

Source: *Economic Report of the President, 1989*: Table B–41.

unemployment spells last more than 27 weeks, although the proportion of such long spells rises during recessions and falls during cyclic expansions. The average spell of unemployment appears to be about three months, although it varies significantly with cyclic expansions and contractions.

Summary

The major points of this chapter include the following.

1. The demand for a productive input such as labor is derived from the market demand for its product.

2. The amount that a firm is willing to pay for a unit of labor per unit of time is limited to the market value of the marginal product of labor. That value declines due to diminishing marginal productivity as more labor is added in production, *ceteris paribus*.

3. The amount of a given type of labor willingly supplied is a positive function of the wage rate, *ceteris paribus*, because leisure is a valued use of time that is subject to diminishing marginal utility and because income from work also has diminishing marginal utility.

4. The normal excess demand mechanism will operate to equilibrate labor markets if allowed (i.e., in the absence of legal impediments, such as minimum wage laws and labor monopolies).

5. Even in the absence of legal impediments, however, labor markets may take longer than most others to clear, particularly when nominal wage reductions are required. Such phenomena as normal variability of output demand (making it difficult to recognize input demand shifts) and worker concern with relative status (the you-go-first problem) help explain this.

6. Many economists use the existence of long-term labor contracting to explain downward nominal wage stickiness. Protection of real wages and incomes often requires nominal wage flexibility, however, which is clearly possible to contract for. Also, formal contracts cover only a relatively small portion of the labor force.

7. Job shifting from lower-valued to higher-valued employment in accordance with market-price signals promotes efficient use of labor.

8. Such normal job shifting between subcomponents of labor markets means that some workers are in transit, and some unemployment (known as frictional unemployment) always exists, even when the overall market is clearing.

9. Employees released from one employment invest time searching out alternate job opportunities until the marginal, or opportunity, cost equals the marginal benefits of additional search.

10. Some normal amount of unemployment is caused by existing structural characteristics of our labor markets, such as the degree of labor monopoly, minimum wage laws, and ongoing changes in the composition of skill demanded.

11. The sum of frictional and structural unemployment, expressed as a ratio to the labor force, is known as the natural rate of unemployment.

12. Most workers are in jobs of long duration and the bulk of job turnover is experienced by a relatively small portion of the labor force, consisting of younger and less skilled workers. Also, most spells of unemployment are usually of rather short duration.

Notes

1. The firm is assumed here to be a price taker in both its input and output markets only for simplicity of exposition and demonstration of the equivalence of the rules for profit maximization. Whatever the market structure conditions assumed, the short-run input side and output side rules can be shown to be equivalent.

2. Leland B. Yeager, "The Significance of Monetary Disequilibrium," *The Cato Journal* 6 (Fall 1986): 369–399, is an excellent essay on monetary economics and sticky wages, which deals with the you-go-first problem among other issues. See also Charles L. Schultze, "Microeconomic Efficiency and Nominal Wage Stickiness," *American Economic Review* 75 (March 1985): 1–15, who characterizes the problem as a prisoner's dilemma.

3. The literature on long–term labor contracting is becoming vast, even for that subset relating such contracting to wage stickiness. For an excellent review article see Benjamin Klein, "Contract Costs and Administered Wages: An Economic Theory of Rigid Wages," *American Economic Review* 74 (May 1984): 332–338.

4. It is well-known that employment relationships in Japan are intended to be lifetime relationships. Many observers have attributed low Japanese unemployment to this cultural attitude. The question is, however, how Japanese firms can preserve employment in the face of fluctuating market conditions. A vital factor is that Japanese law allows a large portion of employee compensation to be paid by the firms in the form of discretionary bonuses. Hourly compensation, the sum of the formal wage plus the bonus, is thus free to vary with demand and supply conditions as needed to equilibrate labor markets, even when formal wages change very little. This demonstrates conclusively that it is indeed possible to write labor contracts in such a way as to make labor compensation flexible.

Formal wage rates are also flexible in Japan. Thomas DiLorenzo, "Lessons from Abroad: Japanese Labor Relations and the U.S. Automobile Industry," Center For the Study of American Business *Contemporary Issues Series* No. 26 (1988): 4, points out that Japanese wage rates vary three times as much as U.S. wages over the business cycle. In this calculation, he was probably referring to both formal and discretionary compensation. John F. Helliwell, "Comparative Macroeconomics of Stagflation," *Journal of Economic Literature* 26 (March 1988): 1–28, admits that this flexibility results in greater stability of employment and lower average unemployment in Japan than in other OECD countries.

5. More than a little empirical evidence has been generated showing that unemployment compensation has raised the basic, or natural, unemployment rate in the United States. See, for example, Gene Chapin, "Unemployment Insurance, Job Search, and the Demand for Leisure," *Western Economic Journal* 9 (March 1971):1094–1091, and Martin Feldstein, "Unemployment Compensation: Adverse Incentives and Distributional Anomalies," *National Tax Journal* 27 (1974).

6. The best essay on the employment effects of technical change is still Yale Brozen, "Automation and Jobs," in V. Orvill Watts, ed., *Free Markets or Famine* (2nd ed., Midland, Michigan: Pendell Printing, 1975): 141–161.

7. The concept originated with Milton Friedman, "The Role of Monetary Policy," *American Economic Review* 68 (March 1968): 1-17, with particular attention to pp. 8 and 9.

8. This may be a response to some fundamental economic factor, such as the substitution effect of a rising real wage, or perhaps the income effect of rising tax rates in the 1970s; see Chapter 16. On the other hand, one-half of teenagers are female, and rising teen labor force participation may in part be another manifestation of rising female labor force participation.

9. See Robert E. Hall, "Employment Fluctuations and Wage Rigidity," *Brookings Papers on Economic Activity* No. 1 (1980): 99.

Student Self-Test

I. True–False

T   F   **1.** An increase in the marginal product of labor reduces the demand for labor, *ceteris paribus*.

T   F   **2.** *Ceteris paribus*, a rise in the real wage rate motivates workers to offer more labor by raising the opportunity cost of leisure.

T   F   **3.** The existence of multiyear labor contracts fully explains downward nominal wage rate inflexibility.

T F **4.** There is no optimal amount of time to be spent in job search for an unemployed individual in a healthy economy.

T F **5.** The sum of those who are unemployed because they are in transition between jobs and those who are unemployed because of structural factors in the labor market, expressed as a percentage of the labor force, is termed the *frictional unemployment rate*.

II. Short Answer (150 words or less each)

1. Explain your answer to True–False number 3.
2. Explain why the market demand curve for a particular type of labor (e.g., machinists, welders, etc.) is probably steeper, or less elastic, than the curve derived by summing horizontally the values of the marginal product curves for all of the firms demanding that type of labor.
3. Given that there are usually many types of firms in different output markets that employ a particular type of labor, briefly explain how the labor market operates as a resource allocation mechanism.
4. Is job shifting the only way in which the labor market operates to allocate labor resources efficiently?
5. Explain the effect of normal variability of output (and hence input) demand on the wage rate response of firms to shifts in output demand.

III. Completion Problems

1. Consider a small firm with given capital and plant, employing a homogeneous work force at a constant wage rate of $W = \$9$ per hour. Labor is the only variable factor. The firm has an hourly fixed cost of $5 and its product can be sold at a constant price of $p = \$1.50$ per unit. Table 4a shows the hourly marginal products for employees 5 to 10.

L	mpl	q	MC	TVC	TC	VMP	TR	π
5	15	35						
6	15							
7	10							
8	6							
9	3							
10	1							

A. From the information given, fill in all of the blanks in the table for the hourly total rate of production, marginal cost, total variable cost, value of the marginal product, total revenue, and net revenue.

   B. If the decision makers of the firm wish to maximize profits in the short run, they should employ _____ workers. At that level of employment and output, are both short-run profit maximizing rules satisfied? _____ (yes/no)

2. Market demand and supply

   A. Since the early days of the industrial revolution, productivity increases have _____ (increased/decreased) the demand for labor relative to the supply. This has _____ (increased/decreased) real wage rates and labor income.

   B. Aggregate man-hours of employment offered in the market has empirically been a _____ (positive/negative) function of the real wage, even though the average number of hours per day or per week worked by individuals have _____ over time due to the _____ effect.

   C. The you-go-first problem is best classed as a _____ source of downward wage rigidity, and the minimum wage rate is best classed as an _____ source.

3. Social and demographic factors

   A. Two groups that entered the labor force in large numbers during the 1970s were _____ and _____. This _____ (increased/decreased) the natural rate of unemployment because these groups have _____ (higher/lower) turnover rates than male adults.

   B. According to Robert Hall, about _____ percent of workers aged 30 to 34 have been employed at the same job for at least three years. About _____ percent of workers aged 50 to 54 have been so employed for three years or more, and _____ percent of workers over age 50 have been employed for at least _____ years at the same job.

   C. About _____ percent of all spells of unemployment last less than 5 weeks and over _____ percent of such spells last less than 15 weeks. The average length of an unemployment spell in the years 1964 to 1987 was about _____ weeks.

PART II

Monetary Theory and the Aggregate Economy

CHAPTER 5

Say's Principle, Walras's Law, and Monetary Equilibrium

This chapter begins the discussion of monetary theory, a vital and major portion of macroeconomics. Indeed, some economists claim that macroeconomics *is* monetary theory and that everything else included in the category is just prelude or epilogue. Whatever the case, it is vital to begin by developing the microeconomic roots of monetary theory— its basis in individual human choice and action. This chapter begins with a review of the excess demand mechanism in commodity markets.

Excess Demand Mechanism

Probably, the central characteristic of modern neoclassical economics is its choice-theoretic and methodologically individualist approach. Beginning with the most basic decision-making units (i.e., individual suppliers and demanders of goods and services) and an assumption of scarcity, requiring value ranking and efficient allocation of resources (i.e., economization), individual demand and supply curves are derived and summed horizontally over all demanders and suppliers of the same item to derive market demand and supply curves, as done previously for the financial capital market and labor markets.

The demand curve derived by this logic shows an inverse relationship between quantity demanded and the *relative* price of the good. The supply function shows a direct relationship. Such curves for good i are shown in Figure 5.1(a). It is important to recognize that supply and demand curves such as these are ex ante (i.e., before the fact) "flow" relationships. That is, they show people's intentions or desires to demand or supply certain quantities at a given price in each time period on an ongoing basis.

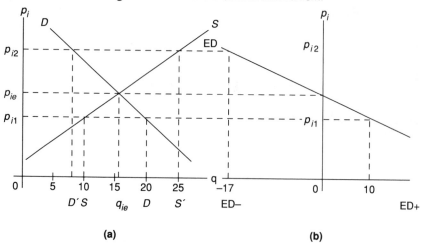

Figure 5.1 Excess Demand Mechanism.

(a)   (b)

It often occurs, however, that ex ante (before the fact) intentions and ex post (after the fact) results are not the same. At price p_{i1} in Figure 5.1(a), quantity demanded per time period is 20,000 units whereas the quantity currently being produced and offered for sale is only 10,000 units. Producers, recognizing this excess demand, will raise the selling price of the good. The rising price will motivate both an increase in the quantity produced and supplied per time period and a decrease in the quantity demanded by consumers until p_{ie} is reached, at which point the excess demand is eliminated.

A similar situation initially exists at price p_{i2}. In this case the quantity that people wish to purchase during each time period, $D' = 8000$ units, is less than the $S' = 25,000$ units that suppliers wish to sell. Over time, competition for sales will result in the market price of the good falling toward p_{ie}, decreasing the quantity supplied and increasing the quantity consumers demand until the excess supply on the market is eliminated.

Note that at any p_i greater or less than p_{ie} the plans of market transactors are not coordinated, but the excess demand and supply mechanism, by moving price toward p_{ie} and motivating transactor adjustment, produces coordination. If excess demand is defined generically as

$$ED_i = D_i - S_i$$

and excess supply is therefore interpreted as negative excess demand, a single excess demand function for the ith market can be derived as shown in Figure 5.1(b). This function is stabilizing in the sense that excess demands, positive or negative, are self-eliminating. A destabilizing excess demand function (i.e., rising toward the right) is imaginable, but would require a perversely sloped demand or supply function such that $ED > O$ for $p_i > p_{ie}$ and vice versa. This is unlikely in real-world markets.

One last point should be made here. It is often useful to express excess demand as a money value rather than in terms of physical units alone. That is, we can consider the difference between the market values of the quantities demanded and supplied at any price p_i, defining the excess demand as

$$ED_i = p_iD_i - p_iS_i$$
$$= p_i(D_i - S_i).$$

Numerically, if the price were $p_{i1} = \$2$ in Figure 5.1(a), the value of the excess demand would be $\$2(20,000 - 10,000) = \$20,000$. Again, excess supply will be a negative magnitude of excess demand so defined. The advantage of expressing excess demand in money value terms is that, conceptually, the excess demands in all markets could be added to obtain a single sum.

Say's Principle

Consider an individual who is not a thief and who wishes to make one or more purchases. Such an individual must plan to finance such purchases by supplying something of identical market value. A $10 purchase, for example, must be financed by selling goods or labor worth $10 or by drawing down one's savings or cash balance (i.e., supplying money), or by borrowing the funds (i.e., selling a bond). This principle, that an individual's intended expenditures must be matched by planned finance, is known as **Say's principle**. If $p_i =$ the nominal prices of goods $i = 1, \ldots n$, d_i is the individual's quantity demanded and s_i is the quantity supplied, Say's principle can be written as

$$p_1d_1 + p_2d_2 + \cdots + p_nd_n = p_1s_1 + p_2s_2 + \cdots + p_ns_n.$$

It follows from Say's principle that the sum of the individual's planned net trades is zero. That is, moving everything on the right-hand side of the equation over to the left-hand side and factoring out the prices,

$$p_1(d_1 - s_1) + p_2(d_2 - s_2) + \cdots + p_n(d_n - s_n) = 0.$$

The terms in this equation are the individual's planned excess demands. If $p_i(d_i - s_i) > 0$ the individual intends to be a net purchaser of the ith good, and if $p_i(d_i - s_i) < 0$ the individual intends to be a net seller. For many goods the individual will be neither a net buyer nor seller but, in any case, the dollar values of the individual's planned excess demands and supplies *must be equal*, such that

$$\sum_{i=1}^{n} p_i(d_i - s_i) = 0.$$

Now suppose that the nth good is money and that we give d_n and s_n slightly different interpretations from those of other economic goods. In particular, s_n shall designate the individual's initial holdings (i.e., stock) of money, and d_n the individual's desired holdings. It follows that if

$$\sum_{i=1}^{n-1} p_i(d_i - s_i) > 0,$$

the equation for all n markets will sum to zero because $p_n(d_n - s_n) < 0$. This means that the individual wishes to purchase goods and services having a larger dollar value than those he or she sells, and finance the difference by drawing down a cash balance. In the opposite case, in which

$$\sum_{i=1}^{n-1} p_i(d_i - s_i) < 0,$$

it must be that $p_n(d_n - s_n) > 0$. Here the individual clearly intends to sell more than he or she purchases and add the difference to a money stock.

Aggregate Say's Principle and Walras's Law _____

If Say's principle holds for any individual, it logically holds for *all* individuals. That is, where there are $j = 1, \ldots, k$ transactors in the economy, we can add the planned excess demand each has for every one of the $n - 1$ goods and services as in Table 5.1.

The bottom row in the table shows the summation of all of the transactor's intended excess demands in the columns, and the entries in that row therefore show the intended market excess demand for each

TABLE 5.1

Transactor	Goods $i = 1, \ldots, n$
1	$p_1(d_1 - s_1) + p_2(d_2 - s_2) + \cdots + p_n(d_n - s_n) = 0$
2	$p_1(d_1 - s_1) + p_2(d_2 - s_2) + \cdots + p_n(d_n - s_n) = 0$
$\vdots$	
k	$p_1(d_1 - s_1) + p_2(d_2 - s_2) + \cdots + p_n(d_n - s_n) = 0$
Market excess demands	$p_1(D_1 - S_1) + p_2(D_2 - S_2) + \cdots + p_n(D_n - S_n) = 0$

good at p_i. The market quantities demanded and supplied are shown as

$$D_i = \sum_{j=1}^{k} d_i \quad \text{and} \quad S_i = \sum_{j=1}^{k} s_i.$$

Since some entries in a given column will be positive, some negative, and some zero, at p_i, the market excess demand can be positive, negative or zero. But since the sum of each row is zero, the far right-hand column must sum to zero. Therefore, while **aggregate Say's principle** does not imply general equilibrium (i.e., all market excess demands being zero), it does say that the sum of the planned market excess demands for all economic goods is zero. That is,

$$\sum_{i=1}^{n} p_i(D_i - S_i) = 0.$$

There is another proposition formally identical to aggregate Say's principle that is known as **Walras's law**. The distinction between the two is that aggregate Say's principle is an ex ante concept describing consistency in individual plans, while Walras's law is an ex post proposition stating that the sum of the actual market excess demands for all economic goods appearing at a given price vector must be zero. Some economists have claimed that aggregate Say's principle, the ex ante relation, holds, but that Walras's law, the ex post relation, does not.[1]

The basis of this claim is that plans may not work out. In particular, it is argued that intended sales that do not occur because prices are above equilibrium in some markets may leave transactors with inadequate income to complete intended purchases in markets where price is below equilibrium. The excess demands in the latter markets will therefore be ineffective and Walras's law will not hold, despite the fact that aggregate Say's principle does.

This argument involves a failure to clearly understand some distinct properties of a monetary economy. First, virtually all purchases are made with money. Second, everyone holds a stock of money, or cash balance, accumulated in the past, with which to make such purchases. Under these conditions the consistency of planned finance and expenditure in the current period—Say's principle—amounts to an intention to add to one's money stock through sales about as much as one spends out of it for purchases, any difference being attributable to an intention to increase or decrease the cash balance at the margin. But the central fact about the use of money as a medium of exchange and store of purchasing power is that it makes current purchases and sales of the $n - 1$ goods and services independent of one another for all individuals.

It is absurd to suppose that purchases to be made by any person this instant depend on the individual's sales to be completed this instant except in a barter system. People make purchases with income earned in the past—and sometimes, employing credit, with income expected to be earned in the future! The current purchasing power of individuals, both separately and collectively, who hold positive cash balances is not restricted to the value of their current sales. So, although some markets may be in excess supply at a particular price vector, the excess demands existing in others are not ineffective and Walras's law holds.[2]

Monetary Equilibrium

Money was defined previously as the nth good. A corollary of the fact that in a monetary economy everything is purchased with money is that the prices of all other $n - 1$ economic goods are quoted in terms of money; it is the unit of account. But what is the price of money itself? The easy answer is that the nominal price of a dollar is $1, so $p_n = 1$. It follows that an individual's excess demand for money is $p_n(d_n - s_n) = d_n - s_n$. If we define the market demand for money as

$$\sum_{j=1}^{k} d_n = M_d$$

and the total supply, or money stock, as

$$\sum_{j=1}^{k} s_n = M_s,$$

then the excess demand for money in the whole economy (i.e., the nth market can be expressed simply as $M_d - M_s$.

If the intention here is to explain the determination of the value of money by its supply and demand, we must be very clear about what we mean by money's "value." Saying that $p_n = 1$ is not enough; that is only its nominal value. What concerns us is its value in terms of other things, that is, its real value or **purchasing power**. Relative prices are always expressed as price ratios, however, and as shown in Chapter 1, real magnitudes can be distinguished from nominal magnitudes by dividing, (or deflating,) the latter by a price index. So the real value, or relative price, of money can be expressed as $1/P$, where P is seen either as the price level itself or as some measurement of it, such as the GNP deflator. This expression allows clear exposition of the fact that as prices rise the value or purchasing power of money falls, and vice versa.

Next, it is crucial to understand what is meant by the demand for money and why it exists. Chapter 6 will deal in depth with the demand for money, but here we need only the basics. It can be argued that the holding of stocks or inventories, including money balances, is a pervasive economic phenomenon that results from a fundamental characteristic of human existence. This ontological condition is that human beings are always subject to some uncertainty about the nature and time-pattern of future events.

Consider an individual driving down a road or highway behind another vehicle. A stock of space is maintained between the individual's car and the car in front because it is not known when the driver in front might slow or stop. The stock of space allows reaction time to match the rates of 'flow' (i.e., movement) of the two vehicles, minimizing the possibility of collision. Individual valuation determines the size of the stock—some people are tailgaters while others hang way back—but everyone keeps one.

Retailers and manufacturers face uncertainties that motivate a similar response. The flow of demand for a firm's products actually has a random character, varying from day to day or week to week, even if the mean of the distribution is not changing, which it may. The flow of deliveries of products or crucial inputs to the firm is also subject to some random variation. Firms, therefore, hold inventories of many inputs and outputs, which can be drawn up or down when the flows of delivery and/or production do not match the flow of sales. Persistent inventory decumulations or accumulations provide signals for needed price changes and adjustments in the flows of deliveries and/or production to that of sales.

Individuals and firms hold money for essentially the same reason. The exact time patterns of income and expenditure flows are uncertain. Transitory components of income and consumption cause both to deviate from their expected values, permanent income, and consumption, as discussed in Chapter 3. Of course, for individuals receiving a salary paid at set times, variation in the income flow may be small. For salesmen and stockholders it may be large. But for everyone there is significant uncertainty about the time pattern of expenditure.

Holding a money stock allows the separation of sale and purchase of the $n - 1$ goods, so transactors can search through time across the distribution of alternative purchases for the best bargains. A cash balance can be drawn down as needed to finance positive transitory consumption or even some permanent consumption, when transitory income is negative, and can be drawn up when $Ct < 0$ or $Y_t > 0$, storing purchasing power for later need. For large and persistent imbalances such a stock allows time to adjust rates of income and expenditure flow to each other.

It is vital to grasp that money primarily yields utility when held rather than when spent[3] and that the magnitude of an individual's average cash balance is subject to economic decision. But is the desired stock simply some number of nominal units of money, d_n? A mental exercise may clarify the matter. Suppose that with prices, real income, and so on, as given, you normally like to keep $500 on average in your pocket and checking account. How much you would want if prices doubled, *ceteris paribus*? An individual's desired holdings would rise to $1000, which makes the point that the underlying demand is for a certain amount of real purchasing power, or a real cash balance, d_n/P.

This exercise yields the vital result that the quantity of nominal units of money demanded by an individual varies directly and proportionately with the price level, *ceteris paribus*. It follows that it varies inversely and proportionately with the value of each unit of money, $1/P$. This is shown in Figure 5.2, where the individual's nominal money de-

Figure 5.2 Individual's Demand for Real and Nominal Cash Balances.

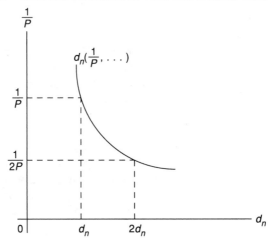

mand is shown as a rectangularly hyperbolic function of its real value per unit, $d_n(1/P, \ldots)$, where the ellipsis indicates omitted variables. At value $1/P$ the individual demands a number of units of money, d_n. But if prices double, reducing the value of money by half to $1/2P$, the quantity demanded rises to $2d_n$.

Taking the product in both cases, we obtain $d_n/P = 2d_n/2P$, so the area under the curve shows the desired *real* money balance and is the same for each point on the curve. Summing the d_n for all individuals at each value of money yields the market demand function, labeled M_d in Figure 5.3(a). Since all individual's demand functions are rectangularly hyperbolic, *ceteris paribus*, this one is also.[4] Summing the s_n for all individuals yields the total stock of money, which can be placed on the graph in Figure 5.3(a) with the demand function as shown. This enables discussion of both the nature of the forces producing monetary equilibrium and its meaning.

Consider the situation when the value of a unit of money is $1/P$ as in Figure 5.3(a). This value is too low (the price level is too high), and $M_d - M_s > 0$. Taking the products of M_d and M_s with $1/P$, we find that $M_s/P < M_d/P$, which means that the real value of the whole money stock is less than people's desired real money balances. Seen in either real or nominal terms then, a positive excess demand for money exists.

By Walras's law, if $M_d - M_s > 0$, then

$$\sum_{i=1}^{n-1} p_i(D_i - S_i) < 0.$$

That is, the excess demand for money must be matched by net excess

Figure 5.3   Exess Money Demand and Excess Supply in a Typical Commodity Market.

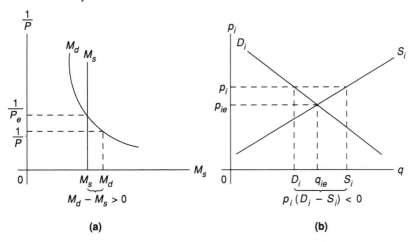

(a)   (b)

supplies in the $n - 1$ markets for goods and services, including labor. If the magnitude of these net excess supplies is large it would be termed a **recession** and, if very large, a **depression**.

Figure 5.3(b) shows the ith commodity market, assumed to represent the typical situation in such markets. As pointed out, prices are too high. This accounts for both the excesses supplies in the $n - 1$ markets and the matching excess demand for money. What will happen? If prices are not artificially immobilized, they will fall over time. This will tend to eliminate the excess supplies in the $n - 1$ markets such as that shown in Figure 5.3(b). Also, as the price level falls, raising the value of each unit of money, the quantity needed in cash balances to maintain the desired level of purchasing power decreases in Figure 5.3(a) until it is equal to the existing stock of money and the excess demand disappears.

Careful consideration of the ith market in Figure 5.3(b) might lead to the conclusion that there is sleight-of-hand in this argument. Both an increase in quantity demanded and a decrease in quantity supplied in such a market are normally predicated on a reduction in the relative price of good i, p_i/P. But if all prices are falling together, then p_i/P is not changing, so why should the excess supply be eliminated?

The answer here is that one nominal price, that of money, is not falling, because $p_n = 1$ and hence a key relative price, the real value of money, $1/P$, is changing. The fall in prices raises the real value or purchasing power of the whole money stock. It is this increase in purchasing power of money held until $M_s/P_e = M_d/P_e$ that increases quantities demanded and decreases quantities supplied in the $n - 1$ commodity markets. This effect is often termed the **real balance effect**.[5] At equilibrium $M_d - M_s = 0$ and

$$\sum_{i=1}^{n-1} p_i(D_i - S_i) = 0.$$

Identical reasoning applies to the opposite situation, in which prices in general are too low, making $M_s/P > M_d/P$ such that $M_d - M_s < 0$ as shown in Figure 5.4(a). By Walras's law it follows that

$$\sum_{i=1}^{n-1} p_i(D_i - S_i) > 0.$$

That is, there must be net excess demands in the commodity markets matching the excess supply of money. Such a commodity market is shown in Figure 5.4(b). In this case prices will tend to rise in such markets. The rise in prices from P to P_e will reduce the real value of the existing money stock until $M_s/P_e = M_d/P_e$, eliminating the excess supplies in the $n - 1$ markets. This also is a real balance effect. In mone-

Figure 5.4 Excess Money Stock and Excess Demand in a Typical Commodity Market.

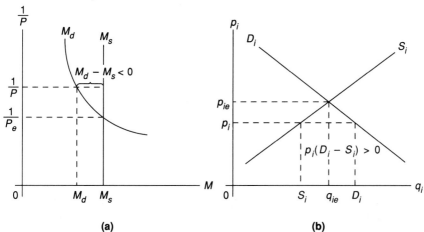

(a)

(b)

tary equilibrium $M_d - M_s = 0$ and therefore

$$\sum_{i=1}^{n-1} p_i(D_i - S_i) = 0.$$

It should be clearly understood, however, that monetary equilibrium does not imply general equilibrium. Excess demand need not be zero in all of the $n - 1$ markets. What *is* implied is that if positive excess demand exists in some markets, it is matched by excess supplies in others and no general tendency toward recession or inflation exists. Note also that all this argument says is that the market economy has a mechanism in the form of real balance effects for eliminating such general recessionary or inflationary conditions, given Walras's law, a demand for money yielding a stabilizing excess demand function, and an absence of artificial impediments to price adjustments. Even given these conditions, nothing is said about how quickly the mechanism operates.

Recession, Expansion, and Monetary Disequilibrium _____

With some justifiable oversimplification it is now possible to say something categorical about the causes of recessionary or deflationary conditions (i.e., net excess supplies in the $n - 1$ markets) on the one hand, and expansionary or inflationary conditions (i.e., net excess demands in the $n - 1$ markets) on the other. All events causing recessions, for example, fall into three categories.

Decreases in the Money Stock Relative to the Demand for Money

For reasons and by methods to be explained in Chapters 6 and 7, the money stock can decline as shown in Figure 5.5(a). At the initial value of money, $1/P$, this decline in the nominal money stock reduces real money balances below real balances demanded. That is, taking the products, $M_s'/P < M_d/P$. This results in individual transactors each attempting to add nominal units of money to their cash balances in order to restore the desired purchasing power, thus collectively, $M_d - M_s > 0$.

How individuals attempt to alter their cash balances is illustrated by the water level in the bathtub in Figure 5.6. The flow of water through the faucet is analogous to income, the flow out of the drain is analogous to expenditure, and the water level itself is analogous to the individual's cash balance. Note that any equivalent rate of flow of both income and expenditure is consistent with the maintenance of any given level of the stock.

There are two controls that can be manipulated to increase the level of the stock, however. Individuals can most easily reduce their flow of expenditures but can also attempt to increase the flow of income by increasing sales of goods or services, and they will usually try both. In the $n - 1$ markets such as those shown for good i in Figure 5.5(b),

Figure 5.5 Effects of a Money Stock Decline on Commodity Supply and Demand.

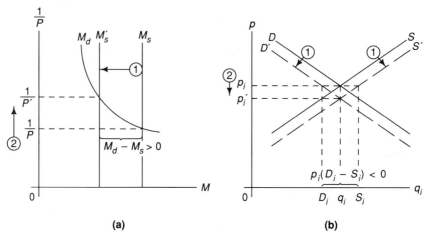

(a)   (b)

Figure 5.6 Stock and Flow Relations in the Demand for Money.

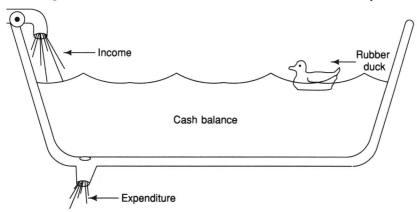

Income

Rubber
duck

Cash balance

Expenditure

these actions imply decreases in demand functions and increases in supply functions, in accordance with Say's principle, creating net excess supplies exactly matching the excess demand for money. This is the economics behind Walras's law.

There is an important point that must be clarified here. Whereas an individual can add to his or her nominal money stock by reducing expenditure and increasing sales, this can only be done by reducing someone else's nominal balance. For a given money stock, a collective excess demand for money cannot be satisfied this way. The collective attempt to add to nominal balance will, however, by causing prices to fall, raise the *real* value of the money stock until $M_s/P' = M_d/P'$ as shown in Figure 5.5(a), and the net excess supplies in the $n - 1$ markets, as shown in Figure 5.5(b) are also eliminated.

Increase in M_d Relative to M_s

There are several economic variables that affect the demand for money. For several reasons, then, the demand for money could shift outward relative to the money stock as shown in Figure 5.7. *Ceteris paribus*, all of the same phenomena previously discussed for case 1 would follow.

Although one of the major arguments of this book is that most recessions, particularly in recent decades, have originated with declines in the money stock relative to the demand for money, it is certainly the case that some have originated with increases in the demand for money. A conspicuous example occurred in 1907, as rapid economic growth raised the demand for real money balances, m_d; see Chapter 6 for an explanation of the causal relationship between real output growth and

Figure 5.7 Increase in the Demand for Money (Real and Nominal Balances).

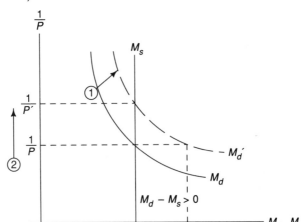

m_d. Because that panic is of some significance for U.S. monetary history, it will be discussed later at various points in this book.

Autonomous Rise in the Price Level

A third possible cause of recession is for prices to rise without an initial shift in M_d or M_s. This could occur following siginificant monopolization of industry or labor, or as a result of government price fixing. Again, an excess demand for money would be created, and simultaneously, net excess commodity supplies. At some point the recessionary condition created by the reduction in real money balances would prevent any further monopoly price increases. For this reason—and for the lack of observable increase in labor or industry monopoly power—it is impossible to blame ongoing price increases on such phenomena alone. Existing monopoly power could be a contributing factor, however, as will be discussed in Chapter 15.

Matching the three general sources of recession are three analogous sources of expansionary or inflationary conditions (both terms are permissible).

Increase in M_s Relative to M_d

If the money stock shifts outward relative to the demand for money, as shown in Figure 5.8(a), people's real money balances exceed their desired magnitude, given other existing conditions. That is, $M_s'/P >$

Figure 5.8 Effects of a Money Stock Increase on Commodity Supply and Demand.

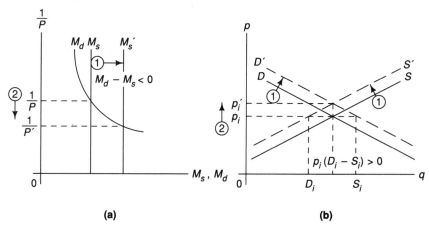

M_d/P. This results in people individually attempting to reduce their nominal balances in order to restore the level of desired real purchasing power. Again, they have two controls that they can manipulate. They can increase the flow of expenditure, decrease the flow of sales, or both. In the $n - 1$ markets such as is shown for good i in Figure 5.8(b), these actions imply increases in demand functions and decreases in supply functions, creating net excess demands, which exactly match the excess supply of money.

Here also there is a difference between the individual attempts and the collective result. A single transactor can run its nominal cash balance down through increased expenditure and reduced sales, but only by thus raising other people's balances. The way the aggregate attempt to reduce nominal money balances will produce equilibrium is by raising prices in the $n - 1$ markets, thereby reducing the *real* value of the existing money stock until $M_s'/P' = M_d/P'$ as shown.

Decrease in M_d Relative to M_s

For a significant number of reasons, several of which are discussed in later chapters, the demand for money could decline relative to the money stock. *Ceteris paribus*, all of the same phenomena previously discussed in case 1 would follow.

Autonomous Decline in the Price Level

If the price level were to be reduced without any initial shift of the demand function or the money stock, the real value of the money stock would be greater than demanded. Matching excess demands would simultaneously appear in the $n - 1$ markets. This really occurs, particularly in Iron Curtain countries, where prices are set by bureaucratic fiat rather than by voluntary market interactions. Soviet and Iron Curtain officials tend to err on the low side in their price setting, with the result that shortages are endemic, black markets—from which the price-setting officials often benefit—are epidemic, and queues are chronic.

The Interest Rate and the Real Balance Effect ⎯⎯⎯⎯

When an increase in the nominal money stock relative to the demand for money (or a decrease in M_d relative to M_s) makes $M_d - M_s < 0$, generating net excess demands in the other $n - 1$ markets, the financial asset market will be among those experiencing excess demand. Because financial asset prices are anticipatory and highly flexible, they will usually rise, say from p_b to p'_b), long before those in most other markets. Because the interest rate on such an asset is $i = d/p_b$, "the" interest rate on a typical asset will fall to some $i' = d/P'_b < i$. This is known as the **liquidity effect** of the money stock change.

Although price indices are not normally defined to include financial asset prices (see the discussions of the CPI and the GNP deflator in Chapter 2), it may be that they should.[6] One simple way of interpreting the effect of the interest rate change is that the rise in financial asset prices begins the operation of the real balance effect. That is, it reduces the real value of the money stock somewhat and causes some increase in the quantity of nominal units of money demanded. Eventually, prices also rise in other markets and complete the reduction of the real money stock to equality with real balances demanded.

As prices rise in other markets, nominal income rises and consequently dividend and interest payments on financial assets will increase. This will occur first on stocks and on bonds with short maturation periods and later on long-term bonds as maturity periods lapse, new bonds are issued, and the stock of such assets turns over. Loan demand will also rise with income and, with the rise in dividends and bond interest payments, will cause "the" interest rate to rise until, *ceteris paribus*, it is restored for the typical asset at $i = d'/p'_b = d/p_b$ when the real balance effect is complete. This is known as the **income effect** on the interest rate.

The opposite sequence of events would result from a decrease in the money stock relative to M_d—or increase in M_d relative to M_s—which made $M_d - M_s > 0$ and generated excess supplies in the $n - 1$ markets. Financial asset prices would fall before other prices, raising the interest rate—but lowering the price level properly conceived—and beginning the process of increasing the real value of the money stock and decreasing the quantity of nominal units of money demanded. Prices of other goods and services would fall later, reducing firm income so that interest and dividend payments would fall, thus lowering the interest rate back to its initial level. The fall in prices of other goods and services would also complete the reduction of the real money stock to equality with real balances demanded, restoring monetary equilibrium.

From this theoretical perspective the initial liquidity and subsequent income effects on the interest rate generated by enduring alterations in the relation between M_d and M_s are both simply phases in the stock adjustment process known as the real balance effect. The initial changes in financial asset prices might appropriately be seen as capitalizing into the present value of debt and equity the anticipated higher or lower nominal firm income flows associated with the later changes in goods and services prices.

In Chapter 6, a slightly contrasting view of the relation between the interest rate and the demand for money will be developed. Also, after the processes by which the monetary authorities alter the money stock are explained in Chapter 8, a more complete discussion of the interest rate effects of monetary policy will be undertaken. The argument above, however, is simple and consistent and should be kept in mind.

International Transactions and Monetary Equilibrium

A crucial assumption of this book has been that an individual could add to or reduce a nominal cash balance by altering sales and expenditure flows, but that collectively people could not do so. Aggregate excess demands for or supplies of money were assumed to be eliminated through real balance effects.

An individual who raises his or her expenditures and reduces sales (so that expenditure on all nonmoney items, goods, services, and financial assets exceeds income earned from sales of such items), in order to reduce a cash balance, may be said to be running a **Balance of Payments (BOP) deficit** with other transactors. In the opposite case, an individual who reduces expenditures and increases sales (so that income exceeds expenditure for some time period) and thereby adds to a nominal cash balance may be said to be running a **Balance of Payments surplus** with other transactors.

From a national perspective it seems clear that an assumption that domestic citizens cannot collectively reduce or add to their nominal cash balances through changes in purchases or sales amounts to assuming either (1) that they are not engaging in trade with citizens of other countries or (2) that something is preventing them from running a collective Balance of Payments deficit or surplus with people in other countries in times of domestic monetary disequilibrium. Today, the citizens of most countries are allowed at least some trade with those of other nations, and Americans engage extensively in international trade; therefore the first condition does not hold. As for the second condition, it does not hold when people in different countries use the same money or when exchange rates between different national monetary units are fixed at a constant magnitude.

To illustrate, suppose that the citizens of all nations use one-ounce $20 gold pieces for money. Further suppose that our nation is only one of many engaged in international trade and is essentially a price taker on world markets. Trade occurs in goods, services, and financial securities on the basis of international comparative cost advantages. Figure 5.9 shows a net domestic import good. The world price, $p_{wi} = \$15$, at which foreigners can cover all of their opportunity costs, is below the domestic market clearing price, $p_{ie} = \$20$.

As a consequence, total domestic consumption, which is 100,000 units (found at the intersection of the world supply curve with the domestic demand curve), exceeds domestic production of 50,000 units (found at that price on the domestic supply curve), and the difference is

Figure 5.9 Excess Domestic Demand for an Import Good at the World Price.

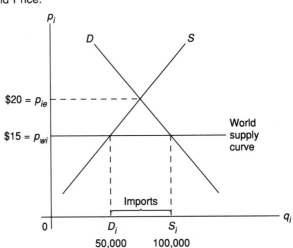

imported. The value of the excess domestic demand, $P_{wi}(D_i - S_i) = $ $750,000$, or 37,500 ounces of gold, is the payment to foreign suppliers.

Figure 5.10 shows a net domestic export good. The domestic equilibrium price, $p_{je} = \$12$, which would cover all opportunity costs of domestic production and would obtain in the absence of foreign demand, is below the world price of $p_{wj} = \$16$. As a consequence total domestic production of 60,000 units (found at the intersection of the world demand curve with the domestic supply curve) exceeds domestic consumption of 35,000 units (found on the domestic demand curve at the world price). The difference between domestic consumption and production, $D_j - S_j = -25,000$ units, is our domestic exports of this good. The value of the domestic excess supply, $p_{wj}(D_j - S_j) = $ $-\$400,000$, or 20,000 ounces of gold, is the value of the payment by foreigners to our producers of good j.

Although the value of our exports and imports shown for these two goods are not equal, they are only two among many such goods. It is crucial to grasp at this point that in a condition of domestic monetary equilibrium, in which domestic citizens are satisfied with their existing real and nominal money balances, the values of our exports and imports of all nonmoney items, goods, services, and financial securities, must be equal, so that the aggregate balance of payments is zero. If the values of exports and imports were not equal, domestic citizens would be exporting or importing gold, decreasing or increasing the domestic money stock relative to the demand for money, and the domestic economy would not be in monetary equilibrium.

Figure 5.10 Excess Domestic Supply of an Export Good at the World Price.

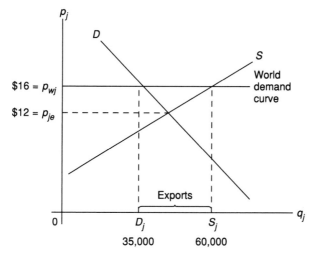

To see the nature and effects of balance of payments flows, suppose that domestic monetary equilibrium is disturbed by a gold discovery which, when coined, increases the domestic money stock as shown in graph 5.8(a). This causes an increase in demand curves and decrease in supply curves in the $n - 1$ markets [see Figure 5.8(b)] as individuals attempt to reduce their nominal balances. As illustrated in Figure 5.11, the same shifts will cause domestic imports to rise and domestic exports to fall.

As domestic citizens begin importing goods, services, and securities of a monetary value larger than their export sales of such items to foreigners, that is, running an aggregate balance of payments deficit such that $EX < IM$ hence $EX - IM < 0$, the difference is money (gold) exported to foreigners in payment. If imports totaled $8 million in a given period, for example, and export sales only totaled $6 million, $EX - IM = -\$2$ million, or 100,000 ounces of gold, represents the net payment to foreigners and the decline in the domestic money stock, *ceteris paribus*. The deficit would continue until the excess domestic money stock was eliminated. At that point people would stop trying to run their cash balances down, supply and demand curves such as those shown in Figure 5.11 would shift back to their inital positions, and the balance of payments deficit would end.

What of the other countries that received the gold in payment? Under the conditions supposed, one in which domestic citizens trade with those in many other countries, it may be supposed that each of these nations receives too small an amount of the new gold to experi-

Figure 5.11 Effects of Relative Money Stock Increase on Domestic Imports and Exports.

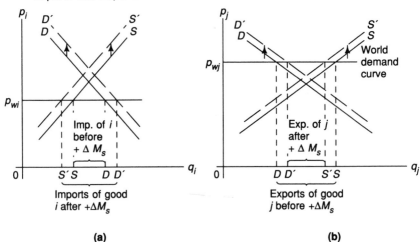

(a)   (b)

ence a significant disturbance to their monetary equilibrium. This is known as the **small country case**, and it immediately implies the **large country case**. The latter would involve a gold discovery large enough relative to the world demand for money to raise the world price level, which happened at the end of the 19th century when strikes were made in near temporal proximity in Australia, the Klondike, and South Africa. From the perspective of a nation in which such a monetary increase originates, the excess money stock is eliminated by a combination of monetary export through the balance of payments and the worldwide real balance effect.

It should be noted, *ceteris paribus*, that this same sequence of events would occur if the initial event that caused an excess domestic money stock was an enduring decline in the domestic demand for money, rather than a rise in the money stock. That is, domestic citizens would run a balance of payments deficit with foreign citizens until the excess money stock was eliminated. In the opposite case, in which an enduring rise in the domestic demand for money occurred, demand and supply curves such as those shown in Figure 5.11 would shift downward as domestic citizens tried to add to their nominal balances by increasing exports and decreasing imports. A balance of payments surplus would emerge ($EX > IM$ so $EX - IM > 0$) and money would be imported until monetary equilibrium was restored, at the initial price level in the small country case.

The reader may doubt that all disturbances to the balance of payments must originate in monetary disequilibrium. It is certainly true that disturbances from the real sector, such as extra large or small crops of export foods at home or abroad, changes in costs of production of traded goods, changes in the composition of demands, and so on, may cause the value of aggregate exports and imports to diverge. But unless such factors affected the demand for money at home or abroad, any BOP deficit or surplus that they generated would be extremely transitory. A domestic BOP surplus generated by such an event, for example, by causing an excess domestic money stock, would motivate domestic transactors to take actions to reduce their excess balances, causing an offsetting payments deficit. Any significant, enduring deficit or surplus originates in a monetary disequilibrium.

The argument, then, is that when nations use the same money, particularly a commodity money (e.g., gold or silver) the amount of money in each country is determined by the domestic demand and adjusted automatically through the balance of payments; this argument is clarified and extended in Chapter 17. This equilibrating mechanism operates partly in place of and partly along with the real balance effect. Today nations employ inconvertible paper currency and demand deposits in distinct units as money, and international trade requires exchange of currencies. In such a system it turns out that a mechanism of money stock adjustment through balance of payments flows operates if nations act to peg the exchange rates between their monetary units in certain ways. Such methods were practiced by Western nations in the post-World War II Bretton Woods system.

Flexible Exchange Rates and Monetary Equilibrium

An alternate way of doing things in an international fiat money system is to allow exchange rates between national currencies to be determined by market supply and demand factors. Since 1973, when the Bretton Woods system ended, that basically has been the method employed. A typical microeconomic foreign exchange market—that for British pound sterling—is illustrated in Figure 5.12. In any such market the price, or **exchange rate** (E), can be expressed as the dollar price per unit of the foreign currency, or $E = \$/f$.

The horizontal axis of Figure 5.12 shows quantities of pound sterling. The demand curve represents the quantities of sterling, read off that axis, that are demanded by U.S. citizens at various exchange rates in order to purchase (import) British goods, services, and financial assets. The curve slopes downward because each pound sterling has a certain purchasing power in Britain over these items, and hence the lower the dollar price of sterling is, the cheaper they are to Americans.

The supply curve shows different amounts of sterling, also read off the horizontal axis, offered by British citizens in exchange for dollars at various exchange rates, so that they can purchase (import) American goods, services, and financial assets. It is shown as an increasing func-

Figure 5.12 The Foreign Exchange Market for Pounds Sterling.

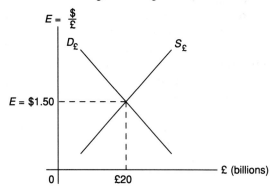

tion of the exchange rate because, for a given purchasing power of the dollar, a higher exchange rate, which implies a lower sterling price per dollar, makes such American items cheaper to the British.

Foreign exchange markets will be discussed in much more detail in Chapter 17. Here only a few points are crucial. First, as long as foreign exchange markets are clearing, the balance of international payments is essentially zero. In Figure 5.12, for example, at equilibrium Americans acquire £20 billion at $1.50 each. The U.S. imports of all items from Britain are therefore $IM_{us} = \$1.50 \times 20$ billion $= \$30$ billion. The British, however, traded £20 billion for $30 billion with which to purchase American goods, services, and securities. Their imports from the United States are our exports to them, however, so (broadly defined) $BOP_{us} = EX_{us} - IM_{us} = 0$.

A second crucial point is that the monetary excess demand mechanism acts on foreign exchange markets the same way it acts on the $n - 1$ domestic markets; indeed, domestic foreign exchange markets must be seen as a subset of the $n - 1$ markets. As shown in Figure 5.13, an initial increase in the domestic money stock, making $M_s/P > M_d/P$ at the initial price level, will not only generate matching excess demands in the markets for domestic goods, services, and financial assets, but also in the typical foreign exchange market.[7]

A third crucial point, however, is that foreign exchange markets are highly organized and efficient information processors. In this respect they are similar to financial asset markets, which quickly assimilate new information on the future prospects of firms and market conditions and capitalize it into the present value of debt and equity. If allowed, exchange rates adjust very rapidly, clearing almost continuously, and

Figure 5.13 Effects of Relative Money Stock Growth on a Foreign Exchange Market.

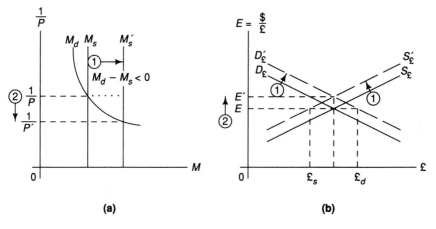

(a)   (b)

no significant balance of payments flows appear. In Figure 5.13(b), for example, the exchange rate would rise quickly from E to E' as the curves shifted upward.

What restores monetary equilibrium in the case under discussion, then, is a reduction in the real domestic money stock to equality with real balances demanded, due to a rise in the prices of domestic goods and services, financial assets, and foreign exchange rates. In this process the dollar prices of domestic financial assets and foreign currencies rise quickly, and the others only later.[8] No balance of payments deficit and monetary outflow occurs, as it would in the fixed-exchange rate or common world money case.[9]

An initial disturbance consisting of either an enduring decline in the domestic money stock or rise in real balances demanded, *ceteris paribus*, would generate the opposite sequence of events. By Walras's law excess supplies would be generated in the $n - 1$ markets. Foreign exchange rates and domestic financial asset prices would fall first, and other prices would decline later, raising the real money stock to equality with real balances demanded. From this perspective, consideration of international transactions under flexible exchange rates adds little complexity to the basic market equilibration mechanism explained previously.

Summary

The vital arguments of this chapter can be summarized as follows.

1. An individual who plans to make one or more purchases must plan to finance them by supplying goods, services, financial assets, or money of identical market value. Thus, the sum of the individual's planned net trades is zero. This is known as Say's principle.

2. If Say's principle holds for any individual then it holds for all, and the sum of the market excess demands for *all* economic goods, including money, is zero. This is known as Walras's law.

3. Everyone has a desired average real cash balance that must be held in the form of nominal dollars of a certain purchasing power each. It follows that the number of dollars demanded for cash balances varies directly and proportionately with the price level (P) and inversely and proportionately with the value of money ($1/P$).

4. By Walras's law an aggregate excess money supply must be matched by excess demands for the other economic goods and assets, and an excess demand for money must be matched by excess supplies of the other economic goods. This is best understood, however, as resulting from economic actions taken by individuals to adjust their cash balances to desired levels.

5. If prices are free to adjust, conditions of net excess supplies of or demands for nonmoney economic goods can be eliminated by price level changes that alter the real purchasing power of the nominal money stock to equality with real balances demanded. This is the real balance effect.

6. When an excess demand for or supply of money pressures a price level change, financial asset prices adjust quickly, which alters the interest rate in an inverse fashion. This is the liquidity effect on the interest rate. When, if not before, other prices complete their adjustment, however, the interest rate is restored to its initial value. This is the income effect on the interest rate. Both effects are components of the real balance effect.

7. If people in different countries used the same money, a domestic excess demand for money would cause Americans to sell more goods, services, and financial assets to foreigners than they bought abroad and to import money until the excess demand was eliminated. A domestic excess money stock would result in Americans buying more from abroad than they sold and in their exporting money until the excess money stock was eliminated.

8. When people in different countries use distinct forms of money and exchange rates between currencies are market-determined, as is now the case, any persistent domestic excess money demand or supply will eventually be eliminated by a price level change that includes the dollar prices of foreign exchange.

Notes

1. See Charles Baird and Alexander Casuto, *Macroeconomics: Monetary, Search and Income Theories* (2nd ed., Chicago: West Publishing Co., 1977), Chapters 3 and 14.

2. The modern notion of effective demand failure is ultimately attributable to Robert W. Clower and Axel Leijonhufvud. For some time their views encountered little opposition, but in recent years a rather large opposing literature has emerged. For a detailed exposition and critique of the notion and references to these literatures, see James Rolph Edwards, "Effective Demand Failure: Critique of an Anti-Monetary Theory," *South African Journal of Economics* 53 (June 1985): 124–140.

3. The satisfaction lies in having money ready to spend as contingencies arise. The marginal utility of money spent is actually that of the good or service obtained, not the money itself.

4. There is an important qualification to this argument that is explained in Don Patinkin, *Money, Interest and Prices* (2nd ed., New York: Harper & Row, 1965): 46–50. Treating Patinkin's "Market Equilibrium" curve as a demand curve is a justifiable simplification at the intermediate level.

5. Although the theoretical validity of the real balance effect as an aggregate equilibrating mechanism has long been accepted, many economists have believed it was a weak force. Modern empirical evidence indicates that the real balance effect is much stronger than such economists have thought, however. See Daniel L. Thornton and Paul E. Smith, "The Empirical Significance of the Real Balance Effect," *Journal of Macroeconomics* 2 (Summer 1980): 213–233, Jason Benderly and Burton Zwick, "Inflation, Real Balances, Output, and Real Stock Returns," *American Economic Review* 75 (December 1985): 1115–1123, and Abdur R. Chowdhury, James S. Fackler, and W. Douglas McMillin, "Monetary Policy, Fiscal Policy, and Investment Spending: An Empirical Analysis," *Southern Economic Journal* 52 (January 1986): 794–806.

6. See Armen A. Alchian and Benjamin Klein, "On a Correct Measure of Inflation," *Journal of Money, Credit and Banking* 3 (February 1973): 173–191) and H. Robert Heller, "Money and the International Monetary System," *Federal Reserve Bank of St. Louis Review* (March/November 1989): 66–67. Aside from the implications for the demand for money and interest rate changes discussed in the remainder of this section, the idea of including asset prices in price level measurements has implications for the theory and measurement of exchange rates (see Chapter 18).

7. The cause of the upward shift in the demand curve in Figure 5.12(b) as the U.S. money stock increases may be obvious, but the reason for the upward shift in the foreign currency supply curve may not because it shows amounts offered by foreigners for dollars at various exchange rates. The supply curve, however, is drawn for a given assumed purchasing power of the dollars they wish to acquire. Given the coming, anticipated decline in that purchasing power, the British will not be willing to purchase as many dollars at each exchange rate as before. That is, supply shifts upward.

8. Since the price of foreign exchange rises quickly, in anticipation of the eventual rise in domestic prices, the first prices consumers generally notice rising are those of import goods. This causes consumer demand shifts to domestic substitutes, hastening the rise in their prices. The opposite would occur in the case of an enduring decline in the domestic money stock, or rise in real balances demanded. Some observers have erroneously concluded from this sequence that exchange rate changes are themselves a cause of inflation or deflation. In fact, they are simply an important element of the monetary transmission mechanism.

9. See Harry G. Johnson, "The Monetary Approach to the Balance of Payments: A Nontechnical Guide," *Journal of International Economics* 7 (August 1977): 251–268.

Student Self-Test _____

I. True–False

T F 1. According to Say's principle, the sum of an individual's planned net purchases and sales must be zero.

T F 2. Every good or service in the economy has a nominal price that can adjust to clear its market with minimal disturbance to other markets.

T F 3. The demand for nominal money varies inversely and proportionately with the price level.

T F 4. If the U.S. Government were to fix all prices at present values while contracting the money stock relative to the demand for money, it would cause permanent net shortages throughout the economy.

T F 5. Because, as the medium of exchange, money circulates, the notion that people *hold* money is meaningless.

T F 6. If everyone everywhere used silver coins as money, Americans still could not reduce their aggregate nominal balances by altering their sales and expenditures but could do so only by changing the U.S. price level.

II. *Short Answer* (150 words or less each)

1. Consider income transfers that are voluntary (e.g., private charity) or involuntry (e.g., theft or governmental transfer). Do such transfers cause aggregate Say's principle to be violated? Explain, using a table for three transactors, one of which is not involved in a transfer, to illustrate your answer.
2. Explain your answer to true–false question 5.
3. Explain what is unique about the nominal price of money, and briefly discuss the economic significance of that fact.
4. Should the real balance effect be seen only as an equilibrating effect of price level changes (i.e., don't ΔM_s with P given and ΔP with M_s given both change M_s/P, with rather different effects on other markets)? Explain, by discussing the relationship between real balance changes of both sorts and Walras's law.
5. Explain the nature of monetary equilibrium. As part of that explanation, contrast that condition with general equilibrium.

III. *Completion Problems*

1. Suppose that the base year value of a price index is defined as $P = 1$ and that in the aggregate people wish to hold real money balances worth \$400 billion. Answer the following questions and plot the answers on the graph.

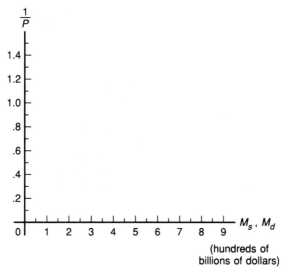

A. In the base year the quantity of nominal units of money demanded is $M_d = \$$_____billion.

B. *Ceteris paribus*, if the price level rose to $P = 1.25$, $M_d = \$$_____ billion.

C. When the value of money rises to $1/P = 1.2$, $M_d = \$$_____billion and $P = $ _____.

D. If the price level were to rise to $P \approx 1.67$, $M_d \approx \$$_____billion and $1/P \approx$ _____.

E. If the value of money continued falling to $1/P = .4$, $M_d = $ _____ billion and $P = $ _____.

F. If the price level fell to $P \approx .714$, $M_d \approx \$$_____billion and $1/P \approx$ _____.

G. If the nominal money stock is $M_s = \$500$ billion, given the demand function already traced, the equilibrium real value per unit of money is $1/P \approx$ _____.

H. If $1/P = 1.2$ instead of its equilibrium value just found, there will be net _____ (excess demand/supply) worth $\$$_____ billion in the markets for nonmoney goods and services.

I. If $1/P = .5$ instead of its equilibrium value, there will be net _____ (excess demand/supply) worth $\$$_____ billion in the markets for nonmoney goods and services.

2. Assume that there are $i = 1, \ldots n$ economic goods and services and that the nth is money.

A. The equation satisfying Walras's law when the price level is above equilibrium is _____.

B. The equation satisfying Walras's law when the price level is below equilibrium is _____.

C. The equation satisfying Walras's law when the price level is at equilibrium is _____.

D. If $n = 5$, $p_1(D_1 - S_1) = \$20$ million, $p_2(D_2 - S_2) = -\$32$ million, $P_3(D_3 - S_3) = \$9$ million and $p_4(D_4 - S_4) = \$4$ million, it follows that $P_n(D_n - S_n) = \$$_____ million. In this case the price level will eventually _____ (rise/fall), although p_2 will _____ (rise/fall).

3. Under an international gold standard,

A. A large, enduring increase in the demand for money in the United States should cause our export sales to _____ (rise/fall) and our imports to _____ (rise/fall), causing us to run a balance of payments _____ (deficit/surplus). This would cause our money stock to _____ (rise/fall) until _____ equilibrium is restored.

B. Suppose that Britain is the only other country in the world and that the same event discussed above occurred. Britain would necessarily run a balance of payments _____ (deficit/surplus), and its money stock would _____ (rise/fall). The price levels in both countries would have to _____ (rise/fall).

C. This is an example of the _____ (large country/small country) case.

CHAPTER 6

The Quantity Theory and the Demand for Money

Chapter 5 introduced the basics of monetary theory. Chapters 6 to 8 will extensively develop the concepts of the demand for and supply of money and the factors affecting their magnitudes. This chapter begins, however, with a brief discussion of the history and development of a theory about the relationships between money and other economic variables that has come to be known as the **quantity theory of money**.

Classical Quantity Theory

The origin of the quantity theory of money often is traced to the 16th century. The Spanish were shipping large quantities of gold and silver from the new world to the old, and prices were rising. The inflation was not large by some historical standards, perhaps 1 percent per year, but it was persistent. Astute thinkers such as the Frenchman, Jean Bodin, noticed that rising prices did not mean that goods were becoming more valuable, but that money was becoming less valuable, and attributed this directly to the increase in the quantity of money. Later 18th- and 19th-century thinkers such as Richard Cantillon, David Hume, and David Ricardo developed this theory into its classical form.

The classical quantity theory reached its highest development in the early 20th century at the hands of the U.S. economist, Irving Fisher, who developed much of the theory of interest discussed earlier. Fisher employed an analytic framework known as the **equation of exchange**. Assume M_s = the quantity of money, P = the price level or an index measuring it, and Q = real aggregate output as before. If V = the velocity of money interpreted as the average number of times each unit of money is used in a transaction during some time period, say a year, it follows that

$$M_s \cdot V = P \cdot Q.$$

The right-hand side of the equation is simply aggregate nominal income and the left-hand side shows total expenditure, so in a tautological sense the equation simply says that expenditure equals receipts for the whole economy. If we apply the percentage change rule, it follows that

$$\% \, \Delta M_s + \% \, \Delta V = \% \, \Delta P + \% \, \Delta Q.$$

This growth rate form of the equation is also a simple tautology. Both expressions are useful, however, for illustrating quantity theory ideas about the relationships between the variables. Usually, four propositions are attributed to classical quantity theorists: (1) proportionality of monetary and price changes, (2) neutrality of money, (3) causality of money, and (4) exogenity of the money stock. Each needs explanation.[1]

Proportionality of Money and Prices

Algebraically, this means that $\% \, \Delta P = \% \, \Delta M_s$, which clearly requires a similar proportionality between the growth rates of V and Q. The simplest interpretation would be to treat V and Q as constants. Indeed, the long-run growth trend was rather flat in Europe over much of the medieval period, although that was not true in the 18th and 19th centuries. An alternate interpretation is that monetary and price changes occur so quickly that output and velocity have no chance to change in the period involved. This seems even more unrealistic.

Neutrality of Money

This proposition says that changes in purely nominal magnitudes like the money stock or the price level have no effect on real variables such as output (Q) or employment. Instead, real variables are functions of other real variables, such as the stock of physical capital, the existing technology, and relative (i.e., real) prices. By this assumption, particularly if combined with proportionality, a change in the money stock would affect only another nominal magnitude, the price level, and in such a fashion as to leave the real money stock (M_s/P) unchanged.

Causality of Money and Exogeneity of the Money Stock

The causality assumption constitutes a claim that causality runs from monetary changes to price level changes, but not vice versa. This is best understood in terms of the exogeneity assumption, however. In the parlance of mathematicians and economists an endogenous variable is one the value of which is determined inside the system and an exogenous variable is one whose value is determined outside the system. The supply of an economic good would be considered endogenous if it were an economic function of its value per unit, that is, a market-determined magnitude. A claim that money is an exogenous variable is a claim that its quantity is essentially determined by a nonmarket institution, such as a Treasury or central bank.

All of these supposedly core assumptions of the classical quantity theory were to some extent unrealistic. Suppose, for example, that $\% \Delta M_s = 5$ and V is constant over one year ($\% \Delta V = 0$). It would be realistic to suppose, however, that real output is growing, say at $\% \Delta Q = 3$. Then

$$\% \Delta M_s \approx \% \Delta P + \% \Delta Q,$$

$$5 - 3 \approx \% \Delta P$$

$$2 \approx \% \Delta P$$

and the price level change is not proportional to the monetary change. Also, monetary changes frequently alter relative prices, and hence output and employment, such that neutrality does not hold. This is true even though it will also be shown that there are forces tending to offset and reverse such relative price distortions, such that neutrality is a reasonable long-run hypothesis.

Also, the causality and exogeneity propositions were unrealistic. During the classical period money largely consisted of metallic coins and banknotes that were claims on such coins; see Chapter 7. Gold and silver were, in fact, endogenous economic goods supplied by private individuals responding to market price signals. Changes in the world price level, by altering the real values of gold and silver, altered resources employed in finding and mining such metals, and hence altered the money stock. Causality clearly ran from P to M_s as much as from M_s to P, in the long run; see Chapter 17 for a detailed discussion.

Also, because national currencies were convertible into gold at fixed rates, and hence exchange rates between such currencies were definitionally fixed, the money supply in each country was demand determined in the short run through the balance of payments, as explained in Chapters 5 and 17. For this reason also, the money stock was an endogenous variable from the perspective of people in any given nation.

Although all these assumptions were unrealistic, it is also unrealistic to claim that classical economists held to them in their rigid forms. Close examination of their writings shows that they were aware of all of the qualifications. When they spoke as if V and Q were constant during a monetary change, they were simply doing what modern economists do, indeed what all economists must do. They were engaging in partial equilibrium analysis, employing the *ceteris paribus* (i.e., all other things equal) assumption, so that the relationship between a single pair of variables could be clearly seen and explained. At other points in their writings the *ceteris paribus* assumption was relaxed.

The same is true of the neutrality hypothesis. In order to explain the elementary relationships between M_s and P in their simplest form, classical theorists often spoke as if monetary changes were instantly neutral. But in the 18th and 19th centuries Richard Cantillon, David Hume, David Ricardo, Henry Thornton, Nassau Senior, and other classical economists analyzed the effects of monetary changes on relative prices, and hence on output and employment so extensively and so lucidly that modern economists have added only marginal improvements.

The reasons for the causality and exogeneity assumptions are interesting. Monetary theorizing is heavily stimulated by monetary crises, which are often associated with warfare. In the preclassical and classical periods, governments at war would often suspend convertibility of banknotes into specie and print money in order to finance wartime expenditures. In so doing they would convert the money stock from an endogenous to an exogenous variable, severing the fixed exchange rates with other currencies and causing the value of domestic money to fall both internally and externally.

The inflation would cause many people to think and write on these events; David Ricardo, who began writing in response to the inflation caused by the Bank of England during the Napoleonic Wars, is a good example. The assumptions of unidirectional causality and exogeneity, which are relevant in these periods, seem to have become engrained in the thinking of classical theorists and carried on to subsequent periods in which convertibility had been restored. Even here, however, it must be argued that most classical economists were aware of the necessary qualifications, as their writings show.[2]

Legitimate Objections to the Classical Quantity Theory

To say that classical theorists were not guilty of adhering rigidly to the unrealistic assumptions listed above is not to say that there are no legitimate objections to the classical quantity theory. One objection from the modern perspective is that the theory is very mechanical. Within the framework of the equation of exchange particularly, highly aggregative macroeconomic variables are interacting directly in a precise quantitative fashion, and the theoretical roots of those interactions in individual human choice and action are weak to nonexistent.

A related criticism is that the theory partakes of what is termed the **classical dichotomy**. Perhaps it should be termed the Neoclassical dichotomy because many economists of the late 19th and early 20th century were using different methods to explain the determination of the value of money on the one hand and the values of other goods and services on the other. The values of nonmoney goods and services were explained by the interaction in micromarkets of supply and demand curves analytically derived on a choice-theoretic and methodologically individualist basis. The value of money, in contrast, was explained on a macroeconomic basis by reference to its supply, or quantity alone.

Some classical quantity theorists did refer to supply and demand in explaining the value of money, but both were seen in flow terms. The right-hand side of the equation of exchange, the flow value of goods and services offered $(P \cdot Q)$ was seen as constituting the demand for money, and the left-hand side, the flow of expenditure $(M_s \cdot V)$ was seen as constituting the supply of money. This is all very confused. The flow value of goods and services does not constitute the demand for money because most are offered for sale with the intent of obtaining other goods and services. That is, goods and services are largely used to demand each other, with money simply acting as the medium of exchange. As for the supply of money, M_s is the obvious candidate, and it is a stock. The demand for money should therefore be seen as a demand for a stock.

Modern Quantity Theory

From each of these criticisms it becomes clear that what is missing in the classical theory is a theory of the demand for money as a demand for a stock, derived in choice-theoretic and methodologically individualist terms. Oddly, several decades before Irving Fisher gave the classical quantity theory its penultimate form, certain economists, who have since become known as **cash balance theorists**, began developing this new approach. Alfred Marshall at Cambridge, and Leon Walras and Carl Menger on the Continent all wrote monetary treatises from the cash balance perspective in the late 19th century. Other great theorists, such as Knut Wicksell and Ludwig von Mises, followed them.

Marshall actually did not publish his work in monetary theory until 1923, but in the second decade of the 20th century his students began publishing his ideas, and historians of monetary thought generally trace the modern quantity theory to these Cambridge thinkers.[3] In a sense this is unfortunate, because the Continental cash balance theorists were in print long before the Cambridge authors, and their role has been overlooked because they did not write in English.[4] However, it is easy to see and illustrate the transition in thought involved by employing the Cambridge approach because they began from the equation of exchange.

If $M_s \cdot V = P \cdot Q$ one can easily isolate the money stock by simply dividing both sides by V and canceling to obtain

$$M_s = \frac{1}{V} P \cdot Q.$$

Because the intent here is to derive an expression of the demand for money as an ex ante desired magnitude and to explain the value of money by its interaction with the stock, the next step is to state the equilibrium condition in that market. That is, set $M_s = M_d$. One can then substitute M_d into the equation to obtain the desired expression,

$$M_d = \frac{1}{V} P \cdot Q.$$

This is termed the **Cambridge variation of the equation of exchange**. In this form the equation says that people wish to hold in their cash balance some number of nominal units of money equal to a fraction $(1/V)$ of their nominal income. It thus expresses the **demand for nominal cash balances**. The next step is to divide both sides of the equation by P and cancel to obtain

$$\frac{M_d}{P} = \frac{1}{V} \cdot Q.$$

In this form the equation says that people want to hold some amount of real purchasing power $(M_d \times 1/P)$ equal to a fraction of their real income. This form of the Cambridge variation thus expresses the **demand for real cash balances**. It can be simplified slightly by defining $M_d/P = m_d$ and $1/V = k$ and then substituting to obtain

$$m_d = k \cdot Q.$$

Two implications can be seen immediately. First, since the demand for money is ultimately a demand for real money balances, the demand for nominal cash balances must be a rectangularly hyperbolic function of its value per unit $(1/P)$, as argued in Chapter 5. Second, from the growth rate rule for a ratio,

$$\% \, \Delta m_d \approx \% \, \Delta k + \% \, \Delta Q$$

and if $\% \, \Delta k = 0$,

$$\% \, \Delta m_d \approx \% \, \Delta Q$$

In other words, *ceteris paribus*, the demand for real money balances will increase over time at the same rate at which real output and income is growing. This is an important result that will be qualified later.

The cash balance approach has developed over time into what is now known as the **modern quantity theory**. In this approach the determination of the value of money and aggregate nominal income are both explained by the interaction of money supply and demand interpreted in stock terms. The theory has five major propositions, and their relationships to those of the classical quantity theory are easily seen.

The Demand for Money Is a Stable, Choice Theoretic Function of a Relatively Small Number of Variables

That is, k is obviously a choice variable with several determinates, so $m_d = f(Q, \ldots)$, where the dots indicate the variables determining k. The claim that this function is stable means that the relationships between the independent variables in the parentheses and the dependent variable are assumed to be reliable and predictable. The claim that the number of independent (i.e., exogenous) variables is relatively small is necessary if it is to be claimed that m_d is in any sense predictable, and hence a reliable guide for monetary policy; see Chapter 8.

Neoclassical Proportionality

This proposition says that, in the long run, an enduring 1 percent change in the growth rate of the money stock $(\Delta M_s / M_s)$ will cause the inflation rate to change by 1 percent in the same direction. For example, suppose that $\Delta V/V = 0$ and $\Delta Q/Q = 3$, while $\Delta M_s / M_s = 6$. Then

$$\% \, \Delta M_s - \% \, \Delta Q \approx \% \, \Delta P$$

so

$$6 - 3 \approx \% \, \Delta P$$

or

$$3 \approx \% \, \Delta P$$

Neoclassical proportionality says that if the monetary growth rate rises to 7 percent, in the long run the inflation rate will simply rise from 3 to 4 percent, and each additional percentage point increase in $\Delta M/M$ will be matched by a percentage point rise in $\Delta P/P$). Note that this is not the same as classical proportionality. The price change is not proportional to the monetary change, only the changes in the money growth rate and inflation rate are proportional, and this result depends on the change in the money growth rate not affecting the growth rate of output in the long run, which is the next assumption.

Long-Run Neutrality of Money

This proposition says that real variables are independent of nominal variables after a transition period. The basis for this assumption will be examined rigorously in Chapter 9 and in later chapters.

Causality of Money

Changes in the monetary growth rate cause changes in the inflation rate and not vice versa.

Exogeneity of the Money Stock

The money stock is ultimately determined by the authorities of a nonmarket institution. Note that the latter two assumptions are identical to those of the classical quantity theory. They are retained in the modern theory because the legal convertibility of currency and deposit money into gold or silver coins at fixed rates, which endogenized the money supply until the 1930s, is now missing. That is, under modern monetary conditions a stronger case can be made for exogeneity and unidirectional causality than before.

Exogeneity and causality are considered in later chapters, but it is worth reporting some recent evidence on neoclassical proportionality and long-run neutrality here. James R. Lothian recently tested these and other quantity theory propositions using cross-country data for the 20 nations in the Organization for Economic Cooperation and Development (OECD).[5] Table 6.1, which essentially duplicates Lothian's Table 1, shows the average annual growth rates of M1, real income, and the price level for the OECD nations in two periods, 1956 to 1973 and 1974 to 1980.

The difference between the means shows the shift in the average growth rates in the second period. For example, average annual real income growth for the OECD nations fell from 5.1 percent in the first

TABLE 6.1   Average Annual Rates of Change and Standard Deviations in 20 OECD Countries, 1956 to 1980

Variable[1]	Means[2]		Standard deviations[2]	
	1956 to 1973	1974 to 1980	1956 to 1973	1974 to 1980
M1	9.11	11.51	6.51	8.52
Consumer Price Index	4.30	11.68	3.06	8.62
Real income	5.10	2.61	2.54	2.63

Source: International Monetary Fund and Darby, Lothian, et al.
[1] Percentage rates of change were computed as first-differences of the natural logarithms of the variables multiplied by 100.
[2] Shown in percent.

period to 2.63 percent in the second, or by 2.47 percentage points. Average annual money growth, in contrast, increased from 9.11 percent to 11.51 percent, or by 2.4 percentage points. The average inflation rate also increased in the second period, by 7.38 percentage points.

Figure 6.1, which replicates Lothian's Figure 1, plots as Cartesian coordinates the real income growth shift for each OECD nation and its money growth shift. The points—shown by the placement of the number of each nation shown on the graph—are clustered around a dashed horizontal line drawn at the average real growth decline, −2.47 percent. Nearly all of the OECD nations suffered about the same real income growth decline. There is clearly no significant positive relationship between money growth shifts and real income growth shifts in the sample. It is such a positive relation that most opponents of the neutrality proposition assert.

One might even be inclined to conclude that higher money growth was responsible for the decline in real income growth if a negative relationship among the points in Figure 6.1 was discernable. Indeed, it will be argued in Chapter 15 that under some institutional conditions, which held for the United States during that period, higher money growth and inflation can reduce real output growth. Most OECD nations are net oil importers, however, and much of the 2.47 percentage point drop in their average real output and income growth in the second period is probably attributable to the OPEC price increases of 1973 and 1979; see Chapter 9.

Lothian concluded that the data were consistent with the neutrality proposition. Further evidence seemed implicit, he argued, in the fact that the variability of money growth increased in the second period

Figure 6.1 Relation of Real Income Growth Shift to M1 Growth Shift for 20 OECD Nations.

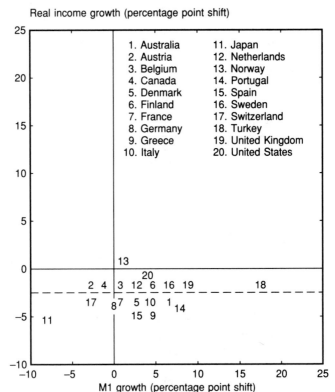

Real income growth (percentage point shift)

1. Australia   11. Japan
2. Austria   12. Netherlands
3. Belgium   13. Norway
4. Canada   14. Portugal
5. Denmark   15. Spain
6. Finland   16. Sweden
7. France   17. Switzerland
8. Germany   18. Turkey
9. Greece   19. United Kingdom
10. Italy   20. United States

M1 growth (percentage point shift)

(the standard deviation increased from 6.51 to 8.52) while the variability of real income growth did not change. Non-neutrality would imply a positive relationship between the standard deviations of these variables, and no such positive relationship is apparent.

Figure 6.2, which replicates Lothian's Figure 2, tests neoclassical proportionality by plotting as Cartesian coordinates the shift in M1 growth and the shift in the inflation rate for each OECD nation. Again, placement of the number of the country on the graph shows the coordinate. In Figure 6.2 a clear positive relationship exists between money growth shifts and increases in the inflation rate. The points are clustered around a 45° line with a negative vertical intercept. Note that with zero money growth and positive output growth, inflation would be negative. Higher money growth shifts are associated with proportionally higher inflation rates in the sample. The evidence seems consistent with neoclassical proportionality.

Figure 6.2   Relation of Money Growth Shift to Inflation Rate Shift.

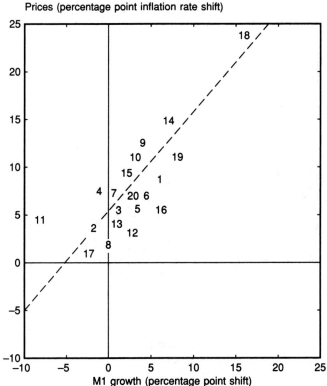

Prices (percentage point inflation rate shift)

M1 growth (percentage point shift)

Nominal Income Determination _____

Just how the quantity theory of money explains the determination of aggregate nominal income requires some elucidation. If $M_d = k \cdot P \cdot Q$ and $P \cdot Q = Y$ by definition, it follows that

$$M_d = k \cdot Y.$$

Note that this expression can be seen as a simple linear equation with an intercept of zero and a slope of k, where $0 < k < 1$. Figure 6.3 plots nominal income, $Y = P \cdot Q$, on the horizontal axis and monetary magnitudes on the vertical axis. In this space the demand for money, $M_d = k \cdot Y$, can be plotted as a ray from the origin. The exogenously determined money stock is shown by a horizontal line at some dollar value, M_s.

Figure 6.3   Nominal Income Determination by Money Supply and Demand.

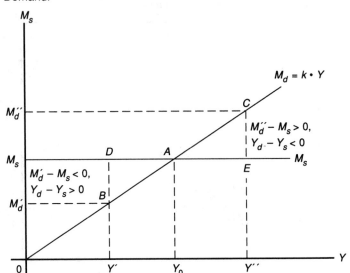

Now suppose that $M_d = M_s$, so that $M_s = k \cdot Y$ at point A on the graph. If that is the case, aggregate nominal income is clearly determined at Y_0. In fact, if real output (Q) is interpreted as final goods and services, Y_o is GNP. Algebraically, $M_s/k = Y$, so by substituting the appropriate values for M_s and k, one can solve for Y. If $M_s = \$800$ billion and $k = .16$, for example, aggregate income is $Y = \$5000$ billion, or 5 trillion dollars. The real question, however, concerns the existence and nature of a mechanism for insuring that $M_d = M_s$. Such a mechanism was presented in Chapter 5 and can be seen in a new light in Figure 6.3.

Consider point B at which $M'_d < M_s$ such that $M'_d - M_s < 0$. By Walras's law there must be net excess demands in the other $n - 1$ markets, that is

$$\sum_{i=1}^{n-1} p_i(D_i - S_i) > 0.$$

This can be written as

$$\sum_{i=1}^{n-1} p_i D_i > \sum_{i=1}^{n-1} p_i S_i,$$

which says that nominal output demanded is greater than nominal output supplied, or $Y_d > Y_s$ such that $Y_d - Y_s > 0$.

In this situation, the excess money stock and excess demand for other economic goods makes prices rise. Quantities demanded in the $n - 1$ markets decrease and quantities supplied increase. So both P and Q rise, raising nominal income from Y' to Y_0, increasing the quantity of money demanded until $M_d - M_s = 0$. Exactly the opposite story could be told beginning from point C at which $M''_d > M_s$ such that $M''_d - M_s > 0$ and $Y_d - Y_s < 0$. This mental exercise is left to the reader.

The effects of shifts in the curves are illustrated in the graph in Figure 6.3. An increase in the money stock, shown by a vertical shift of the horizontal line, say to $M''_s = M''_d$ passing through point C, would raise equilibrium nominal income to Y''. The same thing would occur, however, if k fell instead, reducing the slope of the demand for money function (i.e., reduction in M_d) until it passed through point E. On the other hand, a decrease in the money stock to some $M'_s = M'_d$ passing through point B, would reduce nominal income to Y'. Again, the same thing would result if k increased instead and raised M_d until it passed through point D.

The factors that can cause the money stock to change are discussed in Chapters 7 and 8. The factors affecting k, and hence M_d, are discussed in the remainder of this chapter. First, some fundamental aspects of choice in cash balance size need to be considered.

Microeconomics of Cash Balance Adjustment _____

Table 6.2 shows daily money holdings and expenditures over one pay period for two individuals, Richard and Jane, who are assumed to have the same income, $Y = \$400$, paid weekly. The first day's entry is $600

TABLE 6.2

Day	Jane	Spent	Richard	Spent
1	$ 600	$120	$ 600	$ 60
2	480	100	540	60
3	380	100	480	60
4	280	50	420	60
5	230	15	360	60
6	215	15	300	100
7	200	0	200	0
	$2385	$400	$2900	$400

for each because it is assumed that both carry $200 over from the previous period. The sums at the bottom of the daily balance columns, divided by seven, yield the average cash balance held by each. For Jane this is $2385/7 ≈ $340.71, and for Richard, $2900/7 ≈ $414.29. Note also that each is assumed to spend all of their income during the pay period and to leave $200 to carry over to the next.

It may seem something of a mystery why the average cash balances of these two transactors differ, when they have the same income and both spend all of it during the pay period. The answer is clear from Table 6.2, however. The time patterns within which they spend their incomes differ. Jane spends hers faster at first and more slowly later. Richard spends his more slowly at first and more rapidly later and, therefore, has larger daily balances on average. This is illustrated graphically in Figure 6.4.

Clearly, there is a great deal of psychology and subjective valuation involved in the choice of time pattern, and hence the average cash balance. Note, however, that it is only the $200 carryover that allows

Figure 6.4 Time Pattern of Expenditures and Average Cash Balances.

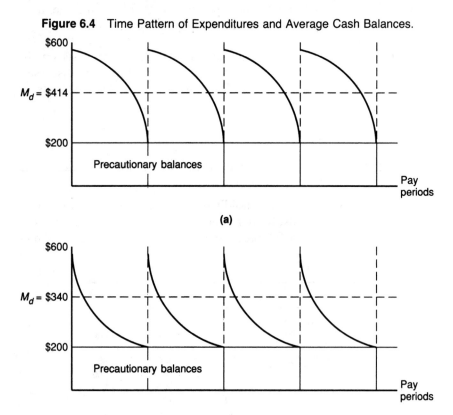

these transactors the possibility of spending more than their current income during the pay period if the necessity arises. This may be termed their **precautionary balances**, and the remainder of their average cash balances may be termed **transactions balances**. A positive precautionary balance can exist only if the individual spent less than his or her income during one or more previous pay periods.

The process by which an individual attains an optimal precautionary balance can be illustrated by supposing total utility to be a function of real money balances held and current expenditure. That is, $U = U(M_s/P, E)$. The individual is assumed to have a given income, and for simplicity, savings other than for additions to the precautionary balance are considered part of the flow of current expenditure (the savings-consumption decision was considered in Chapter 3).

With prices and income given, the individual with $m_s = M_s/P = 0$ faces a choice constraint shown by the lowest budget line in Figure 6.5. Its $-45°$ slope shows a dollar-for-dollar tradeoff between the precautionary balance and expenditure, and its intercepts show the maximum amounts of each possible during that pay period. The individual will actually choose $E < Y$ and real money balance m_s, where the budget line is just tangent to the highest indifference curve reached, U_1.

Figure 6.5 Short-Run and Long-Run Optimal Precautionary Balances.

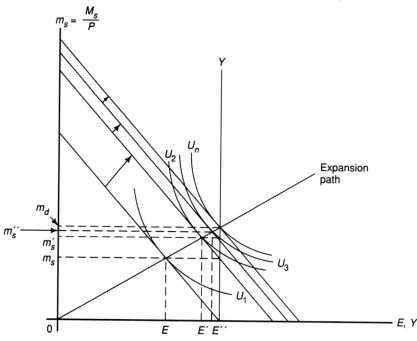

In the next pay period the individual's money balance rises by Y at the instant that income is received. Maximum expenditure possibility within the pay period increases to $Y + m_s$, so the whole budget line shifts outward as shown. The individual will choose expenditure $E' < Y$ and add $Y - E'$ to the precautionary cash balance, raising it to m_s'. Smaller amounts will be added to money balances each time, and expenditure will rise in each period until $E = Y$ and $\Delta m_s = 0$. At that point $m_d = m_s$.

To show that the individual is in long-run equilibrium when $E = Y$, we need to work toward it from the other direction; therefore, suppose that the individual's income falls from Y to Y', *ceteris paribus*, as shown in Figure 6.6. The intercept of the budget line on the vertical axis falls because maximum potential M_s/P (i.e., the amount held if all Y were added to m_s and $E = 0$ during the pay period) is reduced by the fall in income. The intercept on the horizontal axis is also reduced by the fall in income, so the whole budget line shifts back to parallel as shown.

The individual does not maximize utility at either intercept, however, but at E' and m_s' on the expansion path, where $E' > Y'$ is financed by reducing M_s/P from m_s to m_s'. This reduction in real money balances to m_s' means that the budget line shifts back again in the next period. Then the individual maximizes at E'' and m_s'', where $Y'' <$

Figure 6.6 Downward Adjustment to the Optimal Precautionary Balance.

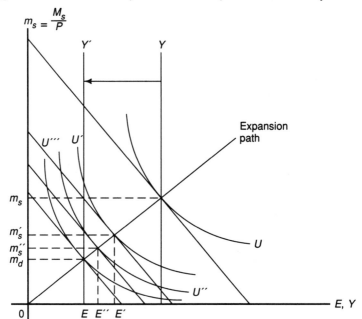

$E'' < E'$ and $E'' > Y$ is financed by reducing M_s/P from m_s' to m_s''. This process continues until $E = Y'$, such that $m_d = M_s/P$ and the individual is in monetary equilibrium.

Two objections are appropriate here. First, the analysis above is useful for distinguishing between the short-run and long-run equilibrium of the individual and for showing adjustment to the optimum cash balance as a process occurring over time. Remember, however, that aggregate adjustment is quite different from individual adjustment. For a given aggregate money stock, one individual can only run his or her nominal cash balance up or down by causing someone else's to change in the opposite direction. As long as foreign exchange rates are not fixed, aggregate changes in domestic real money balances occur through price level changes as Americans in general attempt to alter their nominal balances in order to change their real balances.

Second, the analysis only shows the individual with a nonoptimal cash balance attempting to alter it by altering expenditure relative to a given income. In fact, people also attempt to alter income as well. Supply and demand curves both shift; see Chapter 5.

Portfolio Balance and the Asset Demand for Money

In the previous analysis, the interest rate was implicitly held constant and savings other than for addition to the precautionary cash balance were considered part of the flow of current expenditure, an expenditure on financial assets that might be generically labeled **securities**. Because securities have resale markets, however, they constitute another form in which purchasing power can be stored. Accordingly, many economists see money held as simply one component in a stock of financial assets that includes securities. That is, defining A = the dollar value of such assets, and S = the value of securities held,

$$A = M_s + S.$$

From this perspective the individual is seen as facing a choice problem with regard to the composition of a personal portfolio, that is, what portion of the assets to hold in the form of money (i.e., currency and demand deposits) and how much as securities. The choice is made on the basis of the relative returns to a dollar's worth of purchasing power held in each form at the margin. The return on money held is basically nonpecuniary, consisting of satisfaction, utility, from preparedness for contingencies. The return on securities is pecuniary; they earn interest.

If we define MU_m as the marginal utility of money held and i_s as the interest rate on securities, interpreted here as the total return, the optimum portfolio for the individual occurs where

$$MU_m = i_s.$$

Figure 6.7(a) shows the MU_m schedule for an individual, which falls, *ceteris paribus*, as money held increases on the horizontal axis. Figure 6.7(b) shows the dollar value of securities held on its horizontal axis and measures "the" interest rate on securities, which must actually be interpreted as an average rate, on the vertical axis. The existing market rate (i_s) is shown as a horizontal line on the assumption that the individual is a price taker in the financial capital market.

Figure 6.8 is constructed by taking the horizontal axis of Figure 6.7(b), pivoting it around the vertical axis, and laying it over the horizontal axis of Figure 6.7(a). The total length of the horizontal axis is then adjusted to equality with the dollar value of the individual's liquid assets. The entire portfolio is then expressed in real terms by deflating it by a price index such that $A/P = \mathbf{a}$. The left origin then shows the individual holding all assets in securities and no money balance, and the right origin shows all assets being held as money and none as securities.

By the maximization rule, if the interest rate on securities is i_s, the individual's optimum portfolio consists of money stock M_d and securities with a value of S_d. If the interest rate were to rise to i_s' as shown, the individual's optimal money holdings would decline to M_d', and the optimal holdings of securities would rise to S_d'. This gives a crucial theoretical result: The stock demand for money should vary inversely with the rate of interest. Oddly enough, the same graph gives us

Figure 6.7   The Returns on Money and Securities Held.

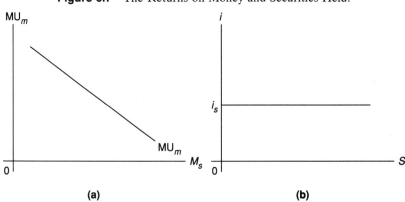

(a)

(b)

Figure 6.8 Money Demanded in the Portfolio Balance.

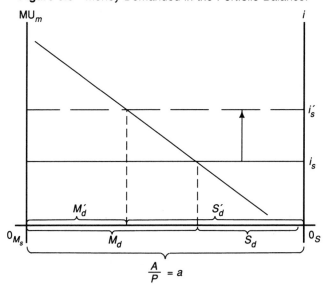

another result. If the real value of liquid assets were to increase, as would be indicated by an increase in the length of the horizontal axis in Figure 6.8, the individual would likely be willing to hold both more money and more securities. Therefore, the stock demand for money should be a positive function of real wealth. More will be said about this below.

Expected Inflation and the Demand for Money _____

The reader may have wondered why the optimum portfolio balance rule stated the returns on both money and securities in purely nominal terms. One might think that such a resource allocation decision would be made by comparing the real returns at the margin. It is, but in the case of both money and securities the real rate of return is expressed by subtracting the expected future inflation rate, $\alpha^* = \Delta P^*/P$, from the nominal rate of return. Because α^* thus enters the equation on both sides with the same sign, no change in the expected rate of inflation will alter the portfolio balance, and the decision can be modeled as if it were made by comparing the purely nominal rates of return.

To say that a change in α^* does not affect the portfolio balance, however, is not to say that it would not affect the demand for money.

Such a change seems likely to affect k directly because the rate at which money held is expected to lose value, $-\alpha^*$, indicates the rate at which nominal balances must be accumulated (i.e., foregoing real goods and services) in order to maintain real balances intact, and hence is a perceived cost of holding such balances. As a discrete rise in that perceived cost occurs, the proportion of people's real income that they wish to hold as real money balances (k) should fall. That is, the demand for real, and hence nominal, money balances should vary inversely with the expected rate of inflation.

Graphic Illustrations and Evidence ——————————

From the previous discussions it can be argued that there are at least four important independent variables in the demand function for real, and hence nominal, money balances; real output and income, the interest rate, real assets, and the expected rate of inflation. Mathematically, the demand for real balances is therefore

$$m_d = m_d(Q, i_s, \mathbf{a}, \alpha^*)$$

and the demand for nominal money balances would be

$$M_d = M_d\left(\frac{1}{P}, Q, \mathbf{a}, \alpha^*\right).$$

The only difference is the inclusion of the expression for the purchasing power per unit of money ($1/P$) defining the shape of the demand for nominal balances in that function.[6] These arguments can be illustrated graphically.

Real Aggregate Output and Real Assets

Both real aggregate output and real assets are positively related to the demand for money. That is, an increase in the magnitude of either will, as already argued, increase M_d. Graphically, the effect of an increase in real output and income, say from some value Q to a higher value Q', can be shown causing an outward shift in the demand for nominal and real money balances, as shown in Figure 6.9.

Such a shift, *ceteris paribus*, would produce recessionary and deflationary conditions. This might seem to be a rather odd form of recession, because it is initiated by increases (i.e., outward shifts) in supply functions in the $n - 1$ markets. This is often termed a **growth**

Figure 6.9 Emergence of a Growth Recession.

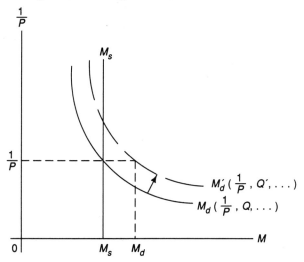

recession. Actually, there is a normal tendency for the demand for money to shift outward in this fashion because capital (i.e., physical) stock growth, labor force growth, and technical change have tended to cause $3\% < \Delta Q/Q < 3.5\%$ per year on average; see Figure 3.7 in Chapter 3.

Indeed, the United States experienced both rapid growth and deflation from the end of the Civil War to the end of the 19th century, a period of rapid industrialization. Other Western countries were also growing and although falling prices raised the real value of gold, world gold production, and hence money stock growth, did not keep up. What has kept this from happening in recent times, under our fiat (inconvertible) money system, has been a tendency for the money stock to shift outward at an even more rapid pace than the demand for money, for reasons to be explained in Chapter 15.

A qualification should be made here to the theoretical argument. Decisions made now relate to actions to be taken in the future, however near. The amount of money people wish to hold now, therefore, is logically related not to current real income (Q) but to what it is expected to be (Q^*). That is, $m_d = k \cdot Q^*$, and m_d will grow over time at the expected trend rate of real output growth, $\Delta Q^*/Q$, *ceteris paribus*. If we assume that this expectation is formed by averaging past observed growth rates, it is therefore much more stable than observed growth.[7] If Q^* is simply **real permanent income**, $\Delta Q^*/Q$ could be termed **permanent real income growth**.

Recognizing that m_d is related to Q^* raises another point. It is probably redundant to include both expected real income and real assets as determinants of m_d because, as explained previously, market supply and demand tend to establish the current real values of assets at the discounted present values of the expected future income flows which they produce or to which they are claims. That is, changes in **a** and Q^* must be highly correlated and the equation could be simplified by deleting one or the other. The practice in the remainder of this book will be to delete the asset variable and list real permanent income.

Rate of Interest and Expected Inflation

Both the rate of interest and expected inflation are inversely related to the demand for money. Figure 6.10 shows money growth, assumed to continue over time, which would, *ceteris paribus*, raise the price level from p to p' in one year. Assuming this inflation rate (α) is higher than previously expected (α^*) it may raise the expectation to $\alpha^{*'} = \alpha$ if it seems likely to continue. This higher perceived cost reduces m_d and hence M_d, as shown. The price level rises to $P'' > P'$, which is enough to reduce real balances to the desired lower level. After that, the inflation rate returns to α, *ceteris paribus*.

This argument is of some historical significance. During the great German hyperinflation of 1918 to 1923, the rate of inflation exceeded the rate of money growth. This observation was widely employed in refutation of the classical quantity theory. Ludwig von Mises and others were able to explain the phenomenon, however, using the

Figure 6.10 Expected Inflation Rate and Real Balances Demand.

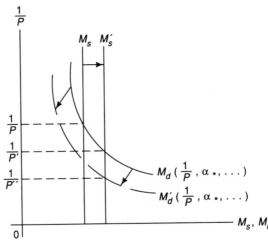

argument just made, which impressively demonstrated the superiority of the cash balance approach.[8]

Much the same thing has happened in the United States in recent decades, although on a smaller scale than that of Germany. Figure 6.11 shows the **income velocity of money** in this country, computed as $V = GNP/M1$, from 1970 to 87. Since $m_d = k \cdot Q^*$, and $k = 1/V$, a rise in velocity indicates a decline in real balances demanded, and a decline in V indicates an increase in m_d.

During most of the post-war period velocity has increased by about 1 percent per year. After 1973 it began rising more rapidly. This was a period of accelerating inflation, during which α^*, the perceived cost of holding money balances, was rising, so it is understandable that desired real balances would fall. Since 1982 velocity has leveled off and declined. This was the period of Reagan administration disinflation, which caused expected inflation to fall and thereby seemed to have raised desired real balances. This history will be discussed in detail in Chapter 15.

Another interpretation of these data is in terms of interest rate changes. Nominal interest rates increased in the 1970s, although real rates declined, and nominal rates fell after 1982, although real rates increased. By portfolio balance reasoning, this could account for some, but not all, of the observed changes in velocity. Numerous studies of the effect of interest rates on the demand for money have found it to be significant. Usually, the interest elasticity of money demand is found to be about $-.015$ for short-term rates, and between $-.2$ and $-.6$ for long-term interest rates.[9]

Figure 6.11 Income Velocity of Money, $V = GNP/M1$.

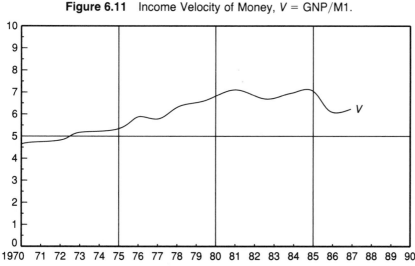

Source: Survey of Current Business (January 1989)

As with real assets and expected real income, it could be argued that it is somewhat redundant to include both the nominal interest rate and expected inflation rate as independent determinants of the demand for money. This is because (see Chapter 8) changes in α^* cause the nominal interest rate to move in the same direction. Also, from the discussion in Chapter 5, it may be remembered that by defining the price level to include financial asset prices, changes in which alter the interest rate, interest rate effects would be already included in the price level variable and be accounted for by movements along the demand curve. Hence the interest rate would not need to be listed as a shift variable.

Standard practice, however, is not to include asset prices in the price index and to list the interest rate separately. Seen this way, an increase in the interest rate would shift the demand function inward, and a decrease in i would shift it outward. From this perspective the demand for real balances would be written as

$$m_d = m_d\,(Q^*, i, \alpha^*)$$

and the demand for nominal money balances would be

$$M_d = M_d\!\left(\frac{1}{P}, Q^*, i, \alpha^*\right).$$

Summary

The major arguments of this chapter include the following.

1. The classical quantity theory of money, consisting of the proportionality, neutrality, causality, and exogeneity hypotheses, explained changes in the price level by reference to changes in the money stock on a *ceteris paribus* assumption, holding output and monetary velocity constant.

2. As an explanation of the value of money, the classical quantity theory was missing a theory of the demand for money to hold. This is added by the modern quantity theory, whose advocates believe that money demand is a stable function of a rather small set of variables. This theory assumes long-run changes in the growth rate of the money stock and the inflation rate to be proportional.

3. Real balances demanded varies directly and proportionately with real output, *ceteris paribus*. People need larger cash balances at any given price level to carry out the additional transactions.

4. By assuming that real variables, not nominal variables, determine real output, and that the money stock and demand for money determine the price level, the modern quantity theory also constitutes a theory of nominal income determination.

5. People can adjust their cash balances to optimal levels by choosing their expenditure pattern within a pay period, and by spending more or less than their income over a sequence of such periods. That they can also vary their money balances by adjusting their income through changes in sales (see Chapter 5) should not be forgotten.

6. Money can be seen as one component in a portfolio of financial assets. The interest rate earnable from investing a dollar in a security can be interpreted as the opportunity cost of holding a dollar in a cash balance. By such "portfolio balance" reasoning the demand for money varies inversely with the nominal interest rate and positively with wealth.

7. The expected rate of inflation, the rate at which money held is expected to lose purchasing power, is a perceived cost of holding real money balances. Real balances demanded should vary inversely with α^*.

Notes

1. The discussion in this section owes much to Thomas M. Humphrey, "The Quantity Theory of Money: Its Historical Evolution and Role in Policy Debates," in Humphrey, *Essays on Inflation* (Richmond: The Federal Reserve Bank of Richmond, 1980): 1–18.

2. On this matter see Robert E. Keleher, "Of Money and Prices: Some Historical Perspectives," in Bluford H. Putnam and D. Sykes Wilford, eds., *The Monetary Approach to International Adjustment* (New York: Praeger Publishers, 1978): 19–48.

3. The "stock" concept of the demand for money first appears in Marshall's work in an 1871 manuscript and appears throughout his later work, although Marshall often reverted to classical "flow" analysis. See Ephrime Eshag, *From Marshall to Keynes: An Essay on the Monetary Theory of the Cambridge School* (New York: Augustus M. Kelley, 1965) 8–10, 22. The first Cambridge work actually published on the stock concept was A. C. Pigou, "The Value of Money," *Quarterly Journal of Economics* 32 (November 1917): 38–65, followed by Edwin Cannan "The Application of the Theoretical Apparatus of Supply and Demand to Units of Currency," *Economic Journal* 31 (December 1921): 453–461.

4. The early contributions of Karl Menger and Leon Walras to the cash balance approach to monetary theory are discussed in Charles Rist, *History of Monetary and Credit Theory: From John Law to the Present Day*. Jane Degras, translator (New York: Augustus M. Kelley, 1966): 345–353. Another early and important continental cash balance theorist was Karl Helfferich, whose *Das Geld* (Leipzig: C. L. Herschfeld, 1903) went through several additions. Knut Wicksell's contributions, although only partly in the cash balance tradition (as with Marshall), are well known. The greatest of these continental monetary theorists, however, was Ludwig von Mises. His *Theorie des Geldes und der Unlaufsmittel* (Munich and Leipzig: Dunker and Humblot, 1912), the revised 1924 edition of which was later translated by H. E. Batson as *The Theory of*

Money and Credit (London: Jonathan Cape Ltd., 1934) was probably the first complete and consistent monetary treatise in the modern cash balance tradition.

5. James R. Lothian, "Equilibrium Relationships Between Money and Other Economic Variables," *American Economic Review* 75 (September 1985): 828–835. See also Robert E. Lucas, "Two illustrations of the Quantity Theory of Money," *American Economic Review* 70 (December 1980): 1005–1014. In a highly readable paper Gerald P. Dwyer and R. W. Hafer, "Is Money Irrelevant?" *Federal Reserve Bank of St. Louis Review* 70 (May/June 1988): 3–16 employ the same essential method as Lothian to a different sample of nations and find striking support for quantity theory propositions.

6. Don Roper has argued that the price level in the nominal money demand function should actually be written in expectational terms as P^*. This is required for consistency with the interpretation of the inflation variable. See Roper, *Monetary Equilibrium, Reification, and the Fundamental Theorem of Calculus* (unpublished essay, 1980).

7. Review the discussion of permanent income in Chapter 3 to refresh your memory of the partial adjustment mechanism for expectations. Alternate explanations of the manner in which expectations are formed are discussed in Chapter 14.

8. See Ludwig von Mises, *The Theory of Money and Credit* (Indianapolis: Liberty Classics edition, 1981): 258–262.

9. See David E. W. Laidler, *The Demand for Money: Theories and Evidence* (Scranton Pa: International Textbook Co., 1969): 105–106. See also John T. Boorman, "The Evidence on the Demand for Money; Theoretical Formulations and Empirical Results," in Thomas M. Havrilesky and John T. Boorman, eds., *Current Issues in Monetary Theory and Policy*, (1st ed., Arlington Heights, Illinois: AHM, 1976): 332.

Student Self-Test

I. True–False

T F **1.** Few classical quantity theorists actually believed that price changes were always proportional to money stock changes or that money was instantly neutral.

T F **2.** The neutrality proposition says that real variables, such as output and employment, are positive functions of purely nominal magnitudes, such as the money stock or the price level.

T F **3.** The amount of money demanded by economic agents to hold in their cash balances should vary positively with the interest rate.

T F **4.** The tendency for nonproportionality between money and price changes during hyperinflation can be explained by an inverse relationship between the demand for money and the expected rate of inflation.

T F **5.** *Ceteris paribus*, the demand for both nominal and real cash balances tends to vary positively with real output and income.

II. Short Answer (150 words or less each)

1. Given the apparent unrealism of the proportionality hypothesis, why did classical quantity theorists often speak as if it were true?

2. What fundamental principle of microeconomics lies behind the notion of the neutrality of money? Explain.
3. What was unrealistic about the causality and exogeneity assumptions of the classical quantity theory in that period of history?
4. How is it that two people who have the same income and both spend it all in each pay period can hold significantly different average cash balances?
5. Explain the basic ideas of portfolio balance theory.

III. Completion Problems

1. The accompanying figure shows a nominal money stock of $400 billion dollars on the vertical axis, and various possible magnitudes of nominal gross national product on the horizontal axis.

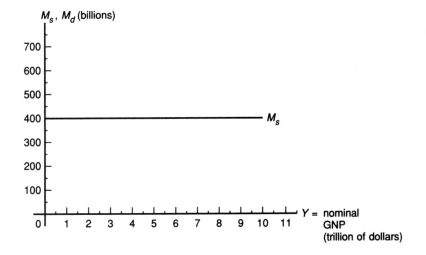

A. Given the Cambridge expression of the demand for nominal cash balances, if $k = .08$, when nominal GNP = $7.5 trillion, M_d = $ _____ billion dollars.
B. If M_d = $400 billion when nominal GNP is Y = $5 trillion, the income velocity of money is V = _____ and k = _____ .
C. Assuming $k = .08$ and M_s = $400 billion as shown, equilibrium nominal GNP is Y = $_____ trillion dollars.
D. If the money stock were to rise to $600 billion, equilibrium nominal income would rise to Y = $_____ trillion, *ceteris paribus*.
E. If the money stock stayed at M_s = $400 billion, but the proportion of nominal income that people wanted to hold as money rose to .12 nominal income would become Y = $_____ trillion dollars.

2. Growth rate problem.
   A. Fill in the blanks in the following table using the information given.

% ΔM_s	% ΔV	% ΔP	% ΔQ	% Δm_d	% Y
5			5	5	
	2	6	4		
8	1		2		
10	-2		3		

   B. In the third row of the table, if the growth rate of the money stock increased by two percentage points, *ceteris paribus*, the inflation rate would become _____ percent. This is termed _____.

CHAPTER 7

The Financial System and Money Supply

In Chapter 5 the basic concepts of the money stock and the demand for money were developed and their relationship with other markets through real balance effects was explained. In Chapter 6 the nature of the demand for money and the factors affecting its magnitude were elaborated further. This chapter begins the discussion of the creation of money by financial deposit institutions and the factors affecting the money supply.

Financial Institutions and Fractional Reserve Banking

For at least the last several hundred years, the evolutions of money and banking have been intimately connected. Banks originated in ancient times primarily as deposit and safekeeping institutions, storing metallic coins for those (i.e., mostly wealthy merchants and aristocrats) who had more money than was safe to keep on hand. For this service the banks charged a fee. In England many of the early deposit bankers were originally goldsmiths, who had vaults in which to store their metal.

Those depositing money with the smiths for safekeeping were given receipts. Because the process of redeeming the receipts either prior or subsequent to purchase added a transaction cost, people eventually began to use the receipts themselves in exchange. The banks then stopped issuing the receipts as payable only to the original depositor and made them convertible on demand by the holder. This occurred in the 17th century and is the origin of modern Western paper currency.[1] Governments soon began specifying the metallic weights in which such receipts, termed **bank notes**, were issued, designating the official units as **legal tender** in which debts and taxes could be paid and eventually even printing the notes and supplying them to the banking system.

It is important to note that the process of issuing receipts for deposit of metallic coins and specie did not in itself alter the money stock. This is because at first all metal deposited was kept on reserve at the bank for conversion on demand by noteholders. Coins formerly held in transactors's cash balances and used in exchange were simply replaced in those cash balances and transactions by notes of identical nominal and real value.

This situation can be expressed symbolically. Suppose that $B =$ the monetary base. Because notes were created by deposit, in those days the monetary base consisted of all metallic coins, including those held on reserve against deposits. Where M_s has already been defined as the money stock, at that time it consisted of currency (i.e., banknote claim checks) plus coins not held in bank reserves. Now define $M_s/B = \phi$, where ϕ is termed the **money multiplier**. As long as all money deposited in the banks was held on reserve and no claims on specie were issued without prior deposit, $M_s = B$ and $\phi = 1$. This is termed **100 percent reserve banking**.

The significance of the symbolic definition of ϕ lies in its generality. One-hundred percent reserve banking did not persist. The widespread holding and use of paper currency claims in transactions meant that money could be created at virtually no opportunity cost. Since there was and is a large demand for credit by both private parties and government, and hence an opportunity to earn interest at low cost by supplying this demand, deposit bankers began doing so by printing and issuing additional notes.

This additional currency was "backed" only by the written promises of the borrowers to repay the loans. These notes consisted, however, like all others, of claims on specie held on reserve, hence its issuance without prior deposit increased the money stock and made it larger than the monetary base, such that $\phi > 1$. This is termed **fractional reserve banking**, because under such a system reserves held are less than the claims issued against them.

Financial Intermediation and the Banking System _____

With the emergence of fractional reserve banking, banks became both deposit and lending institutions, acting as financial intermediaries connecting borrowers and lenders. Financial intermediation is a vital function in modern market economies. By providing central location and specialized knowledge, financial intermediaries reduce the transaction costs for both savers and borrowers and significantly increase the efficiency of resource use. If those with surplus income (i.e., savers) and those needing funds for investment or purchase of consumer durables had to seek each other out individually, the efficiency of resource use would be drastically reduced.

A word or two of qualification is needed here. First, since income is earned by the production and supply of goods and services, saving involves more than simply not spending a portion of current income on current consumption. It involves a literal release of physical inputs and outputs for redirection to the production of future goods and services through the process of investment. Financial intermediation connecting voluntary savers and lenders aids this process. Credit supplied through money creation only, however, does not involve the voluntary release of resources. Command over physical resources (i.e., purchasing power) is supplied to the borrower, and these resources are transferred from others, but the process, known as **forced saving**, involves inflation and an arbitrary wealth redistribution that is much less efficient than that of voluntary saving.[2]

Second, it is not obvious that deposit banks had to evolve into financial intermediaries, because other institutions can and do perform this function. Stock brokers act as financial intermediaries, for example, without creating money in the process. It is often argued correctly that banks offer small savers an advantage of lower risk over investment through brokers, because banks pool the funds of many such savers and invest them in a broad portfolio of assets, spreading the risk. However, mutual funds do the same thing for small savers without altering the money stock. For these and other reasons some prominent economists, such as Irving Fisher and Milton Friedman, have advocated a return to 100 percent reserve banking.

Today the primary financial intermediaries in the U.S. economy are banks and similar depository institutions such as mutual savings banks, savings and loans and credit unions, all of which were created legislatively to specialize in certain kinds of lending (e.g., home mortgages in the case of savings and loans). By their very nature these firms interact with each other in a way that makes it appropriate to speak of a banking system.

Much of this interaction stems from the widespread use of **demand deposits** (i.e., checking accounts) in cash balances and transactions. Checks have advantages as money. They can be any denomination as long as sufficient funds are on deposit, and they are also riskier for thieves to steal and use than cash is, because signatures must be forged. There are also disadvantages, of course, since demand deposit transactions are traceable and usually take longer, as anyone standing in a supermarket express lane behind a person writing a check for an 89-cent purchase knows.

The widespread use of demand deposits in the United States began shortly after passage of the **National Bank Act** in 1863. This Act created a system of nationally chartered banks to compete with state-chartered banks. The former issued national bank notes. State-chartered banks issued their own distinctive notes, although they were also denominated in dollars and convertible into gold and silver at the specified legal rates. The federal government wanted to unify the currency, however, so in 1864 it amended the 1863 Act to tax the state bank notes out of existence.[3]

The tax forced state banks to use the national bank notes for all of their customer's needs and prevented them from making loans by creating notes, but it did not prevent them from making loans or creating money. They began making loans by creating a demand deposit for the customer and issuing a check or a checkbook in implicit recognition that demand deposits were a close if not perfect substitute for currency. Check usage expanded rapidly for several decades thereafter.

If banks were not willing to cash or accept as deposits checks drawn on other banks, this extension of deposit money usage could not have occurred, because people would have been restricted to using checks in payment to other customers of their own bank. A check is an order to transfer ownership of funds, however, and interbank acceptance of checks requires an interbank mechanism for completing these transfers. To do this, certain large commercial banks developed into **clearing houses**, in which other banks would deposit part of their reserves.

Imagine two banks. Customers of each bank write checks and make payments to customers of the other, who either cash or deposit them at their own bank. Each bank now has checks drawn on the other. The checks are sent to the clearing house, where both banks have accounts. The clearing house totals the amounts each owes the other, debits the account of the net debtor by the difference and credits the other bank's account by the same amount. The checks are then sent back to the banks of origin, where the deposits of their writers are debited. This clearing process drastically reduces the accounting and other costs incurred in the use of demand deposits as money.

Balance Sheet of a Bank

Banks and other depository institutions are profit-seeking and loss-avoiding firms. There are unique aspects to their operation, but they provide services, incur costs, and earn revenues, and as in any other business, short-run variable input usage is extended to the point that marginal revenue is equal to marginal cost.

Many of the basic characteristics of the banking business can be seen by examining the balance sheet of a bank. Table 7.1 shows such an account, which is based upon the time-honored principles of double-entry bookkeeping. The assets of the firm are listed on the left-hand side of the account and its liabilities are shown on the right-hand side. Because assets normally exceed liabilities, the difference, known as net worth, is added to the right-hand side to balance the account. If the firm did poorly, such that assets < liabilities, the net worth entry would be negative and the account would still balance. The dollar values shown are only representational.

The major liabilities of a bank consist of demand deposits and time deposits. Demand deposits have been discussed previously. They are checkable and generally pay no interest. In fact, customers are usually charged a fee for this service, although recently the law was changed to allow depository institutions to issue a type of demand deposit called a **Negotiable Order of Withdrawal** or **NOW account**, which pays interest.

Savings accounts are a form of time deposit. The term stems from the fact that the law does not require requests for withdrawal to be honored immediately, but gives the banks up to 30 days in which to do so. Savings accounts pay interest. Here again, recent changes in the law have somewhat blurred the distinction by allowing the issuance of **Automatic Transfer Savings deposits** (ATS Accounts), which automatically transfer funds to the customer's demand deposit to cover over-drafts. The distinction between time and demand deposits will be retained in this book, however, by listing all checkable deposits, including NOW and ATS accounts, as demand deposits.

Whereas funds deposited with the bank constitute liabilities in the sense that they are the property of and are owed to the depositors, they also become assets to be used. Part of the assets are held as reserves and the rest are used to make loans and investments, from

TABLE 7.1

Assets	Liabilities
Reserves	Demand deposits
$3,000,000	$10,000,000
Loans and Investments	Time deposits
$17,000,000	$8,000,000
	Net worth
	$2,000,000

which interest is earned to cover the wages of employees, pay interest on time deposits, pay taxes, and make dividend payments to investors.

Money held on reserve, part as vault cash and part on deposit at a clearing house, earns no interest. It is economically necessary to hold such a reserve stock, however, for the same reasons that other transactors hold a cash balance. Basically, the bank needs a reserve cushion so that it can match flows of deposit and withdrawal, the magnitudes of which are subject to random variation. In a period over which withdrawals exceed deposits, for example, the net withdrawals can be covered by drawing down reserves.

The major factors affecting the magnitude of bank reserves will be discussed in detail in Chapter 8. Here only the basic point is essential: The magnitude of reserves relative to deposits is a choice variable, subject to economic decision by the managers, and it can change for both an individual bank and the banking system as a whole. This fact turns out to be highly significant.

The Monopoly Bank Model of Deposit Money Creation

The manner in which the banking system creates money can be illustrated by a series of models of decreasing simplicity. The models employ the following definitions, some of which have been given previously.

D = deposits, where $D = D_d$ (demand deposits) + D_t (time deposits)

Cu = currency

M_s = the money stock

B = the monetary base

ϕ = the money multiplier

Z = the dollar value of legally required reserves

X = the dollar value of excess reserves (above Z)

R = the value of total reserves, where $R = Z + X$

v = the legal reserve ratio (percentage of deposits required), where $v = Z/D$ and $v \cdot D = Z$

e = the excess reserve ratio (percentage of deposits), where $e = X/D$ and $e \cdot D = X$

TABLE 7.2 GMB&T

Assets		Liabilities	
R	$ 40,000	D	$200,000
L&I	$160,000		
	$200,000		$200,000

For the simplest model, imagine a country in which the government has granted a monopoly in the provision of banking services to a single firm, which may be assumed to have several branch offices. Suppose also that no currency is used and all payments are made by check. Further, assume that all deposits are demand deposits. Last, assume that the government, out of concern for the safety of deposits, specifies $v = .2$ and that the firm wants to hold no excess reserves. Summarizing, we are assuming

1. A single monopoly bank.
2. $Cu = 0$ so $M_s = D$ (and $D = D_d$).
3. $v = .2$.
4. $X = 0$ so $R = Z$.

Let us call our firm the Greedy Monopolist Bank and Trust, or GMB&T. The initial situation is shown on the balance sheet of the GMB&T in Table 7.2, where all entries are denominated in dollars. For simplicity, the net worth entry has been eliminated, and it is implicit that an identical sum has been deducted from assets. Given that initially $D = \$200,000$, $R = \$40,000$ because $v = .2$.

Now suppose that the People's Republic bordering our imaginary country is not a nice place and that a refugee slips under the barbed wire, dashes across the border, and deposits $2000 in life savings in the nearest branch of the GMB&T. This shows up as an addition to deposit liabilities of +$2000 in Table 7.3. Because the moment that the money

TABLE 7.3 GMB&T

Assets		Liabilities	
R	$ 40,000	D	$200,000
	+2,000		+2,000
L&I	$160,000		

crosses the teller's window, it also becomes an asset of the firm, an identical entry is made under reserves, and the books balance.

The first thing to notice is that the GMB&T now has excess reserves on hand. That is, where

$$v = \frac{Z}{D}$$

$$.2 = \frac{Z}{\$202,000}$$

$$.2(\$202,000) = Z$$

$$\$40,400 = Z.$$

Total reserves, however, are \$42,000, and because

$$R = Z + X,$$

$$\$42,000 = \$40,400 + X$$

$$\$42,000 - \$40,400 = X$$

$$\$1600 = X.$$

Now by assumption the bank does not wish to hold excess reserves and there is a simple way to get rid of them. The bank does this by making additional loans equal to $\Delta L = \frac{1}{v} \cdot X$

$$= 5(\$1600)$$

$$= \$8000.$$

These additional loans are shown in Table 7.4. The loans are made by creating deposits for the borrowers in the amounts of the loans and giving them checkbooks, so an addition to deposits of identical magnitude is also shown and the books balance.

TABLE 7.4   GMB&T

Assets		Liabilities	
R	$ 42,000	D	$202,000
L&I	$160,000		+ 8,000
	+ 8,000		
	$210,000		$210,000

The derivation of the formula for changing loans is not readily apparent until one notices that where

$$v = \frac{Z}{D}$$

$$.2 = \frac{Z}{\$210,000}$$

$$.2(\$210,000) = Z$$

$$\$42,000 = Z$$

and all of the excess reserves have now been converted to required reserves. In fact, expanding loans in this fashion is the only way the bank can get rid of the excess reserves.

Why the bank can get away with creating loans and deposits that are a multiple of an initial deposit may seem a mystery until it is realized that the bank faces no possible drain on its funds. All checks written by borrowers and used in payment will be deposited at either the same or another branch of the same bank by their recipients. The ownership of the deposits will change hands, but that is all. And since no currency exists, no drain can occur due to recipients cashing, but not depositing, their checks.

Note two more things: First, if we remember that $M_s = D$ because $Cu = 0$, the initial money stock of $200,000 has increased by a multiple of the $2000 deposit to $210,000. Second, the whole process also works in reverse. If the refugee were to get homesick, withdraw the $2000 and leave, the bank would have to reduce loans and deposits by the same multiple until actual reserves were once again legally sufficient. It would do this by refusing to extend any new loans while existing loans were being paid off through the debiting of deposits.

The Competitive Banking Model and the Simple Multiplier

The second model differs from the first only by removing the assumption of monopoly banking and assuming the existence of competition. Specifically, suppose our country has ten banks, each with deposits of $20,000 so that the initial total of $D = M_s = \$200,000$ as before. All other assumptions are the same, so the initial position of each bank is as shown in Table 7.5.

Suppose now that the refugee deposits the $2000 in the First National Bank, as shown by the entry of +$2000 under deposits in Table 7.6.

TABLE 7.5

Assets		Liabilities	
R	$ 4,000	D	$20,000
L&I	$16,000		

Note that the $2000 increase in deposits is not matched by a $2000 increase in reserves. Of course, reserves instantly go up by $2000, causing the bank to have excess reserves, but the question is how the bank responds to this situation.

The First National Bank is not in the same position the GMB&T was in. It cannot create new loans (by creating deposits) equal to a multiple of the new deposit because checks written by the borrowers might be deposited in other banks, and when the checks cleared it might not be able to cover them all. What it can do is keep the legally required percent of the new deposit (.2 times $2000 = $400), adding it to reserves and lending the $1600 remainder. The loan is made by creating another deposit of $1600, but that entry disappears when the checks clear, so it is not shown in Table 7.6.

Now suppose that the checks are used in payment to customers of the Second National Bank, where they show up as an addition of $1600 to deposits. The Second National is in the same position as the First National. They cannot do as the GMB&T did and make loans equal to a multiple of the initial deposit for fear of a drain, so they keep .2($1600) = $320, adding it to reserves, and lend out the remaining $1280 as shown in Table 7.7.

The borrowers write checks making payment to customers of the Third National Bank, which show up as an addition of $1280 to its deposits. The Third National adds .2($1280) = $256 to its reserves and lends out $1024 as shown in Table 7.8. Note that deposits have already been created that are a multiple of the initial $2000 deposit. Each additional deposit is smaller, because of the portion added to reserves in each case, but the series continues. How far will it go? The series

TABLE 7.6 First National Bank

Assets		Liabilities	
R	$ 4,000	D	$20,000
	+400		+2,000
L&I	$16,000		
	+1,600		

TABLE 7.7 Second National Bank

Assets		Liabilities	
R	$14,000	D	$20,000
	+320		+1,600
L&I	$16,000		
	+1,280		

continues until the reserves of the banking system have increased by $2000, deposits have increased by $10,000 (including the initial $2000 deposit), and the money supply reaches $210,000, exactly as in the monopoly bank case. Again, it would work in reverse for a withdrawal.

The point of these exercises is to demonstrate the nature of multiple deposit creation and derive the value of the money multiplier. The latter can be found by simple algebra. Given the initial assumptions that $M_s = D$ because $Cu = 0$, and $X = 0$ so $R = Z$, we can begin with the definition $M_s/B = \phi$. Under the institutional conditions assumed, the monetary base consists only of the reserves of the banking system. ϕ can be derived by making the appropriate substitutions:

$$\frac{M_s}{B} = \frac{D}{R} = \frac{D}{Z} = \frac{D/D}{Z/D} = \frac{1}{v} = \phi.$$

Therefore,

$$\frac{M_s}{R} = \frac{1}{v}$$

and

$$M_s = \frac{1}{v} \cdot R$$

TABLE 7.8 Third National Bank

Assets		Liabilities	
R	$ 4,000	D	$20,000
	+256		+1,280
L&I	$16,000		
	+1,024		

Figure 7.1 The Money Multiplier.

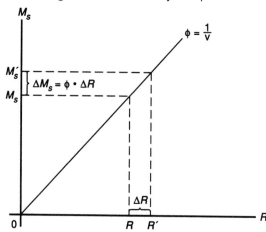

This means that the money stock will be a multiple of the reserves of the banking system given by the inverse of the legal reserve ratio under the institutional conditions assumed. It follows that

$$\Delta M_s = \frac{1}{v} \cdot \Delta R$$

which is exactly what happened in the previous cases. Given $v = .2$, $\Delta R = +\$2000$ caused $\Delta D = \Delta M_s = +\$10,000$. Given this form of the expression, the money multiplier can be written as $\Delta M_s/\Delta R = 1/v$. Expressing the money multiplier as the slope of a function specifying the rate at which the money stock changes as bank reserves change makes it easy to illustrate the argument graphically, as in Figure 7.1.

Excess Reserve Holding and the Money Multiplier _____

The model employed previously can be brought another step closer to reality by removing the assumption that banks hold no excess reserves. There is a very good reason why they do hold such reserves: Legally required reserves are not really reserves in the economic sense of the term. That is, precisely because the banks are required to keep them on hand, such reserves are not available to be paid out during period of heavy withdrawal. In order to be prepared for such contingencies, it makes sense for banks to keep more than the legally required amount of reserves on hand, and they normally do so.

Allowing $X > 0$, so that $R = Z + X$, changes the model in only one way. The assumption that $Cu = 0$ such that $M_s = D$, and all $D = D_d$, can be retained. Beginning again with the fundamental definition of the multiplier, we can derive its form by the appropriate substitutions. That is, $M_s/B = \phi$, and since $M_s = D$ and $B = R$,

$$\frac{M_s}{B} = \frac{D}{R} = \frac{D/D}{R/D} = \frac{1}{R/D} = \phi.$$

Therefore,

$$\frac{M_s}{R} = \frac{1}{R/D},$$

$$M_s = \frac{1}{R/D} R,$$

and

$$\Delta M_s = \frac{1}{R/D} \Delta R.$$

Since $R = Z + X$, this multiplier could also be transformed and expressed as

$$\phi = \frac{1}{R/D} = \frac{1}{(Z + X)/D} = \frac{1}{Z/D + X/D} = \frac{1}{v + e}.$$

There are two important points here. First, $1/(v + e) < 1/v$ because $e > 0$; that is, the holding of excess reserves reduces the multiplier. Second, the ratio R/D expresses two choice variables, one under the control of the government and one whose value lies at the discretion of the banking system. Changes in either of these will alter ϕ and hence the money stock. This can be seen from the general form of the multiplier: $M_s/B = \phi$, so $M_s = \phi \cdot B$. Applying the growth rate rule to this expression, we obtain

$$\frac{\Delta M_s}{M_s} \approx \frac{\Delta \phi}{\phi} + \frac{\Delta B}{B},$$

and if $\Delta B/B = 0$, $\Delta M_s/M_s \approx \Delta \phi/\phi$. This is illustrated in Figure 7.2, where (remembering that $B = R$) $\Delta R = 0$, but an increase in R/D,

Figure 7.2 A Decline in the Money Multiplier.

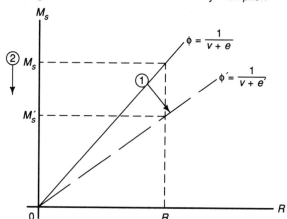

perhaps due to a rise in the excess reserve ratio, lowers ϕ to ϕ', and hence reduces the money stock to M'_s.

The Complete M1 Money Multiplier _____

The last and most important abstraction that needs to be removed in developing a realistic money multiplier for the purposes of this book is the assumption that all money consists of demand deposits. The assumption that no time deposits exist can also be removed, although because it is the M1 multiplier that is being developed here, the deposits referred to in the equation will be existing demand deposits, D_d.

It is now assumed, therefore, that $Cu > 0$ such that $M_s = Cu + D_d$ and $B = Cu + R$. As before, $X > 0$ so $R = Z + X$. The M1 multiplier is now developed from its generic definition by the appropriate substitutions:

$$\frac{M_s}{B} = \phi,$$

$$\frac{M_s}{B} = \frac{Cu + D_d}{Cu + R} = \frac{Cu/D_d + D_d/D_d}{Cu/D_d + R/D_d} = \frac{Cu/D_d + 1}{Cu/D_d + R/D_d} = \phi,$$

$$M_s = \frac{Cu/D_d + 1}{Cu/D_d + R/D_d} B.$$

The new ratio in this expression, Cu/D_d, the ratio of currency to demand deposits, refers to the relative composition of the money stock. In November 1988, this ratio averaged about .371, with $M_s \approx \$211$ billion in currency and \$569 billion in demand deposits. The reserve ratio, R/D_d, was about .1275 at that time. Figure 7.3 shows that ϕ has been rather stable over time. Although it declined from the mid-1960s to 1980, leveled off until 1984, and began rising thereafter, annual variations usually have been very small. The average annual percentage change in ϕ during this period is only .018, or 1.8 percent, although relatively large changes of .049, $-.056$, and .055 did occur in 1977, 1978, and 1986, respectively.

At least three distinguishable groups make decisions that affect ϕ, and hence the money stock. The first is the Federal Reserve system, which has the authority to set and alter the legal reserve ratio (v), as is discussed in Chapter 8. The second is the banking system itself, which can alter the reserve ratio, R/D_d, by its discretion over the excess reserve ratio. The third group is the public, which can alter Cu/D_d at will by either depositing currency, making cash withdrawals, or switching funds between demand deposits and time deposits, and thus raising or lowering D_d, *ceteris paribus*.

The effects of such changes on ϕ are also discernable. Suppose, to take an extreme example, that Cu/D_d approaches infinity. Then ϕ would tend to become

$$\phi = \frac{\infty + 1}{\infty + R/D_d} \approx 1.$$

A rise in Cu/D_d, then, tends to reduce ϕ *ceteris paribus*, and a fall in Cu/D_d tends to raise ϕ. In fact, as the ratio approaches zero, the multiplier tends to approach the value of

$$\phi = \frac{0 + 1}{0 + R/D_d} = \frac{1}{R/D_d}$$

Figure 7.3 The Empirical Money Multiplier (M1/B = ϕ), 1965 to 1986.

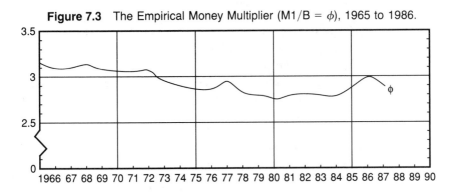

as shown previously. Historically, the currency ratio was rising in the 1970s (see Chapter 16) and this was largely responsible for the fall in ϕ during that period, as shown in Figure 7.3. A fall in the currency ratio after 1982 was also partly responsible for the rise in the money multiplier during that period.

Now suppose that the reserve ratio rises toward unity $(R/D_d \rightarrow 1)$. The multiplier would tend toward

$$\phi = \frac{Cu/D_d + 1}{Cu/D_d + 1} = 1,$$

as would be expected under 100 percent reserve banking. If the reserve ratio approached zero, in contrast, the multiplier would get larger, although exactly what value it would approach depends on the value of the currency ratio at the time. Clearly, ϕ varies inversely with the reserve ratio, and changes in reserves relative to deposits have frequently been a crucial factor causing changes in the multiplier.

As pointed out previously, government can alter the reserve ratio by altering the legal reserve ratio $(v = Z/D_d)$ and decision-makers in depository institutions may also alter the reserve ratio by altering their desired excess reserve ratio $(e = X/D_d)$. The primary factor determining the optimal level of excess reserves is probably the interest rate. A dollar invested earns interest, but a dollar held in reserve does not, so interest foregone is the opportunity cost of adding a dollar to reserves. Consequently, higher interest rates motivate bankers to economize on excess reserves, reducing e and raising ϕ. On the other hand, lower interest rates may result in bankers raising e and reducing ϕ.

The potential significance of fluctuations in ϕ can be illustrated by combining the money multiplier graph with a money supply and demand graph as shown in Figure 7.4 by placing their common axes together. Here the fourth (lower right) quadrant is not a positive–negative $(+, -)$ quadrant as such graphs are normally interpreted, but is positive–postive, as is quadrant one.

Figure 7.4 shows a rise in ϕ, which must be due to a reduction in v, e, or Cu/D_d. The graph also shows the associated multiple deposit expansion by the banking system. In the case shown, this expansion occurs rapidly enough so that the money stock grows relative to the demand for money, creating excess real balances and matching excess demands in commodity markets by Walras's law. Under a gold standard, base money would flow out through the balance of payments and reduce the money stock until equilibrium was restored. Under the current fiat money system, however, prices, including foreign exchange rates (i.e., the dollar prices of foreign currencies), eventually rise enough to reduce real balances to the desired level. This is the sequence shown by the numbered arrows in Figure 7.4.

The opposite case can be imagined also. A sharp fall in ϕ would reduce the money stock such that $M_s/P < M_d/P$, creating a recession until prices fell enough to raise real balances to the desired level. Just how important such fluctuations are would seem to depend on their magnitude and how quickly they occur. Figure 7.3 seems to indicate that, although it is usually relatively stable, large fluctuations in ϕ can occur. Clearly, as long as fractional reserve banking exists there is a potential source of macroeconomic instability latent in the market economy.

As a matter of historical record, 19th-and early 20th-century banking was characterized by intermittent monetary expansions and associated inflations, although these were very mild by recent standards, and

Figure 7.4 Destabilizing Effect of a Large Change in the Money Multiplier.

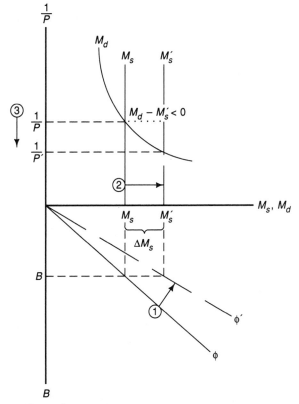

Source: Economic Report of the President, 1989: 385 and 388

gold outflows, followed by sharp monetary contractions and recessions as people, worried about the financial condition of depository institutions, "ran on the banks" and traded their depreciating currency for gold. In such cases the banks would temporarily restrict, although seldom totally suspend, currency convertibility. This gave them time to increase their reserves relative to monetary liabilities, both by selling other assets and thus increasing reserves directly and by calling in loan payments due, reducing the amount of money in circulation.

Such system-wide bank runs did not occur frequently, however. From 1850 to 1933, general bank runs requiring convertibility restriction occurred only five times. These were in October 1857, September 1873, August 1893, October 1907 and March 1933. This averages out to about every 17 years. Indeed, several recessions occurring during this period generated no concern over the financial health of the banking system and/or bank runs.[4]

The surest cure for macroeconomic instability resulting from endogenous fluctuations in ϕ would, of course, be 100 percent reserve banking. The cure eventually sought by the government was not 100 percent reserve banking, however. Interpreting the liquidity crises as a problem of periodic inadequate reserves in the banking system, rather than one of intermittant excess money creation through reduction of the reserve ratio by the banks[5], what was sought was the creation of a quasi-governmental institution to feed reserves to the system when needed to prevent the resulting recessions. This institution, the Federal Reserve system, will be discussed in Chapter 8. It may be noted here, however, that by far the worst of the banking crises listed and, indeed, in U.S. history, was the one that occurred in 1933, *after* the Federal Reserve had been created.

Summary

The primary arguments of this chapter can be summarized as follows.

1. Paper money originated as claimchecks for specie deposited for safekeeping. People began trading the claimchecks in place of much of the specie.

2. Issuance of such claimchecks did not affect the money stock until depository institutions began putting additional currency into circulation through loans, at interest, without prior deposit. This was the origin of fractional reserve banking.

3. By definition the money stock exceeds the deposit base under fractional reserves. The ratio of the two, M_s/B, is the "money multiplier."

4. The widespread use of demand deposit money in the United States followed the National Bank Act of 1863, when state banknotes were taxed out of existence.

5. A net change in the reserves of the financial system has a multiplied effect on the money stock through a process of multiple deposit creation or destruction.

6. Governments specify by law or regulation the portion of deposits that financial institutions must hold on reserve, but depository firms decide for themselves, on economic considerations, the proportion they hold as excess reserves. Changes in either of these ratios can alter the money stock and affect economic activity for quite some time.

7. The public determines, as a matter of choice, the proportion of currency and deposits composing their cash balances. Changes in this proportion can also affect the money multiplier and hence the money stock.

8. Annual changes in the money multiplier have not been large in recent decades, but some instability in money and credit at least partly attributable to fractional reserve banking is part of our historical record.

Notes _____

1. The Chinese had paper currency as early as the 10th century, but little is known of its historical origin. See Elgin Groseclose, *Money and Man: A Survey of the Monetary Experience* (4th revised ed., Norman Oklahoma: University of Oklahoma Press, 1976): 115.

2. See F. A. Hayek, "A Note on the Development of the Doctrine of Forced Saving," in Hayek, *Profits, Interest and Investment* (reprint of 1939 edition, New Jersey: Augustus M. Kelley, 1975): 183–197.

3. See Robert D. Auerbach, *Money, Banking and Financial Markets* (2nd ed., New York: Macmillan Publishing Company, 1985): 130.

4. See Gerald P. Dwyer, Jr., and R. Alton Gilbert, "Bank Runs and Private Remedies," *Federal Reserve Bank of St. Louis Review* (May/June 1989): 43–61, Table 6.

5. It is noteworthy that the reserve ratio in the banking system was declining for a significant period preceding each of the liquidity crises listed. One reason a fractional reserve banking system may have a tendency to reduce the reserve ratio and engage in excess money creation over time, precipitating periodic liquidity crises, seems clear. Bankers and the public and even many economists—fail to distinguish between the demand for credit, which is a flow, and the (stock) demand for money. Any increase in the demand for credit that raises the interest rate thereby raises the opportunity cost of holding reserves. This motivates bankers to increase loans, reducing the reserve ratio and expanding the money stock. If no equivalent increase in the demand for money occurs, the value of money tends to decline.

Student Self-Test

I. True–False

T F 1. Financial intermediation could not be supplied without fractional reserve banking.

T F 2. The emergence of paper money meant that money could be created at an opportunity cost of almost zero.

T F 3. The widespread use of demand deposits as money in the United States began before passage of the National Bank Act of 1863.

T F 4. The process of reciprocal cancellation and crediting or debiting of net differences owed by banks to each other was first introduced by the Federal Reserve system because widespread check usage was impossible without this function and the market would not create institutions to perform it.

T F 5. The demand for money and the demand for credit are the same thing.

II. Short Answer (150 words or less each)

1. Explain: (a) why banks begin to hold reserves that are less than 100 percent of deposits. (b) why they still keep some reserves, and (c) why required reserves are not really reserves in the economic sense of the term.

2. Although paper money originated as claimchecks on specie deposited, governments have specified standard denominations ever since. Is there good reason for believing—or disbelieving—that competitive market processes would have resulted in a system of uniform standardized denominations in the absence of goverment intervention?

3. Explain why both the holding of excess reserves by banks and the holding of currency by the public reduce the money multiplier in the banking system.

4. What central factor might motivate many banks at a given point in time to reduce their reserve to deposit ratios and to raise the money multiplier? (*Hint*: Think of a bank's ratio of reserves to other assets as a portfolio balance.) What might result in such a case and eventually cause the banks to shift gears and raise R/D again?

5. Explain why, in an economic system without currency, in which no excess reserves are held, a monopoly bank could create loans and deposits that were a multiple of an initial deposit, whereas a competitive bank could not.

III. Completion Problems

1. Assume a multibranch monopoly bank that lends out to its required reserves as quickly as possible. All payments are by check (Currency = 0).
   Case 1: The assets and liabilities are as shown, $v = .25$, and an immigrant deposits $400.

   A. Excess reserves instantly = _____.
   B. Loans increase by $_____.

Assets	Liabilities
R $100	D $400
L $300	

C. Deposits increase by $_____ (not including the immigrant deposit)

D. The money supply becomes $_____ and ϕ = _____.

Case 2: The assets and liabilities are shown, v = .4, and an immigrant deposits $100.

A. Excess reserves instantly = _____.

B. Loans increase by $_____.

C. Deposits increase by $_____ (not including the immigrant deposit)

D. The money supply becomes $_____ and ϕ = _____.

Assets	Liabilities
R $400	D $1000
L $600	

2. Now assume a modern financial and monetary system in which both currency and demand deposits are held and used to make payments and banks hold excess reserves in accordance with their preferences. Assume also that Cu/D_d = .6, R/D_d = .2, and B = $250 billion. Refer to the following graph in solving Problems A–D.

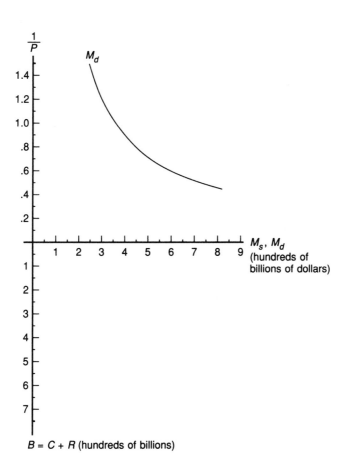

A. The numerical value of ϕ = _____. Draw this on the graph above in its correct location.
B. The nominal money stock is M_s = $_____ billion. Draw this in its correct location on the graph.
C. The *real* money stock is m_s = $_____ billion and P = _____.
D. Suppose the banks reduce the reserve ratio to R/D_d' = .04. This would change the money multiplier to ϕ' = _____. Show this change on the graph.
E. The change in ϕ alters the money stock to M_s' = $_____ billion. Show this change also.
F. The price level will _____ (rise/fall) to P' = _____.
G. Now suppose that the events described in questions D to F cause depositors to run on the banks and convert deposits to currency until the currency-deposit ratio reaches Cu/D_d' = .92. This _____ (raises/lowers) the money multiplier to ϕ'' = _____.
H. Until prices adjust, the economy should experience a temporary _____ as a consequence of this last event.

CHAPTER 8

The Federal Reserve and Monetary Policy

The creation of the Bank of England in 1693 began the emergence of special banking institutions with quasi-monopolistic powers over national money supplies—modern central banks. For some time the legal necessity for both commercial and central banks to convert national currencies into gold or silver at fixed rates on demand severely limited central bank power to control money stocks. The elimination of the gold standard and subsequent reliance of governments on fiat (i.e., inconvertible) money since the 1930s has removed that important constraint. Central banks have evolved into official instruments of national monetary control and, in many cases, regulation of the domestic banking industry.

This chapter discusses the nature and use of the monetary control instruments of the U.S. Federal Reserve system, which is the central bank of the United States. It is also crucial to consider the institutional incentives that affect Federal Reserve policy because changes in the money stock have such enormous impact on the economy. It may help, therefore, to begin with a brief discussion of the origin and structure of the Fed.

The Federal Reserve and the Banking System

The United States has actually had three central banks in its history: the First and Second Banks of the United States, and the **Federal Reserve system**. From the elimination of the Second Bank of the United States as a governmental institution in 1836 until 1913 the United States functioned—and functioned quite well—without a central bank. Indeed, in this period, particularly after the Civil War, real per capita output growth was very rapid and the United States became a world-class industrial power.

This was a period, however, in which there was considerable monetary instability centrally dependent on fractional reserve banking.[1] At intermittent intervals depositors, fearful of bank insolvency, would panic and simultaneously attempt to convert deposits for cash. The currency ratio, Cu/D_d, would rise. Banks would suspend conversions and scramble for reserves, calling in all payments due and ceasing new loans, often raising R/D_d despite reserve loss. The rise in both ratios would reduce ϕ, causing a multiplied contraction of the money stock, creating an economic contraction.

Following a sharp contraction of this type, in 1907 Congress created the **National Monetary Commission** to suggest measures for monetary reform. The commission reported in 1912 and the Federal Reserve system was created in 1913. The function of the Fed, as conceived by Congress, was to eliminate monetary instability and to prevent contractions by acting, in accordance with its name, as a "lender of last resort," supplying reserves to the banking system as needed.

Over time changes in the law have altered much of the Federal Reserve structure and operation, but many of its original features remain. The 1913 Act divided the United States into 12 geographic districts and created a **district Federal Reserve Bank** for each. Commercial banks joining the system purchase stock in and literally own the district Fed. For many years the Federal Reserve did check clearing free of charge and provided free wire transfer of funds and other fringe benefits, but this ended in 1980. Since then all banks have been required to keep a portion of their reserves on deposit at the district Federal Reserve bank and are paid no interest on those deposits.[2]

The most powerful institution in the Fed is the **Board of Governors** (BOG), consisting of seven members including a chairman, all of whom are appointed by the President of the United States with the consent of Congress. The Board establishes various regulations for the banking system. The Board members also sit on the 12-member **Federal Open Market Committee** (FOMC) with five presidents of district banks. It is this committee that determines and carries out U.S. monetary policy.

Reserve Requirement Policy

The Federal Reserve has three primary instruments of monetary policy, which will be discussed in reverse order of their current importance. The first of these is **reserve requirement policy**. The Board of Governors determines legal reserve requirements against different kinds of deposits and can alter them at will. Remembering that

$$\phi = \frac{Cu/D_d + 1}{Cu/D_d + R/D_d}$$

$$= \frac{Cu/D_d + 1}{Cu/D_d + v + e},$$

we find that if the Board of Governors, in concert with the FOMC, decided to reduce the legal demand deposit reserve ratio (v), ϕ would rise, *ceteris paribus*.

From the perspective of the commercial bankers, the reduction in v would mean that they found themselves holding larger excess reserves than they desired. They would therefore lend out such "excess" excess reserves, and the multiple deposit expansion process would increase the money stock. That is, because $M_s = \phi \cdot B$,

$$\frac{\Delta M_s}{M_s} \approx \frac{\Delta \phi}{\phi} + \frac{\Delta B}{B},$$

and even if $\Delta B/B = 0$, $\Delta M_s/M_s \approx \Delta \phi/\phi$. The effect would be as shown in Figure 7.4; see Chapter 7.

If the Fed decided to raise v, banks would find themselves with less excess reserves than they desired. They would constrict new loans and allow the multiple deposit contraction process to operate as existing loans were paid off, until excess reserves were again adequate, reducing the money stock in the process. The primary problem with such a policy, however, is that because the level of excess reserves is discretionary to the commercial bankers, the Fed does not know exactly what the multiplier response to a change in v would be.

Discount Policy

The second of the Fed's instruments of monetary control is **discount policy**. In its ostensible role as the ultimate supplier of reserves to the banking system, the Fed often makes short-term collateralized loans to banks that find themselves with inadequate reserves. These loans are made through the district banks at an interest rate, ultimately set by the Board of Governors, which is termed the **discount rate**. This process is illustrated in Tables 8.1 and 8.2. Table 8.1 shows the balance sheet of the Fed. Currency and coin in circulation are listed as a liability. Since the United States is no longer on the gold standard this is, of course, an

TABLE 8.1   Federal Reserve

Assets	Liabilities
Government securities	Currency and coin
Loans to commercial	Reserves of commercial
banks	banks
+$5 billion	+$5 billion

accounting fiction. They are not liabilities in any economic sense. No one presenting a Federal Reserve note for conversion at the Fed will receive in exchange anything but another note, or perhaps change. The other major entry on the liability side is commercial bank reserves, kept on deposit at the Fed as required. Together, these entries constitute the monetary base, $B = Cu + R$. The Fed can therefore alter the monetary base through certain transactions that alter its liabilities.

The Fed has a large amount of U.S. government securities on the asset side of its ledger. The second asset entry shown consists of loans made by the Fed to commercial banks. For expositional purposes, the initial dollar values of these entries are not shown. The dollar magnitudes listed are the initial changes on the books resulting from Federal Reserve actions. Also, while there are other entries on both the asset and liability sides of the Fed's books, the fact that base money is matched in the balance sheet by an identical value of assets can be illustrated graphically by a 45° line as in Figure 8.1.

Table 8.2 adds all of the assets and liabilities of the commercial banking system onto one combined balance sheet. Together with the entries discussed in Chapter 7 there must be a new entry on the liability side, showing the dollar value of commercial bank borrowings from (and hence indebtedness to) the Fed. Again, however, the initial dollar magnitudes of these entries are not shown. What is shown are the dollar values of changes resulting from a discount policy change.

At any given time the Fed is extending some loans and others are being paid off. Imagine an initial balance or equilibrium in which the

TABLE 8.2   Combined Commercial Bank Accounts

Assets	Liabilities
R	D
+$5 billion	Borrowings from the Fed
	+$5 billion
L&I	

Figure 8.1 Federal Reserve Balance Sheet Equality of Monetary Base Items and Matching Assets.

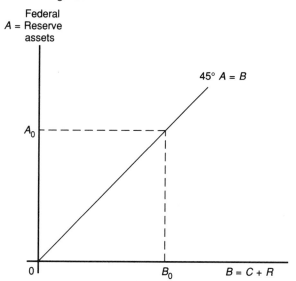

value of payments and new loans extended are equal, so that the value of loans outstanding is not changing. Now suppose that the Fed decides to increase the money stock. To do so it can encourage additional borrowing by lowering the discount rate banks must pay on such loans. In particular, the Fed must reduce the discount rate relative to the **Federal Funds rate**, which is a market interest rate at which commercial banks borrow excess reserves from and lend to each other as needed.

The +$5 billion addition to loans on the asset side of Table 8.1, the Fed's balance sheet, shows the result of such a relative discount rate reduction. The Fed makes these loans by crediting the reserve accounts of the commercial banks on the liability side of its ledger, which is the reason for that entry. These reserves, however, are both a liability to the Fed and assets to the banks, so commercial bank reserves rise by the same amount on their own books while their liabilities in the form of indebtedness to the Fed increase simultaneously, as shown.

The increase in total bank reserves means two things: First, the monetary base has increased and second, the banks are holding additional excess reserves. Commercial bank loans will therefore be increased and the money stock will rise by a multiple of the increase in the monetary base. That is, as previously shown, $M_s = \phi \cdot B$ and $\Delta M_s = \phi \cdot \Delta B$.

If the Fed wished to contract the money stock instead, it could raise the discount rate relative to the Federal Funds rate and discourage borrowing. All of the entries in Tables 8.1 and 8.2 would then be negative as loan payments to the Fed exceeded new loans extended and payment was taken by debiting commercial bank reserve deposits on the Fed's books, reducing bank reserves and indebtedness to the Fed. There is a problem with discount policy of either type, however, in that the Fed does not know the exact interest elasticity of commercial bank demand for its credit and hence does not know the exact quantitive effects on the monetary base or money stock of a given change in the discount rate.

Open Market Policy

When the imprecision of both reserve requirement and discount policy became evident early in its history, the Federal Reserve invented a third method of monetary control, which has become by far the most important. This method is called **Open Market Operations**. Consider Tables 8.3 and 8.4, which once again show the balance sheet of the Fed and the combined accounts of commercial depository institutions. Note that in Table 8.4 banks are shown as holding U.S. government securities among their assets. Actually, a large portion of bank investment is in such securities.

The Federal Open Market Committee meets about ten times per year to decide on monetary policy. If the FOMC decides to expand the money stock, it can direct its agents to enter the market and purchase securities from the banking system, say in the amount of $10 billion. This adds that amount to the Fed's asset portfolio, as shown in Table 8.3. The securities portfolio of the commercial banks is reduced by the same amount in Table 8.4.

The Fed pays for the securities purchased by crediting the reserve deposits of the commercial banks on its books with the amount of the purchase, raising the reserve entry on both sets of books. Since banks now have excess reserves, new loans will be made and the multiple deposit expansion process will increase the money stock by a multiple

TABLE 8.3 Federal Reserve

Assets	Liabilities
Government securities +$10 billion	Cu
	B
	R +$10 billion

TABLE 8.4 Commercial Banks

Assets	Liabilities
R +$10 billion	D_d
	D_t
Loans	
	Borrowings from the Fed
Investments	
Government securities −$10 billion	

of the change in the monetary base $(Cu + R)$ produced by the open market purchases.

If the Fed wished to decrease the money stock instead, it could engage in open market sales of securities from its asset portfolio to the commercial banks. In that case the entries in Tables 8.3 and 8.4 would have the opposite signs of those shown, and the multiple deposit contraction process would reduce the money stock by a multiple of the decline in the monetary base as the Fed took payment by debiting the bank reserve deposits on its books.

This method of monetary control is much more precise than the others. The Fed can purchase or sell exactly the dollar value of securities it wishes and hence exercise nearly perfect control over the monetary base.[3] There is still some imprecision in its control over the money stock, however, because the money multiplier may be changing due to alterations in the currency ratio by the public, by alterations in the reserve ratio by the banks, or both.

Just how much imprecision changes in ϕ introduce into Federal Reserve monetary control depends on the magnitude and rapidity of such changes. Open market operations are highly flexible, and if the data presented in Figure 7.3 (see Chapter 7) is indicative, significant changes in ϕ generally occur only over periods of several months or a year; in fact, the increase in ϕ from 1985 to 86 was unusually large. Over such a period the Fed could undertake offsetting open market operations if it wished to do so.

Open market purchases or sales aimed at offsetting changes in ϕ are termed **defensive** open market operations. Figure 8.2 illustrates one such operation by combining Figure 8.1 with Figure 7.4 (see Chapter 7). All quadrants are positive–positive. Here a decline in ϕ over time which, *ceteris paribus*, would reduce the money stock from M_s to M_s' and, by Walras's law, create a recessionary condition, is offset by an open market purchase that raises Fed assets from A to A', increases the

Figure 8.2 Defensive Open Market Operation.

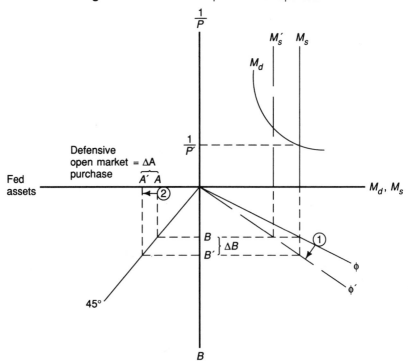

monetary base from B to B' and prevents the decline in the money stock.

In the real world this could not be done perfectly. Some time is required for the Fed to gather, assimilate, and act on information. But, in fact, the banks are required to report all the relevant data to the Fed weekly, it is processed rapidly, and open market policy can respond as soon as a trend movement in ϕ can be observed. Repeated studies have shown that the Fed can control the money stock within fairly narrow margins over periods as small as a quarter.[4]

Perhaps it is less relevant to ask whether the Fed can offset the effects of $\Delta\phi$ on the money stock than whether it wants to do so. As a matter of fact, much of the time autonomous changes in ϕ will be causing changes in the money stock that are in accord with the dynamic policy goals of the Fed. At such times the Fed will desist from defensive open market operations and may even act to augment the effects under way. An important advantage here, from the Fed's perspective, is that it can disassociate itself from any detrimental effects resulting from its monetary policy by blaming them on the money multiplier. For these reasons autonomous changes in ϕ must be recognized as frequently constituting a fourth important monetary policy instrument of the Federal Reserve. There are yet others, but it is now time to discuss the aims of monetary policy.

Abstract Goals of Monetary Policy

Economists usually identify three abstract or "ideal" goals of monetary policy: The first involves eliminating or (even better) preventing severe unemployment; the second is the attainment of an acceptable level and growth trend of real GNP; and the third is the preservation of price level stability. These may be summarized in terms of stabilizing employment, output, and the price level at acceptable values. How these goals can be attained is a matter of heated debate. The debate focuses on whether the Fed should exercise purely discretionary control over the money stock, altering it at will, or be subject to externally imposed rules for monetary control.

The nature of the debate is illustrated in Figure 8.3, which is like Figure 8.2 except that, with the money stock at M_s and the value of money at $1/P$, it shows an initial situation of excess demand for money and hence, by Walras's law, a recession. Without asking why this gap appeared, note first that if prices were highly flexible and the real balance effect operated quickly—or if the money stock was demand-determined and adjusted quickly by an automatic mechanism, as under the gold standard—there would be little role for monetary policy. Suppose, however, as shown, that a price level adjustment has not yet begun. If the Fed knew the magnitude of the excess demand it could, in principle, undertake open market purchases or discount policy sufficient to increase the money stock from M_s to M_s' and eliminate the gap. This would not only get rid of excess unemployment but also preserve price level stability.

An identical argument could be made for an initial situation in which $M_s/P > M_d/P$, creating inflationary pressures in commodity markets. Here again, if the Fed had accurate knowledge of the magnitude of the excess real money stock, it could undertake open market *sales*, raise the discount rate, or even raise the reserve requirement and reduce the nominal money stock enough to eliminate the gap. Because of their greater precision, open market operations are generally relied upon in Fed efforts to eliminate inflationary and recessionary gaps, and these are termed **dynamic** (in contrast with defensive) **open market operations**.

Look again at Figure 8.3 to determine what created the initial recessionary situation. There are essentially two possibilities if we exclude

Figure 8.3 Eliminating a Recessionary Gap with Monetary Policy.

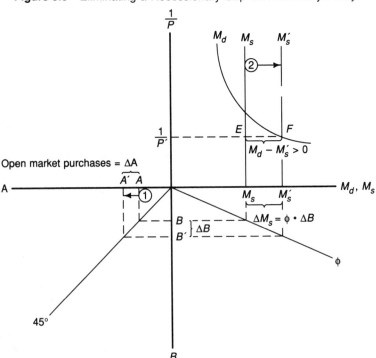

an autonomous rise in prices, as discussed in Chapter 5. First, the economy could have been in equilibrium with $M_s = M_d$ at point E and then M_d could have shifted outward to the position shown. Note also that if it had shifted back instead, an inflationary gap would have been created. Many economists argue strongly that if the business cycle is primarily the result of such intermittent, random shifts in M_d, no rational monetary policy alternative exists to discretionary adjustments of the money stock aimed at closing the resulting gaps.

The second possibility is that the system was initially in equilibrium at point F, and the nominal money stock then declined to M_s. In this case, whether the decline was due to contractionary policy or a fall in ϕ which the Fed chose not to offset at the time, subsequent Fed policy restoring the money stock to M_s' would simply be correcting a past policy error. Note also that, beginning from point F, an increase in the money stock could create an inflationary gap, and the same argument would apply to a correction in that case. Clearly, if business fluctuations are primarily a consequence of fluctuations in the money stock, a superior policy would be one in which the Fed was required to stabilize the money stock at a target value.

The question whether the money stock or the demand for money is the primary source of macroeconomic instability is primarily an empirical issue. Good men and true disagree on the matter. However, nearly every major economic contraction since the Civil War has been preceded by a decline in the money stock, and an increase in the money stock typically precedes expansions. Milton Friedman and Anna Jacobson Schwartz have shown, for example, that the onset of the Great Depression was associated with a decline in the money stock by one-third between 1929 and 1932.[5] In a more recent example, the 1982 recession was initiated by a monetary contraction.[6] Such cyclic money stock changes can typically be shown to be the result of deliberate policy action or inaction and not a result of prior income change. No such regular cyclic pattern for the demand for money, in which its changes lead the cycle, is apparent.

Policy Goals in Dynamic Form

Here it is necessary to complicate the analysis by one step. In Chapter 6 it was shown that by transforming the equation of exchange into its Cambridge variation, the demand for real money balances could be expressed as $m_d = k \cdot Q^*$, from which it followed that $\Delta m_d/m_d \approx \Delta k/k + \Delta Q^*/Q$. Real output growth has a positive and well-anticipated trend value near 3.5 percent per year, and unless the trend value of k is negative and as large or larger than that, m_d and hence M_d is normally shifting outward over time at a fairly regular rate.

Given this normal growth in m_d caused by normal economic growth, the monetary policy problem of maintaining the stability of employment, output growth, and the value of money becomes one of matching the growth rate of the money stock to that of the demand for money. This is illustrated in Figure 8.4 in which the demand for money shifts from M_d to M_d' and is assumed to keep shifting out over time.

If the Fed caused the money stock to grow at the same rate, the value of money would be kept stable at $1/P$ and no recession or inflation would occur. Chronically slower money growth would result in a recession, which would be cured when prices began falling fast enough to make the real money stock grow at the desired rate, and chronically excessive money growth would create an expansion, which would stop when prices began rising fast enough to reduce the growth rate of the real money stock to the desired level.

In this dynamic framework the rules-versus-discretion issue concerns whether the Fed should be allowed to adjust the nominal money stock growth rate at will in (ostensible) attempts to eliminate gaps appearing when the money demand growth rate varies, or be required by law to

Figure 8.4 Stabilizing the Economy by Matching M_s Growth to Secular M_d Growth.

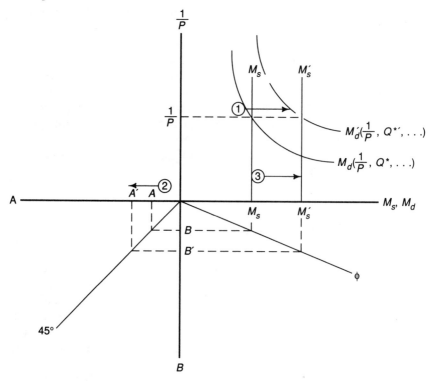

target money stock growth on the long-run trend growth in M_d. Put in these terms it is hard to make the case for discretion. First, considerable evidence indicates that such adjustments in money growth are more frequently a source of disturbance than correction to the system, although some stabilizing examples can be found. In 1985 and 1986 the Fed caused the money stock to grow very rapidly to feed an obvious increase in m_d that was occurring. Even in this case the Fed overshot slightly and inflation increased somewhat from 1987 to 89, necessitating a contractionary policy response. Second, it is much easier to keep money growth at a constant target value than to adjust it repeatedly to shifting target values.

More important, however, M_d can only be observed ex post, not ex ante, hence only its long-run trend growth value can be predicted accurately; short-run future values cannot be. The data required to make such accurate predictions are not available, because they exist only in the minds of money holders. Therefore, the precise monetary growth rate changes required to eliminate temporary gaps stemming from fluctuations in the growth rate of m_d cannot be known, even if money growth rates could be readjusted accurately in the short run. Of course, special circumstances causing a large shift in M_d may require some monetary response, but that is not an argument for general discretion.

Monetary Effects on the Interest Rate ⸻

In Chapter 3, the interest rate and the credit market were discussed without mentioning anything about changes in the money stock. In this chapter and in Chapter 7 monetary changes through the credit mechanism are discussed without much being said about the interest rate. Certain effects of monetary changes on the interest rate were briefly discussed in Chapter 5, but since neither the processes by which changes in the money stock were brought about nor the nature of inflation were explained in Chapter 5, that discussion was somewhat incomplete. A fuller discussion of the interest rate effects of monetary policy is now in order.

In discussing the primary factors affecting the demand for money in Chapter 6, it has been argued that the nominal demand function could be written as $M_d = f(1/P, Q, i, \alpha^*)$, where $\Delta M_d/\Delta Q > 0$, $\Delta M_d/\Delta i < 0$, and $\Delta M_d/\Delta \alpha^* < 0$. Graphically, real output, the interest rate, and the expected rate of inflation have been treated as shift variables in a money-demand function related inversely to the real value, or relative price, of money, $1/P$. Although there are good reasons for preferring to express the quantity of money demanded as a function of its relative price, for certain analytical purposes it is feasible to list Q or i or α^* first and graphically express the functional relationship between that variable and M_d, treating the others as shift variables. This is done for the interest rate in Figure 8.5.

The stock demand for nominal cash balances is shown in Figure 8.5 as an inverse function of the interest rate in accordance with the portfolio balance reasoning of Chapter 6. By that theory the interest foregone on alternative assets or securities represents the opportunity cost of a decision to hold a marginal dollar in the cash balance. Logically, the quantity of money demanded for cash balances should be smaller the higher that cost is, and higher the smaller that cost is, *ceteris paribus*.[7]

With the demand for money expressed this way, P, Q and α^* are now the shift variables. There is a useful simplification here, however. Because P and Q are both positively related to M_d, and because their

Figure 8.5 Money Supply and Demand and the Interest Rate.

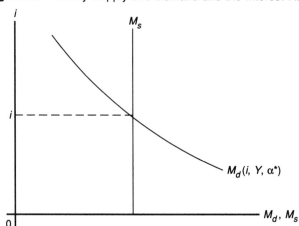

product is $P \cdot Q = Y$, or aggregate nominal income, the money demand function can then be written $M_d = f(i, Y, \alpha^*)$ as shown, where
$\Delta M_d/\Delta Y > 0$. That is, a net rise in nominal income, due either to a
rise in the price level, an increase in real output, or both, shifts the
money-demand function in the graph outward, and a net decline in
nominal income shifts it toward the left.

A nominal money stock is also shown in Figure 8.5, and because in
equilibrium people must be satisfied with their nominal cash balances,
the interest rate must be at the level shown. There are at least two
incorrect notions implied by the graph, however. The first is that the
interest rate is a purely monetary phenomenon, which could be eliminated by simply increasing the money stock enough. Much of the point
of this section is to demonstrate the fallacy of that notion. The interest
rate really is a credit and capital market phenomenon, as explained in
Chapter 3, representing the price paid in accordance with time preferences for early availability of goods and services. Almost nobody—
except, at times, a commercial banker—borrows money and pays
interest on it with intent to hold it in a cash balance. The second and a
closely related fallacy is that the interest rate is the primary factor
equilibrating M_d and M_s. The real value of money, $1/P$, ultimately
does that through changes in the price level, as previously explained.

In order to illustrate the effects of monetary policy on the interest
rate, consider Figure 8.6, which differs from graphs such as those
shown in Figures 8.2, 8.3, and 8.4 only by employing Figure 8.5 in the
upper right-hand quadrant. Suppose that the Federal Reserve expands
the monetary base and increases the money stock from M_s to M_s' by

Figure 8.6 The Liquidity and Income Effects of Expansionary Monetary Policy.

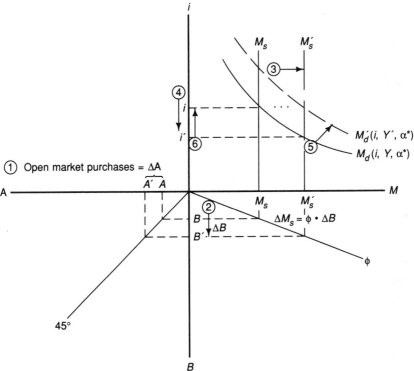

accumulating assets through open market purchases or discount policy as shown in steps 1 to 3. The first implication of the graph is that the resulting excess money stock shows up as an excess demand for bonds, raising their prices and reducing the interest rate (step 4).

The second implication is that the decline in the interest rate toward i' increases the quantity of money demanded until equilibrium with the existing stock is reached. This initial inverse relation between the money stock and the interest rate, such that $\Delta i/\Delta M_s < 0$, is termed the **liquidity effect**, and would work for both increases and decreases in the money stock. In the latter case, open market sales or discount policy which reduced the money stock would (initially) raise the interest rate.

Certain amplifications and qualifications are in order. In the case of open market purchases by the Fed, it is actually its offer of base money to the banking system for securities that raises their prices and hence reduces their yields because, from Chapter 3, $i = d/P_b$. The banks then reduce loan rates in order to lend out their "excess" reserves, and the multiple deposit expansion process subsequently operates to increase the money stock. In the case of discount policy the discount rate is reduced directly by the Fed, and again the banks subsequently reduce their own loan rates, causing multiple deposit creation. In either case the actual sequence of events involved in the liquidity effect is slightly different than that implied in the graph.

A more important qualification is that the resulting excess money stock does not show up only as excess demand for bonds, but also as excess demands across the spectrum of nonmoney goods and services. This increases sales and prices, raising nominal income. As income rises, the demand for money will begin shifting outward M'_d (i, Y') as shown by step 5. Consequently, before the interest rate reaches i' and fully equilibrates M_d and M'_s, it will start rising again and will eventually be restored to its initial value.

This is termed the **income effect** of monetary policy. In the case of a contractionary policy, in which the liquidity effect initially raised the interest rate, the resulting excess supplies of nonmoney goods and services, by reducing sales, prices and hence nominal income, would cause the demand for money to decline, reducing the interest rate back to the initial level. Empirically, the income effect usually offsets the liquidity effect and restores the interest rate to its initial value three to nine months following the onset of an expansionary or contractionary monetary policy.[8]

A third interest rate effect of monetary policy stems from the distinction between the purely nominal interest rate and the real interest rate pointed out in Chapter 3. That is, where $\alpha = \Delta P / P$, the real interest rate is

$$r = i - \alpha$$

Actually, this is best termed the ex post real rate of interest, because only in looking backward over the period of a credit contract or investment can both the contract or nominal interest rate and the inflation rate be observed and hence the resulting real interest rate known.

Suppose that $\bar{r}$ = the ex ante desired real rate of interest. That is, $\bar{r}$ is the real rate that is acceptable to both parties of a credit contract, constituting the least that credit suppliers will voluntarily lend for and the most that borrowers will willingly pay in equilibrium. Because α can take on different values, the ex post real rate can deviate from the ex ante desired real rate. To minimize this risk, in settling on a nominal contract interest rate, borrowers and lenders will attempt to set it at a value that not only covers the mutually acceptable real rate, but also correctly anticipates and allows for changes in the value of money over the period on the contract. That is, if α^* is the expected rate of inflation, $\Delta P^*/P$,

$$\bar{r} + \alpha^* = i \qquad \text{ex ante.}$$

The crucial point is that every $\Delta\alpha^*$ will cause an adjustment in the nominal interest rate on new contracts and on financial assets through changes in stock and bond prices. Suppose, for example, that $\bar{r} = .03$ and $i = .03$ because $\alpha^* = 0$, but that ex post $\alpha = .03$, such that $r = 0$. As soon as this is generally known, both borrowers and lenders, if they expect α to continue, will realize that it takes $i' = .06$ to yield $\bar{r} = .03$, and contracts will settle on that nominal rate, *ceteris paribus*. Graphically, α^* must be written in as a shift variable in both the saving and credit demand functions, with a negative sign for the former and a positive sign for the latter. The example just given is illustrated in Figure 8.7, which shows the inflation adjust (i.e., real) value of credit on the horizontal axis.

The same argument could also be shown in Figure 8.6 as an additional outward stock demand shift of the same type by which the income effect restored the initial interest rate, following the liquidity effect of an expansionary open market operation. Such an additional outward shift, following the income effect, would occur if the monetary expansion appeared likely to continue and generate ongoing inflation and would raise the interest rate above the initial level restored by the income effect.[9] This long-run positive relationship between expected inflation and the

Figure 8.7 The Fisher Effect in the Credit Market.

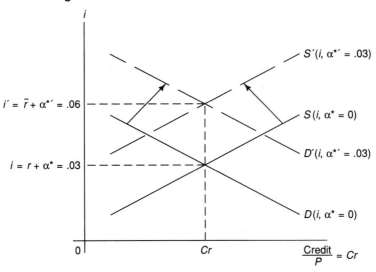

interest rate is termed the **Fisher effect**, after Irving Fisher, and works for both increases and decreases in α^*.[10]

Intermediate Targets and Monetary Control

In pursuing its goals the Fed must use one or more gauges or indicators of the expansionary or contractionary character of its monetary policy, making adjustments when the observable values of these indicators deviate from the chosen target values. Such indicators are termed the **intermediate targets** of monetary policy. During the 1960s and 1970s the Fed used the market interest rate as an intermediate target, specifically by setting a target value for the Federal Funds rate and adjusting the monetary base as required to keep the rate within a narrow band around that chosen value.

Interest rate targeting is not entirely illogical. Knut Wicksell, a great Swedish economist at the turn of the century, argued that there was one **natural rate of interest**, the equilibrium rate, that was consistent with price level stability. Consider Figure 8.8, in which a rise in the ratio of reserves to deposits, R/D, by commercial bankers reduces ϕ and hence the money stock, *ceteris paribus*, causing a recessionary condition. Suppose that the original interest rate (i), was the natural rate and that the Fed responded quickly with open market purchases that increased the monetary base enough to keep the interest rate at i. Clearly, the disturbing effect of the change in ϕ would be reduced if the Fed pegged the natural rate in this manner. This would work also for increases in ϕ.

It turns out, however, that there are severe difficulties with interest rate targeting. First it is very difficult to know what the natural rate of interest is, and even if the Fed targeted the right value initially, the natural rate can change as time preferences or productivity change, making the target rate wrong. Worse, the very existence of interest rate targeting results in strong political pressures to set the target rate, low, and the effects can be devastating.

Consider Figure 8.6 in which the income effect of an expansionary open market operation was shown offsetting the liquidity effect and restoring the initial interest rate (i). Suppose that the initial monetary base expansion was intended to target the interest rate at i', and that when the income effect began to operate, the Fed responded by expanding the monetary base again to maintain the target. If the Fed offset each operation of the income effect this way, the effect would be continuous excess money growth and inflation as the income effect kept shifting the demand for money out and the Fed kept increasing the base

Figure 8.8   The Stabilizing Effect of Natural Interest Rate Targeting.

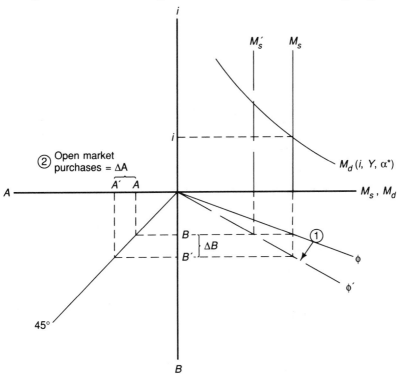

to prevent the interest rate from rising. In fact, because this would cause the Fisher effect to operate, shifting M_d outward even more, progressively larger base expansions would be required to peg i'. Consequently, the inflation would accelerate over time. This is known as the **Wicksellian cumulative process**, and the accelerating U.S. inflation of the 1970s may have resulted in part from such interest rate targeting.

This process has operated in many countries, such as France, which experienced heavy destruction in World War I. The government established a separate budget for restoration expenditures financed by reparation payments from Germany and by borrowing in anticipation of such payments. The debt was incurred primarily through sales of national defense bills (i.e., "bons") at fixed interest rates. Funds that could not be obtained that way were obtained through monetary advances from the central Bank of France. This excess money growth generated inflation.

As inflation accelerated and the income and Fisher effects operated, it became harder to sell additional bons at the fixed nominal interest rates. Consequently, the monetary advances increased, causing further acceleration of inflation from 1925 to 1926. Stabilization of the price level occurred suddenly in 1926 when Premier Poincaré raised tax rates to put the budget in surplus and ended the pegging of interest rates.[11]

Monetarist economists, who came into prominence in the 1960s, have long opposed interest rate targeting and advocated that the Fed be required to target the growth rate of the money stock at a value set by law or constitutional amendment. This argument for a **money growth rule** stems from modern quantity theory reasoning. The equation of exchange implies that

$$\% \ \Delta M_s + \% \ \Delta V \approx \Delta P + \% \ \Delta Q,$$

so

$$\% \ \Delta M_s + \% \ \Delta V - \% \ \Delta Q \approx \% \ \Delta P$$

and

$$\% \ \Delta M_s - [\% \ \Delta Q - \% \ \Delta V] \approx \% \ \Delta P.$$

From the Cambridge variation—assuming $Q = Q^*$ and $\Delta Q^*/Q = \Delta Q/Q$ for simplicity—the demand for real money balances can be expressed as

$$m_d = k \cdot Q$$
$$= \frac{Q}{V},$$

because $k = 1/V$.

It follows that

$$\% \ \Delta m_d \approx \% \ \Delta Q - \% \ \Delta V,$$

and therefore, by substitution,

$$\% \ \Delta M_s - \% \ \Delta m_d \approx \% \ \Delta P,$$

which means that the inflation rate is given by the difference between the growth rates of the nominal money stock and the demand for real money balances.

The monetarist argument essentially has three facets: First, the demand for money is a relatively stable function, (see Chapter 6). Second, money stock growth should be stabilized to prevent it from being a source of disturbance to the economy; third, because at least the long-run $\% \Delta m_d$ is fairly predictable, the law should set $\% \Delta M_s = \% \Delta m_d$ so that $\% \Delta P = 0$ on average. Essentially, this would involve setting the money growth rate equal to the sum of our best estimates of the long-run trend growth rates of real output and velocity and keeping it there.

Monetarist arguments and political pressure motivated the House to pass concurrent resolution 133 in 1975, requiring the Fed to begin reporting annual target ranges for money growth. This provided no constraint on Fed behavior, however, and money growth was outside the announced growth targets for M1 almost half of the time between 1975 and 1979. It is evident that the Fed was still targeting the interest rate. In 1979 the inflation rate for consumer prices reached 13.3 percent. In October of that year Paul Volker, the new Chairman of the Board of Governors, formally announced a shift from interest rate targeting to focus on controlling the monetary aggregates.

From the Fed's announcement through 1987, money growth rates were more variable than in any other post-war period. The Fed immediately reduced money growth in 1979 and produced a recession in 1980, although it was short because the Fed raised money growth rapidly after July of that year. The Fisher effect raised the prime rate to 18 percent in 1981, and in January 1982 the Fed again drastically reduced money growth to less than 2 percent per annum, causing the largest recession since 1974. This monetary instability continued, and this has led many commentators to conclude that monetarism has been tried and failed.

Two responses are in order. First, the Fed was never subject to a legal monetary rule, and never made any serious effort to stay within its announced targets. Second, the German and Swiss central banks, under the influence of the monetarist Karl Brunner, not only set monetary targets but normally stay within them. Not accidentally, these two countries have had the best records of price stability among Western industrial nations.

The most important recent criticism of the monetarist argument concerns the stability of the demand for money. Real balances demanded declined at a relatively slow and steady pace for most of the post-war period. From 1984 to 1986, in contrast, a large increase in the demand for money (i.e., decline in velocity) occurred, as mentioned previously. This large change, which few economists—including monetarists—predicted, has convinced some economists that the demand for money is unstable, weakening the case for a fixed money growth rule.

In retrospect, however, perhaps this shift was predictable. The post-war rise in velocity was probably itself at least partly a consequence of steadily accelerating inflation, which raised α^* over time. The recession of 1983, in contrast, produced a large decline in the inflation rate, as just noted, which should have reduced α^* and raised m_d.[12] Besides, both of these money demand shifts are the result of large swings in monetary policy of precisely the sort that a money growth rule is designed to eliminate.

Monetarists are not the only ones advocating changes in the Fed's methods, and other intermediate targets have been mentioned. Some economists have argued that the Fed should target the price level directly, reducing monetary base, and hence M_s growth when prices are rising and raising base, and hence M_s, growth when prices are falling. The problem with this view is that there is a variable lag, from nine months to two years, between changes in money growth rates and their effect on prices. Price changes occurring now are the result of monetary actions taken at some indeterminate time in the past, and monetary base adjustments made now will have their effect at some indeterminate time in the future. Adjusting base growth now in response to price changes occurring now would probably be destabilizing.

The Reverse Causation Hypothesis

In recent years evidence that the growth rate of the money stock varies procyclically (i.e., falling below the inflation rate so that the real money stock falls during contractions, and rising above α, so that m_s rises rapidly during expansions) has probably convinced most macro-monetary economists that a money growth rule of some type is desirable. It has come to be accepted that stable, predictable policy is beneficial. Many types of rule have been proposed, each with its supporters, although none have achieved as much acceptance as the fixed growth rate rule.

Not everyone is convinced, however. An important objection to this line of thinking is known as the **reverse causation hypothesis.** As noted in Chapter 7 interest foregone is the opportunity cost to depository institutions of holding reserves. Consequently, the reserve ratio may vary inversely with the interest rate, and hence the money multiplier may vary directly. Proponents of reverse causation argue that as income falls during a recession, the demand for credit and financial capital falls, reducing the interest rate. This motivates depository institutions to hold larger reserves relative to deposits, making the multiplier fall. The decline in the multiplier reduces the money stock, or at least its growth rate, *ceteris paribus*.

In the opposite case, rising income during an expansion causes increased demand for loanable funds, raising the interest rate. This motivates depository institutions to hold smaller reserves relative to deposits, raising the money multiplier. The rise in ϕ increases the money stock or its growth rate, *ceteris paribus*. By this reasoning money growth varies procyclically as quantity theorists claim, but their claim that money growth changes are usually the cause of cyclic expansions and contractions is denied. Instead, autonomous income changes cause the associated changes in money growth.

As might be expected, quantity theorists have objected to many aspects of the reverse causation argument. For one thing, it implies that changes in money growth rates lag business cycle turning points, whereas to quantity theorists the evidence seems clear that such monetary changes lead cyclic peaks and troughs. For another, the theory leaves the source of income changes unclear. Money demand changes might work in theory, and such changes have been important in certain historical cases, but as pointed out previously, no clear and consistent

TABLE 8.5

Year	% ΔM1	% $\Delta\phi$
1965	4.7	−0.6
1966	2.5	−1.5
1967	6.6	0.3
1968	7.7	0.9
1969	3.2	−1.8
1970	5.2	−0.6
1971	6.6	−0.3
1972	9.2	0.3
1973	5.5	−2.2
1974	4.4	−3.0
1975	4.9	−1.7
1976	6.6	−0.7
1977	8.0	4.9
1978	8.3	−5.6
1979	7.7	−0.7
1980	6.5	−1.4
1981	6.4	1.0
1982	8.6	0.7
1983	9.5	0.3
1984	5.8	−1.8
1985	12.5	3.6
1986	16.5	5.5

procyclic pattern of money demand changes leading turning points exists in the empirical record.

One also has to wonder about the *ceteris paribus* assumption. The reverse causation argument implies either that the Federal Reserve does nothing to offset procyclic money stock changes, or that its defensive open market operations are inadequate. In either case the question apparently reduces to one of whether the money multiplier or the base is the primary influence on the nominal money stock.

Table 8.5 and Figure 8.9, which relate annual percentage M1 growth and percentage changes in ϕ during the period 1965 to 1986 by plotting them as Cartesian coordinates, cast some light on the issue. Even if the extreme observations for 1977, 1978, 1985, and 1986, are ignored, there is a definite positive relationship between the two variables, although it is not very tight. Given that $M_s = \phi \cdot B$ and $\% \, \Delta M_s \approx \% \, \Delta \phi + \% \, \Delta B$, however, such a discernable but loose relationship is wholly consistent with effective Federal Reserve control of the money stock. This seems particularly clear when it is remembered that only

Figure 8.9 The Relation Between Monetary Growth Rates and Money Multiplier Growth Rates, 1965 to 1986.

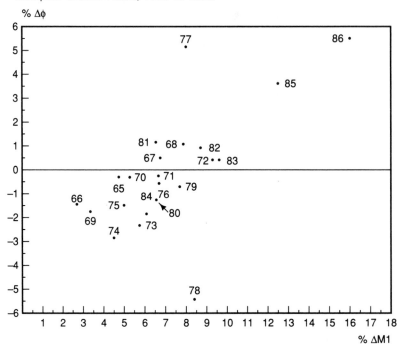

changes in ϕ that are moving money growth in directions the Fed does not want it to go will be offset through defensive alterations of the base.

Figure 8.10 and Table 8.6 relate annual M1 growth to monetary base growth during the same period. It is immediately observable that the positive relationship between these variables is much stronger than in the other case. Base growth appears to dominate multiplier growth in determining money stock growth. This is further indicated by the fact that money growth was positive each year throughout the period, although the money multiplier fell in 13 of these years. The average annual percentage growth in M1 was about 7.14. The average annual % $\Delta\phi$ was approximately 1.8. The average annual % $\Delta B \approx 7.4$.

In order to argue that the money stock is endogenous and not controlled by the Fed, it would seem necessary to argue that the base is endogenously determined. Now there are clear institutional conditions under which this is the case, although they are not conditions under which money stock changes are systematically procyclic. Under the

Figure 8.10 Relation Between Money Stock Growth and Monetary Base Growth, 1965 to 1986.

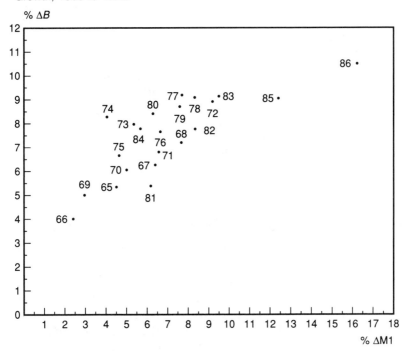

Source: *Economic Report of the President, 1988*: 325, 328.

TABLE 8.6

Year	% ΔM1	% ΔB
1965	4.7	5.3
1966	2.5	4.0
1967	6.6	6.2
1968	7.7	7.0
1969	3.2	5.0
1970	5.2	6.1
1971	6.6	6.7
1972	9.2	8.8
1973	5.5	8.0
1974	4.4	8.2
1975	4.9	6.5
1976	6.6	7.5
1977	8.0	9.0
1978	8.3	9.0
1979	7.7	8.6
1980	6.5	8.2
1981	6.4	5.3
1982	8.6	7.6
1983	9.5	9.0
1984	5.8	7.75
1985	12.5	8.9
1986	16.5	10.2

gold standard, as explained in Chapter 5, the domestic money stock and monetary base are demand-determined through the balance of international payments. A similar condition exists for a small country employing a fiat currency under an international regime of fixed exchange rates; see Chapter 18. The central point, however, is that these conditions have not applied to the United States since the demise of the gold standard.

The Political Economy of Federal Reserve Policy Making

The abstract goals of monetary policy have been discussed previously. It can be argued that decision makers at the Fed have other goals that are often pursued along with or even in place of the abstract goals. Indeed, it would be naive to presume otherwise. Individuals do not, upon attaining positions of power and influence, automatically become angels whose only intentions are to pursue the abstract public good. Of course, they do not automatically become devils either, despite Lord Acton's dictum. The reasonable assumption is that the distribution of moral tendencies among members of the FRB and FOMC over time is not different from that of the population as a whole. But other members of the population, partly excepting commercial bankers, cannot alter the money stock at will in pursuit of personal objectives.

The economist's approach to analyzing the behavior of individuals in any particular institutional setting is to suppose that they are basically self-interested beings in whose personal value systems the abstract public good may or may not rank highly and to inquire into the particular structure of pressures and constraints they face. In this light the crucial features of the Fed are that it is a quasi-monopolistic, semi-governmental regulatory agency with vast powers, which was deliberately designed to be politically independent. Its decision makers are thus relatively free of both competitive and political constraints and are able to pursue their own chosen ends, whatever they are.

What unofficial ends might the Fed pursue? For one thing, the Fed has a built-in structural bias toward excess money growth and inflation because all of its salaries, expenses, and perquisites are paid from interest earned on loans made and securities purchased with money it creates at will. The Fed has been able to brilliantly prevent recognition of and criticism for this by deliberately returning a large portion of its annual earnings to the Treasury. As a result, politicians frequently praise the Fed as one of the few governmental agencies that more than covers its own costs. They fail to grasp the method by which the revenue was obtained, or that—for any given portion the Fed chooses to return, because it can set the gross it wants—it can set the net it wants.

Other unofficial ends might be political in nature, because the ability to alter the monetary growth rate and create recessions and expansions at will is a potent tool of political power and influence. Several economists have found evidence for a "political business cycle," noting, for example, that monetary policy is almost always expansionary during presidential election years.[13] In only one election year since 1960 (i.e., 1974) has monetary policy failed to turn expansionary. In that year Gerald Ford lost the election. The chairman of the Federal Reserve Board at that time was Arthur Burns, a Democrat who had been appointed by President Eisenhower.

Some observers argue that the alleged independence of the Fed is only apparent, not real. The late Robert Weintraub, a monetarist, argued strenuously that the Fed had catered so much to administration wishes over the years that, in essence, the President had always made monetary policy.[14] Others claim that the Fed tailors monetary policy to the dominant views in the House and Senate Banking Committees.[15]

In response, even if it were true that the Fed was essentially a slave of such political authorities, it does not follow that monetary policy would be constrained to follow the "public interest." Such political authorities are themselves self-interested individuals. Indeed, the combination of such political control with the appearance of independence on the part of the Fed might lead to an even greater tendency for monetary policy to be used for personal or partisan gain because responsibility for damaging consequences could be denied and blame placed on the Fed. This seems to occur frequently.

Perhaps the crucial datum indicating that monetary policy.is at least sometimes used to pursue unofficial goals is the unwillingness of the Fed to accept any legislated rule. Implicit in the Fed's claim that its monetary manipulations have a net stabilizing effect on employment, output, and prices is a claim that it both knows how and intends to respond to macroeconomic disequilibria in a stabilizing fashion. As such, it should be willing to write its own reaction function and accept the codification of that function into law. Instead, the Fed is willing to accept only absolute, unfettered discretion, and even keeps its monetary policy deliberations secret. In light of all of this, the monetarist call for an externally imposed money growth rule would seem to be a modest reform proposal.

Summary

Here are the primary arguments of this chapter.

1. The Federal Reserve was created in 1913 to eliminate monetary instability and prevent economic contractions. The history of business cycles since then, beginning with the sharp recession of 1921 and the Great Depression in 1930, hardly indicates that it succeeded.

2. Originally, the Fed exercised its monetary control through discount policy, involving loans to the banking system that alter reserves, and to a lesser extent through changes in legally required reserves. In recent decades open market securities transactions to alter bank reserves have become the primary monetary policy tool.

3. Defensive open market operations aim at offsetting the effects of non-Fed influences on the money stock through the money multiplier. Dynamic open market policy aims at adjusting the money stock to obtain some other goal.

4. The abstract or "ideal" goals of dynamic monetary policy involve stabilization of output, employment, and the price level, or their growth rates, at acceptable magnitudes.

5. Obtaining these goals involves adjusting the money stock in the same direction and magnitude in response to shifts in the demand for money.

6. If instability in money demand is the primary source of cyclic disturbances to the economy, no alternative apparently exists to discretionary monetary policy aimed at offsetting such demand shifts.

7. If fluctuations in the money stock, relative to money demand, are the primary source of cyclic disturbances, the best policy would be one requiring the Fed to stabilize the money stock. Empirically, most disturbances seem to have had this character, even though some monetary policy actions have had a stabilizing effect.

8. In a dynamic setting, one in which the demand for money has a known growth trend, stabilization appears to involve matching the growth rate of the money stock to that of money demand. Because fluctuations in m_d growth around that trend are impossible to predict and hard to estimate, monetarists argue that discretionary policy is destabilizing on net and that money stock growth should be kept steady by law.

9. Dynamic monetary policy operations have a short-run inverse effect on the interest rate. This is the liquidity effect. There are two long-run effects of such policy on the interest rate, however, both of which are positive. The income effect tends to offset the liquidity effect, with a lag. The Fisher effect alters the nominal interest rate to compensate for changes in the expected rate of inflation.

10. In pursuing its goals, the Fed must use indicators of the expansionary or contractionary character of its policies. These indicators are known as intermediate targets. The Fed has usually targeted some value of the nominal interest rate. Such interest rate targeting can lead to accelerating deflation or inflation, however, whenever the target rate is set, respectively, above or below the "natural" rate of interest. Consequently, many economists advocate other targets, such as a legally fixed growth rate of the nominal money stock itself.

11. Most economists now admit the desirability of stable, predictable monetary policy. Some have objected to a fixed money growth rule, however, by arguing that the observed positive correlation between money growth and income over the business cycle is a result of income changes altering money growth, rather than the opposite. This is the reverse causation hypothesis. To monetarists and other quantity theorists, however, there seems little empirical or theoretical validity to a claim that the Fed does not effectively control the money stock.

12. Recognizing that monetary policymakers are self-interested individuals as private citizens are, and are faced by a particular structure of incentives and constraints in the institutional setting in which they operate, forces the recognition that monetary policy may often be employed for purposes other than macroeconomic stabilization.

Notes

1. Fractional reserve banking is the crucial condition for this kind of instability, but certain peculiar U.S. banking regulations, such as the prohibition of branch banking, certainly aggravated the situation. See Lawrence H. White, "Regulatory Sources of Instability in Banking," *The Cato Journal* 5 (Winter 1986): 891–897.

2. In 1980 Congress passed *the Depository Institutions Deregulation and Monetary Control Act*. Until that time only *member* banks had to keep a portion of their reserves on deposit at the Fed. The Act made that requirement universal and simultaneously eliminated free provision of services to member banks. The Federal Reserve had experienced declining membership for many years and was worried about losing its control over the money stock. For a discussion of the motives, provisions, and economics of this act, see Richard H. Timberlake, "Legislative Construction of the Monetary Control Act of the 1980," *American Economic Review* 75 (May 1985): 97–102.

3. For a detailed description of the mechanics of open market policy, see Auerbach, *Money, Banking and Financial Institutions*: 294–296.

4. See, for example, Albert Burger, "Money Stock Control," *Federal Reserve Bank of St. Louis Review* (October 1972): 10–18, and James M. Johannes and Robert H. Rasche, "Predicting the Money Multiplier," *Journal of Monetary Economics* 5 (1979): 301–325.

5. See their book, *A Monetary History of the United States, 1867–1960* (Princeton, N.J.: Princeton University Press, 1963), Chapter 7.

6. In this case, as is typical during inflationary periods, it was a decline in the *real* money stock that caused the recession. The nominal money stock growth rate did not become negative but fell below the inflation rate, so that $\% \, m_s \approx \% \, \Delta M_s - \% \, \Delta P < 0$.

7. This argument has been losing much of its strength in recent years because the innovation and expansion of NOW and ATS accounts has resulted in more than half of the total dollar value of money in checkable deposits paying interest. A decision to hold dollars in such accounts is therefore not a decision to forego interest, except to the extent that interest rates are higher on alternate assets. As long as the interest rates on such accounts track changes in other rates, this event must have severely reduced the interest elasticity of the demand for money, *ceteris paribus*.

8. See William E. Gibson, "The Lag in the Effect of Monetary Policy on Income and Interest Rates," *Quarterly Journal of Economics* 84 (May 1970): 288–300.

9. For empirical evidence on the Fisher effect, see Milton Friedman and Anna J. Schwartz, *Monetary Trends in the United States and the United Kingdom, Their Relation to Income, Prices, and Interest Rates, 1867–1975* (Chicago: University of Chicago Press, 1982).

10. Under deflation ($\alpha < 0$), however, the rule breaks down for $\alpha \geq \bar{r}$ because the nominal interest rate cannot become zero or negative. Suppose $\bar{r} = .03$ and $\alpha = \alpha^* = -.04$, for example. The rule implies that $i = -.01$, but nobody would pay people 1 percent to borrow money, and thereby earn a 2 percent return, when they could get a 3 percent return just by holding it while deflation raised its real value.

11. Gail E. Makinen and G. Thomas Woodward, "A Monetary Interpretation of the Poincare Stabilization of 1926," *Southern Economic Journal* 56 (July 1989): 191–211.

12. This interpretation was raised early by some monetarists. See John A. Tatom, "Was the 1982 Velocity Decline Unusual?" *Federal Reserve Bank of St. Louis Review* (August/September 1983): 5–15. Other economists have argued that the recent velocity decline reflects increased interest rate sensitivity of the demand for money. It should be remembered, however, that i and α^* are correlated through the Fisher effect.

13. See, for example, David Meiselman, "Is There a Political Monetary Cycle?" *The Cato Journal* 6 (Fall 1986): 565–579.

14. Robert E. Weintraub, "Congressional Supervision of Monetary Policy," *Journal of Monetary Economics* 4 (April 1978): 341–362.

15. See Kevin B. Grier, "Congressional Preference and Federal Reserve Policy," *Working Paper Number 95* (St. Louis: Center for the Study of American Business, Washington University, 1985).

Student Self-Test

I. True–False

T F 1. Currency and coin in circulation are correctly understood as constituting an economic and financial liability of the Federal Reserve.

T F 2. Most economists agree that the primary goals of monetary policy should be to stabilize the growth rates of output, employment, and the price level and to debate only the methods to be employed.

T F 3. In the short run the growth rate of the demand for money can be predicted accurately, but the long-run growth rate cannot be predicted accurately.

T F 4. The best intermediate target of monetary policy probably would be the price level itself.

T F 5. Almost all significant contractions in this century have been preceded by an increase in the growth rate of the demand for money, and most expansions have been preceded by a decline in % ΔM_d.

II. Short Answer *(150 words or less each)*

1. Many people, including some economists, believe that individuals acting in the private sector are motivated primarily by self-interest, but that public servants are motivated primarily by the selfless pursuit of the public good. Comment on this view, particularly as it applies to the Federal Reserve officials who determine monetary policy.

2. It is widely believed that the Federal Reserve can control the interest rate and that a low rate of interest is economically beneficial. Comment on this belief and on the probable results of basing monetary policy on it.

3. Pertaining to monetary policy, explain (a) why policy actions that produce a particular increase or positive growth rate in the money stock might not actually be expansionary and (b) why a literal decline in the money stock might not be required to produce contractionary effects.

4. "The business cycle results from intermittent, random shifts in the growth

rate of the demand for money, hence no rational monetary policy alternative exists to discretionary adjustments of the money stock by the monetary authorities, aimed at closing the resulting inflationary and deflationary gaps." Support or critique this statement logically and/or empirically.
5. Distinguish between dynamic and/or defensive open market operations.

III. Completion Problems

1. The first T account shown in the following table represents the books of the Federal Reserve and the second represents the combined accounts of the commercial banks. Suppose that the Fed reduces the discount rate and increases its loans outstanding to the banking system by $10 billion.
   A. Show on the T accounts here, or on a copy, all immediate changes that would occur on both sets of books as a result of the Fed's actions.

Fed		Commercial banks	
Assets	**Liabilities**	**Assets**	**Liabilities**
Securities	Currency and coin	R	D
Loans from member banks	Reserves of member banks	Loans and investments	Borrowings from the Fed

   B. The T accounts in the following table have the same interpretation as in part A. Now suppose that the Fed sells $5 billion worth of securities to the banking system. Again show all immediate changes that would result on both sets of books.

Fed		Commercial banks	
Assets	**Liabilities**	**Assets**	**Liabilities**
Securities	Currency and coin	R	D
Loans from member banks	Reserves of member banks	Loans and investments	Borrowings from the Fed

2. Walras's law and monetary policy: Assume that the graph in the following figure depicts conditions in the economy.
   A. Given the conditions shown in the graph, the value of $\phi =$ _____ .
   B. Assuming that the price index was at $P = 100$ in the base year and the value of money is currently as shown in the graph, then the price level has _____ (risen/fallen) by _____ percent since that base year.

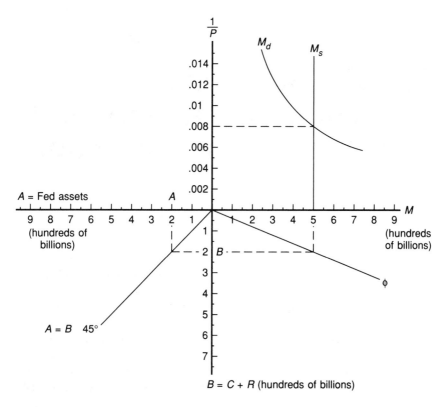

$B = C + R$ (hundreds of billions)

This means that the money stock has _____ (increased/decreased) relative to the demand for money.

C. If the Fed wanted to decrease the money stock to $400 billion through open market operations, then it would have to sell $_____ worth of securities to the banking system.

D. If the Fed bought $80 billion worth of securities, *ceteris paribus*, it would cause an _____ (excess supply/excess demand) worth $_____ in the markets for nonmoney goods and services. This is termed _____.

E. If M_d is expected to shift rightward at the normal long-run trend rate of real growth in the economy, and ϕ is not expected to change, then the Fed should purchase $_____ worth of securities this year if it wishes to stabilize the value of money.

CHAPTER 9

The *AD–AS* Model: Aggregate Demand for and Supply of Labor and Output

In this chapter a model known as the **aggregate demand and supply** (*AD–AS*) **model** is developed. This model is useful for illustrating several aspects of the operation of the macroeconomy. As stressed in Chapter 1, such models are highly aggregative and their heuristic character should be kept in mind. The microeconomic roots of the model will be carefully developed, however, beginning with a discussion of the neutrality conditions for microeconomic supply and demand functions, which ties in with the monetary macro model previously developed.

The Neutrality of Supply and Demand Functions _____

Microeconomic supply and demand functions are considered to be functions of relative prices. The demand function for good i, for example, is usually written as $D_i = D_i(p_i, p_s, p_c, y, \ldots)$, where p_s and p_c are the prices of substitute and complement goods, y is transactor income, and the ellipsis indicates the possible presence of other variables. The **demand law** is then derived by analytically altering p_i, *ceteris paribus*, that is, while holding the other variables constant so that p_i is changing relative to other prices, causing the substitution and income effects to alter the quantity demanded.

The same argument can be made by expressing p_i as a ratio to the price level, thus including all prices (even those of goods sold by transactors to obtain income) in the denominator, such that $D_i = f(p_i/P, \ldots)$. The shape of the demand curve for good i is normally analytically derived by altering the numerator of this ratio, *ceteris paribus*. But what if it is the denominator that changes?

Consider the demand function $D_i(p_i/P)$ shown in Figure 9.1(a). At nominal price p_i' quantity q_i is demanded. It is implicit, however, that other prices have some given magnitude P, such that q_i is actually the quantity demanded at relative price p_i'/P. Now suppose that the price level either doubles or is expected to double soon to $2P$. If we assume that commodity demand functions really are functions of relative price, what nominal price per unit should transactors now be willing to pay for quantity q_i? The logical answer seems to be $2p_i'$, because $2p_i'/2P = p_i'/P$.

In other words, suppose that the price level was initially $P = 1$ and people were willing to pay $p_i = \$5$ per unit for quantity q_i. If the price level then doubled to $P' = 2$, they should willingly pay $p_i' = \$10$ per unit for the same quantity, *ceteris paribus*, because $\$10/2 = \$5$. The same analysis could be carried out beginning with any price and quantity combination on $D_i(\cdot)$ and a change in the price level in either direction. The conclusion seems to be that a change, or an expected change, in the absolute price level by some percentage would shift commodity demand functions in the same direction (upward or downward) by the same percentage, *ceteris paribus*.

This analysis also applies to supply functions such as $S_i(p_i/P)$ shown in Figure 9.1(b), where quantity q_i is willingly offered for sale at nominal price p_i'. Again this assumes some price level P such that qi is actually the quantity supplied at relative price p_i'/P. Suppose, however, that the price level doubles or is expected to double soon. What

Figure 9.1 Neutral Price Level Shifts of Supply and Demand Curves.

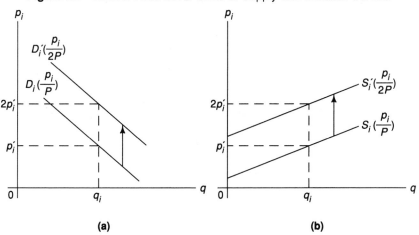

(a)   (b)

nominal price should suppliers then require to willingly sell q_i, *ceteris paribus*? As before, the answer seems to be $2p_i'$, because that would represent the same real (i.e., relative) price since $2p_i/2P = p_i/P$ and, by assumption, values, technology, population, and so on have not changed. Because the same logic applies beginning with any price and quantity combination on the supply function, it seems that a change or expected change in absolute P would shift commodity supply functions in the same direction by the same percentage.

The initial supply and demand functions for good i are placed together in Figure 9.2(a), where it is supposed that p_i' and hence p_i'/P, and q_i are equilibrium prices and quantities. If we assume that the price level doubles or is expected to double to $2P$ as before, the symmetric upward shifts in both the supply and demand functions to D_i' $(p_i/2P)$ and $S_i'(p_i/2p)$ should increase the equilibrium price from p_i' to $2p_i'$.

The argument here is about neutrality, however, not equilibrium. Consider Figure 9.2(b) in which, at p_i', and hence at p_i'/P, given $D_i(p_i/P)$ and $S_i(p_i/P), p_i'(D_i - S_i) > 0$, that is, positive excess demand exists. Assuming that the price level then doubles or is expected to double as before, at what price should the same state of excess demand involving the same real quantities appear? Again the logical answer is at $2p_i'$ because $2p_i'/P = p_i'/P$, implying symmetric upward shifts in the demand and supply functions as shown. In Figure 9.2 the conclusion is that, *ceteris paribus*, microeconomic markets should be neutral to changes in the absolute price level that leave relative prices, including the interest rate, undisturbed.

Figure 9.2 Price Level Supply and Demand Shifts with Neutral Relative Price Effects.

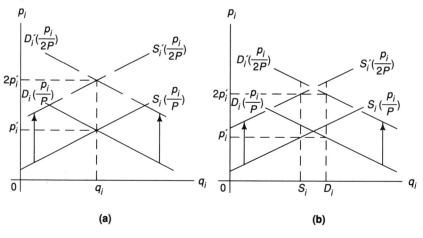

(a) (b)

Real Balances and Neutrality _____

It now will be demonstrated that the conclusion just reached is false or, at least, incomplete and misleading. The reader has been led deliberately down the primrose path to error, although only with the intention to lead to better understanding. Indeed, the reader who clearly understands Chapter 5 may have caught the mistake already. To see the problem, imagine—for simplicity of analysis—an initial condition of general equilibrium. Excess demand is zero not only in the $n - 1$ markets, of which the ith, shown in Figure 9.3(a), is representative, but also in the nth or "money market" shown in Figure 9.3(b).

Now suppose that the price level doubles or is expected to double, *ceteris paribus*, with no change in relative prices—for the $n - 1$ goods—or in the nominal money stock; this might be imagined to result from a governmental edict. By previous argument commodity supply and demand functions, as functions of relative price, should shift upward symmetrically. That would leave all $n - 1$ markets still in equilibrium with the same real quantities supplied and demanded. There is one relative price that would change, however: The real price of money, $1/P$, would be reduced to $1/2P$. This would reduce the real value of the money stock from M_s/P to $M_s/2P$, creating an excess demand for money.

This change in the real value of money, per unit and in total, as prices increased would cause nonneutral effects in the $n - 1$ markets. Instead of commodity supply and demand functions shifting upward symmetrically as shown in Figure 9.3(a), they would shift upward only

Figure 9.3 Real Balances and Neutrality.

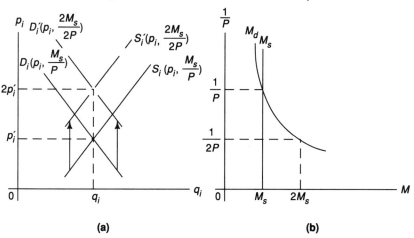

(a)   (b)

partially. Transactors would increase the quantities of goods and services offered for sale and decrease quantities demanded in an attempt to add to their cash balances. This would result in an excess supply in the ith market, and for all $n - 1$ markets the sum of the excess supplies would be exactly equal to the excess demand for money, satisfying Walras's law.

Clearly, it is erroneous to claim that commodity supply and demand relations are functions of relative prices alone and are neutral in the absolute level of prices if, in the *ceteris paribus* condition—for technology, the capital stock, population, tastes, and so on—the nominal money stock is included. Put another way, commodity supply and demand functions must be written literally as functions not only of relative prices, including the interest rate, but of real money balances, such that $D_i = D_i(p_i, M_s/P, \ldots)$ and $S_i = S_i(p_i, M_s/P, \ldots)$.

This gives a more correct statement of the neutrality condition. As shown in Figure 9.3(b), if the money stock increased to $2M_s$ simultaneously or following the rise in P to $2P$, then the excess demand for money would be eliminated and with it, the excess supplies in the $n - 1$ markets by Walras's law. This is shown by the complete upward shift in the supply and demand functions in Figure 9.2(a) that leaves unchanged the real quantities initially supplied and demanded.

A more accurate statement of the neutrality condition, then, is that commodity supplies and demands are neutral not in the absolute level of nominal prices alone, but only, *ceteris paribus*, for symmetric changes in both M_s and P, leaving real money balances—and relative prices, including the interest rate—unchanged. Most economists believe this condition is seldom realized, at least initially, so much is left to be explored concerning the ways in which real-world monetary changes alter relative prices (and hence real quantities demanded and supplied) and the nature of the forces tending to restore such real relationships. This exploration may begin by examining possible effects of monetary changes on the demand for and supply of labor.

The Aggregate Labor Market

The analysis in Chapter 4 and in this chapter provide the microeconomic background for a model of the aggregate labor market. Suppose that there are $j = 1, \ldots, z$ types of labor and $i = 1, \ldots, n - 1$ nonmoney goods and services and that each firm adds man-hours of employment until $W_j = p_i \cdot \mathrm{mpl}_j = \mathrm{vmp}_j$, as explained in Chapter 4. If we assume that all employers act this way, then for the economy-wide aggregate labor market,

$$Wa = P \cdot \text{MPL}$$
$$= \text{VMP}_\text{L}.$$

Here the symbol Wa = the wage level, or some index designed to measure that level, just as P = the price or GNP deflator. MPL is also an aggregate concept designed to represent the weighted average of the microeconomic marginal products. Multiplying and canceling, we obtain

$$\frac{Wa}{P} = \text{MPL},$$

which tells us that the real (i.e., purchasing power) wage is equivalent to the marginal product of labor. We could therefore write the **aggregate demand for labor** (AL_d) as a function of its relative price, the real wage. Remembering, however, that all microeconomic demand functions, and hence any macroeconomic demand function derived by aggregation, are functions of real money balances as well as of relative prices, we find that this function should be written as

$$\text{AL}_d = f(\underset{-}{Wa}, \underset{+}{P}, \underset{+}{M_s}, \ldots),$$

where the ellipsis again indicates the presence of other variables such as the capital stock, technology, and so on, here omitted by inclusion in the *ceteris paribus* condition.

The minus sign on the aggregate nominal wage variable indicates that a change in the wage level, *ceteris paribus*, which therefore alters the real wage, has an inverse effect on labor demanded in the economy. That is, a rise in the real wage, which makes labor more costly to firms, decreases the amount demanded by firms, and a fall in the real wage increases the amount demanded, as demonstrated in Chapter 8. The positive sign on the money stock variable indicates that a change in M_s, *ceteris paribus*—including M_d—which therefore alters the real money stock, shifts labor demand in the same direction as the money stock change (upward or downward), just as it does the demand functions for other goods and services. Firms, after all, are also transactors that want to hold money balances of a desired real magnitude.

The sign on the price level variable is more problematic. Most economists assume that it is unambiguously positive because a rise in P raises the value of the marginal product of labor, $\text{VMP}_L = P \cdot \text{MPL}$, thereby increasing the demand for labor, and vice versa for a fall in P. But this ignores that, for a given nominal money stock, a rise in P reduces M_s/P below desired real holdings, which tends to reduce quantities of goods and services (including labor) demanded as transactors (including firms) attempt to add to their nominal money stocks.[1]

If M_s and P are rising or falling together, or if M_d and P are moving inversely, however, demand and supply functions logically shift in the direction in which prices are moving as a matter of neutrality. In what follows, M_s and P will be assumed to be moving in the same direction—or M_d and P moving inversely—so the sign of P will be assumed to be positive as shown, and the monetary variable can be suppressed for the sake of simplicity. Therefore, the aggregate labor demand function can be written

$$AL_d = f^{-1}\left(\frac{Wa}{P}\right).$$

One more algebraic manipulation of this function turns out to be useful. By assuming that labor demand is **monotonic** (i.e., uniformly downward sloping), it is permissible to rewrite the function, swapping the dependent and independent variables.[2] Thus

$$\frac{Wa}{P} = f(AL_d)$$

from which it follows that

$$Wa = P \cdot f(AL_d).$$

The latter expression is highly useful because it allows the price level to be interpreted as a simple proportional demand shifter.

The aggregate labor supply function can be developed with similar logic. From the reasoning developed previously, microeconomic labor supplies are functions of the real wage and real money balances. If we again suppress the monetary variable by assuming that M_s and P move in the same direction, we can write aggregate labor supply as

$$AL_s = g^{-1}\left(\frac{Wa}{P}\right).$$

The small g^{-1} is functional notation designed to distinguish the supply function. Assuming monotonicity, we obtain

$$\frac{Wa}{P} = g(\mathrm{AL}_s)$$

or

$$Wa = P \cdot g(\mathrm{AL}_s).$$

The aggregate labor market thus developed is shown in Figure 9.4, where the aggregate nominal wage $Wa_1 = \$10$ initially equates the quantities supplied and demanded at L_f, given price level $P_1 = 1$ and hence real wage $w_1 = \dfrac{Wa_1}{P_1} = \$10$). Now suppose that a decline in the money stock (M_s) with M_d constant—or a rise in M_d with M_s constant—causes the price level to fall or to be expected to fall soon from P_1 to $P_2 = .6$. This shifts the demand and supply functions for labor downward as required, *ceteris paribus*, for the same real quantities to be offered and demanded at the same relative but lower absolute prices.

If labor markets are competitive and wage rates are flexible, the aggregate wage rate would fall smoothly with prices, and little or no unemployment would appear. On the other hand, if the aggregate wage rate were completely rigid and immobile, perhaps because of a minimum-wage law setting $\overline{W}a = Wa_1$ or because a single monopoly

Figure 9.4 Neutral Price Level Shifts of Labor Supply and Demand.

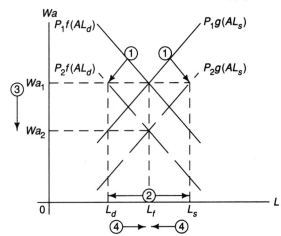

union to which all workers belonged fixed the wage at that level, the downward shift of AL_d and AL_s would raise the real wage to $Wa_1/P_2 = \$10/.6 \approx \$16.67$. This would produce unemployment as shown, and it would be permanent.

As noted in Chapter 8, wage rates in real labor markets are neither perfectly flexible nor perfectly inflexible. Minimum-wage laws and multiyear union contracts produce rigidity in certain industries, but other industries are not covered. Many workers caused to be unemployed under deflationary conditions could shift from covered to uncovered industries, bidding down wage rates there enough to obtain employment. Union contracts would eventually terminate and be renegotiated, although unions, as actual or aspiring labor monopolies, are notorious for resisting required wage rate reductions. The average wage would eventually fall to $Wa_2 = \$6$, such that $Wa_2/P_2 = \$6/.6 = \$10 = Wa_1/P_1$.

Still, such artificial obstructions decrease wage flexibility, prolonging unemployment. Even in the absence of such impediments some unemployment would appear as a signal for the necessity for wage reductions, and adjustment to equilibrium would take some time, although just how much is hard to say. This is the sequence of events shown by the numbered arrows in Figure 9.4, and the model is ultimately neutral to the monetary change.

The same set of events can be usefully modeled in an alternate graph such as that in Figure 9.5. Here AL_d and AL_s are modeled as functions of the real wage by explicitly measuring $w = Wa/P$ on the vertical axis. Note that the price level shifter is therefore missing from the demand

Figure 9.5 Real Wage Version of the Aggregate Labor Market.

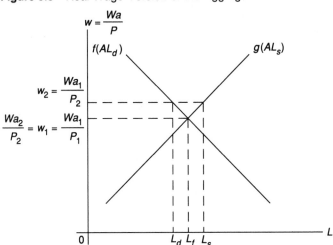

and supply functions, which interact to establish the real wage at $w_1 = Wa_1/P_1$. Again suppose that the money stock declines, or M_d rises instead, causing the price level to fall from P_1 to P_2 and thereby raise the real wage to $w_2 = Wa_1/P_2$. In Figure 9.4 the decline in the money stock and price level shifted the demand and supply functions vertically downward, decreasing demand and increasing supply. In Figure 9.5, however, the functions do not shift, but *quantity demanded* declines and *quantity supplied* increases as the real wage rises, producing unemployment as before.

If the nominal wage level then declined to Wa_2 such that $w_1 = Wa_2/P_2 = Wa_1/P_1$, the unemployment would be eliminated. That is, where

$$w = \frac{Wa}{P}$$

it follows from the rule for the growth rate of a ratio that

$$\frac{\Delta w}{w} \approx \frac{\Delta Wa}{Wa} - \frac{\Delta P}{P},$$

and if the terms on the right-hand side have the same value, then the one on the left-hand side must be zero. In other words, if the nominal wage were to fall proportionately to the price level, the equilibrium real wage and quantity (w_1 and L_e) would be restored and the monetary change would be neutral. Again, how long this would take depends on the natural and artificial impediments to nominal wage flexibility.

Note that the term *full employment* does not quite mean what it says. Even when the aggregate labor market clears at L_f, some unemployment exists because of dynamic job shifting among the micro markets composing it, labor market entry and exit, recent technological change, and so on. As defined in Chapter 4, this almost irreduceable minimum unemployment, expressed in percentage terms, is referred to as the natural rate of unemployment.

The Labor Market with Money Illusion

The conclusion is that if supply and demand are functions of relative prices and real money balances, and wages and prices are flexible, then changes in the money stock and the demand for money will be neutral, altering no real variables except for transition periods. Relaxing the second assumption by assuming downward wage rigidity results in significant non-neutrality from deflationary monetary changes. But what if the first assumption were relaxed?

Suppose that the labor supply function is simply written as

$$AL_s = g^{-1}(Wa)$$

and after deriving the inverse function as

$$Wa = g(AL_s).$$

According to this specification, labor supply decisions are made purely on the basis of the nominal wage established in the market and are not a function of the real wage. This failure of workers to distinguish between real and nominal magnitudes is an example of what is called **money illusion**. In general, money illusion exists whenever transactors in any market make supply or demand decisions purely on the basis of nominal rather than relative prices.

Figure 9.6 duplicates Figure 9.4, except that labor supply is subject to money illusion, as indicated by the absence of the price level shifter from that function, although the vertical axis measures only the nominal wage rate. Now suppose that a decline in the money stock—or, alternatively, a rise in M_d—reduces the price level as before from P_1 to P_2. In this case the aggregate demand for labor shifts downward but, because of the money illusion, the aggregate labor supply function does *not*. Assuming that the wage rate is flexible we find that unemployment appears only briefly, after which the wage rate falls to clear the market

Figure 9.6 Price Level Decline with Money Illusion in Labor Supply.

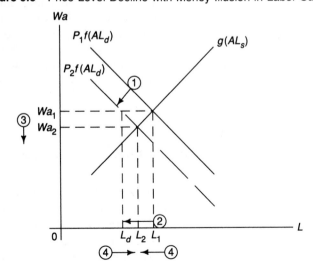

at Wa_2. This is the sequence indicated by the numbered arrows in Figure 9.6.

Note that although the market clears at Wa_2, the new equilibrium quantity is L_2, which is less than L_1. The money illusion in the labor supply has resulted in the monetary change being non-neutral. This is because, although the wage rate fell as demand declined, it did not fall as much as it would have had the supply function also shifted downward, and hence it did not fall as much, proportionately, as prices did. Where $w = Wa/P$ and $\% \Delta W \approx \% \Delta Wa - \% \Delta P$, the money illusion resulted in $\% \Delta Wa < \% \Delta P$, and since both terms are negative this means that the real wage increased.

To illustrate, suppose that in this case $\% \Delta Wa = -.05$ and $\% \Delta P = -.10$. Then

$$
\begin{aligned}
\% \Delta w &\approx \% \Delta Wa - \% \Delta P \\
&\approx -.05 - (-.10) \\
&\approx -.05 + .10 \\
&\approx +.05.
\end{aligned}
$$

It is this increase in the real wage, raising the real cost of labor to firms, that accounts for the smaller employment.

Further implications of money illusion will be explored, but the reader may be curious whether or not this is a real-world phenomenon. After all, that supply and demand decisions are made on the basis of relative prices is a core theorem of economics. Under some conditions, however, money illusion might appear. If the output prices in general were stable for some time, for example, workers might get so accustomed to looking at nominal wage changes that they forget to pay attention to the price level.

There is a vital point here. It has been stressed that people's decisions in the present about actions to be taken are based on current expectations of present and future conditions. People attempt to offer or demand certain real quantities of economic goods and services (e.g., labor) at certain real prices (p_i/P), but what they are really doing is offering or demanding those quantities at their estimated relative prices (p_i/P^*) and in any particular case that expected price level value may be incorrect.

Now, incorrect expectations may not be quite the same as pure money illusion, but they are certainly a first cousin and have the same effects. Suppliers having an expectation $P^* < P$, for example, are obtaining a lower real price per unit than they want for the commodity they sell. Put another way, they are supplying a larger quantity than they want at the given real price and need to raise the nominal price. The opposite would be true for an expectation $P^* > P$. All things considered, however, since money illusion and incorrect expectations both impose costs on transactors through wealth and resource misallocation, it is difficult to believe that they can persist indefinitely. Such costs must eventually force transactors to pay close attention to real relationships and to make the required adjustments in quantities and nominal prices.

The same argument applies to inflationary conditions. Those wishing to obtain relative price per unit p_i/P for a certain real quantity of a good or service supplied will attempt, *ceteris paribus* (in particular, assuming $\% \, \Delta M_s = \alpha$, so that the real money stock is constant), to raise its nominal price over time at the rate $\% \, \Delta p_i = \alpha$. What they actually do, however, is raise the price at rate $\% \, \Delta p_i = \alpha^*$, which will result in unintended relative price changes and resource misallocation whenever $\alpha^* \neq \alpha$.

Accelerating inflation during the 1970s seemed to have fooled transactors in the credit markets, for example. The Fisher effect, explained in Chapter 8, operated to raise nominal interest rates during this period but, as explained in Chapter 15, not enough to keep real interest rates from falling below their values of the 1950s and 1960s.[3] This imposed losses on many financial market transactors, however, and the credit markets finally raised nominal rates enough to restore real interest rates by 1981. Labor markets seemed to have correctly adjusted to the inflation much sooner; see Chapter 14.

The Aggregate Production Function

Having developed two models of the aggregate labor market, our next step in developing a model of aggregate demand for and supply of output for the entire economy is to link the employment of labor to the production of output through an aggregate production function. Figure 4.1 (c), (see Chapter 4) illustrated the total product curve for a single firm, showing the quantities produced as labor usage was varied while the firm's capital stock was fixed. Such changes input proportions eventually exhibited diminishing returns, as shown in Figure 4.1 (a) and in the shape of Figure 4.1 (c).

If we assume that all firms are operating in the Marshallian short run and consider variations in aggregate employment, then output in the whole economy should vary in a pattern similar to that of a single firm's total product curve. Figure 9.7 shows such a short-run aggregate production function, $Q(L, \bar{K}, \dots)$ in which $\bar{K}$ indicates the assumption of a fixed national physical capital stock and the ellipsis indicates the presence of other variables (e.g., technology, raw materials, etc.) that are also held constant. The slope of the curve at any point, such as

Figure 9.7   The Short-Run Aggregate Producton Function.

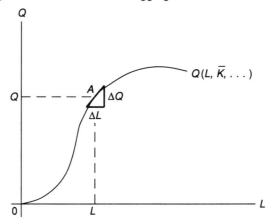

point A, shows the marginal product of employment, $(\Delta Q/\Delta L)$ at that point. The shape of the curve shows the standard assumptions about diminishing returns.

Two major shift variables in the aggregate production function are the capital stock and the level of embodied technology; population has its effect on output through employment. The distinction is between the quantity and the quality of tools and equipment. An increase in the quantity of capital employed as a result of significant net investment tilts the production function upward, raising both the marginal productivity and total output of labor. Such an increase in the nation's capital stock is illustrated in Figure 9.8 (a).

Figure 9.8   Capital Stock Growth and Neutral Technical Change in the Aggregate Production Function.

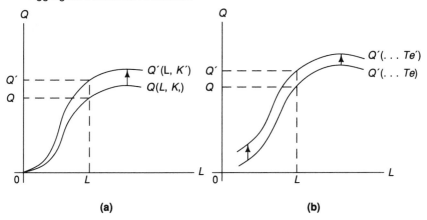

(a)   (b)

An increase in embodied technology, *ceteris paribus* (e.g., replacement of old machines and equipment with improved types), essentially shifts the whole production function upward, and may increase, decrease, or leave unchanged the marginal product of labor. Figure 9.8 (b) is designed to illustrate a **neutral technical advance**, leaving marginal productivity of labor unchanged. An increase in human capital (i.e., a more educated and skilled workforce) has qualitative aspects like technical change but also raises the MPL like a change in physical capital. Raw materials are also important in production, and changes in their availability and usage shift the production function in the same way as ΔK. For now, however, all of these variables will be assumed constant and only the labor input will be varied.

Aggregate Demand and Supply and Walras's Law _____

We can now develop the concepts of aggregate demand and supply for final output as functions of the price level. The basic question is why would aggregate demand vary inversely and aggregate supply vary directly with the price level (P) when, conceptually at least, no relative price—including the interest rate or the real wage—in the $n - 1$ markets may be changing. Where do the substitution and income effects come from? The answer is that, for a given M_s, such a price level change is altering the relative price of money and hence the real money stock away from desired real balances.

Suppose that the price level is determined at P and hence the value of money at $1/P$, as in Figure 9.9 (a). Because $M_d - M_s = 0$, net excess demand in the $n - 1$ markets, which are all aggregated into one

Figure 9.9 Real Balance Effects in the *AD–AS* Model.

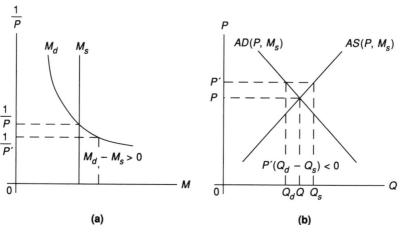

(a)   (b)

in Figure 9.9 (b), is also zero at price level P. Now if the price level were raised from P to P', *ceteris paribus*—perhaps by legislative or bureaucratic fiat—people's real cash balances would be reduced below desired levels, making $M_d - M_s > 0$. In each of the $n - 1$ micro markets, and hence in the aggregate, individuals would reduce quantities of goods and services demanded and raise quantities supplied in an effort to restore money balances, making

$$\sum_{i=1}^{n-1} p_i(D_i - S_i) < 0$$

and equal to the excess demand for money. This is shown by and is equivalent to $P'(Q_d - Q_s) < 0$ in Figure 9.9 (b). Repeating the logic for a reduction in the price level to some value below P would complete the explanation for why the aggregate demand and supply functions have the shapes shown.

Because the derived neutrality results apply for each micro market, they also apply in the aggregate. A proportional rise in M_s and P, m_d given—or a rise in P that was proportional to a decline in the demand for real balances, M_s given, which therefore reduced the real money stock to the new desired level—would shift the aggregate demand and supply functions upward symmetrically, leaving unchanged the initial real quantities supplied and demanded. This is the sequence of events shown in Figure 9.10. A line connecting the neutral equilibrium points of AD and AS at different price levels is hereafter labeled LRAS for **long-run aggregate supply**. For distinction, the upward sloping supply function is labeled SRAS for **short-run aggregate supply**.

Figure 9.10   Neutral *AD–AS* Shifts and the *LRAS* Curve.

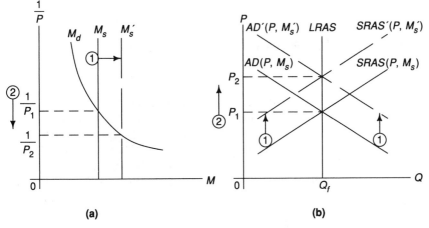

Aggregate Demand and the Interest Rate _____

Previously, all ΔP have been assumed to involve no alteration in relative prices in the $n - 1$ markets. Many economists argue, however, that a *ceteris paribus* change in the price level would automatically alter the interest rate. The argument proceeds as follows: An increase in the price level, M_s constant, increases the amount of money demanded. This causes the interest rate to rise—apparently, as people try to borrow money to add to their cash balances—and the rise in the interest rate reduces investment and increases saving, both of which reduce the aggregate real quantity of goods and services currently demanded.

The opposite occurs with a fall in the price level, M_s constant. This reduces the demand for nominal units of money—because people need fewer units to maintain desired real balances—reducing the rate of interest by reducing credit demand. The interest rate reduction increases investment and reduces savings, both of which add to the quantity of real goods and services demanded in the other $n - 2$ markets.

The effect of this postulated direct relationship between the price level and the interest rate, and the inverse relationship between the interest rate and aggregate demand, is to reinforce the real balance effect in causing aggregate demand to be inversely related to the price level.[4] In completion of the argument it needs to be pointed out that any discrete proportional *ceteris paribus* change in both P and M_s such that $\Delta(M_s/P) = 0$ would leave the interest rate and the real quantities of goods and services demanded and supplied unchanged, as explained in Chapter 5.

The *AD–AS* Model with Money Illusion in Labor Supply _____

The *AD–AS* model can be completed by combining the aggregate markets for labor and final output with the aggregate production function, placing their common axes together as in Figure 9.11. All relationships are shown as previously theorized. In this case money illusion is assumed as in Figure 9.6. This is clear from the absence of the price level shifter on the labor supply function in the third quadrant in Figure 9.11. The initial equilibrium quantities assumed are P_1, Q_1, L_1, and Wa_1.

Figure 9.11 Deriving the *SRAS* from Money Illusion in Labor Supply.

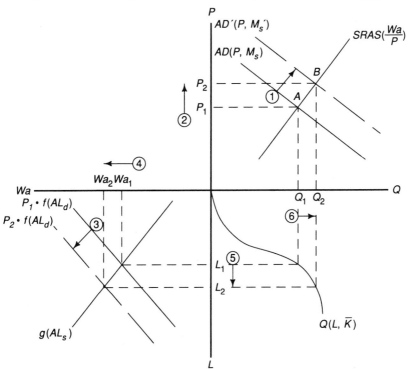

The initial event disturbing equilibrium is an increase in the money stock from M_s to M_s'—although a decrease in k, reducing M_d, could serve as well—which raises aggregate demand to AD', causing prices to rise from P_1 to P_2. This increases the demand for labor from $P_1 \cdot f(\text{AL}_d)$ to $P_2 \cdot f(\text{AL}_d)$, but because of the money illusion, the labor supply function does not decrease (i.e., shift upward). The wage rate does increase somewhat, from Wa_1 to Wa_2, increasing employment from L_1 to L_2. The increased employment raises output through the production function from Q_1 to Q_2. This sequence of events is shown by the numbered arrows, and by drawing a line between points $A = (Q_1, P_1)$ and $B = (Q_2, P_2)$ in the first quadrant, the SRAS function is derived.

There are two important non-neutralities in the model with a common source. First, because money illusion prevented the labor supply function from shifting along with AL_d, $\Delta Wa/Wa < \Delta P/P$ and the real wage fell. This accounts for the increased employment and output. We might suppose, for example, that the price level rose from $P_1 = 1$ to $P_2 = 1.2$, or $\Delta P/P = .2$, whereas the weighted average wage increased only from \$10 to \$11, or $\Delta Wa/Wa = 1.1$, such that the real wage fell to $\$11/1.2 \approx \$9.17$. That is, $\Delta w/w \approx \Delta Wa/Wa - \Delta P/P \approx .10 - .20 \approx -.10$.

Second, note that the price level did not rise by as much as the vertical shift in aggregate demand. If AD is seen in terms of the equation of exchange as the total level of expenditure, then

$$AD = M_s \cdot V$$

and it follows that

$$\frac{\Delta AD}{AD} \approx \frac{\Delta M_s}{M_s} + \frac{\Delta V}{V}.$$

By assumption, the initial disturbance involved $\Delta M_s/M_s > 0$ and $\Delta V/V = 0$, so $\Delta AD/AD = \Delta M_s/M_s$. But the real money stock is $m_s = M_s/P$, so

$$\frac{\Delta m_s}{m_s} \approx \frac{\Delta M_s}{M_s} - \frac{\Delta P}{P},$$

and because prices did not rise by as much as the M_s increased—as shown by the vertical shift in AD—the real money stock increased. To illustrate, if the money stock increase was from \$1000 billion to \$1250 billion or 25 percent, while the price level rose only from $P_1 = 1$ to $P_2 = 1.2$, or 20 percent, then the real money stock increased to $M_s'/P_2 = \$1250/1.2 = \$1042$ billion. That is, $\% \Delta m_s \approx \% \Delta M_s - \% \Delta P \approx .25 - .20 = .05$.

The explanation is observable in Figure 9.12. The initial increase in the nominal money stock to M_s' first made $M_d - M_s' < 0$ such that prices started rising. *Ceteris paribus*, they would have risen all the way to P_3, reducing the value of money to $1/P_3$, at which point $\Delta P/P = (P_3 - P_1)/P_1 = (M_s' - M_s)/M_s = \Delta M_s/M_s$ such that $\Delta m_s = 0$. But the increased output caused by money illusion increased the demand for money slightly because, as explained in Chapter 7, $m_d = k \cdot Q$ and $\Delta m_d/m_d = \Delta Q/Q$ when $\Delta k/k = 0$), such that prices only increased to P_2, and

$$\frac{M_s'}{P_2} > \frac{M_s'}{P_3} = \frac{M_s}{P_1}.$$

It is this rise in real money balances that accounts for the increase in quantity demanded along AD' in Figure 9.11 sufficient to purchase the additional output.

Figure 9.12 Nonneutral Effect on Real Balances from Money Illusion in Labor Supply.

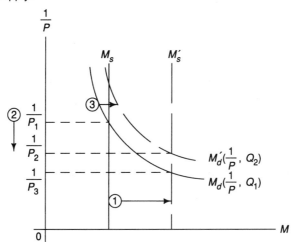

The Complete *AD–AS* Model Without Money Illusion ___

The initial conditions in Figure 9.13 duplicate those in Figure 9.11 except that both labor supply and demand are assumed to be free of money illusion. The initial equilibrium values are P_1, Q_f, L_f and Wa_f, where the f subscript denotes full employment values, and Q_f, L_f, and Wa_f are identical to Q_1, L_1, and Wa_1 in Figure 9.11. Now suppose that the same disturbance occurs: The money stock increases, *ceteris paribus*. *AD* shifts up by $\Delta AD/AD = \Delta M_s/M_s$ as before, creating excess demand in the product markets and causing prices to rise. The rise in product prices also raises the demand for labor. Because workers are free of money illusion, however, their supply function also shifts upward proportionately. Realizing the effect of rising prices in reducing real wages, they demand higher nominal wages for each real quantity supplied.

Because AL_d and AL_s shift proportionately, % ΔWa = % ΔP and the real wage does not change (i.e., $Wa'/P_3 = Wa_f/P_1$) and the model is completely neutral. Quantity employed does not change, nor does output. The SRAS curve defined for real money balance changes shifts upward to SRAS' and prices rise to P_3, such that % ΔP = % ΔM_s and Δm_s = 0, leaving the money market in equilibrium as in Figure 9.12 at the intersection of M_d and M_s'. The long-run aggregate supply curve is vertical. This would also, of course, be the eventual outcome in Figure 9.11 as the money illusion assumed there disappeared. There is

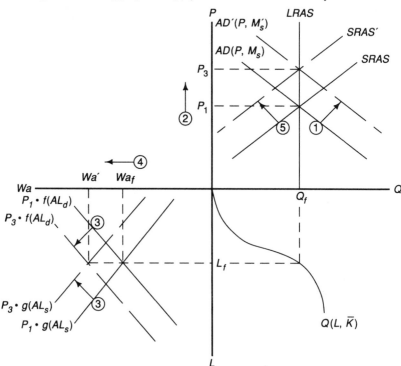

Figure 9.13 Aggregate Supply in the Absence of Money Illusion.

another important source of non-neutrality to discuss, however, before considering disturbances to the system from the supply side.

The *AD–AS* Model with a Downwardly Rigid Nominal Wage Rate

Figure 9.14 differs from Figures 9.11 and 9.13 in two respects: First, while it assumes no money illusion in the labor market, the real wage is measured on the axis in the third quadrant, hence the price level shifters are missing from both the labor supply and demand functions, as in Figure 9.5. Second, a rectangular hyperbola labeled Wa_1 is drawn in the second quadrant. With $w = Wa/P$ on the horizontal axis and P on the vertical axis of that quadrant, each Cartesian coordinate on a rectangular hyperbola represents a product $(Wa/P) \cdot P = Wa$ with the

Figure 9.14 *AD* Decline with a Downwardly Rigid Nominal Wage.

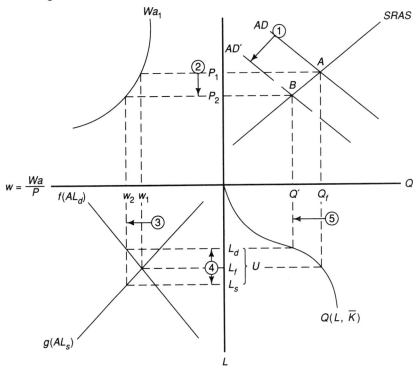

same magnitude as the others. Such a line represents a given nominal wage rate then, and in fact each nominal wage rate could be represented by its own rectangular hyperbola in that space, higher ones being further from the origin. The one shown is the existing nominal wage and is assumed to be downwardly inflexible.

The initial equilibrium values in Figure 9.14 are Wa_1, P_1 (yielding $Wa_1/P_1 = w_1$), L_f, and Q_f. Again we can assume that either a contractionary open market operation or an increase in the demand for money disturbs the system by reducing aggregate demand from AD to AD'. Prices begin to fall but the aggregate nominal wage, being downwardly rigid, does not. This raises the real wage above equilibrium as shown, creating unemployment $= u$. The short side of the labor market determines employment at L_d and output is reduced to Q'. Prices stop falling at P_2. The shape of the SRAS is then found by drawing a line connecting points $A = (Q_f, P_1)$ and $B = (Q', P_2)$.

The system cannot be said to be truly in equilibrium at these subsequent values, however. Excess supplies exist in the labor market, and excess plant capacity exists also. These excess supplies must be matched by an excess demand for money, so deflationary pressures still exist; they are simply stalled by the refusal of wage rates to fall. As discussed previously, however, such rigidity cannot be permanent. Over time contracts will terminate and unemployment will force renegotiated wage rates downward. Meanwhile, many unemployed workers will shift to occupations and employments with more flexible wage rates, bidding them down.

The eventual result is shown in Figure 9.15 which duplicates the first and second quadrants of Figure 9.14. The nominal wage level will fall to Wa_0, shifting the SRAS down to SRAS', allowing output to rise from Q' to Q_f and prices to fall from P_2 to P_3. At that point $Wa_0/P_3 = w_1 = Wa_1/P_1$, and the economy is back in equilibrium. The monetary change is ultimately neutral with regard to real output and employment.[5]

This "classical" stabilizing mechanism seems to have operated effectively in our economy before the Great Depression, as was demonstrated recently by Lowell Gallaway and Richard K. Vedder.[6] These economists examined the relation between the movements of the real wage and employment during the sharp recession of 1920 to 1922, and then did the same for the Depression. For this empirical work they employed a variation of the real wage known as the **productivity adjusted real wage**, $w_r = Wa/(P \cdot APL)$, where APL is the average hourly product of labor.

The significance of this conceptual adjustment can be seen by applying the percentage change rule, to obtain

$$\% \, \Delta w_r \approx \% \, \Delta Wa - (\% \, \Delta P + \% \, \Delta APL).$$

Figure 9.15 *AD Decline with Neutralizing Wage Adjustment.*

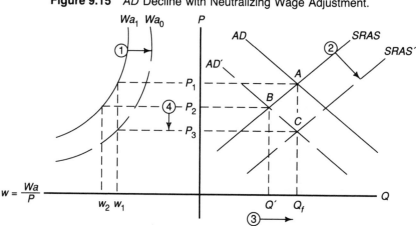

Assuming that $\% \, \Delta P = 0$, it can be seen that any nominal wage increase that is matched by a rise in productivity will have no effect on w_r. Also, a decline in nominal wage rates matched by a decline in APL would leave $\% \, \Delta w_r \approx 0$. Because labor productivity is a prime determinant of labor demand, some positive correlation between these variables is normal and must modify the effect of any change in the relation between nominal wage rates and the price level. This complication has been avoided previously by making the short-run assumption that $\% \, \Delta \text{APL} = 0$.

Vedder and Gallaway found that the recession of 1920 to 1922 presented an almost-classic case of labor markets responding to and helping to correct a macroeconomic disequilibrium generated by a contractionary AD shock. As prices fell, nominal wage rates initially adjusted slowly and the real wage increased, decreasing employment and output over a period of a little more than five quarters or 15 months. In mid-1921 the price level began to stabilize while money wage rates continued falling. The real wage began declining and employment steadily recovered.

The time pattern and magnitudes of these changes in employment and the productivity adjusted real wage over this cycle are shown in Figure 9.16, which replicates Vedder and Gallaway's Figure 2. The

Figure 9.16   The Adjusted Real Wage and Employment over the 1920 to 1922 Cycle.

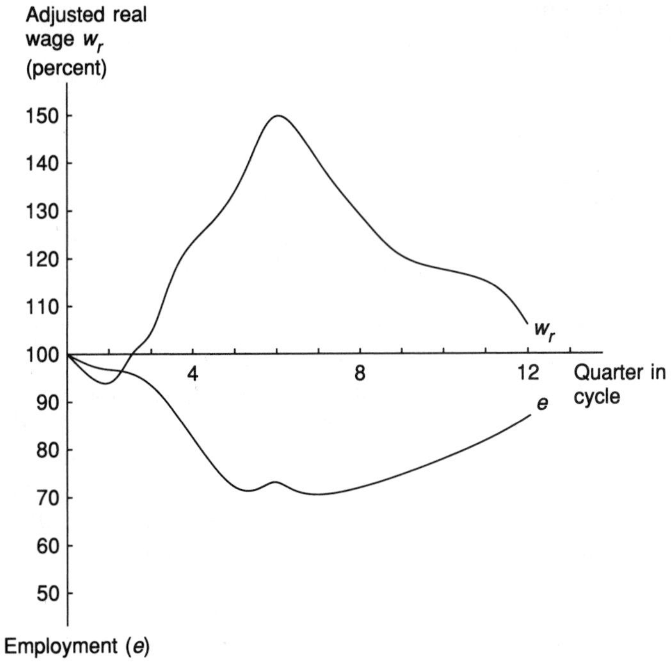

initial values of w_r and employment are set at index number values of 100, so that the vertical scale shows percentages of those initial values. The experience of the Great Depression, discussed in Chapter 10, confirms in several respects the importance of nominal wage adjustments for the stability of the macroeconomy. By that time, however, U.S. political authorities had rejected and begun to impede this sort of classical adjustment mechanism that worked so well in 1920 to 1922 and earlier.

Alternate Antirecession Policies

Two government policies aimed at hastening the restoration of equilibrium are implicit in the recessionary situation described in Figure 9.14. One is for government to take action aimed at removing artificial impediments to wage adjustment, so that market forces might act as efficiently as possible. Some economists reject this policy for two reasons: First, because they believe union power makes it politically impossible to institute such a program and second, because they believe the bulk of wage rigidity may be a natural characteristic of labor markets and not the result of legislated impediments.[7]

The preferred policy of such economists is to simply restore AD to its initial level, either by increasing the nominal money stock or by some other method aimed at increasing total expenditure in the economy; see Chapters 10 and 11 about Keynesian economics for a detailed discussion of such methods. This policy seems to avoid any long wait and prolonged unemployment while falling wages and prices increase the real money stock enough to restore equilibrium.

The appeal of this policy lies in its apparent simplicity, which is deceptive, however. For reasons partly elaborated in Chapter 8 and to be augmented in Chapter 11, such a policy of countercyclical demand management is much more difficult than the graphics make it seem, and more often may be a source of disturbance to the economy than a source of stability. A preferable policy would be one that prevented such declines in AD relative to AS in the first place.

To the extent that such deflationary AD shocks originate in monetary policy, this might be accomplished by keeping the money stock constant in the previous static growth case or by growing at a rate consistent with the trend of real economic growth. The employment effects associated with remaining fluctuations in AD resulting from instability of M_d, rather than M_s, could then be minimized by policies making wages and prices as flexible as possible.

These issues will be discussed more fully in later chapters, but one reason it may be bad policy to fight unemployment by raising AD can be explained here. Static graphics, such as those in Figures 9.14 and 9.15, partly falsify the modern situation since they deal only in levels and not in rates of change of the variables. In the last several decades U.S. inflation has meant that both wage rates and prices were rising. Under these conditions a literal decline in AD, causing a literal fall in P (raising Wa/P because of rigid wages) is not required in order to create unemployment. A reduction in the growth rate of AD (cause by say a reduction in the rate of growth of M_s), which makes $\% \Delta P < \% \Delta W_a$ such that $\Delta w > 0$, will, *ceteris paribus*, cause unemployment and reduced output.

In this real-world case it is downward rigidity in the rate of wage *inflation*, more than in the absolute wage level, that causes the real wage distortion. Under these conditions, an argument that unemployment should always be fought by raising aggregate demand relative to aggregate supply—rather than by targeting policy on wage and price flexibility—really amounts to an argument that inflation should never be fought, at least never by reducing the excess growth rate of the nominal money stock. It quite literally seems to be an argument for interminable inflation.[8]

Supply Shocks in the *AD–AS* Model

Macroeconomic disturbances, originating either as shifts in the money stock or in the demand for money, are known as **aggregate demand shocks**. Most shocks are of this type. It is possible, however, for a macroeconomic shock to originate from the supply side of the market. Such disturbances are termed **aggregate supply shocks**.

A major shock of this type occurred in 1973 when the Yom Kippur War broke out between Israel and Syria. The war disrupted the flow of crude oil from the Middle-East and the OPEC cartel, an organization of governments (i.e., not private firms) of major third-world oil exporting nations, took the opportunity to restrict their production and drastically increase the price of petroleum. This generated a large recession in most of the industrial, oil-importing nations of the world, including the United States. The same occurred on a smaller scale in 1979 and 1980 when the Iranian revolution again allowed OPEC the opportunity to restrict output and raise the price of oil.

One of the nice things about the *AD–AS* model is that it can be easily employed to illustrate such an *AS* shock and its consequences. This is attempted in Figure 9.17. If we remember that raw materials should be written as an input in the aggregate production function, a good way of modeling the initial effect of a partial withdrawal and increase in price of an input such as petroleum is by a downward shift in

Figure 9.17 Negative Aggregate Supply Shock in the *AD–AS* Model.

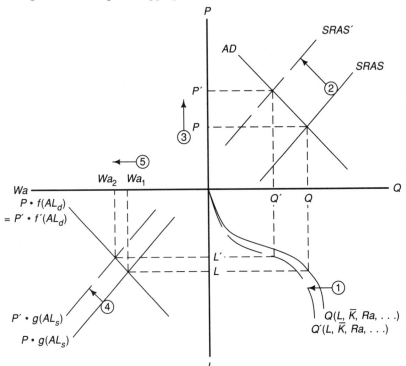

the production function, say from $Q(L,\bar{K},R_a,\ldots)$ to $Q'(L,\bar{K},R'_a,\ldots)$ as shown. This is because, *ceteris paribus*, the effect of partial loss of an input in production is to reduce the marginal productivity of the complementary inputs, such as labor.

As the aggregate production function declines, the LRAS (not shown) and the SRAS curves begin shifting leftward and the price level starts rising, as shown in the first quadrant of Figure 9.16. This is due to rising production costs being passed through to final prices. In the third quadrant, the decline in the production function has two opposite effects on labor demand. Where the value of the marginal product of labor is $VMP_L = P \cdot MPL$, the decline in output and marginal productivity tends to reduce labor demand, but the rise in the price level tends to raise it. For simplicity it is assumed here that these effects roughly cancel, leaving $P' \cdot f(AL_d) \approx P \cdot f(AL_d)$.

Assuming labor demand unchanged does not mean that employment does not change, however. If workers lack money illusion and accurately anticipate the price level change, as assumed here, the labor supply function must decline to $P' \cdot g(AL_s)$, resulting in smaller employment and a rise in the wage rate to Wa_2.[9] The final equilibrium output (Q') is a result of both the decline in the production function and the reduced employment. This is roughly the sequence of events shown in Figure 9.17.

A negative AS shock of this sort is often thought to result in a dilemma for policy makers, because it involves a combination of reduced employment and output with a rise in the price level. The output decline could be fought by raising AD and moving up the SRAS curve, but that would work only if there were money illusion, or sticky price expectations, in the labor supply, and in any case the long-run effect would be even higher prices. On the other hand, the price level increase resulting from the negative AS shock could be fought instead, by employing a contractionary AD policy. If prices and wage rates are at all sticky downward, however, that will cause an even worse recession in the short run.

Perhaps the lesson to learn from this supposed dilemma is that demand management is not the appropriate policy response to a supply shock in the first place. In the case of OPEC, actions to break up the cartel quickly or to prevent it from being able to restrict world petroleum supply in the first place, might have been more rewarding. Second, policy tools are available to the government that could be employed to reduce business costs and shift the production function outward. The economics and political economy of such "supply-side" policies are examined in Chapter 16.

At this point it is time to leave the $AD–AS$ model and deal with a different (although in many senses related) form of macroeconomic model developed by the great British economist, John Maynard Keynes. Keynesian economic enriched our understanding of macroeconomic modeling and introduced a set of theories and issues that need to be examined closely. The $AD–AS$ model is highly useful, however, and will be employed again in later chapters.

Summary _____

Among the many important points of this chapter are the following.

1. Commodity supply and demand functions are functions of relative prices and real money balances.

2. Such functions will shift vertically (upward or downward) in a neutral fashion when symmetric changes in both M_s and P occur, such that $\Delta m_s = 0$, *ceteris paribus* (m_d constant).

3. This proposition applies equally to labor markets as long as both supplies and demands are assumed to be functions of the real wage. Further, if we assume that the money stock and price level move in the same direction, the price level can be usefully modeled as a vertical supply and demand shifter.

4. An alternate method of describing the aggregate labor market, which yields the same analytic results, is to model supply and demand expressly as functions of the real wage measured on the vertical axis and to leave the price level shifter off both functions.

5. Non-neutral effects of monetary changes would result if workers were subject to "money illusion," that is, if labor supply was a function of the nominal wage only. (This literally means that workers are not concerned with the goods-value of their hourly wage payment.) Incorrect price level expectations will yield the same results.

6. The aggregate labor market can be linked to the aggregate output market through the concept of the aggregate production function. By assuming that all firms are operating in the Marshallian short run, changes in aggregate employment will alter national production in a pattern similar to that of the short-run total product curve of a firm.

7. Using the economics of Walras's law (see Chapter 5), we find that aggregate demand for and supply of final output can be modeled as negative and positive functions of the price level respectively, even if no relative price changes occur among the $n - 1$ goods as P changes. This is because such a price level change would generate an excess demand for or supply of real money balances, *ceteris paribus*.

8. A second method of explaining non-neutrality of money and price level changes, resulting in a positively sloped aggregate supply function, is to assume money illusion, or inelastic expectations, in labor supply, such that a price level change alters the real (i.e., relative) wage.

9. A third method of explaining non-neutrality and deriving a positively sloped *AS* function is to assume a downwardly rigid nominal wage under deflationary conditions.

10. Virtually all conditions actually or allegedly generating non-neutrality of money, whether money illusion, incorrect expectations, long-term contracts, and so on, generate costs for the transactors making such errors. Such conditions must therefore, be temporary, as efforts are undertaken to avoid and correct these costly errors.

11. In the past, U.S. prices and wage rates adjusted with reasonable dispatch to eliminate recessionary conditions generated by negative *AD* shocks. Since the Great Depression, policymakers have preferred a strategy of raising *AD* to eliminate recessionary conditions.

12. Not all macroeconomic disturbances come in the form of aggregate demand shocks. Aggregate supply shocks, such as the OPEC actions of 1973 and 1979, reducing petroleum output and raising its price, also occur. Such supply shocks and their effects can also be usefully modeled in the *AD–AS* framework.

NOTES

1. See Don Patinkin, *Money, Interest and Prices* (2nd ed., New York: Harper and Row, 1965): 76–77.

2. The rules says that if a function $Y = f(X)$ is monotonic, there must exist an inverse function $X = f^{-1}(Y)$. See Alpha C. Chiang, *Fundamental Methods of Mathematical Economics* (2nd ed., New York: McGraw-Hill, 1974): 181. (**Note**: In the text above, the inverse sign is on the initial function so that it would not be present on the inverse function.)

3. See Frederic S. Mishkin, "The Real Interest Rate: An Emperical Investigation," *Carnegie-Rochester Conference Series on Public Policy: The Costs and Consequences of Inflation* 15 (Autumn 1981): 151–200.

4. Indeed, this explanation is sometimes used in place of the real balance effect in deriving the *AD* curve. The most extreme example of this is Robert E. Hall and John B. Taylor, *Macroeconomics: Theory, Performance, and Policy* (New York: W. W. Norton, 1986), from which all mention of the real balance effect is rigorously and deliberately excluded.

5. But only in the aggregate, unless all wage rates and prices are flexible. In the case in which wage rigidity in some micro labor markets causes job shifting and gradual erosion of the aggregate wage rate, wage rates in the micro markets are certainly changing relative to one another, as is the pattern of employment and hence the composition of output. So even if the aggregate wage rate did decline to the initial level and the real value of output was restored, there would be significant distributional non-neutralities.

6. See Lowell Gallaway and Richard K. Vedder, "Wages, Prices and Employment: Von Mises and the Progressives," *Review of Austrian Economics* 1 (1987): 33–80.

7. There is evidence, however, that wage rates and prices were much more flexible before the 1930s, which was the great period of labor legislation. See Daniel J. B. Mitchel, "Wage Flexibility in the United States: Lessons From the Past," *American Economic Review* 75 (May 1985): 36–39.

8. At the American Economic Association meetings in New Orleans in December 1986, during a seminar on the contribution of John Maynard Keynes after 50 years, about 200 economists heard R. J. Gordon, then the most prominent neo-Keynesian economist, state that he would be "perfectly happy to see 3 percent inflation forever" (i.e., the rate at that time) rather than suffer even a temporary recession.

9. The student may note that despite the increase in the nominal wage to W', the real wage has declined, because this increase is not as large as that in the price level, shown by the vertical (or, in this case, horizontal) shift in the labor supply curve. So we have the seemingly odd combination of a lower real wage and lower, rather than higher, employment. This makes sense, however, since the reduced real output must mean reduced per capita real income all around. Investors are also worse off, because the price level does not rise by as much as the unit rise in business costs, given by the vertical shift in the SRAS curve, hence profits are squeezed. In the case under discussion, these losses occurred as wealth was transferred to OPEC.

Student Self-Test _____

I. True–False

T F **1.** A change or expected change in the absolute price level by some percentage would shift commodity supply and demand functions in the same direction, by the same percentage, *ceteris paribus*, including M_s and m_d.

T F **2.** In the absence of money illusion, proportional shifts of the money stock and the price level in the same direction would result in aggregate labor supply shifting in the same direction by the same percentage, *ceteris paribus*.

T F **3.** A rise in the nation's capital stock tends to increase the marginal product of labor, *ceteris paribus*.

T F **4.** If wage rates are downwardly rigid, a decline in the money stock will be neutral to real output, employment, and the real money stock, even in the short run.

T F **5.** The withdrawal of petroleum supplies from Western economies by OPEC in 1973 and again in 1979, with its attendant price increases, raised the MPL in the West and shifted *AD* toward the right.

II. Short Answer *(150 words or less each)*

1. Explain why *commodity* supply and demand functions must logically list real money balances as an independent variable.

2. Does the logic in Question 1 apply to financial asset supply and demand functions? What are the implications for the interest rate?

3. What is the significance for money neutrality and macro policy if the rate of wage inflation exhibits significant downward "stickiness?"

4. Distinguish clearly, in the case of a rise in the price level and money stock, between money illusion in labor supply, and incorrect price level expectations on the part of workers.

5. What is the policy dilemma associated with negative aggregate supply shocks?

III. Completion Problems

1. Suppose that when the price level is $P = 100$, the market supply function for good x can be written as $q_{s,x} = -20,000 + 16,000 \cdot p_x$, where $q_{s,x}$ is the quantity supplied and p_x is the nominal price of good x.

   A. Under these conditions firms supplying good x will be willing to supply 100,000 units at a unit price of (to the nearest cent) $p_x = \$$ _____. They will supply 140,000 units at $p_x = \$$ _____, and 200,000 units at $p_x = \$$ _____.

   B. Given the stated conditions, if the equilibrium quantity in the market was 100,000 the relative price of good *x* would be _____. At an equilibrium quantity of 140,000 the relative price would be _____.

C. Suppose that the money stock declines, causing wage rates and prices to decline in proportion, such that $P' = 87$. Suppose also that market participants are aware of this and suffer no money illusion. Under these conditions suppliers of good *x* should be willing to supply 100,000 units at a unit price of $p_x = \$$ _____, 140,000 units at $p_x = \$$ _____, and 200,000 units at $p_x = \$$ _____.

2. The *AD–AS* graph below shows the initial equilibrium values of an imaginary economy. The third quadrant incorporates in its notation certain assumptions about the aggregate labor market. The *AS* curve is not shown in the first quadrant because its shape is to be derived. Assume that prices and wage rates are flexible and that the central bank causes a permanent reduction in the money stock.

A. Draw on the graph, or on a copy, all shifts of the curves and changes in quantities that would occur as the system moved toward its new equilibrium.

B. Illustrate the sequence of the changes with numbered arrows.

C. Write a one-sentence explanation of the cause of each shift.

D. Find in the first quadrant the point of intersection of the new equilibrium output and price levels and derive the shape of the aggregate supply curve.

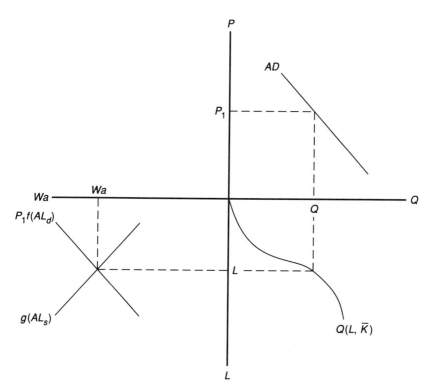

    E. At the end of this process the real money stock is _____ (greater than/smaller than) its initial magnitude.

    F. The real wage is _____ (greater than/smaller than) its initial magnitude after the new equilibrium is reached.

3. The *AD–AS* model in the following figure shows a hypothetical economy that differs from that shown in Question 2 only by its labor market behavior, which can be determined by inspection of the notation in the third quadrant. Assume that the same macroeconomic disturbance occurs as in Question 2.

    A. Draw on the graph, or on a copy, all shifts that would be produced by the disturbance and lead to a new equilibrium.

    B. Illustrate the sequence of the shifts with numbered arrows.

    C. Write a one-sentence explanation of each shift.

    D. Find the point of intersection between the new equilibrium output and price levels, and derive the shape of the *AS* curve.

    E. At the end of this process the real money stock is _____ its initial magnitude.

    F. The real wage is _____ its initial magnitude.

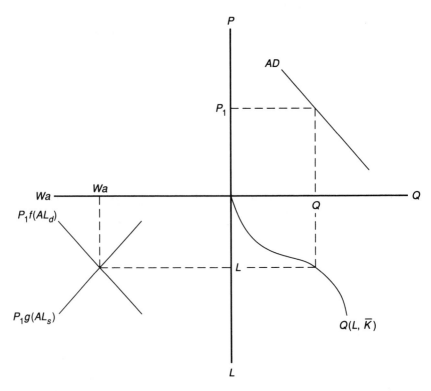

4. The *AD–AS* graph in the following figure is a real wage model with no money illusion, which incorporates an assumption that nominal wage rates are downwardly inflexible for the period under analysis. Assume, *ceteris*

paribus, that a positive supply shock occurs to the economy, perhaps in the
form of increased availability of raw materials ($Ra' > Ra$) at low cost.
- **A.** Show the attainment of the new equilibrium values by showing the shifts
  of the curves and variables that occur. Keep in mind the downward
  inflexibility of the wage rate.
- **B.** Illustrate the sequence with numbered arrows.
- **C.** The increase in quantity demanded along the *AD* curve in this case is
  accounted for by the _____ in the _____ as the price level _____.
- **D.** The real wage rises due to the rise in _____ and the fall in _____.

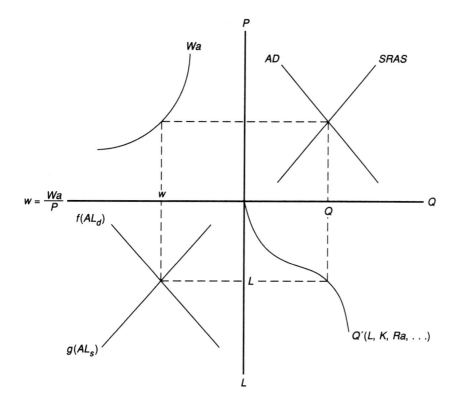

PART III

Keynesian Macroeconomics

CHAPTER 10

The Basic Keynesian Model

The most traumatic event in 20th-century U.S. history has been the Great Depression. Although real output and employment did not fall much until 1930, the depression began in 1929. A contractionary monetary policy and an announcement by President Hoover that he would sign the Hawley–Smoot Tariff then in Congress, caused an enormous drop in stock prices. When the tariff was signed in 1930, other nations responded with similar barriers to imports of our products. American agriculture, in particular, was dependent on foreign sales for major portions of its crops.

Farmers were indebted heavily at that time because the Fed had kept interest rates low during the 1920s. The loss of overseas markets meant that they could not pay their debts and many rural banks began to go broke. Frightened citizens ran on the banks to convert deposits to currency, raising Cu/D_d. Waves of rural bank failures spread to the city banks through correspondent relationships. The banks, liquidating assets to pay depositors, raised their reserves relative to deposits (R/D_d). The increases in the ratios of currency to deposits and reserves to deposits reduced the money multiplier (ϕ) and the money stock declined by one-third over three years. The Federal Reserve, which could have supplied sufficient reserves to the system to stop the contraction, failed to do so.[1]

It is not well known, but a monetary contraction that was almost as large occurred in 1920, creating the recession of 1920 to 1922. It was short lived, however, as prices and wages fell and equilibrium was restored. Prices and wage rates also fell in the early 1930s, but equilibrium was not restored. Why? In retrospect, many of the measures taken to alleviate the harsh conditions of the depression acted to prolong it. President Herbert Hoover, for example, made strenuous efforts to keep wage rates from falling, on a theory that maintaining wage rates maintained purchasing power. The result was that, although wage rates fell, they did not fall as much as prices did, and the real wage rate increased significantly. This fact alone should eliminate any misunderstanding about the magnitude of depression unemployment.[2]

Elected in 1932, Franklin Roosevelt began an extremely activist set of governmental measures intended to help the economy. In fact, they administered a series of recessionary shocks. Major sections of industry were cartelized for a time under provisions of the National Industrial Recovery Act of 1933 and encouraged to reduce output, terminating an expansion begun earlier in that year. Public works, welfare programs, and unemployment compensation helped the unemployed but reduced incentives to work, which raised the natural rate of unemployment. The income tax was greatly increased in both 1933 and 1936, further reducing production incentives. Just as the economy was beginning to recover, the Wagner Act (1935) was passed, forcing several million workers into unions.[3] A large series of strikes followed, which increased unemployment and reduced real output to deep depression levels.[4]

Despite the failure of these governmental policies to end the depression, Franklin Roosevelt was reelected three times and hailed as a hero, and the severity and length of the contraction came to be interpreted as a failure of the free market. Public attitudes toward the relative roles of the private and public sectors changed drastically. It became accepted that governmental action was necessary to stabilize the macroeconomy and to insure private citizens against virtually every possible detrimental contingency. Just why this interpretation was put on events and these conclusions reached is difficult to understand in retrospect, but probably had to do with the attitudes of intellectuals and opinion makers of the day. The greatest and most influential of these was John Maynard Keynes.

Fundamentals of the Keynesian Model

Keynes published a book in the midst of the depression that many economists found highly pursuasive.[5] The book provided a theoretical explanation and cure for the depression which was, while complex in detail, simple in essence. Basically, he argued that national income and employment were determined by the level of aggregate demand (AD), interpreted as total expenditure, but that private spending was unstable. Fluctuations in such spending resulted in recessions and expansions. Government, however, could alter both its own and certain private components of expenditure through alterations in its budget and could do so in such a way as to maintain total spending, and hence the level of income and employment, at the full employment level.

Keynes's theory is best explained beginning with the equation describing the measurement of GNP developed in Chapter 2. Upon substituting the generic aggregate income symbol for GNP,

$$Y = Co + I + G + (EX - IM).$$

The terms on the right-hand side are the components of total expenditure that constitute current aggregate demand. The term on the left-hand side is interpreted as current income. The simple identity becomes a theory by recognizing that current expenditure can be greater or less than current income. It follows that if $AD > Y$ national income rises, and if $AD < Y$ it falls. The equilibrium level of national income, from which the economy does not tend to deviate, *ceteris paribus*, therefore exists when $Y = AD$.

Two more vital assumptions of the Keynesian model should be identified before proceeding. First, when Y_f = the level of national income existing at full employment, Y_f is assumed constant. The model is therefore a short-run model, relating to periods over which the aggregate production function does not change significantly. Second, where in equation of exchange terms $Y = P \cdot Q$, the Keynesian model assumes the price level to be *given* and *constant* for all values of $Y \leq Y_f$, such that all $\Delta Y = \Delta Q$ over that range. The model is therefore a model of real output and income determination.

If the economy is in equilibrium when $AD = Y$ and changes in income result from changes in AD conceived as the sum of a set of expenditure categories, it is vital to explain the factors determining the magnitudes of the various components of expenditure. Keynes began by developing a theory of consumption and savings from the observation that all income is either spent on current consumption or saved. That is,

$$Y = Co + S.$$

It follows that any incremental change in income is divided the same way. That is,

$$\Delta Y = \Delta Co + \Delta S,$$

and if we divide through by ΔY we obtain

$$\frac{\Delta Y}{\Delta Y} = \frac{\Delta Co}{\Delta Y} + \frac{\Delta S}{\Delta Y}.$$

The term on the left-hand side is unity. The ratio $\Delta Co/\Delta Y$, termed the **marginal propensity to consume** (MPC) is the slope of a functional relationship between income and consumption spending. This hypothesized relationship is known as the **consumption function**. The ratio $\Delta S/\Delta Y$, or **marginal propensity to save** (MPS), is the slope of a similar relationship between savings and income. Because MPC + MPS = 1, as long as both are positive they are both numbers smaller than one. Keynes justified this assumption with his psychological law, which said that as people's incomes rise their consumption increases, but not by as much as the rise in their income.

Note the apparent circularity here: The magnitude of national income is to be explained as determined by the magnitude of expenditure, and the single largest component of expenditure, consumption, is immediately argued to be a function of income, $Co = Co(Y)$. The simplest form of the consumption function is a straight line, $Co = a + bY$, where a is the vertical intercept of the function, assumed to be positive, and b is the slope parameter, or MPC. Such a function is shown in the graph in Figure 10.1. Table 10.1 shows representative values of Y, a, bY and Co for a particular linear consumption function, $Co = a + bY = 20 + .75Y$. All dollar magnitudes are assumed to be in billions, for a modicum of realism.

Figure 10.2(a) shows a 45° line in $Co-Y$ space. If we assume that the scales are the same on both axes, the Cartesian coordinates on this line represent points at which income received and consumption expenditures are the same. Figure 10.2(b) interposes the consumption function with the 45° line and adds a new line labeled $S(Y)$, which is the **saving function**. If the consumption function is given as $Co = a + bY =$

Figure 10.1 The Consumption Function.

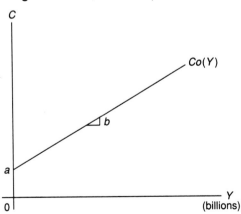

TABLE 10.1

Y	a	bY	C
0	20	0	20
20	20	15	35
40	20	30	50
60	20	45	65
80	20	60	80
100	20	75	95
120	20	90	110

$20 + .75Y$, then the saving function must be $S = -a + (1 - b)Y = -20 + .25Y$. This is because consumption of $20 billion at the intercept of the consumption function when income is zero can be financed only by drawing down past savings, so that current saving is $-$20 billion. Also, if the MPC $= b = .75$, then the MPS $= 1 - b = .25$ because MPS + MPC = 1. Note also that the point at which the consumption function crosses the 45° line (at $Y = $80 billion), so that $Co = Y$, S must be zero because $Y = Co + S$.

It makes little sense to talk of saving without discussing investment. The simplest way to treat investment in the model is to assume that it is a constant, independent of income. The level of investment can then be represented by a horizontal line of the appropriate dollar magnitude. Keynes's reasoning was that savers and investors were different people; hence not all savings necessarily got invested. Empirically, he observed that investment was highly variable, which led him to believe that it

Figure 10.2   The 45° Line and the Saving Function.

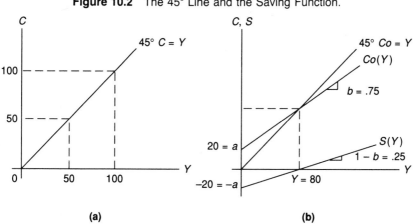

(a)   (b)

Figure 10.3 Investment As a Component of Aggregate Demand.

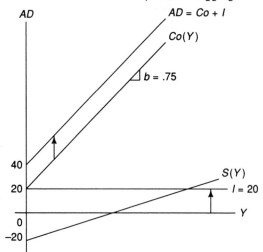

constituted the most active variable, changing the level of aggregate demand, and hence income.

Figure 10.3 shows a constant level of investment of \$20 billion. Adding this constant amount to the dollar value of consumption raises expenditure by \$20 billion at each income level. If we assume that all other components of expenditure are zero (which amounts to assuming a worldwide anarchic utopia), $Co + I = AD$, and the aggregate demand function has the same slope as $Co(Y)$.

Table 10.2 amends table 10.1 by adding columns for I and AD. The consumption function assumed is still $Co = 20 + .75Y$. Given the

TABLE 10.2

Y	Co	I	AD
0	20	20	40
20	35	20	55
40	50	20	70
60	65	20	85
80	80	20	100
100	95	20	115
120	110	20	130
140	125	20	145
160	140	20	160
180	155	20	175
200	170	20	190

equilibrium condition, $AD = Y$, the equilibrium level of aggregate income can be found by simple reading across the rows and comparing the values in the Y and AD columns. The equilibrium value is $160 billion. The economic process by which equilibrium is attained in this model can be seen better in Figure 10.4, which interposes an AD function with a 45° line, points on which now represent equality between AD and Y.

Suppose that the economy is at national income level Y. If this were the equilibrium value, aggregate demand would be AD, read on the 45° line. At income level Y, however, people wish to spend a larger amount (AD'), read on the aggregate demand line. Expenditure AD' raises income to $Y' = AD'$ in the next period. But the increase in income from Y to Y' raises desired expenditure through the MPC to AD'', which is larger than Y'. Expenditure of AD'' raises income in the next period to $Y'' = AD''$, at which point desired expenditure is still larger. The difference between income and desired expenditure keeps declining as income rises because MPC < 1, but income will keep rising until income level Y_e is reached, where $AD_e = Y_e$.

The opposite occurs for initial income levels greater than Y_e, such as Y_1. At Y_1, desired total expenditure is not $AD_1 = Y_1$, but $AD_1' < Y_1$. Income therefore falls over time to $Y_1' = AD_1'$. The fall in income, however, reduces desired total expenditure through the MPC to

Figure 10.4 Attaining Equilibrium Aggregate Income in the Keynesian Cross Model.

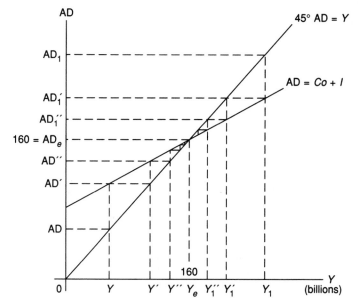

$AD_1'' < Y_1'$. Income falls again, therefore, to $Y_1'' = AD_1''$, which reduces desired expenditure again. Because MPC < 1, the difference between income and desired expenditure diminishes, but income keeps falling as long as $AD < Y$ until $Y_e = AD_e$.

An important clarification is needed here. For income levels less than Y_e, such that $AD > Y$, people must be reducing past savings to make the additional purchases, but another stock adjustment is also occurring. Income is earned through production, and aggregate income equals the aggregate value of goods and services produced. Expenditure in excess of income means the value of goods and services purchased exceeds the value of goods and services produced. The extra sales must be made from inventories. Therefore, whenever $AD > Y$, inventories must be falling, even if income, employment, and production are rising. The opposite is true for values of $Y > Y_e$, such that $AD < Y$. Expenditure less than income means that the value of goods purchased is less than that being produced and the difference must be accumulating in inventories.

The Savings–Investment Approach ─────────────

The process determining the equilibrium national income in the Keynesian model can also be shown by employing the savings and investment functions. If $Y = Co + I$ in equilibrium, and it is also the case that $Y = Co + S$ by definition, then in equilibrium

$$Co + S = Co + I$$
$$Co + S - Co = I$$
$$S = I.$$

Now suppose that $Y < Y_e$, as shown in Figure 10.5. That means that $Y < AD$, so $Co + S < Co + I$ or $Co + S - Co < I$, and therefore $S < I$ as also shown. The reason that total expenditure exceeds income is because the dollar value of investment exceeds saving. The extra AD makes income rise, which increases savings through the saving function until $S = I$ and $AD = Y_e$. If the initial situation was one in which $Y > Y_e$, it would follow that $Y > AD$, or $Co + S > Co + I$, such that $S > I$. In this case the failure of firms to invest an amount equal to current saving is the reason for the inadequate aggregate demand. Keynes thought that this was generally the cause of recessionary conditions. In such a case income would fall, reducing saving through the MPS until $S = I$ and $AD = Y$.

Figure 10.5 Saving-Investment Equilibrium in the Keynesian Model.

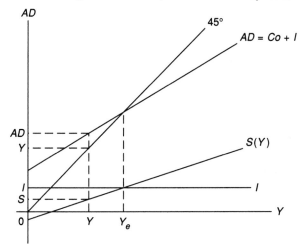

The rather odd character of this Keynesian equilibration mechanism can be illustrated by comparison with a more orthodox mechanism. Consider an initial income level Y_1 at which $S > I$, as shown in Figure 10.6 (b). Figure 10.6 (a) replicates the credit and capital market graph developed in Chapter 3, simplified only by ignoring consumer credit demand, so that the demand curve reflects only the demand for credit and capital for investment purposes, and is relabeled $I(i)$. Of course, if the functional relationships among savings, investment, and the interest rate shown in Figure 10.6 (a) hold, the interest rate

Figure 10.6 Classical and Keynesian Saving-Investment Equilibration Mechanisms.

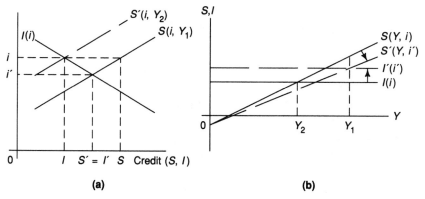

(a)   (b)

must be listed as a shift variable in those functions in Figure 10.6 (b), as shown.

The initial situation of $S > I$ at Y_1 in Figure 10.6 (a) can be shown to mean that the interest rate (i) is above the equilibrium implied by the initial functional relationships, $I(i)$ and $S(i, Y_1)$. Seen in terms of Figure 10.6 (a), the Keynesian mechanism means that income falls to Y_2 and shifts the saving function leftward until $S = I$ at interest rate i. There is another possibility, however. The interest rate could simply fall to i before income changed. This would increase the quantity of credit and capital demanded for investment purposes and decrease the quantity of savings until $S' = I'$ as shown. In Figure 10.6 (b) the interest rate decline would shift the investment line up to $I'(i')$, and the decline in savings at the initial income level Y_1 would mean a literal decline in the MPS, reducing the slope of the savings function until $S' = I'$ at Y_1.

The question seems to be which of these mechanisms logically operates quickest. Put in these terms, it is hard to give credence to the Keynesian mechanism. One of the most notable facts about credit and financial capital markets is the extremely high degree of price flexibility they exhibit. Also, there is another problem here. Seen in terms of Figure 10.6, the Keynesian mechanism depends on the investment function being written $I(i)$ so that it does not shift leftward with the saving function as income falls. If investment was a function of both the interest rate and income, or $I(i, Y)$, and investment declined as rapidly as the saving function did as income fell, falling income would not produce equilibrium.

Actually, more sophisticated Keynesian models do give investment some income elasticity, as we shall see. But all Keynesian models depend crucially on an assumption that investment has lower income elasticity than savings. The problem here is that there is no good theoretical justification for this assumption, at least not in the long run.[6]

Injections and Withdrawals

The saving–investment approach can easily be generalized to include the other components of total expenditure that have not yet been considered. Keynesians consider saving a **withdrawal** from the stream of expenditures, and investment an **injection** into that spending stream. Other items can be placed in the same categories, however. Taxes reduce spendable income, *ceteris paribus*. Expenditures on imports raise foreign, not domestic income. If **W** = the dollar value of with-

Figure 10.7 Equilibrium of Withdrawals and Injections in the Keynesian Model.

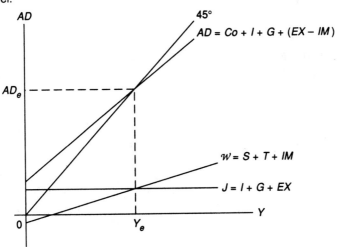

drawals, then,

$$\mathbf{W} = S + T + IM.$$

If we assume that government was financed by a lump-sum tax, so that taxes were not functionally related to income, adding the lump sum to the saving function would shift it upward without causing its slope to change from the MPS. If imports are independent of domestic income, their dollar value could also be added to the other withdrawals with the same effect.

As with investment, government expenditure can also be considered an injection and can be treated as independent of income. Adding the dollar value G to I will therefore yield a horizontal injection function with an intercept equal to the sum. The dollar value of exports of goods and services, which primarily depends on foreign, not domestic income, can be added in the same way. If $\mathbf{J}$ = injections, therefore,

$$\mathbf{J} = I + G + EX.$$

A critical assumption here is that injections and withdrawals are independent of one another and are equilibrated only in the aggregate through income changes, in the same way that saving and investment were equilibrated previously. In this generalized version of the model the equilibrium condition is not $S = I$, but $\mathbf{W} = \mathbf{J}$. The $AD = Y$ corollary still holds, although now $AD = Co + I + G + (EX - IM)$. These relationships are shown in Figure 10.7.

Inflationary and Recessionary Gaps in the Keynesian Model

So far, the discussion has centered on the nature of the mechanism determining the equilibrium value of national income in the Keynesian model with nothing said about recessions or expansions. Yet explaining such phenomena was precisely what Keynes intended, and his explanation provided two of the unique claims of his theory. What Keynes argued was that the equilibrium value of national income (Y_e) could be either less than or greater than Y_f, the full employment value, and that no automatic market mechanism existed to guarantee the restoration of Y_f in such cases.

Figure 10.8 shows a situation in which $Y_e < Y_f$. The horizontal difference between the two is the way the recessionary gap is shown in the Keynesian model, although some Keynesian texts define it as the vertical difference between AD and the dashed-line AD' at Y_e, or the amount by which aggregate demand needs to rise to restore Y_f. It should be pointed out that Y_e has a special interpretation here. By definition, equilibrium does not exist in the sense that markets are

Figure 10.8   Monetary Disequilibrium and a Keynesian Recessionary Gap.

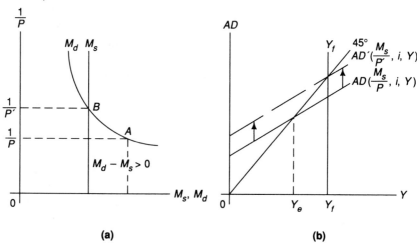

(a)   (b)

clearing if widespread unemployment and large unsold inventories of goods exist. This was why Y_e was defined previously as a value that had no tendency to change.

Serious questions arise as to whether $Y_e < Y_f$ really can be claimed to constitute an equilibrium value even in the restricted sense of not showing a tendency to change, however. A recession implies that $P(Q_d - Q_s) < 0$, or $Y_d - Y_s < 0$ (because $P \cdot Q = Y$); see Chapter 9. This is roughly equivalent to the $Y_e - Y_f < 0$ shown in Figure 10.8 (b). By Walras's law this implies that $M_d - M_s > 0$, as shown for the initial price level and value of money, $1/P$, in Figure 10.8 (a).

Chapter 5 makes it clear that such an excess demand for money would result in a balance of payments surplus, causing money to be imported from other countries if they used the same money or the exchange rates between different national monetary units were fixed. In Figure 10.8 (a) the domestic money stock would increase to some $M_s' = M_d$ at point A. In Figure 10.8 (b) the effect of the rise in the domestic money stock, as net exports became positive and foreign investment in the United States increased, would be to shift the aggregate demand function upward to AD' as shown, restoring equilibrium. This mechanism has operated many times in U.S. history, such as in the 1880s when the domestic demand for money increased, following restoration of the gold standard in 1879; see Chapter 17.

If different countries use distinct monetary units and exchange rates are flexible (as is currently the case for major Western nations), or if the money stock cannot automatically adjust through the balance of payments, because other nations are also experiencing excess demands for money, there is still the real balance mechanism. The price level, including the dollar prices of foreign currencies, would eventually fall, raise domestic real money balances to equality with real balances demanded, and restore equilibrium, as at point B in Figure 10.8 (a). Again, aggregate demand would rise as shown in Figure 10.8 (b), where AD is properly shown as a function of M_s/P.

For some decades Keynesian economists failed to recognize these mechanisms. Britain was off the gold standard when the general theory was written. Also, the Keynesian model takes the price level as given and holds it constant (for all $Y < Y_f$) by assumption. If prices are analytically held constant, it is hard to recognize the equilibrating effects of price changes. This is not to say that Keynesians never recognized the possibility of falling prices during a recession. Pressured on the matter by opponents, they often explicitly denied that reductions in wages and prices would produce equilibrium.[7]

In 1948 an economist named Don Patinkin rigorously demonstrated the real balance mechanism.[8] Patinkin was successful in defending the mechanism against Keynesian critics, and in the 1960s the monetarist

Figure 10.9 Monetary Disequilibrium and a Keynesian Inflationary Gap.

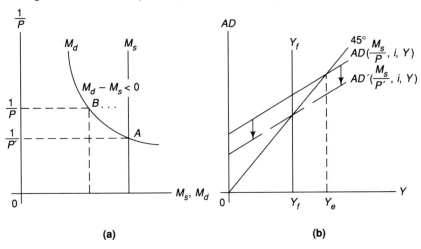

(a)   (b)

school emerged and began strongly defending the basic stability of the market. Currently, few sophisticated Keynesians deny that the market has an aggregate stabilizing mechanism. The sophisticated objection now is that it may take too long to operate, and that faster methods of eliminating unemployment, involving governmental policy, are available.

In the Keynesian model an expansionary or inflationary gap means that $AD = Y_e$, where $Y_e > Y_f$. This implies excess aggregate demand for commodities at Y_f, as shown in Figure 10.9 (b), and by Walras's law, an excess domestic supply of money, as shown in Figure 10.9 (a) for the initial price level P and value of money $1/P$. In early interpretations of the Keynesian cross model $AD > Y$ at Y_f caused nominal income to rise by raising prices, but not output or employment.

Today it is recognized that real output and employment can rise temporarily above the full employment level and that a rise in the level of wages and prices, by reducing M_s/P would tend to eliminate such an excess demand and restore equilibrium, *ceteris paribus*. Here again an alternate possibility, under a system of fixed exchange rates or common international money, would be for the excess domestic money stock to be eliminated through a balance of payments deficit (shifting leftward in Figure 10.9 (a) to equilibrium at point B). In a simple Keynesian cross model the effect of this decline in the domestic money stock would also be shown by a downward shift in AD until $AD' = Y$ at Y_f, as net exports became negative and foreign investment in the domestic economy declined.

The Mathematics of Equilibrium and Investment Multipliers _____

Given the basic assumptions of the Keynesian model, specification of the parameters allows the equilibrium level of national income to be solved for algebraically. For simplicity, assume a worldwide anarchic utopia as before, such that $AD = Co + I$ (because G, EX and IM all $= 0$). When the equilibrium condition is $Y = Co + I$ and $Co = a + bY$, let us also assume that $a = 20$ billion, $b = .75Y$, and $I = 20$ billion. By substitution,

$$Y = 20 + .75Y + 20$$
$$Y - .75Y = 40$$
$$Y(1 - .75) = 40$$
$$.25Y = 40$$
$$Y = \frac{1}{.25}(40)$$
$$= 160 \text{ billion.}$$

This is the value found in Table 10.2 for the same parameters.

In general, what may be termed the **structural form** of this model is given by three equations.

1. $Co = a + bY$.
2. $I = \bar{I}$ (where $\bar{I}$ indicates the fixed dollar value of investment).
3. $Y = Co + I$.

In order to solve for Y, we must construct a **reduced form** of the model, substituting **1** and **2** into **3** as follows:

$$Y = a + bY + I$$
$$Y - bY = a + \bar{I}$$
$$Y(1 - b) = a + \bar{I}$$
$$Y = \frac{1}{1 - b}(a + \bar{I}).$$

Also, because $b = \text{MPC}$ and the MPS $= 1 - b$, $Y = 1/\text{MPS}(a + \bar{I})$.

Next, note that given $Co(Y)$ and the 45° relationship a comparatively small ΔAD produces a significantly larger ΔY. Employing the same parameters as in the example above, $Co = 20 + .75Y$ and $\bar{I} = 20$, suppose that $\Delta \bar{I} = +10$ occurs, raising investment to $\bar{I}' = 30$, where $Y = Co + \bar{I}'$. This gives us

$$Y' = 20 + .75Y' + 30$$

$$.25Y' = 50$$

$$Y' = \frac{1}{.25}(50)$$

$$= 200.$$

In this case $\Delta I = +10$ yields $\Delta Y = +40$, so that $\Delta Y = 4\ \Delta I$ and $\Delta Y/\Delta I = 4$. Also note that $\Delta Y/\Delta I = 1/\text{MPS}$. The ratio $1/\text{MPS}$ is termed the **multiplier** (actually the **investment multiplier** in this case). The argument is that an injection of investment spending of this type increases income initially by the amount of the injection, then raises it further as each recipient of the expenditure spends a portion determined by that individual's MPC and saves a portion determined by the MPS. The ultimate ΔY is given by the limit of this process. Figure 10.10 illustrates the specific example just given. Also, the argument works in reverse. If investment were to fall back to 20, *ceteris paribus*, the equilibrium solution to the equation would once again be 160 billion.

At this point one of the oversimplifications of the basic model may be removed by assuming that investment also is a positive function of income. That is, $I = I(Y)$, and in linear form, $I = \bar{I} + zY$, when

Figure 10.10 The Keynesian Investment Multiplier.

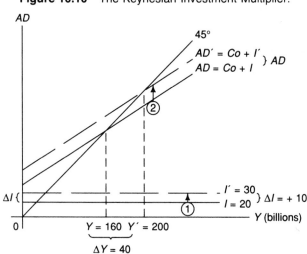

$\Delta I/\Delta Y = z$ is the **marginal propensity to invest** (MPI). A necessary stricture here, of course, is that the value of the MPI must be smaller than the MPS, (i.e., that investment is less income-elastic than saving, as previously argued). The effect of assuming that $0 < z <$ MPS is to give the investment line a positive slope and to make the slope of the AD line, $\Delta AD/\Delta Y = b + z$ (where $b + z < 1$) as shown in Figure 10.11.

The structural form of the model is now

$$
\begin{aligned}
&(1) \quad Y = Co + I, \\
&(2) \quad Co = a + bY, \\
&(3) \quad I = \bar{I} + zY.
\end{aligned}
$$

The reduced form of the model is therefore

$$Y = a + bY + \bar{I} + zY$$
$$Y - bY - zY = a + \bar{I}$$
$$Y(1 - b - z) = a + \bar{I}$$
$$Y = \frac{1}{1 - b - z}(a + \bar{I}),$$

and the multiplier is $\Delta Y/\Delta I = 1/(1 - b - z)$. Note that this is larger than $1/(1 - b)$.

Figure 10.11 Investment As a Positive Function of Income.

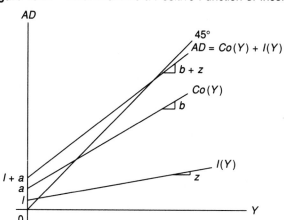

The Governmental Sector Multipliers _____

Because successful anarchic societies are infrequent, it is useful to add a governmental sector to the model. On the assumption that governmental spending is not a function of income, adding a fixed dollar value of expenditures $= G$ shifts the AD function upward vertically without changing its slope, as previously argued. Because governmental expenditures must be financed, the existence of taxation should also be assumed. The simplest form of taxation to include in the model is a lump-sum tax, $T = \bar{T}$. With $T > 0$, consumption becomes a function of after-tax income, usually termed **disposable income**. That is, $Co = Co(Y^d) = a + bY^d$, where $Y^d = Y - T$.

By maintaining the assumption that investment is a function of income, the structural form of the model now becomes

$$(1) \quad Y = Co + I + G,$$

$$(2) \quad Co = a + bY^d,$$

$$(3) \quad Y^d = Y - T,$$

$$(4) \quad T = \bar{T},$$

$$(5) \quad I = \bar{I} + zY, \text{ and}$$

$$(6) \quad G = \bar{G}.$$

The reduced form of the model becomes

$$Y = a + b(Y - \bar{T}) + \bar{I} + zY + \bar{G}$$

$$Y - bY - zY = a - b\bar{T} + \bar{I} + \bar{G}$$

$$Y(1 - b - z) = a - b\bar{T} + \bar{I} + \bar{G}$$

$$Y = \frac{1}{1 - b - z}(a - b\bar{T} + \bar{I} + \bar{G}).$$

The multipliers are easily found. The investment multiplier is still

$$\frac{\Delta Y}{\Delta I} = \frac{1}{1 - b - z}.$$

The governmental expenditure multiplier is

$$\frac{\Delta Y}{\Delta G} = \frac{1}{1 - b - z},$$

the same as the investment multiplier.

The tax multiplier looks somewhat different, however. Tax changes in this model affect AD and hence Y by altering Y^d, and hence consumption spending, in the opposite direction of the ΔT. The vertical shift of the consumption function (and of the AD line) in dollar terms is $-b \cdot \Delta T$, that is, $-b$ times the change in the lump sum. A \$10 billion increase in the tax, for example, with $b = .75$, would reduce Co (hence AD, *ceteris paribus*) by \$7.5 billion, the portion that would have been spent on consumption without the ΔT. From the equation above, the tax multiplier is

$$\frac{\Delta Y}{\Delta T} = \frac{-b}{1 - b - z}.$$

Note that the absolute value of the tax multiplier is smaller than that of the government expenditure multiplier because $b < 1$. In this model, therefore, identical increases in both government expenditure and the lump-sum tax would have a net positive effect on aggregate income, because the contractionary effect of the tax increase would be smaller than the expansionary effect of the $+\Delta G$. Identical decreases in both G and T would have a net contractionary effect on income for the same reason. This effect is termed the **balanced budget multiplier**, and its magnitude can be computed by specifying the relevant parameters. Where βu is the dollar magnitude of the budget, $\Delta Y/\Delta \beta u = \Delta Y/\Delta G + \Delta Y/\Delta T$. With this and other results, it is easy to see why government officials and policy advisers found themselves highly favorable to the Keynesian model.

Summary _____

The Keynesian model constructs the macroeconomy in a way that is different from both preceding and subsequent models. Before proceeding with the discussion of fiscal policy making in the Keynesian model, it may help to summarize its major assumptions.

1. Output and employment respond passively to the level of aggregate demand, at least until Y_f is reached.
2. Y_f is assumed constant for the period under analysis.
3. The price level is exogenously determined and is fixed for all $Y \le Y_f$.
4. Consumption and serving are functions of income.
5. The interest rate adjusts slowly under disequilibrium conditions.
6. The income elasticity of investment is lower than that of saving.
7. Injections and withdrawals are independent of one another.

Notes

1. Friedman and Schwartz attribute this failure of monetary policy to a struggle for power within the Federal Reserve following the death in 1928 of Benjamin Strong, who had headed the system from its inception. See *A Monetary History of the United States, 1867–1960*: 407–419. If this is true, it is a testament to the danger of placing larger discretionary power in the hands of fallible human beings.

2. Lowell Gallaway and Richard K. Vedder, "Wages, Prices, and Employment: Von Mises and the Progressives," *Review of Austrian Economics* 1 (1987): 33–80. Worse, the real wage kept rising throughout the Depression, rather than adjusting down to equilibrium. Vedder and Gallaway estimate that if the real wage had stayed at its 1933 level, unemployment in 1937 would have been 2.4 percent rather than 14.3 percent.

3. See Morgan O. Reynolds, *Power and Privilege: Labor Unions in America* (New York: Manhattan Institute for Public Policy Research, 1984): 92–132.

4. Gallaway and Vedder, op. cit., estimate that union activity following the New Deal labor legislation added five percentage points to the unemployment rate. On all these events see Karl Brunner, *Contemporary Views on the Great Depression* (New York: Martinus Nijhoff, 1980), and Benjamin M. Anderson, *Economics and the Public Welfare: A Financial and Economic History of the United States, 1914–1946* (New York: D. Van Nostrand Co., 1949).

5. John Maynard Keynes, *The General Theory of Employment, Interest and Money* (New York: Harcourt Brace Jovanovich, 1936).

6. A theoretical justification for high short-run income elasticity of saving is provided, oddly enough, by the modern permanent income hypothesis that permanent consumption is a function only of permanent income, where that expectation adjusts only partially to income surprises in the current period, as explained in Chapter 3. This appears to be a case of monetarist theory actually rehabilitating Keynesian economics.

7. On the theoretical debate between Keynesians and their opponents over the equilibrating effects of wage and price flexibility, see Mark Blaug, *Economic Theory in Retrospect* (3rd ed., Cambridge, England: Cambridge University Press, 1978): 675–691.

8. Don Patinkin, "Price Flexibility and Full Employment," *American Economic Review* 38 (September 1948): 543–564. For a far more complete exposition, however, see his *Money, Interest and Prices: An Integration of Monetary and Value Theory* (2nd ed., New York: Harper and Row, 1965).

Student Self-Test

I. True–False

T F **1.** In the Keynesian model a condition in which investment expenditure exceeds the amount saved out of current national income implies that aggregate equilibrium income is above the full employment level.

T F **2.** In the basic Keynesian cross model, saving is assumed to be a positive function of the interest rate.

T F **3.** If total injections equal total withdrawals in the Keynesian model, saving need not equal investment and imports need not equal exports.

T F **4.** The marginal propensity to consume (MPC) describes the rate at which consumption expenditure changes as the interest rate changes.

T F 5. According to the basic Keynesian model, a reduction in a lump-sum tax raises income by raising disposable income and hence investment spending.

II. *Short Answer (150 words or less each)* _____

1. What is the logic and perception behind Keynes's view that private aggregate expenditure is unstable because private investment is unstable?
2. What view of aggregate supply appears to inhere in the Keynesian model? (You may illustrate your argument by drawing an aggregate supply curve in P–Q space exhibiting the properties implied by the Keynesian view.)
3. Write a brief Keynesian interpretation of the origin and duration of the Great Depression.
4. Suppose equilibrium national income is $Y_e < Y_f$ because $I < S$. Keynes believed that no aggregate equilibrating mechanism existed to guarantee that income, output, and employment would be restored to the full employment level. Briefly describe two mechanisms.
5. Beginning with a decline in private investment at some initial aggregate income level, write a brief Keynesian description of the process by which the economy reaches its new equilibrium. Focus specifically on the key theoretical relationships assumed by Keynes, particularly saving and investment.

III. *Completion Problems*

1. Assume that $Y = Co + I + G$, where $I = \$200$, $G = \$300$, $T = \$250$ (lump sum), $Co = \$1000 + .8Y^d$, and all dollar magnitudes are in billions.
   A. The equilibrium values are
   $Y = \$$_____ $Co = \$$_____ $S = \$$_____ $I + G =$ _____.
   B. Given $\Delta G = +\$50$, *ceteris paribus*, the new equilibrium values are
   $Y = \$$_____ $Co' = \$$_____ $S' = \$$_____ $I + G' =$ _____.
2. Given the following definitions, assume a worldwide anarchic utopia in which investment is a function of income.

Co = consumption expenditure

I = investment expenditure

G = government expenditure

Y = aggregate income

T = tax function

Y_d = aggregate disposable income

a = autonomous consumption

b = MPC

z = MPI

t = marginal income tax rate

A. Write the structural form of the Keynesian model that describes this economy.
B. Derive the reduced form of the model.
C. Symbolically, the investment multiplier is $K_I =$ _____ .
D. Now assume that the economy has a government that is financed by a lump-sum tax and write the structural form of the Keynesian model of this economy.
E. Derive the reduced form of this model.
F. The government expenditure multiplier is $K_G =$ _____ and the tax multiplier is $K_T =$ _____ .

CHAPTER 11

Fiscal Policy in the Keynesian Model

The Keynesian model explains recessionary gaps as the result of a decline in total expenditure, such that aggregate demand is less than income at full employment, and inflationary gaps as the result of increases in AD, making it greater than income at full employment. Two views of aggregate demand interpreted as total expenditure have been presented in this book. In terms of the equation of exchange, where $M_s \cdot V = P \cdot Q$, $AD = M_s \cdot V$. In the Keynesian formulation, $AD = Co + I + G + (EX - IM)$. These statements must be equivalent in some sense, and they are. The Keynesian statement implies the existence of a money stock in its dollar magnitudes and lists in broad categories, for analytical purposes, the types of expenditures that money is spent on.

In Chapters 5 to 8 recessionary gaps were analyzed in terms of fluctuations in the money stock or the demand for money, and issues in the employment of monetary policy for macroeconomic stabilization were explored. By assuming the money stock and full employment level of output to be constant (or, in dynamic terms, growing at the same rate), any ΔAD causing a recessionary or inflationary gap, even if seen in Keynesian terms as originating with a change in some expenditure category, must involve a change in the velocity of money (i.e., in m_d, because $M_d/P = 1/V \cdot Q^*$). Also, M_s given, any governmental policy to be successful in eliminating such a gap, must do so by altering velocity. Indeed, one of the great theoretical contributions of Keynesian economics was a claim that government could alter AD through a policy completely separate and distinct from monetary policy. This method is termed **fiscal policy**.

The Budget and Fiscal Policy ───────────────────

Where $\mathbf{W} = S + T + IM$ and $\mathbf{J} = I + G + EX$, notice that one component of each (taxation and government expenditure) is related to the federal budget. It seems a straightforward conclusion that the government can alter the levels of injections and withdrawals and hence alter AD by changing the magnitude and/or relative state of its own budget. There are three states of the budget distinct from its magnitude. First, equality of government expenditure and tax revenue, $G = T$, at whatever relative (to the rest of the economy) or absolute magnitude, is termed a **balanced budget**. Second, a condition of $G > T$, such that $T - G < 0$, is termed a budget **deficit**. Last, a condition of $G < T$, such that $T - G > 0$, is termed a **surplus** in the budget.

Any change in the budget aimed at increasing AD in order to raise national income and employment is termed an **expansionary fiscal policy**. In Keynesian terms, there are basically four such policies.

1. *An increase in G, with T constant or increasing less than G.* This involves creating a deficit (if $G = T$ initially), increasing an existing deficit (if $G > T$ initially), or reducing a surplus (if $G < T$ initially).

2. *A reduction in T, with G constant or decreasing much less* (so that the expansionary effect of the tax reduction exceeds the contractionary effect of the reduction in G). This also involves creating a deficit, increasing an existing deficit, or reducing an existing surplus.

3. *An increase in G, combined with a decrease in T.* The same budgetary effects would result here.

4. *An equal increase in both G and T.* In the Keynesian model this would have an expansionary effect due to the balanced budget multiplier discussed in Chapter 10.

A fiscal policy aimed at reducing AD, inflation and income is termed a **contractionary fiscal policy**. There are four types of such policy.

1. *An increase in T, with G constant or increasing much less.* This would create a surplus if $G = T$ initially, increase an existing surplus, or reduce an existing deficit.

2. *A decrease in G, with T constant or decreasing less.* This also would either create or increase a surplus, or reduce a deficit.

3. *A decrease in G, combined with an increase in T.* Here again the same budgetary effects would result.

4. *An equal decrease in both G and T.* In the Keynesian model the balanced budget multiplier would be contractionary in this case.

One of the impressive things about the Keynesian model has been the simple and precise solutions this framework seems to offer for stabilization problems. If we assume that the theory is correct, all that is required is knowledge of the relevant parameters and the magnitude of the recessionary or expansionary gap. The necessary policy adjustments are immediately obvious. If $Y_f - Y_e$ is the magnitude of the gap, what is needed is $\Delta Y = Y_f - Y_e$. Defining the governmental expenditure multiplier as $\Delta Y/\Delta G = K_G$, we find that the $\Delta G = \Delta AD$ necessary to eliminate the gap is computed as follows.

$$\Delta Y = K_G \cdot \Delta G$$

$$Y_f - Y_e = K_G \cdot \Delta G$$

$$\frac{Y_f - Y_e}{K_g} = \Delta G$$

A numeric example may help. Suppose that $Y_e = \$200$ billion, Y_f is estimated to be \$240 billion, and it is estimated that $K_G = 5$. The recessionary gap is $Y_f - Y_e = \$40$ billion. \$40 billion/5 = $\Delta G = \$8$ billion is the increase in government expenditure needed to produce full employment and prosperity, *ceteris paribus*. This example, is illustrated in Figure 11.1 with one modification: The first event shown is an

Figure 11.1 Raising Government Expenditure to Eliminate a Recession.

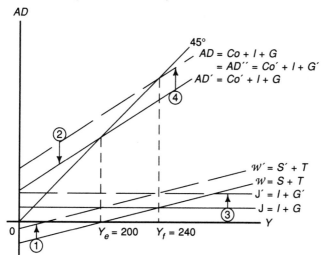

increase in private saving, which creates the recessionary gap by reducing Co to Co' and AD to AD'.

As an alternate policy, AD could be raised through a tax reduction, where $\Delta AD = \Delta Co = -b \cdot \Delta T$. If we define the lump-sum tax multiplier as $\Delta Y / \Delta T = K_T$, it follows that $\Delta Y = K_T \cdot \Delta T$, and $\Delta Y / K_T = \Delta T$ is needed to eliminate the gap. Suppose that the tax multiplier is $K_T = -4$. $\$40/-4 = -\$10$ billion is the lump-sum tax reduction needed to raise AD enough to eliminate the gap.

Because a lump-sum tax is unrealistic, it may be useful to complicate the model slightly at this point by introducing an income tax. To avoid excessive complexity, however, let us give the tax function a linear form by assuming that the government is financed by a combination lump-sum and proportional income tax in which everyone pays the same percentage. This alters the form of the consumption function somewhat. Where previously $T = \bar{T}$,

$$Co = a + bY^d$$
$$= a + b(Y - T).$$

Now the tax function is $T = \bar{T} + tY$, and $t =$ the (flat) marginal tax rate. So the consumption function becomes

$$Co = a + b(Y - \bar{T} - tY)$$
$$= a + bY - b\bar{T} - btY$$
$$= a - b\bar{T} + b(1 - t)Y.$$

Figure 11.2 Lump Sum and Proportional Income Tax in the Keynesian Cross.

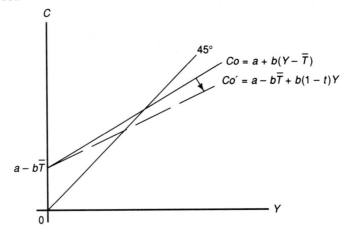

The effect of adding a proportional income tax to the lump sum is to reduce the slope of the consumption function (and hence the AD line, *ceteris paribus*) as shown in Figure 11.2, because $b(1 - t) < b$ if $t > 0$. The structural form of the model now becomes

$$(1) \qquad Y = Co + I + G,$$

$$(2) \qquad Co = a + bY^d,$$

$$(3) \qquad Y^d = Y - T,$$

$$(4) \qquad T = \bar{T} + tY,$$

$$(5) \qquad I = \bar{I} + zY,$$

$$(6) \qquad G = \bar{G}.$$

The reduced form is therefore

$$Y = a + b(Y - \bar{T} - tY) + \bar{I} + zY + \bar{G}$$
$$= a - b\bar{T} + b(1 - t)Y + \bar{I} + zY + \bar{G}$$
$$Y - b(1 - t)Y - zY = a - b\bar{T} + \bar{I} + \bar{G}$$
$$Y[1 - b(1 - t) - z] = a - b\bar{T} + \bar{I} + \bar{G}$$

$$Y = \frac{1}{1 - b(1 - t) - z} (a - b\bar{T} + \bar{I} + \bar{G}).$$

Note that the multipliers in this model are smaller than when $T = \bar{T}$, as expected, because $1 - b(1 - t) - z > 1 - b - z$.

With this form of the tax function, there are now two methods of changing taxes in order to alter aggregate demand in the Keynesian model. Consider the recessionary gap in which $Y_e = 200$, $Y_f = 240$, and $\Delta Y = 40$ is needed to eliminate the gap. Suppose that the tax function is $T = \bar{T} + tY = 20 + .25Y$ and that the government wants to eliminate the gap by reducing the income tax rate rather than by reducing the lump sum as before.

The first step is to estimate what the tax revenue would be if the economy were at Y_f, given the initial tax structure. Because $Y_f = 240$,

$$T = \bar{T} + tY$$
$$= 20 + .25(240)$$
$$= 20 + 60$$
$$= 80 \text{ billion.}$$

If the lump-sum tax multiplier was $K_T = -4$, a reduction of the lump sum by 10 billion would eliminate the gap. That would result in tax revenue at Y_f of

$$T' = \bar{T}' + tY$$
$$= 10 + .25(240)$$
$$= 10 + 60$$
$$= 70 \text{ billion.}$$

Given this information, it is simple to calculate the Δt that will yield the same ΔT and hence the same level of disposable income and aggregate demand at Y_f.

$$T' = \bar{T} + t'Y$$
$$70 = 20 + t'(240)$$
$$70 - 20 = t'(240)$$
$$\frac{50}{240} = t'$$
$$.2083 \approx t'$$

A reduction of the income tax rate to just under 21 percent would therefore eliminate the gap. Instead of shifting the whole AD function upward, however, as the ΔG did in Figure 11.1, the lower income tax rate would raise the slope of the AD line (without changing the intercept) such that it passed through the 45° line at Y_f.

Automatic Stabilizers and the Full Employment Budget

With taxation modeled as a function of income, it should also be pointed out that a significant portion of federal expenditures also bear some functional relationship to the level of aggregate income. In particular, income maintenance expenditures such as welfare, farm subsidies, unemployment compensation, and social security, which have come to compose the bulk of the budget in recent years, are inversely related to aggregate income, rising as income falls during recessions and falling as income rises during expansions.

Note that an inverse relationship between G and Y and a positive relationship between T and Y (an income tax) both have the effect of reducing the slope of the AD function, making the multiplier smaller, and reducing the ΔY resulting from a given shift in the function. As a consequence, Keynesians term such expenditures and taxation **automatic stabilizers**. The idea is that recessionary conditions cause G to rise and T to fall, both of which add to aggregate demand and reduce the decline in income. Expansionary conditions, in contrast, cause G to fall and T to rise, both of which act to reduce AD and hence inflationary pressures. Thus with no active governmental policy at all the business cycle is smoothed. However, this and other features of the Keynesian model rely crucially on the assumption of independence of injections and withdrawals, which will be argued to be highly dubious.

Another way in which treating taxation and government spending as functions of income changes things may be mentioned here. So far, the term *expansionary* has referred to any increase in the budget that, in the Keynesian model, raises income from an initial level. The term *contractionary* has meant the opposite. These definitions are essentially correct, but the expansionary or contractionary character of government fiscal policy cannot be judged simply by observing the state of the budget itself at a given income level because the state of the budget can change over the business cycle, even in the absence of a policy change.

For a given level or function of government expenditures, an income tax tends to reduce the deficit as income rises (because revenues increase and expenditures decrease). Also, a budget surplus tends to decline as income falls, because of falling revenue and increasing federal expenditures. For given tax and expenditure functions, then, (and a given aggregate production function) there is a particular income level that would balance the budget. Two such budget functions, labeled βu and $\beta u'$, are shown in Figure 11.3

Figure 11.3 The Full Employment Budget.

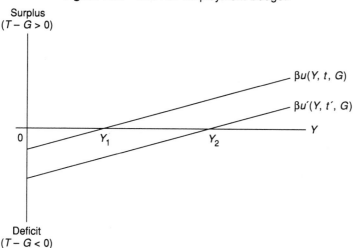

Note that budget function βu is balanced at income level Y_1, while it takes a higher income level Y_2 to balance budget function $\beta u'$. The difference is that the income tax rate in $\beta u'$ is t', where $t' < t$. Clearly, for a given level or function of governmental expenditures, the lower the income tax rate is, the higher income must be for the budget to be in balance. It follows that a decrease in the tax rate shifts the budget function downward and an increase in the tax rate shifts it upward, *ceteris paribus.* On the other hand, for a given tax function, the higher G is, the higher Y must be to raise T enough to balance the budget. A policy raising G therefore shifts the budget function downward and a policy reducing G shifts it upward, *ceteris paribus.*

In order to distinguish such policy-induced changes in the budget from changes caused by the state of the business cycle, Keynesian economists developed the notion of the **full-employment budget**, which is an estimate of the surplus or deficit that would exist if the economy were at Y_f. Suppose, for example, that the economy is at Y_1 in Figure 11.3, that $Y_2 = Y_f$ and that the existing budget function is $\beta u'$. Although the budget would be in deficit, a Keynesian economist would argue that policy was neither contractionary nor expansionary, because the budget would be in balance if the economy were at Y_f. If the existing budget function were βu, such that $G = T$ at Y_1, it would be argued that policy was highly contractionary, because the budget would be in surplus at Y_f. Only if the full-employment budget was estimated to be in deficit would Keynesians characterize policy as expansionary.

A few weak points in the argument should be noted. For one, statistical estimates of revenues and expenditures at different income levels often turn out to be highly inaccurate. Second, estimates of Y_f have the same tenuous character. The estimate of the high-employment budget therefore rests on two highly dubious estimates. Graphically, whether policy is expansionary or contractionary depends upon the estimated budget function and on where Y_f is placed on the horizontal axis. Estimates of this type are easily manipulated for political purposes because they rest on many arbitrary assumptions, and some economists place little faith in policy conclusions drawn from them.

Fiscal Finance and the Multiplier _____

Here the character and certain problems of the Keynesian model can be clarified by asking and answering two questions: In the case of a deficit, where does the federal government obtain the funds to finance expenditure in excess of tax revenue, and in the case of a surplus, what does it do with the extra funds? The answers to these questions cast severe doubt on the Keynesian assumption that injections and with-drawals can be considered to be independent of one another (such that a change in one does not cause an offsetting change in another) and that pure fiscal policy can therefore alter aggregate demand.

Beginning with the first question, suppose that the budget is initially in balance and that the government then decides to run a deficit of $100 billion. The first thing to occur is that the Treasury tells the Govern-ment Printing Office to print up $100 billion worth of goverment bonds. The government obtains the money by selling the bonds, and the only options it faces concern to whom it sells the bonds. The first option is to sell them to the Federal Reserve. In this case the bonds enter the books of the Fed as assets, as shown in Table 11.1. The Fed pays the Treasury for the bonds by crediting the Treasury's deposit on its books with the amount of the purchase as shown.

The Treasury now has $100 billion more on deposit than before the bond sale. At this point it writes checks and spends the $100 billion on whichever programs, military or domestic, that Congress had intended the money to finance. The recipients of the checks cash them at their commercial banks, which then send the checks to the Fed for clearing. The Fed, upon receiving the checks, debits the deposits of the Treasury by $100 billion and credits the reserve deposits of the commercial banks with the same amount; this sequence of entries is illustrated by circled numbers in Table 11.1. At that point the monetary base is increased and the money stock rises by $\Delta M_s = \phi \cdot \Delta B$.

This method of deficit finance, by which the sale of U.S. government securities to the Fed increases the money stock, is called **debt monetiza-tion**. In this case, monetary policy and fiscal policy are combined, and because $AD = M_s \cdot V$, no problem exists in understanding how AD may rise. A combined policy confuses matters, however, because what is at issue here is whether policy-induced changes in the federal budget are expansionary or contractionary in and of themselves. In order to distinguish fiscal policy from monetary policy, then, the option of

TABLE 11.1 Federal Reserve

Assets	Liabilities	
U.S. Government Securities	Currency and coin	
① +$100 billion		$B = C + R$
	Reserves of commercial	
Loans to commercial	banks	
banks	④ +$100 billion	
	Treasury deposits	
	② +$100 billion	
	③ −$100 billion	

monetizing debt must be excluded from consideration, although in the real world, some portion of a deficit is almost always monetized.

The government's second option is to sell its bonds to the commercial banks and the public. In this case, after all checks are written, cashed, and cleared the monetary base and the money stock are uneffected. This may be termed a **pure fiscal policy**. Such government borrowing competes with private demand, however, for a limited available supply of financial credit and capital. Figure 11.4(a) shows private demand, D_p, and the saving function interacting to determine the initial interest rate. The quantities saved and invested by private parties are equated at I, which is the initial level of investment shown in Figure 11.4(b), the Keynesian cross diagram.

The entry of government into the market to obtain financing for the deficit shifts the total demand function outward to D_{p+g}, the sum of the private and governmental demand. This large increase in demand raises the interest rate to i', which causes a reduction in the quantity of private credit demanded, reducing private investment to I'. This is termed **crowding out**. In the absence of such crowding out the increase in government expenditure would raise aggregate demand to $AD' = Co + I + G'$. The decline in investment from I to $I' < I$, however, at least partially offsets the increase in G.

Now note that if the saving function were perfectly interest-inelastic (vertical), the resulting reduction in private investment would exactly equal and hence totally offset the increase in government expenditure. It does not, because the saving function is upward sloping, such that saving increases to S'. By Keynes's own logic, however, where $Y = C_o + S$, a rise in saving at the initial income level implies a matching decline in consumption, say to $Co' < Co$. Logically and graphically,

Figure 11.4 Pure Fiscal Policy and Crowding Out.

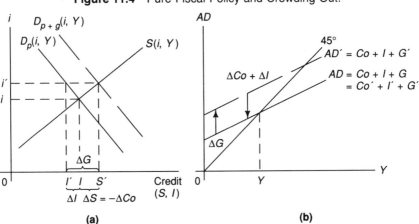

(a)

(b)

the declines in investment and consumption exactly match the $+ \Delta G$, such that neither AD nor Y are increased by the rise in the deficit.

A similar story could be told about a surplus generated, say by a reduction in government expenditure from an initial balanced budget. The government essentially has two optional uses of the extra funds: It could deposit them in the Treasury account at the Fed or pay off past accumulated debt. Excluding the first option because it would reduce the money stock (and we are concerned with the effect of pure fiscal policy), paying off government bondholders would result in increased consumption and investment matching the reduction in government spending, such that $\Delta AD = 0$.

The only way to save the Keynesian story about $\Delta \beta u$ causing ΔAD is through the effect of interest rate changes on the demand for money. In monetary terms, a Keynesian story of recession and fiscal correction might read as follows: A decrease in investment demand or an increase in saving causes the interest rate to fall, increasing M_d relative to M_s (in the equation of exchange terms, reducing V and hence AD) and, by Walras's law, causing a recession, as shown in Figure 5.6 (see Chapter 5), or Figure 10.8(a) (see Chapter 10). The government then increases the deficit, raising the interest rate back to the initial level as it borrows the funds. The rise in the interest rate reduces the demand for money (raising V and hence AD), eliminating the recession.

A version of this argument is, in fact, embodied in the sophisticated Keynesian $IS-LM$ model developed in Chapter 12. In that model the effects of deficit finance in raising AD are only partly offset by crowding out because of the effect of the associated Δi on desired money balances. There is a long-term effect that is ignored by this argument, however, because all versions of the Keynesian model concern themselves only with the short run, in which the capital stock does not change. Ongoing deficit finance, by reducing investment, can reduce capital stock growth over time, thus reducing the growth rates of productivity and output. Indeed, chronic and increasing deficits combined with poor performance in such variables since the early 1970s, have recently caused even the Democrats in Congress (traditionally the advocates and defenders of Keynesian policies) to become worried about the effects of crowding out.

The Ricardian Equivalence Doctrine ⎯⎯⎯⎯⎯⎯⎯⎯⎯

Another problem with the Keynesian story stems from a new crowding-out argument. Because the market establishes the price of a bond at the discounted present value of its future income flow and the income from government bonds is paid from tax revenues, several economists have recently pointed out that bond issuance to cover a deficit implies future taxation of identical present value. Therefore, bond issuance does not increase wealth in the present. The failure to recognize this constitutes **bond illusion**, which is an irrationality like money illusion.

Rational consumers, recognizing the future taxes implied by debt finance, will increase savings in the present by enough to generate just the additional future income required to pay the future taxes. Graphically, as government borrowing shifted the credit demand function outward in Figure 11.4, the saving function would shift outward by an equal amount. The interest rate would not change, but the increased government expenditure would be matched by an identical drop in present consumption expenditure, preventing any change in AD or Y. This is termed **tax discounting**, or the **Ricardian equivalence doctrine**, after David Ricardo, who argued that people might be indifferent to a choice between taxation or bond finance of deficits.

One objection to this line of reasoning is that people have finite lifespans. Much of the population living at the time of Federal debt issuance will not have remaining lifespans long enough that they might expect to experience all of the implied future taxation. For such people, it is argued, some fraction of the value of federal government bonds issued will represent net wealth. Hence aggregate expenditure will increase, causing aggregate income to rise through the multiplier.

Critics are not persuaded by the finite lifespans argument, however, if people with finite lifespans intend to bequeath wealth and assets to their children from altruistic motives, as seems widely the case, then they would act in the present as if they had infinite lifespans. They would discount all future taxation implied by present federal debt issuance and increase their present saving to offset the implied decline in the future living standard of their descendents (who will bear some part of the taxation).[1]

If tax discounting occurs and is total, it may explain one of the puzzles of modern macroeconomics: the failure of repeated empirical studies to find a significant positive relationship between the magnitude of deficits and the interest rate.[2] The fact that the large deficits of the Reagan administration were associated with a decline and not a rise in the gross private saving rate (i.e., the sum of private and business saving divided by GNP), however, and that there were high real interest rates, has cast some doubt on the notion that tax discounting is complete.

Some economists have argued that there is a logically consistent reason for bond illusion—that tax discounting should not be total. This is because holders of government bonds can be almost completely certain that their interest and principle will be paid. It follows that the present value of government debt will be set by the market at the value of the future interest and principle payments discounted by a low, no-risk interest rate. For taxpayers, however, the amount to be paid in the future is uncertain, so the tax payments will be discounted at a higher interest rate. It follows that the reduction of perceived wealth for taxpayers will be smaller than the increase for bondholders and that government debt issuance will generate net wealth.[3]

This counterargument is subtle and persuasive, although the issue is still hotly debated. Whether right or wrong, it should be noted that this is not an argument that implies particulary strong effects of budget changes on AD, but rather weak effects. This is because the addition to net wealth generated by bond issuance, for example, will only equal the difference between the discounted present values of the future interest payments and the future expected taxes. Also, this may mean that crowding out will occur by the conventional process.

International Transactions and Crowding Out _____

The reader who remembers the discussion of international investment flows and portfolio adjustments in Chapter 3 might perceive another aspect of the crowding out debate that is highly relevant for recent U.S. history. As shown in Figure 11.5 (which is derived from

Figure 11.5 Limited Interest Rate Effect of a Deficit with International Investment.

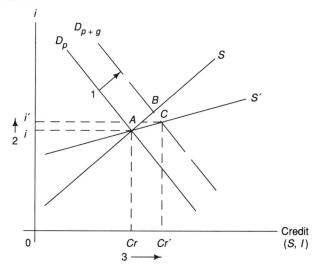

Figure 3.11), if Americans are free to invest at home and abroad and foreigners are free to do the same, the credit and financial capital supply function in the U.S. economy is more elastic than it would be in the absence of such opportunities. That is, it would look more like S' than S.

In such a case a given increase in demand for financial capital resulting from an increase in the federal deficit, as shown, raises the domestic interest rate by a smaller amount than it would if the new interest rate were determined at point B rather than at point C. This is because the rise in the U.S. interest rate relative to those in other countries causes two things to happen: Some U.S. investment abroad shifts homeward, and some foreign investment abroad shifts to the United States.

This may cause the United States to experience what is termed a **capital account surplus**, in which the dollar value of U.S. government and private securities and assets sold to foreigners exceeds the value of foreign securities and assets purchased by Americans. This happened in the 1980s. As the federal deficit expanded, foreign net investment in the United States from people in countries such as Britain and Japan reached large magnitudes.

At first glance it might appear that such an inflow of foreign (and domestic) funds through the Capital Account in the U.S. balance of international payments as the deficit rises allows escape for the Keynesian model from crowding-out phenomena. The lower increase in the interest rate reduces the crowding out of private investment (compare Figures 11.5 and 11.4(a) and reduces the increase in private saving, so that less domestic consumption is crowded out. The inflow of foreign funds covers the disparity between domestic saving (which is actually reduced, because the deficit is a form of *dissaving*) and investment.

This escape is illusory, however. As pointed out in Chapter 5, the major international trading nations now employ a flexible exchange rate system. If allowed, exchange rates between national monetary units adjust almost continuously to clear those markets, such that national balances of payments are zero. That is, the value of U.S. sales to foreigners of all $n - 1$ items, goods, services, and financial assets, will equal the value of their aggregate purchases of such items from foreigners.

In such a case, a domestic capital account surplus, in which we sell a higher value of our financial assets to foreigners than we buy from foreigners (as net foreign investment here occurs) will be matched by a domestic **current account deficit**. That is, the flow of funds into the United States through the capital account is matched by a flow out as Americans purchase a larger dollar value of goods and services from foreigners than they sell to foreigners. In essence, the dollars acquired by foreigners through net sales of goods here are being invested here.

This is precisely what happened to the United States as the federal deficit expanded in the 1980s. With minor qualifications due to intermittent and sporadic central bank interventions in the foreign exchange markets, the enormous inflow of foreign investment funds was matched by huge trade and current account deficits. This is a perfect example of dollar-for-dollar crowding out. In such a case the deficit logically affects the pattern, but not the total, of aggregate expenditure.

This logic also affects another aspect of the Keynesian theory. Because international financial flows limit the interest rate increase associated with an increase in the deficit, they limit the force of any argument that such a deficit increase (where $AD = M_s \cdot V$ and M_s is given) can raise AD, output, and employment by raising the interest rate enough to cause a significant increase in velocity. In fact, as federal deficits grew and both inflation and α^* fell in the 1980s, there was a large decline in the velocity of money, so that large increases in the growth rate of the money stock were required in 1985 and 1986 to keep AD from falling.

This large decline in velocity is discussed more fully in Chapter 15, because it was not predicted by many economists and has been interpreted as casting doubt on monetarist models. See also Chapters 17 and 18 for much fuller discussions of the balance of payments, current and capital account imbalances, flexible exchange rates, and exchange-rate intervention than are conducted here.

Policy Lags

A significant difficulty with governmental countercyclical policy, whether monetary or fiscal, stems from the existence of what may be termed **policy lags**. The first of these can be called the **information lag**. The government must rely on statistical data for information about the state of the economy and where it is headed. Some of these data, such as the money and credit information collected by the Federal Reserve, is only a few days or weeks old. Most data, however, are several months old, at best. In a sense the government never knows the present but only the past state of the economy. It can make inferences about present and future states from such data, but they usually turn out to be highly inaccurate. The central point here, however, is that it takes time to obtain even a tenuous estimate of the state and tendency of the economy.

A second lag may be termed the **decision and implementation lag**. Once the information has been collected and processed, it takes additional time to determine the correct policy response to and enact it into law. The political process, in particular, is slow to operate, taking months at best to deal with a particular policy proposal. Worse, under democratic decision-making processes different parties and interest groups, often having completely different goals, must be satisfied. The most carefully and rationally constructed executive branch proposal may bear little resemblance to the original upon emergence from Congress. The key point here is, however, the time involved, and it should be noted that this lag is much shorter for monetary policy, because the Fed does not have to submit its proposals for Congressional approval.

A third lag may be termed **lag in effects**. Even admitting the validity of the Keynesian mechanism, where income changes can be found instantly by simply changing a parameter of a simultaneous equation, real changes in expenditures have their effects on income, output, and employment only over significant periods of time. The same is true of changes in the money stock.

The lag in effects is primarily a consequence of the normal variability of demand and the holding of stocks. As pointed out in Chapter 5, people's cash balances have some normal fluctuation as their income and expenditure flows vary. It takes time after a ΔM_s before they realize that their cash balances are persistently higher or lower than desired and alter their supply and expenditure behavior in response. When they do, the initial effect is primarily on business inventories, which are also held as cushions between production and the variable flow of demand. Here also it takes time for businessmen in micro markets to realize that the mean of demand has changed, making their inventories persistently low or high, and to respond by altering employment, production, and prices. The lags in effects of monetary or fiscal policy resulting from such cushions and slack linkages seem to vary in length from case to case.

Together these lags make countercyclical policy very difficult and somewhat hazardous. Consider Figure 11.6 in which the solid line shows aggregate real output fluctuating over time in a somewhat cyclic pattern. The slight upward slope of this line indicates the positive growth trend of real output. Keynesians argue that the business cycle is inherent in the market economy but can be smoothed out, as shown by the dashed line, through monetary and fiscal policies that reduce excessive aggregate demand during the expansion phase and increase AD in the contraction phase when it is too low.

To illustrate the difficulty, suppose that the economy reaches the peak of the second expansion shown and starts down the contraction phase. Due to the information lag, it may well reach point A before administration policy makers are even sure a recession is in progress. The recession may deepen to point B before an appropriate expansionary fiscal policy is formulated and legislated. Worse, the expansionary

Figure 11.6 Policy Lags and the Business Cycle.

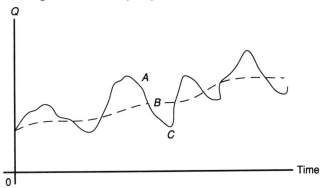

effects of the increased expenditures, fiscal or monetary, may just start being felt at point *C*, when the economy is ready to begin the expansion phase. In that case the policy would aggravate the inflationary characteristics of the expansion rather than reduce the effects of the contraction.

Keynesian economists and policy makers have traditionally denied significance to these difficulties, claiming the empirical data show the variance of the business cycle to be smaller in the post World War II period of Keynesian demand management than in the period preceding the depression. Recent data suggests, however, that these results were due to incorrect treatment of the data for the earlier period, and that the magnitude of the business cycle has not been smaller in the later period.[4]

The Keynesian argument seems misleading, because demand management through monetary policy has been in operation since the creation of the Federal Reserve, and both the 1921 recession and the Great Depression must be counted at least in part as failures of such policy. Including both would significantly raise measured cyclicity in the period of countercyclical demand management.

Political Economy of Keynesian Fiscal Policy ⎯⎯⎯⎯

In recent decades a group of economists called the **public choice school** has begun applying economic reasoning and models to aid in understanding political phenomena. The leader of this school is James Buchanan, who won the Nobel prize for economics in 1986. Buchanan and his followers have argued that the worst features of Keynesian economics is its political naivety.[5] Keynes was a British lord and a member of the elite upper-class intellectual set. As such, it was natural for Keynes to assume that macroeconomic policy would be made by the sort of Platonic "philosopher kings" he saw himself and his friends to be; that is, by people who were highly intelligent, disinterested, altruistic, and unconstrained by political pressures. Keynes's biographer called this attitude the "presupposition of Harvy Road."[6]

The problem with this presumption is that it bears little correspondence to the realities of decision makers and decision making in democratic states. In the first place, although public officials may be more intelligent than average, they often make glaring errors. Second, even high intelligence is no guarantee of altruistic intent (e.g., Hitler) or a lack of personal interest in policy outcomes. As pointed out in Chapter 8, the most realistic assumption is that public officials are self-interested individuals in whose value systems the abstract public good may or may not rank highly. And last, decision makers in democratic states are hardly unconstrained by external political pressures.

The reality is that politicians in democratic states operate within a particular environment that faces them with particular pressures, incentives and constraints. The necessity for election requires that they compete with one another by offering alternative programs of expenditure and finance aimed at satisfying diverse constituencies and interest groups in order to maximize the votes obtained. Almost by definition, in this environment it is difficult for the politician to avoid paying more attention to the desires of the most highly organized interest groups than to the abstract public good. Also, the necessity for reelection, although it protects the public by allowing the removal of bad apples, also motivates politicians to have short time horizons, that is, concerned primarily with the immediate rather than the long-run effects of policy.

Public choice economists argue that the incentives and constraints inherent in the democratic political process are biased toward deficit spending. Politicians offering programs of expenditure benefiting various consituencies usually find that they gain more votes than they lose. When they offer programs of taxation to finance such expenditures, however, they generally lose more votes than they gain. Hence there is a highly natural temptation to offer the expenditures, but defer the taxation forward in time (preferably, beyond the next election) through debt finance. This allows them to give the appearance of offering costless benefits in the present.

Before this argument can be accepted, it must be squared with an obvious fact: The United States ran a basically balanced budget policy for over 150 years, during which time it had the same democratic political structure it has now. Only in recent decades have chronic and expanding deficits emerged. Public choice economists Richard Wagner, Robert Tollison, et al., have no problem explaining this, however.[7] To say that democratic political incentives are biased toward deficits is not to say that these incentives cannot be offset by other pressures. From the inception of the Constitution, U.S. culture was imbued with a Protestant ethic of household frugality, an attitude that people should live within their means, which carried over to government. It was thought that government should not go heavily into debt, except under extraordinary circumstances, such as war.

Before the Great Depression there was a clear pattern to federal deficits and surpluses in which the government ran persistent deficits only during war, to be followed by a series of surpluses by which the accumulated war debt would be retired. In fact, this pattern began with the Revolutionary War, and continued through the War of 1812, the Mexican–American War, the Civil War, the Spanish–American War, and World War I. While the debt accumulated during the Great Depression and World War II was not retired in this manner, Wagner and Tollison argue that this basic pattern continued, because from 1947 to 1960 there were seven years of surplus and seven years of deficit in the federal budget.

Things began to change during the depression, however. Before then it was not only the Protestant ethic of household frugality, but also a widespread attitude that the function of government was to maintain individual rights, peace, and order, not to redistribute wealth, which acted to suppress the deficit running tendencies of the democratic political process. As pointed out in Chapter 10, the Great Depression changed this attitude, causing acceptance of the incipient welfare state. Thus pressures for deficit spending grew, while simultaneously the propagation of Keynesian economics destroyed the intellectual respectability of the notion that budgets should be kept in balance. From 1960 to 1980 Keynesians dominated policy advisory positions in the federal government.

It is important to recognize that Keynesian economics does not advocate continual deficits nor, by Keynesian theory, does the existence of Keynesian policymaking involve a prediction that such deficits will appear. Pure Keynesian theory says that a business cycle is inherent, that expansion phases can be moderated by running surpluses, and that contraction phases can be moderated by running deficits. The (Keynesian) prediction based on the existence of Keynesian policymaking, therefore, is that annually balanced budgets would be replaced by budgets that were balanced over the business cycle. The public choice theory, in contrast, predicts that once the intellectual and attitudinal constraints have been removed, democratic states will tend to generate continuous and increasing deficits. Which prediction has turned out to be correct?

Figure 11.7 The Federal Budget Balance ($T - G$).

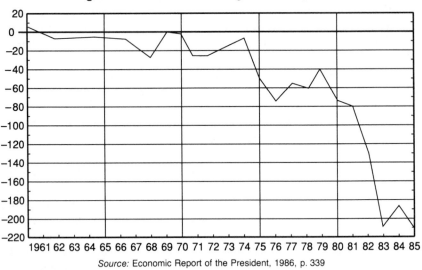

Source: Economic Report of the President, 1986, p. 339

Figure 11.7 shows the dollar value of the federal budget deficit or surplus, $T - G$, in each year from 1960 to 1985. During that period the budget has been in surplus only twice, in 1960 and 1969. It has been in deficit in every other year, whether the economy was expanding or contracting, and the magnitude of the deficits has grown over time. Because the economy has grown also, it is important to compare the magnitude of the deficit to that of the economy. Figure 11.8 shows the budget balance as a percentage of GNP by calculating the ratio of the deficit or surplus to Gross National Product. As the graph shows, the deficit has been growing relative to the economy over time.

Figure 11.8 Ratio of Federal Budget Balance to GNP $\left(\dfrac{T - G}{GNP}\right)$.

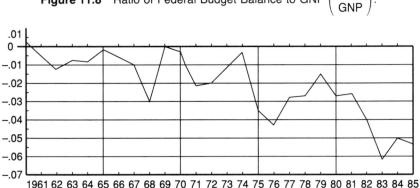

In retrospect, it seems rather surprising that normally sensible economists would ever believe that the federal budget could be manipulated in a rational, Keynesian countercyclical manner. Government expenditures are easily increased to fight recession, but expenditures always have recipients and hence automatically create constituencies with vested interests in their preservation and increase. It is almost impossible to reduce such expenditures in order to fight inflationary expansions. If, despite political resistance, tax increases are sometimes employed, then a ratchet effect, by which expenditures rise during contractions and tax rates rise during expansions, operates to increase the size of government relative to the private sector over time. On the other hand, if tax revenue is not raised to match expenditure increases, deficits grow over time. Both of these effects seem to have operated since 1960.

The strength of the political forces generating deficits is perhaps best illustrated by the course of budgetary events since 1980. Ronald Reagan, a vocal advocate of balanced budgets, became President that year, and Republicans took control of the Senate, yet deficits increased enormously. This occurred despite the miraculous conversion of congressional Democrats, at the time of the first large Republican deficit, to the notion that crowding out is significant and harmful, resulting in nearly unanimous vocal opposition to deficit spending.

That at least some of this opposition represents a genuine change of heart is indicated by passage of the **Gramm–Rudman–Hollings Act** in 1985, mandating automatic expenditure reductions to occur if Congress failed to meet specified declining deficit targets in subsequent years. Adverse court interpretations left the success of the law in doubt for a while, but its genuine intent has been clear. Although the Act may have been accepted by Congress to avoid the greater restrictions of a balanced budget amendment to the Constitution, such as advocated by President Reagan, Gramm–Rudman seems to have provided incentives for Congress to reduce the deficit, and until the time of this writing (early in the Bush administration) the deficit/GNP ratio has fallen significantly.

Summary

Here are the essential points of this chapter.

1. Aggregate demand interpreted as total expenditure can be defined either as the sum of the expenditure components, $Co + I + G + (EX - IM)$, or as the product of the money stock and velocity,

$M_s \cdot V$. A change in total expenditure expressed in Keynesian terms, assuming that $\Delta M_s = 0$, must involve a change in the velocity of (or, more properly, the demand for) money.

2. Keynesian fiscal policy aims at altering AD by altering the federal budget through changes in taxation and/or government expenditure. The idea is to offset the destabilizing effects on output and employment allegedly resulting from fluctuations in the private expenditure components of AD (i.e., instability in the demand for money).

3. Due to progressive income taxes and transfer payments, the state of the federal budget has a tendency to change systematically over the business cycle, moving toward deficit during contractions and toward surplus during expansions. Because by Keynesian theory deficit expenditure tends to raise AD and surpluses tend to reduce AD, Keynesians argue that progressive taxes and transfers have an automatic stabilizing effect on the macroeconomy.

4. In order to run a budget deficit (i.e., spend more than its tax revenue), the federal government must acquire the additional funds elsewhere. Its basic options are to create the money or borrow it—or a combination of the two.

5. The first method, termed *debt monetization*, is a mixture of fiscal and monetary policy, which involves selling government debt instruments (i.e., bonds) to the Federal Reserve. When the government checks for the expenditures clear, the monetary base is increased and multiple deposit expansion occurs.

6. The second method involves selling its debt instruments to the public and not to the Fed. This is pure fiscal policy. Most non-Keynesians believe such policy partially or totally crowds out private investment and/or consumption expenditure, however, such that AD rises little or not at all. Economic growth may actually be reduced in the long run.

7. Even assuming that pure fiscal budget changes actually can alter AD, the feasibility of employing such fiscal and/or monetary policy in a countercyclical fashion is reduced by the existence of long and variable lags in information acquisition, decision, and effects of such policy action.

8. The concept of rational countercyclical fiscal policy seems to presume a Platonic "philosopher king" or benevolent director who is supremely intelligent, altruistic, and unconstrained by external political pressures. Actual policymakers in democratic states, however, are fallible, self-interested human beings who are subject to political pressures and constraints. Consequently, rational policy may not prevail.

9. The nature of democratic political competition arguably subjects political agents to pressures that are biased toward deficit expenditure. Reduction of ideological and theoretical constraints on deficit expenditure in recent decades has observably been associated with a pattern of chronic and increasing deficits that does not accord with the budgetary pattern predicted from the application of Keynesian policy.

10. Perhaps the best evidence of the deficit-generating tendency of the democratic political incentive structure is the expansion of deficits during the first Reagan term, although members of *both* parties almost unanimously expressed opposition to such deficits. Serious efforts to alter the incentive structure were undertaken, however, in the form of pressures for a balanced budget amendment to the Constitution and resulting passage of the Gramm–Rudman–Hollings Act in 1985.

Notes

1. The seminal modern source on this idea is Robert J. Barro, "Are Government Bonds Net Wealth?" *Journal of Political Economy* 82 (November/December 1974): 1095–1117. A Nice essay on crowding out for the intermediate-level student is John A. Tatom, "Two Views of the Effects of Government Budget Deficits in the 1980s," *Federal Reserve Bank of St. Louis Review* (October 1985): 5–16.

2. There is another explanation, however. Federal deficits have usually involved some debt monetization deliberately intended to offset, through monetary expansion, the interest rate effects of the deficit. That this is the primary reason the predicted effects seemed absent may be indicated by the rise in real interest rates after 1981, as deficits increased but debt monetization decreased; see Chapter 15.

3. It should be noted that this argument is counterfactual in a crucial respect. As shown in Chapter 15, people who purchased government bonds in the period from the late 1960s to the 1970s were not compensated by the full, implicitly contracted *real* value of their interest and principle. This massive, undeniable, covert debt repudiation casts severe doubt on the notion that the value of government debt will be set by discounting at a lower interest rate than that applied to future taxation.

4. See Christina D. Romer, "Is the Stabilization of the Postwar Economy a Figment of the Data?" *American Economic Review* 76 (June 1986): 314–334.

5. Buchanan's best work on this subject is *The Consequences of Mr. Keynes* (London: Institute of Economic Affairs, 1978).

6. Sir Roy Harrod, *The Life of John Maynard Keynes* (New York: Macmillan Publishing Company, 1951): 192–193.

7. Richard Wagner, Robert Tollison, Alvin Rabushkal and John T. Noonan, *Balanced Budgets, Fiscal Responsibility, and the Constitution* (Washington D.C.: The Cato Institute, 1982): 5–9.

Student Self-Test

I. True–False

T F 1. In the Keynesian model an equal increase in both government expenditure and lump-sum taxes would fail to affect aggregate demand or income.

T F 2. If the economy is at $Y < Y_f$ and the full employment budget is estimated to be in deficit, Keynesian economists would term current policy expansionary.

T F 3. Treasury sales of bonds to the public to obtain funds to finance a rise in the deficit necessarily cause the money stock to expand.

T F 4. The decision lag is the time it takes to collect and process information.

II. Short Answer (150 words or less each)

1. Ignoring political economy issues, what is the central source of doubt about the Keynesian view that pure fiscal policy can be used to manage aggregate demand and stabilize the economy? Explain.
2. It is easy for the federal government to raise expenditures during the contraction phase of the cycle as advocated by Keynesian theory but difficult for it to reduce such expenditures in the expansion phase, as the theory also advocates. Explain.
3. How does the normal variability of microeconomic demand functions affect the efficacy of demand management policy?
4. Write a simple description of the process of debt monetization, listing at least five separate steps.
5. What basic similarities and differences exist between the equation of exchange and the Keynesian macroeconomic equilibrium equation? What central insight does consideration of the first give us about the Keynesian view of macroeconomic disturbances?

III. Completion Problems

1. Assume an economy at aggregate income $Y = \$1600$, where $Y_f = \$2000$. The government employs a combination lump-sum and flat-rate income tax $T = \bar{T} + t(Y) = \$200 + .2(Y)$ and the lump-sum tax multiplier is $K_T = -3.2$. All dollar magnitudes are in billions.
   A. If the government accepts Keynesian theory and wishes to eliminate the recessionary gap through lump-sum tax policy, it should alter the lump sum by $\Delta T =$ _____.
   B. Before the alteration, total tax revenue at Y_f would be $T = \$$ _____.
   C. After the alteration, total tax revenue at Y_f would be $T' = \$$ _____.
   D. If the government wishes to use a marginal tax rate adjustment to end the recession, it should change it to $t' =$ _____.
2. For the economy described in question 1, assume that investment is a function of income with both a lump sum and marginal rate component but that government expenditure is not.
   A. Write the structural form of this economy.
   B. Derive the reduced form of the model.
   C. The government expenditure multiplier is $K_G =$ _____ and the lump sum tax multiplier is $K_T =$ _____. (*Note*: Mathematical forms, not numerical magnitudes, are required here.)

3. Miscellaneous:
   A. The time it takes to formulate a policy response to a macroeconomic condition and enact it into law is termed the _____ .
   B. The theorized process by which Treasury bond sales aimed at raising revenue to cover an increase in the federal deficit might raise current saving and reduce current consumption is termed _____ .
   C. During the decades of the 1960s, 1970s and 1980s, the only surpluses in the federal budget were in _____ and _____ . For most of that time deficits kept _____ (increasing/decreasing) both in absolute dollar magnitudes and in proportion to GNP.

CHAPTER 12

The Fixed-Price *IS–LM* Model

Although the simple Keynesian cross model developed in Chapter 10 captures the essence of many of Keynes's analytical contributions, certain others are not included. A more complete and fair representation of Keynesian economics, known as the *IS–LM* model, was developed by John R. Hicks in 1937.[1] In the primary version of this model, which was the only version employed in textbooks for many years and is the one developed here, the price level was assumed to be predetermined and constant as in the simple Keynesian cross model. The doctrinal significance of the complete Keynesian model is that it was the first to formally integrate the financial and commodity sectors of the economy into a general equilibrium framework. Its impact on actual policy after 1960 was enormous.

The *IS–LM* model formally integrates the money market with the commodity market for goods and services, including investment goods, in such a manner as to determine both the interest rate, which was absent from the Keynesian cross model, and income. Conditions in a third market, the bond market, are often argued to be implied by Walras's law. In this chapter the model will be derived and manipulated for the purposes of expositing fiscal and monetary policy in a Keynesian framework. Certain problems with that framework and this model will also be discussed.

The *IS* Curve: The Interest Rate and the Commodity Market _____

As long as the price level is assumed constant, there is no difference between real and nominal interest rates. It is shown in Chapter 3 (see particularly Figure 3.5(b)) that investment varies inversely with the interest rate, and in Chapters 3 and 11 (particularly Figure 11.4(a)) it is shown that consumption varies inversely with the interest rate. Where $Y = Co + S$, if saving out of current income has any positive response to the interest rate, then for any initial income level increased saving as the interest rate rises must mean reduced expenditure on consumption. Thus both investment and consumption are inverse functions of the interest rate.

The implications of interest rate changes for aggregate demand can be illustrated as in Figure 12.1(a). If the effects of income on consumption and investment are already incorporated into the slope of the AD function, and the foreign and governmental sectors are ignored for simplicity, it can be written $AD = Co(i) + I(i)$. Figure 12.1(a) shows separate AD functions for two such possible interest rates, i_1 and i_2. If

Figure 12.1 Deriving the *IS* Curve.

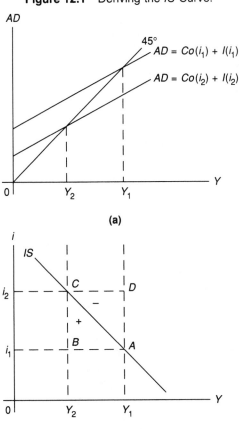

we assume that $i_2 > i_1$ and that the higher interest rate reduces consumption and investment, *ceteris paribus*, it follows that $AD(i_2) < AD(i_1)$.

With the interest rate at i_1, equilibrium occurs at income level Y_1, where $AD = Co(i_1) + I(i_1) = Y$ at the intersection of the AD line and the 45° line. This corresponds to point $A = (Y_1, i_1)$ in Figure 12.1(b). On the other hand, if the interest rate were i_2, the commodity market would be in equilibrium at income level Y_2, where $AD = Co(i_2) + I(i_2) = Y$ at its intersection with the 45° line. This corresponds to point $Co = (Y_2, i_2)$ in Figure 12.1(b). Points A and C, therefore, both represent combinations of the interest rate and income yielding equilibrium in the commodity market.

Clearly, there is a unique AD curve for each possible interest rate, *ceteris paribus*, and hence an infinite number of equilibrium interest rate and income combinations, such as points A and C. A line drawn as shown in Figure 12.1(b) to connect all such equilibrium interest rate and income pairs is called the **IS curve**, in reference to the equality of saving and investment that occurs in this restricted system when $AD = Y$. The curve has a negative slope, because higher interest rates are paired with lower income levels.

Suppose, however, that the economy was at a point such as $B = (Y_2, i_1)$ in Figure 12.1(b), to the left of the IS curve. In Figure 12.1(a) that would mean that aggregate income was Y_2 but that the existing level of aggregate demand was $AD(i_1)$, so that $AD > Y$ and a condition of excess demand existed in the market for commodities. All points such as B, to the left of the IS curve, represent income and interest rate combinations yielding positive excess demand in the market for commodities, as indicated by the plus sign in Figure 12.1(b).

Now consider point $D = (Y_1, i_2)$ in Figure 12.1(b). This represents a situation in which, interpreted from the perspective of Figure 12.1(a), the income level in the economy is Y_1, but the level of aggregate demand is at $AD(i_2)$, so that when compared on the vertical axis $AD < Y$ and a condition of excess supply (i.e., negative excess demand) exists on the output market. All points such as D to the right of the IS curve represent interest rate and income combinations yielding excess supply in the market for commodities. This is indicated by the negative sign to the right of the IS.

The shape of the IS curve depends crucially on the responsiveness of investment and saving (and hence consumption) to changes in the interest rate. Consider an increase in the interest rate from i_1 to i_2. If saving and investment were highly elastic functions of the interest rate, so that their quantitive responses to this change were very large, $AD(i_2)$ would lie even farther below $AD(i_1)$ than is shown in Figure 12.1(a). This would move points B and C horizontally further to the left of points A and D than they are now shown, and the IS curve would be flatter. On the other hand, if saving and investment were interest-inelastic, such that their quantitative responses to the interest-rate change were very small, $AD(i_2)$ would not be as far below $AD(i_1)$ as it is now shown, and points B and C would be shifted horizontally toward the right, closer to points A and D, making the IS curve steeper.

It is also important to recognize that the IS curve can shift. Suppose, for example, that the amount that people wish to invest at each interest rate increases from $I(i)$ to $I'(i)$. This would occur if the credit demand curve developed in Chapter 3 shifted outward; Figure 3.4(b) or Figure 10.6(a). *Ceteris paribus*, this would raise AD at each interest rate, as shown in Figure 12.2(a). The result would be that points A, B, C, and D would all shift rightward to A', B', C', and D' as in Figure 12.2(b), shifting the whole IS curve outward as shown. Clearly, a decrease in

Figure 12.2 Deriving Shifts in the IS Curve.

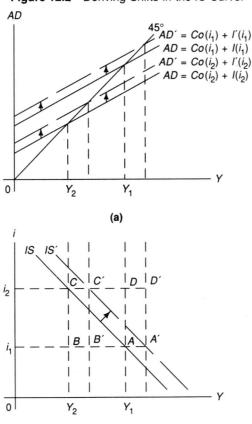

(a)

(b)

desired investment at each interest rate would have the opposite effect, shifting the *IS* curve leftward, *ceteris paribus*.

Theoretically, other factors can also shift the *IS* curve. If we admit the governmental sector into the analysis (the foreign sector could also be included, but that is discussed in Chapters 17 and 18) and explicitly recognize the effect of income in the functional notation, aggregate demand should be written as $AD = Co(Y, i) + I(Y, i) + G$. *Ceteris paribus*, a change in government expenditure alters AD in the manner described in Chapter 10, shifting the *IS* curve in the same direction. The remaining question would then be to what extent the *ceteris paribus* condition can hold, that is how much crowding out or crowding in of investment and consumption occurs to offset the ΔG.

The *LM* Curve: The Interest Rate and the Money Market

Throughout this book it is stressed that the demand for money and money stock interact to determine the value of money by determining the price level. In Chapter 6 the demand for nominal money balances is expressed as a function of four variables. M_d is argued to vary positively with the price level as the purchasing power of the dollar changes, inversely with the interest rate as portfolio adjustments are required, positively with real income in order to affect transactions, and inversely with the expected rate of inflation as that cost of holding money changes. The demand for real money balances differs from that for nominal balances only by the exclusion of the price-level variable.

Because the advanced Keynesian model under consideration here assumes the price level to be predetermined and constant, much of this is altered. The $1/P$ and α^* variables can be entirely deleted and the demand for money can be written as $M_d = L(Y, i)$. The L here is the traditional functional notation employed in Keynesian analysis for the demand for money and should not be confused with the demand for or supply of labor, L_d and L_s. Remember that ΔY in this model always represents a change in real output and income, because $Y = P \cdot Q$ and P is fixed.

The demand for money in this framework can be represented as in Figure 12.3(a). M_d is plotted as an inverse function of the interest rate, and income is listed as a shift variable, so that $M_d = L(Y)$. The graph shows separate demand for money functions for two different income levels, Y_1 and Y_2. If we assume that $Y_2 > Y_1$ as shown in Figure 12.3(b), it follows from the positive relationship between real income and the demand for money that $L(Y_2) > L(Y_1)$.

Figure 12.3   Deriving the *LM* Curve.

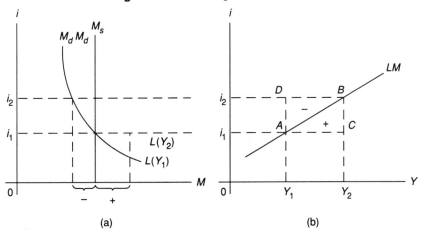

(a)   (b)

A nominal money stock is also shown in Figure 12.3(a). If aggregate income is assumed to be Y_1, so that the existing money demand function is $L(Y_1)$, moneyholders will be satisfied with their existing nominal balances when the interest rate is at i_1, when $L(Y_1) = M_s$. This corresponds to point $A = (Y_1, i_1)$ in Figure 12.3(b). On the other hand, if aggregate income were Y_2, so that the existing demand for money function was $M_d = L(Y_2)$, the money market would only be in equilibrium at interest rate i_2, where $L(Y_2) = M_s$. This corresponds to point $B = (Y_2, i_2)$ in Figure 12.3(b). Points A and B therefore both represent combinations of income and the interest rate that equate desired money holdings with the existing stock.

There is obviously a unique demand for money function for each income level, *ceteris paribus*, and hence an infinite number of equilibrium interest rate and income combinations such as points A and B. A line drawn as shown in Figure 12.3(b) to connect all such equilibrium interest rate and income pairs is called the **LM curve**. The curve has a positive slope because higher income levels require higher interest rates to equilibrate the money market, *ceteris paribus*.

Suppose, however, that the economy was at a point such as $D = (Y_1, i_2)$ in Figure 12.3(b), to the left of the *LM* curve. In Figure 12.3(a) that would mean that the existing demand for money function was $L(Y_1)$, but that the interest rate was above equilibrium, resulting in an excess supply of money. All points such as D, to the left of the *LM* curve, represent interest rate and income combinations generating excess supply in the money market, as indicated by the minus sign on the left-hand side of the *LM*.

Now consider point $C = (Y_2, i_1)$ to the right of the *LM* curve in Figure 12.3(b). From the perspective of Figure 12.3(a) this represents a situation in which the existing demand for money function is $L(Y_2)$, and the quantity of money demanded for cash balances exceeds the existing nominal stock because the interest rate, i_1, is below equilibrium. All such points as C on the right of the *LM* curve represent combinations of the interest rate and income yielding excess demand in the money market. This fact is represented by the plus sign to the right of the *LM* curve.

The shape of the *LM* curve depends primarily on the interest elasticity of the demand for money (horizontally flatter M_d curves in Figure 12.3(a) would be more elastic that those shown). In particular, the more responsive the quantity of money demanded for cash balances is to changes in the interest rate, such that smaller interest rate changes are required to equilibrate the money market for each given income level, the flatter the *LM* curve is. Oddly, despite the emphasis that many text books give to allegedly different assumptions about this elasticity on the part of Keynesians and monetarists, there is little disagreement on the part of empirical researchers. Almost all such researchers, Keynesian and monetraist, find empirical magnitudes for this elasticity (defined as $\% \, \Delta M_d / \% \, \Delta i$) to be significantly less than unity (or by definition, inelastic).[2]

Like the *IS* curve, various factors can act to shift the *LM* curve. An increase in the money stock such as shown in Figure 12.4(a), for example, would clearly reduce the interest rates required to equilibrate the money market, both for $L(Y_1)$ and $L(Y_2)$. In other words, points A and B would shift downward as shown in Figure 12.4(b), as would

Figure 12.4 Deriving Shifts in the *LM* Curve.

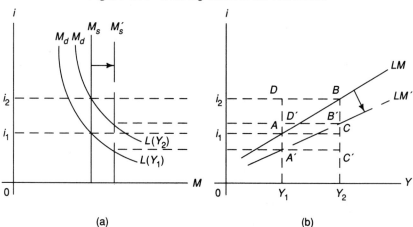

(a)　　　　　　　　　(b)

points C and D, shifting the LM downward and toward the right. Just as clearly a decrease in the money stock would have the opposite effect, *ceteris paribus*, shifting the LM curve upward and toward the left.

Changes in the demand for money work in the opposite direction of changes in the stock. If, for example, people decided that they wished to hold more money at each income level, such that $L(Y_1)$ and $L(Y_2)$ both shifted upward symmetrically, it would take higher interest rates to equilibrate the money market for each function, *ceteris paribus*. Points A and B would both shift vertically (as would points C and D), shifting the LM upward and toward the left. A decrease in people's desired money holdings would have the opposite effect, *ceteris paribus*. To summarize then, either an increase in the money stock or a decrease in the demand for money will shift the LM downward and toward the right, while either a decrease in M_s or an increase in M_d will shift the LM upward and toward the left.

Walras's Law and Equilibrium in the *IS–LM*

With the IS and LM curves derived and defined, the $IS–LM$ model can be completed by placing the two together in the same $i–Y$ space, as in Figure 12.5. If we assume that the vertical intercept of the LM curve lies below that of the IS curve, the two must intersect, and there will be a single interest rate and aggregate income combination, such as $A = (Y_e, i_e)$ in Figure 12.5, which yields equilibrium in both the output

Figure 12.5 Equilibrium in the *IS–LM*.

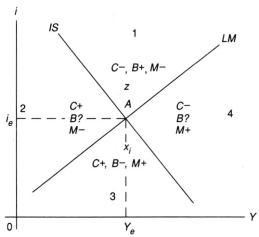

and money markets. The question, then, is whether a set of economic forces exists and acts to generate that interest rate and income combination.

Note that the *IS* and *LM* neatly divide the *i–Y* space into four rough quadrants, as labeled. Points in the first quadrant, such as point *z*, are to the right of the *IS* curve, such that excess supplies exist in the commodity market. This may be indicated by $C-$. Points in this quadrant are to the left of the *LM*, however, hence the money market must also be in excess supply. This can be indicated by $M-$. In order to satisfy Walras's law, many economists argue that a third market, the bond market, is implicit in the model, and that its conditions are implied by those of the other markets. By this reasoning in the case of a point such as *z* in the first quadrant where $C-$ and $M-$, there must be matching excess demand in the bond market ($B+$), such that the excess demands for all three sum to zero.

Under these circumstances the excess demand for bonds will cause bond prices to rise. The rise in P_b will not only eliminate the excess demand for bonds, but because $i = d/P_b$ (see Chapter 3), it will also reduce the interest rate, eliminating the excess money stock by increasing the quantity of money demanded. The falling interest rate will also reduce the excess supply in the output market by increasing aggregate demand. Eventually the intersection of the *IS* and *LM* will be reached, where $C = 0$, $B = 0$ and $M = 0$.

Now consider point *x* in the third quadrant. All such points in this quadrant are to the left of the *IS* curve, such that excess demand exists in the output market ($C+$). They are to the right of the *LM* curve, however, indicating that excess demand also exists in the money market ($M+$). By inference from Walras's law there must be a matching excess supply of bonds ($B-$). In this case bond prices would fall, raising the interest rate and reducing *AD* until the excess demands for money and goods and the excess supply of bonds were all eliminated. Until point *A* was reached, there would definitionally still be pressure for bond prices to fall and the interest rate to rise.

The movement to point *A* from points in the second and fourth quadrants is a little harder to explain. Points in the second quadrant are to the left of both the *IS* and the *LM*, such that the output market is in a state of excess demand and the money market is experiencing excess supply. The condition in the bond market is therefore not obvious *a priori*. Excess demand in that market could be positive, negative, or zero. Most logically, it would be positive, and the excess demand in both the bond and commodity markets would be matched by the excess money stock, although that would imply the operation of a real balance effect, which few Keynesians would like to admit.

It may be impossible to avoid such an implication, however, since it also seems implicit if the $C+$ matches the $M-$ such that $B = 0$.[3] In either case, the excess output demand will cause output and income to rise, moving the economy toward point A. The rise in real output and income will eventually raise the demand for money, until $M = 0$. As for the commodity market, because consumption is a function of income, expenditure rises as output and income rise in the Keynesian model, but because the MPC < 1 such that demand for output is rising less than the supply of output, excess demand will go to zero when point A is reached.

The opposite would occur from points in the fourth quadrant. Here $C-$, $M+$, and the sign of B is indeterminate (although most likely negative), again implying the operation of a real balance effect. From such points income and output would fall, reducing M_d to eliminate the excess demand, and reducing expenditure at a lower rate than output itself until $C = 0$ when point A is reached. In all of these cases, in the four quadrants the exact path of the economy toward point A is impossible to predict from the model, as is the amount of time involved. The argument here claims only that the model describes forces moving the economy to that point from other points in each sector, or from points on the IS or LM other than point A.

Shifts in the *IS* Curve

Figure 12.6 combines Figures 12.1 and 12.3 into an even more complete three-quadrant version of the *IS-LM* model suitable for examining the causes and consequences of shifts in the *IS* and *LM* curves. The first stage in its construction involves reversing the vertical ordering of Figures 12.1 (a) and (b), so that 12.1 (b) is on top. Figure 12.1 (a) is then rotated on its horizontal axis so that it is upside down and the income axes of the two graphs can be combined. The next step involves rotating Figure 12.3 (a) on its vertical (interest rate) axis and combining that axis with that of Figure 12.3 (b). Figures 12.1 (b) and 12.3 (b) are then superimposed, so that the *IS* and *LM* curves are in the same space. In this process only spatial relationships, not economic relationships, are altered.

Aggregate demand in Figure 12.6 is initially $AD(i_1, Y)$, the demand for money is $M_d = L(Y_1)$, and the initial equilibrium values are i_1 and Y_1 at point A. Now suppose that either government expenditure falls, or desired private investment falls, reducing aggregate demand in the lower right quadrant of the graph to $AD'(i_1, Y)$. This shifts the *IS*

Figure 12.6 Leftward Shift in the *IS* Curve.

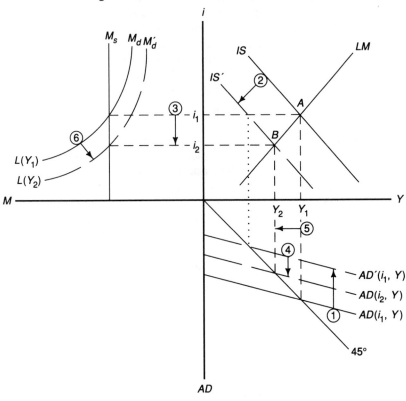

curve leftward to *IS'* as shown. Point *A* is now to the right of the *IS* curve (although it is still on the *LM*), such that excess supplies exist in the output market, as can be easily seen from the lower right quadrant. Because $M = 0$ and $C-$ at point *A*, there must be an excess demand for bonds ($B+$, either because the government is paying off debt, in accordance with the fall in *G*, or because private corporations have reduced bond issuance, in accordance with a decline in desired investment).

The excess demand makes bond prices rise, reducing the interest rate. The falling interest rate increases consumption and investment spending, eventually raising aggregate demand to $AD(i_2, Y)$, thus partially offsetting the initial reduction in *AD*. The falling interest rate would also cause an excess demand for money, *ceteris paribus*, of course, but because the effect of falling *i* on *AD* only partly offsets the initial decline, income falls to Y_2 and reduces the demand for money to

$L(Y_2)$, so that no excess demand for money appears. This is the sequence of events shown by the numbered arrows in Figure 12.6.

In this form it is easy to see the difference between the simple Keynesian model of Chapters 10 and 11 and the *IS–LM* version. Because the simple version did not incorporate the interest rate effects on M_d and AD, the simple model would have ended the analysis of the initial AD decline with a fall in income to the point at which the dotted line in Figure 12.6 intersects the income axis and not shown the partially offsetting rise in AD as the interest rate fell. It can also be seen from Figure 12.6 that the reason the offset is only partial is because the fall in the interest rate increases the quantity of money demanded. Put another way, it causes the velocity of money to fall, so that a net decline in AD and income occurs.

Figure 12.7 illustrates the effects of the opposite initial disturbance, beginning again with the equilibrium values of Y_1, i_1, $L(Y_1)$ and $AD(i_1)$. In this case some event such as a rise in government expenditure, reduction in taxation, or rise in desired private investment causes

Figure 12.7 Rightward Shift in the *IS* Curve.

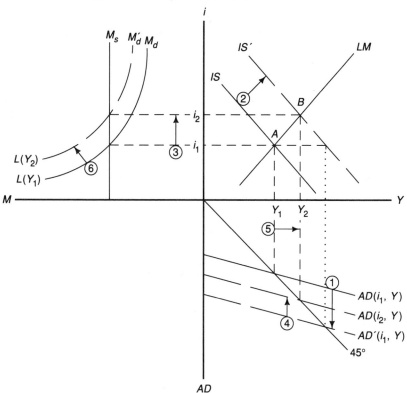

aggregate demand to rise from $AD(i_1, Y)$, shifting the *IS* curve toward the right. At the initial income and interest rate levels, point A, the money market is in equilibrium, but point A is now to the left of the *IS* curve, so that an excess demand for output exists $(C+)$, and because $M = 0$, there must be an excess supply of bonds $(B-,$ as government offers bonds to cover the increased deficit, or as private corporations increase bond issuance to finance their desired increase in investment).

The excess supply makes bond prices fall to clear the market, raising the interest rate in the process. The rising interest rate crowds out some private consumption and investment, eventually reducing aggregate demand to $AD(i_2, Y)$, partially offsetting the initial increase in AD. The rising interest rate would also tend to cause an excess supply of money, *ceteris paribus*, but because income rises from Y_1 to Y_2 the demand for money increases to $L(Y_2)$ and prevents the appearance of an excess supply in the money market.

Again, comparison between the simple Keynesian model of Chapter 10 and the *IS–LM* version is made in Figure 12.7. Without the interest rate effects the rise in aggregate demand to $AD'(i_1, Y)$ would raise income to the intersection of the dotted line in Figure 12.7 with the income axis. The crowding out resulting from the interest rate increase, however, results in income only rising to Y_2. One way of looking at this is that the magnitudes of the multipliers, $\Delta Y/\Delta G$, $\Delta Y/\Delta T$, and $\Delta Y/\Delta I$ have been reduced by the interest rate increase. Another is to see that the crowding out is not total because the rise in the interest rate has decreased the quantity of money demanded, increasing the velocity of money so that a net increase in AD results.

Shifts in the *LM* Curve

The nature and consequences of factors shifting the *LM* curve can be illustrated and explained with graphs such as Figure 12.8, which assumes the same initial equilibrium values as before. Because money demand and supply allow for four possible initial shifts (excluding simultaneous shifts in M_d and M_s), but the *LM* can only either shift in or out, matters will be simplified here by considering only money stock shifts, leaving for the reader the exercise of working out the consequences of demand shifts.

Suppose, therefore, that the money stock increases from M_s to M_s', as shown in the upper left-hand quadrant of Figure 12.8. This shifts the *LM* downward and to the right, as argued previously. The economy is still at point A, however, which is on the *IS* curve so that $C = 0$ but is

Figure 12.8 Rightward Shift in the *LM* Curve.

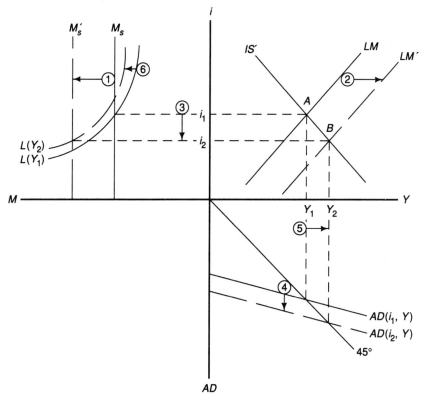

now to the left of the *LM*, such that $M-$ at the initial interest rate, as can be seen in the upper left-hand quadrant. It logically follows that the bond market must be in excess demand, $B+$, (which makes sense if it is assumed that the money stock increase is the result of open market purchases).

The excess demand for bonds raises P_b, reducing the interest rate and causing aggregate demand to rise. The rise in AD makes $C+$ at Y_1, so that production and income rise to Y_2. The rise in income causes consumption and investment to rise also, of course, but not as fast as income, so that $C = 0$ again at Y_2. The fall in the interest rate tends to eliminate the excess money stock, but the new equilibrium cannot be at the intersection of $L(Y_1)$ and M'_s, because the rise in income must increase the demand for money to $L(Y_2)$ as shown. This is the sequence of events shown by the numbered arrows in the graph, and at point $B = (Y_2, i_2)$ all three markets must once again be in equilibrium.

Now return to the initial equilibrium position, point $A = (Y_1, i_1)$, and suppose that the system is disturbed by a decrease in the money stock from M_s to M_s', as shown in Figure 12.9. Everything works in reverse of the previous case. The money stock decrease shifts the LM toward the left, so that point A, where $C = 0$, is now to the right of LM', so that $M+$ at the initial interest rate, i_1. Bonds are therefore in excess supply (perhaps because the monetary contraction is due to the Fed selling government bonds).

In this case P_b must fall to clear the market, raising the interest rate in the process. The rise in the interest rate reduces consumption and investment, lowering AD to $AD(i_2)$ and making $C-$ at Y_1. Output and income therefore fall to Y_2, decreasing M_d to $L(Y_2)$ in the process. Point $B = (Y_2, i_2)$ is eventually reached, at which $M = 0$, $C = 0$, and $B = 0$. This is the sequence of events shown by the numbered arrows in Figure 12.9.

Figure 12.9 Leftward Shift in the LM Curve.

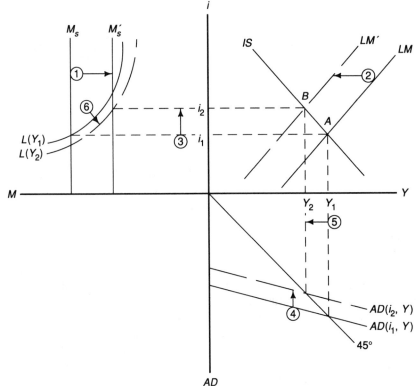

Full Employment and Countercyclical Policy in the *IS–LM* _____

The basic *IS–LM* model as developed here has long been thought by its advocates to provide great insight into the sources and persistance of disturbances to the macroeconomy, as well as the appropriate counter-cyclical policies. A typical recessionary situation can be illustrated as the *IS–LM* graph in Figure 12.10, in which the equilibrium level of income is less than the full employment value, Y_f, which is also shown. In this framework the possible causes of a recession or depression break down into two broad categories. The first consists of events such as decreases in desired consumption or investment expenditure which shift the *IS* toward the left, reducing both income (and output and employment) and the interest rate in the process. The second consists of increases in the demand for money or decreases in the money stock which shift the *LM* leftward, decreasing income, output and employment while raising the interest rate.

Keynesians have traditionally assumed events in the first category to be the most important and frequent source of recessionary disturbance. Modern neo-Keynesians such as Peter Temin maintain this tradition and still explain the Great Depression, for example, as due to a decline in desired consumption or investment that decreased the *IS* curve.[4] Monetarists, of course, have countered by pointing to the decline

Figure 12.10 Recessionary Gap in the *IS–LM*.

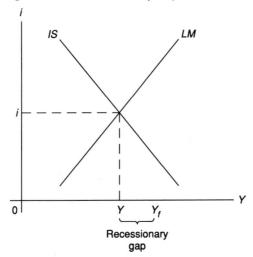

in the money stock that occurred between 1929 and 1932 as the initial disturbance.

Keynesians responded by arguing that the banking crash that reduced the money supply was the result, not the cause, of the income decline, in essence arguing that the leftward shift of the *IS* eventually caused the *LM* to shift leftward also. Monetarists deny this reverse causality. A key sticking point in the argument concerns the behavior of the interest rate, which declined in accordance with the Keynesian argument that an *IS* shift was the initial disturbance, but increased in real terms as prices fell, which is more in accordance with the monetarist argument. Clearly, the historical event was highly complex and is subject to varying interpretations.

The persistence of recessionary phenomena, and particularly that of the Great Depression, was long explained in the Keynesian model by claiming that $Y < Y_f$ could be an equilibrium level of income. That is, point (Y, i) in Figure 12.10 is a point on both the *IS* and *LM* curves, so in terms of the model no pressure exists to make income, output, and employment rise. This hypothetical situation was long referred to as an **unemployment equilibrium**, and the demonstration of its existence was thought to be the most original and important contribution of the Keynesian model. Is implication (often expressly stated) was that the market economy had no automatic aggregate stabilizing mechanism.

In recent decades critics have made the point that this unemployment equilibrium is a rather artificial result of assuming a fixed-price level in the Keynesian model. As shown in Chapter 13, the existence of a permanent unemployment equilibrium cannot survive an assumption of flexible prices. This point has been accepted, and the term "unemployment equilibrium" (which was a self-contradiction) has disappeared from the literature. The *IS–LM* model is still defended, however, even with its fixed-price assumption, by reference to the existence of empirically observable downward price rigidity.

This observation hardly distinguishes the Keynesian model, however, as most non-Keynesian economists long accepted price and wage rigidity as a partial explanation of the persistence of recessionary phenomena (indeed, price inflexibility has been analyzed in both the *AD–AS* and monetary models), while disagreeing with Keynesians over the magnitude and primary source of this rigidity. Other explanations of the persistence of the Great Depression have also been offered, such as the series of recessionary shocks administered to the economy by the Roosevelt administration in the name of antirecessionary policy, as discussed in Chapter 10.

The policy implications of the *IS–LM* model are straightforward. The recessionary condition illustrated in Figure 12.10 calls for an expansionary fiscal policy (i.e., an increase in G and or a decrease in T)

sufficient to shift the *IS* rightward to an intersection with the *LM* at Y_f, raising the interest rate in the process, as shown in Figure 12.11. Alternately, an expansionary monetary policy could be employed to shift the *LM* rightward until it reached an intersection with the *IS* curve at Y_f, lowering the interest rate in the process, as shown in Figure 12.12.

Another alternative would involve combining expansionary monetary and fiscal policy through debt monetization. Many Keynesians view this an ideal expansionary policy because by shifting both the *IS* and *LM* curves outward together, an interest rate change with its associated crowding out is avoided and the full multiplier effect is obtained. In the case of an initial situation in which income and employment exceed the full employment level, the *IS–LM* calls for policies producing a leftward shift of the *IS* or the *LM* or both. By these types of discretionary policy actions, deviations of the *IS* or *LM* from intersection at Y_f can theoretically be countered.

It should be pointed out that all of the criticisms and qualifications to such discretionary demand management policies made in previous chapters, such as the problem of lags, the difficulty of measuring such gaps, the political economy of policy making in democracies, the likelyhood that policymakers have other goals than rational stabilization, and the frequency with which instability seems to result from such policies, still hold. In recent years recognition of such problems, and of the existence of alternative nondiscretionary policy solutions such as the Friedman rule, have reduced the enthusiasm for discretionary monetary and fiscal policy among economists.

Figure 12.11 Antirecession Fiscal Policy.

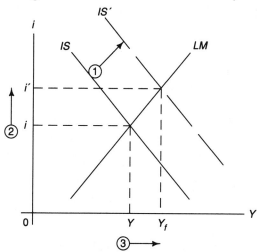

Figure 12.12   Antirecession Monetary Policy.

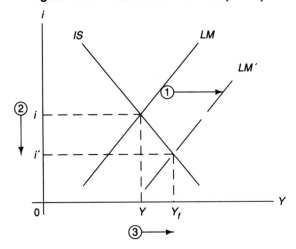

Other Problems with the Fixed-Price *IS–LM* Model

Certain other problems with the standard *IS–LM* framework have been recognized in recent decades, resulting in a search for new and hopefully better models. Awareness of many of these problems resulted from the appearence of inflation as the primary macroeconomic problem after the mid-1960s. First, a model that takes the price level as predetermined and constant and that shows money supply and demand determining the interest rate, lacks an explanation of the price level itself, and it is highly difficult to say much about inflation from such a viewpoint.[5] Other important phenomena related to inflation, such as the Fisher effect on interest rates and the adjustment of inflation rate expectations could not be analyzed in a fixed-price model.

Related to this, an important problem with standard Keynesian theory is that it is primarily a theory of aggregate demand. Aggregate supply and employment adjust passively and positively to *AD* changes in this framework. This passive response of output and employment is a result of not only assuming the price level to be predetermined and fixed, but also fixed above equilibrium. Events in the late 1960s and 1970s, such as simultaneously increasing prices and unemployment (known as **stagflation**), showed that output and employment did not respond passively and positively to *AD* changes. This was difficult for Keynesians to explain, because in their model rising prices imply excessive aggregate demand, whereas rising unemployment implies inadequate *AD*.

Fundamentally, the problem is that real output and employment respond crucially to changes in relative prices (including the real wage) and real money balances, none of which, by definition, can be analyzed adequately in a fixed-price Keynesian framework. For this reason economists have increasingly developed and relied on the *AD–AS* model exposited in Chapter 9, which not only shows price level determination but also allows analysis of the effects of relative and absolute price changes and can even explain stagflation.[6]

Another problem concerns the short-run nature of the Keynesian model. The *IS–LM* holds the capital stock and technology constant in an implicit *ceteris paribus* assumption. It also shows crowding out from expansionary fiscal policy to be only partial and not to completely prevent such policy from raising *AD*. But even partial crowding out of private investment, if continued over time, can result in slowed capital stock and productivity growth, threatening the national standard of living in a manner much more fundamental than that of mere business cycle phenomena.

Such reduced capital stock and productivity growth actually seemed to occur during the 1970s as chronic deficits expanded.[7] In consequence, economists became increasingly disenchanted with a model that focuses attention myopically on short-run demand management for the relief of immediate distress to the exclusion of long-run growth considerations. The fact that capital stock and productivity growth are more easily analyzed in terms of the *AD–AS* model was one more reason its popularity has increased while that of the *IS–LM* model decreased.

None of this is to say that an *IS–LM* type model cannot be developed to deal with many if not all of the problems and issues mentioned here. Explicitly introducing a labor market and allowing price and wage flexibility allows examination of many issues in inflation and employment (and even, potentially, growth, although consideration of that issue is deferred to later chapters). This is the purpose of Chapter 13, and as we shall see, the resulting model produces results that contrast considerably with those of the fixed-price *IS–LM*.

Summary

The primary points of this chapter include the following.

1. Continuing the standard Keynesian assumption of a predetermined price level, the fixed-price *IS–LM* model integrates the money and commodity markets in such a way as to simultaneously determine both the interest rate and aggregate real income.

2. The *IS* curve connects combinations of interest rates and income yielding equilibrium in the commodities market. It slopes downward in *i–Y* space because *AD* is assumed to be a positive function of income (through the consumption function) but a negative function of the interest rate.

3. The *IS* curve is steeper the less interest-elastic saving and investment are. Any increase in *AD* resulting from a rise in one or more of its expenditure components, *ceteris paribus*, will shift the *IS* curve toward the right. A decline in *AD* will shift it leftward.

4. The *LM* curve connects combinations of interest rates and income yielding equilibrium between the demand for and supply of money. It is positively sloped in *i–Y* space because higher incomes raise money demand, such that higher interest rates are required to equilibrate the money market.

5. The *LM* curve is flatter the greater the interest elesticity of the demand for money. An increase in the money stock shifts the *LM* toward the right, and a decrease shifts it toward the left, *ceteris paribus*. An increase in the demand for money shifts the *LM* toward the left, and a decrease in money demand shifts it toward the right, *ceteris paribus*.

6. The attainment of a single *i–Y* combination yielding equilibrium in both markets from points above or below the intersection of the two curves (such that, viewed horizontally, it is between the two) can be explained by employing Walras's law to infer conditions in a third market, the bond market, which yield equilibrating changes in the interest rate.

7. Attainment of equilibrium from points to the left or right of both curves is best explained by reference to a real balance mechanism.

8. Fiscal policy multipliers are reduced by interest rate changes which cause crowding out in the *IS–LM* model, but fiscal policy changes *AD* because the interest rate changes alter the amount of money demanded (i.e., total expenditure changes because monetary velocity changes).

9. In the *IS–LM* model a recessionary situation can be cured either by an expansionary fiscal policy (raising the interest rate) or through an expansionary monetary policy (lowering the interest rate). Given the fixed-price assumption, the best policy is to combine the two, running a deficit and monetizing the debt (or independently increasing the money stock through open market operations), because that avoids crowding out and maximizes the expenditures multiplier.

10. The fixed-price *IS–LM* model has very limited usefulness for analyzing macroeconomic events and problems in an inflationary era such as the one that has existed since the 1950s.

Notes

1. J. R. Hicks, "Mr. Keynes and the 'Classics'; A Suggested Interpretation," *Econometrica* 5 (April 1937): 147–159.

2. See Laidler, *The Demand For Money*: 105.

3. Even the third possible case ($C+$, $B-$, and $M-$) does not entirely avoid this implication. These observations should dispense with the commonly held notion that the fixed-price version of the *IS–LM* is completely devoid of real balance effects.

4. Peter Temin, *Did Monetary Forces Cause the Great Depression?* (New York: W. W. Norton and Co., 1976). See also, however, Thomas Mayer, "Money and the Great Depression: A Critique of Professor Temin's Thesis," *Explorations in Economic History* (April 1978).

5. To be fair, the statement usually made in expositing the Keynesian model is that the price level is assumed to be constant for values of income output and employment less than the full employment values, Y_f. As Y rises above Y_f, the price level is assumed to be rising because, by assumption of the model, Q cannot be increasing. Such price changes immediately cause problems for the model, however, because all aggregate demand components are expressed as nominal magnitudes and, in fact, little is said in terms of either the Keynesian cross or the *IS–LM* about inflation.

6. The negative supply shock case discussed in Chapter 9 is a prime example of "stagflation". However, prices and unemployment can rise together also, following a positive *AD* shock. To see this, reread the explanation of *AD–AS* Figure 9.11, then suppose that expectations readjust and the money illusion disappears from the labor supply. As $g(AL_s)$ shifts upward, the SRAS in the upper right-hand quadrant will shift leftward. Employment and output will decline toward L_1 and Q_1 as the price level rises to P_3. This is the stagflation phase of the adjustment toward neutrality.

7. See J. R. Norsworthy, Michael J. Harper and Kent Kunze, "The Slowdown in Productivity Growth: Analysis of Some Contributing Factors," *Brookings Papers on Economic Activity* No. 2 (1979): 387–471.

Student Self-Test

I. True–False

T F **1.** The *IS–LM* model incorporates the notion that consumption expenditure varies inversely with the interest rate.

T F **2.** Points on the *LM* curve represent combinations of income and the interest rate yielding equilibrium between the demand for and supply of money.

T F 3. A fall in the demand for credit, *ceteris paribus*, would shift the *IS* curve toward the left, reducing the interest rate and income in the *IS–LM* model.

T F 4. In the *IS–LM* model, *ceteris paribus*, a given reduction in government expenditure will reduce aggregate income by a smaller amount than it would in the Keynesian cross model.

T F 5. By the reasoning of the *IS–LM* model, the best possible antirecession policy is to increase the deficit and monetize the debt.

II. Short Answer *(150 words or less each)*

1. Consider the "unemployment equilibrium" shown in Figure 12.10. How does this notion square with the 'Walras's law reasoning by which the attainment of the intersection of the *IS* and *LM* curves was explained?
2. Is the real balance effect entirely missing from the fixed-price *IS–LM*? Explain.
3. Explain the relationship between the fixed-price assumption and the passive response of output and employment to *AD* changes in the *IS–LM* model.
4. List and briefly discuss four problems with the *IS–LM* model.
5. How would a Keynesian economist explain the banking collapse and money stock decline between 1929 and 1933?

III. Completion Problems

1. From the analytical process by which the *IS* and *LM* curves are derived, figure out the shapes of the *IS* and *LM* curves, given different assumptions about income and interest-rate sensitivity of the relevant variables and answer the questions.
   A. The less interest-elastic the demand for money is, the _____ (flatter/steeper) the *LM* curve is.
   B. A demand for money that was interest-inelastic (rather than elastic) would _____ (increase/decrease) the change in income and employment resulting from a given horizontal shift in the *IS* curve.
   C. The interest elasticity of M_d is usually estimated by both Keynesian and non-Keynesian economists to be about _____, which is definitionally _____ (elastic/inelastic).
   D. The less interest-elastic that investment and consumption are, the _____ (flatter/steeper) the *IS* curve is.
   E. In comparison with the *IS* curve resulting from interest-elastic consumption and investment, one that resulted from interest-inelastic consumption and investment would _____ (increase/decrease) the change in income resulting from a given shift in the *LM* curve.
2. You are a Keynesian policy advisor to the president of your country. You have drawn the following graph to show the president, who has a smattering of economic training, how the present situation looks to you.

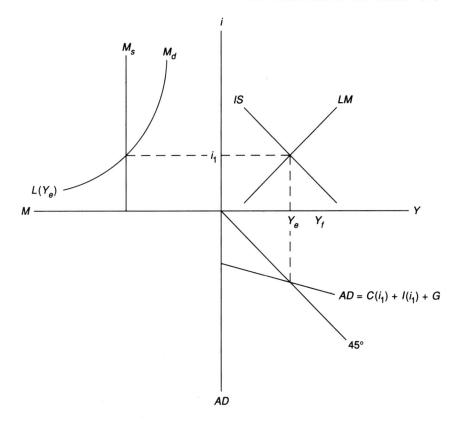

A. Suppose you believe that the problem can and should be cured through pure fiscal policy. Draw on the graph, or on a copy, all of the shifts of the curves that you believe would occur, showing their sequence with numbered arrows.

B. On another copy of the graph, show what you believe would happen if fiscal and monetary policy were employed together to eliminate the gap.

C. Now try pure monetary policy.

CHAPTER 13

The Flexible-Price *IS–LM* Model

The purpose of this chapter is to relax the strict assumption of a predetermined price level and to examine the effects of price flexibility in an *IS–LM* framework. To begin with, however, the effects of price-level changes on the behavioral equations defining the model must be carefully examined. A determinate, flexible-price *IS–LM* model can then be developed and applied to analyze the responses of a flexible price system to different macroeconomic shocks.

Incorporation of real balance effects into this model can be shown to answer certain objections to the notion that flexible prices are macroeconomically stabilizing. The model will also be employed to illustrate the interest rate effects of monetary policy, another task for which the fixed-price *IS–LM* model is inadequate.

Price-Level Changes and the *IS–LM* Curves _____

Consider the *IS* curve. Ignoring the existence of government and the foreign sector for simplicity, the equilibrium condition in the commodity market ($Y = AD$) implies an equality of saving and investment, $S = I$. That is (from Chapter 10), because

$$Co + I = AD$$

and hence

$$Y = Co + I$$

in equilibrium, it follows that

$$Y - Co = I,$$

and because by definition any income left after consumption is saved,

$$S = I.$$

In the fixed price *IS–LM* model saving and investment are written as functions of nominal income and the nominal interest rate, $S = S(Y,i)$ and $I = I(Y, i)$. Because $Y = P \cdot Q$, however, and the price level was assumed predetermined and constant, all ΔY were really changes in real output and income (Q). Hence both saving and investment were actually functions of real income and the nominal interest rate in that fixed-price model.

Allowing the price level to change means, among other things, that the price level (P) must be included as an independent variable in the saving and investment functions. Doing so expresses real saving and investment as functions of real income and the nominal interest rate. That is,

$$S = S\left(\frac{Y}{P}, i\right)$$

and

$$I = I\left(\frac{Y}{P}, i\right).$$

Alternately, they could be expressed as $S(Q,i)$ and $I(Q,i)$ because $Y/P = Q$. In either case, the two equations collapse to one in equilibrium, where

$$S\left(\frac{Y}{P}, i\right) = I\left(\frac{Y}{P}, i\right).$$

From the form of these equations it follows that, as written, changes in the price level will have no effect on real saving and investment, *ceteris paribus*. They are both functions of real income, and for a given Q, a change in the price level changes the numerator of the ratio Y/P in exactly the same proportion as it does the denominator. That is, since $Y = P \cdot Q$, assuming Q constant during ΔP means that $\% \ \Delta Y = \% \ \Delta P$. This is particularly clear from the alternate forms of the functions, $S(Q,i)$ and $I(Q,i)$, from which the price level is apparently absent because it cancels with the P implicit in nominal income.

Now consider the *LM* curve. In the fixed-price *IS–LM* model the demand for nominal money balances is written, in consistence with the *IS* equations, as a function of nominal income and the nominal interest rate. That is, $M_d = L(Y, i)$. Equilibrium in the money market then requires that

$$L(Y, i) = M_s.$$

Treating the price level as a variable means that the demand for money is best explicitly interpreted as a demand for real money balances, and the price level must be included as an independent variable in the demand function. This makes the demand for real balances a function of real income and the nominal interest rate. That is (where $M_d/P = m_d$), the equation should be written as

$$m_d = L(Y/P, i)$$

or alternately as $L(Q, i)$ because $Y = P \cdot Q$. The money stock must also be stated in real terms, as M_s/P. Equilibrium along the *LM* curve then requires that

$$L\left(\frac{Y}{P}, i\right) = \frac{M_s}{P}.$$

Here also, it should be noticed that, from the form of the function, a change in the price level will have no effect on the demand for real money balances, *ceteris paribus*, because $\% \Delta Y = \% \Delta P$. A change in the price level will affect the magnitude of the real money stock, however, causing the *LM* curve to shift. The nature of such shifts can be illustrated with graphs such as in Figure 13.1.

If we assume that real income and output is Q_1, as shown in Figure 13.1(b), the associated demand for real money balances $m_d = L(Q_1)$ is shown in Figure 13.1(a), and because the quantity of real money balances demanded is plotted as an inverse function of the interest rate, i need not be listed in the parenthesis. An initial nominal money stock, M_s is assumed, as is an initial price level (P_1), yielding the initial real money stock M_s/P_1 also shown in Figure 13.1(a). The interest rate that initially clears the money market is therefore i_1, such that the initial *LM* curve in Figure 13.1(b) is LM_1.

Now suppose that the price level were to fall to some $P_0 < P_1$, *ceteris paribus*. This would increase the real money stock to M_s/P_0 as shown in Figure 13.1(a). At the initial income level (Q_1) the interest rate would have to fall to i_0 to clear the money market. In other words, the *LM* would shift outward to LM_0 as shown in Figure 13.1(b). On the other hand, if the price level were to rise rather than fall to some $P_2 > P_1$,

Figure 13.1 Shifts in the Flexible Price *LM* Curve.

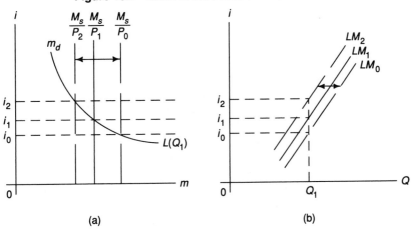

(a)   (b)

ceteris paribus, the real money stock would decline as shown to M_s/P_2. It would then take a higher interest rate i_2 to clear the money market. In other words, the *LM* curve would shift leftward from LM_1 to LM_2.

One more matter should be clarified before proceeding. The reader may have noticed that the form of the money demand function employed here, $m_d = L(Q, i)$, differs from that developed in Chapter 5 and employed in Chapter 7 in one respect: The expected rate of inflation, α^*, is missing from the list of independent variables in the parentheses. This may seem puzzling in a model in which the price level is to be assumed variable. This absence can be justified, however, by simply assuming until further notice that $\alpha^* = 0$.

A Determinate Flexible-Price *IS–LM* Model ————————

Thus far the flexible-price *IS–LM* model being developed here has two equations: a commodity market equilibrium defining the *IS* curve,

$$S\left(\frac{Y}{P}, i\right) = I\left(\frac{Y}{P}, i\right)$$

and a money market equilibrium defining the *LM* curve,

$$L\left(\frac{Y}{P}, i\right) = \frac{M_s}{P}.$$

Unfortunately, this two-equation form is not sufficient, because there are now three variables to be determined: real income, the interest rate, and the price level. This is the problem of the missing equation.[1] It can be solved either by assuming one of the variables to be determined exogenously (which is essentially the fixed-price *IS–LM* solution), or by adding another market equation to the model.

Because the existence of a labor market and a production function are implicit even in the fixed-price *IS–LM*, a sensible solution is to include a labor market explicitly, as in the *AD–AS* model of Chapter 9. Assuming that the labor market is free of money illusion, we find that the demand for and supply of labor are both functions of the real wage: $W/P = f(AL_d)$ and $W/P = g(AL_s)$. Adding these equations results in a model that has a **recursive** or causal character that automatically tends toward full employment. The determination of the variables in the model can be demonstrated as follows and is illustrated as in Figure 13.2.

1. Given labor supply and demand as functions of the real wage, the equilibrium values of employment and the real wage (L_f and w_f) are determined in the labor market, where $f(AL_d) = g(AL_s)$.

Figure 13.2 The Determinate Flexible-Price *IS–LM*.

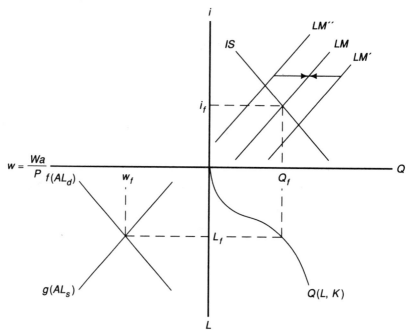

2. Given L_f and the production function, $Q = Q(L, \bar{K})$, the full employment level of real income and production, Q_f, is determined.

3. Given Q_f, i_f (i.e., the full employment interest rate) is determined in the commodity market by the *IS* equation, $S(Q_f, i) = I(Q_f, i)$. That is, because Q_f is given, the interest rate is the only remaining unknown in the *IS* equation, so its value is determined at i_f.

4. Given the full employment values of real output and the interest rate determined in the real sector, a nominal money stock M_s, which is exogenously determined by the Federal Reserve, and a demand function for real money balances $m_d = L(Q_f, i_f)$, then money market equilibrium determines the price level. That is, if

$$\frac{M_s}{P} = L(Q_f, i_f),$$

P_f is determined because the reciprocals are also equal,

$$\frac{P}{M_s} = \frac{1}{L(\cdot)},$$

and hence

$$P_f = \frac{M_s}{L(\cdot)}.$$

5. Given P_f and w_f (the full employment *real* wage), the full employment *nominal* wage is determined at $Wa_f = P_f \cdot w_f$ (because $w_f = Wa/P_f$). Thus all of the variables in the system are determined (and when all three markets are in equilibrium, the bond market can also be argued to be in equilibrium by Walras's law, as in Chapter 12).

Note the similarity of this model to modern quantity theory reasoning. Real variables such as employment, output, and the interest rate are determined by other real variables, such as the capital stock and the real wage. Even the demand for real money balances is ultimately determined in the real side of the market. Then m_d interacts with the exogenously given nominal money stock to determine the price level (and hence the real money stock), shifting the *LM* curve passively from the right or left in the process, as shown in Figure 13.2, until it intersects the *IS* curve at point (Q_f, i_f). The model is neutral and, *ceteris paribus* (particularly holding tastes, technology, and the capital stock constant), exhibits proportionality between price level changes and money stock changes.[2]

Disequilibrium and Adjustment in the Model _____

If price flexibility is perfect and adjustments are instantaneous, no problem of macroeconomic disequilibrium can ever exist and the model is useless for examining such phenomena. Only one modern school of thought (the rational expectations school, examined in Chapter 15) accepts such instantaneous price adjustment and continuous market clearing as a real-world phenomenon. Most economists believe that the excess demand mechanism takes at least some time to produce complete adjustment to macroeconomic shocks and to clear all markets. With this restricted definition of *price flexibility* the model just developed can be employed to examine the process of adjustment to *AD* shocks.

For the first case, assume that an initial general equilibrium is disturbed by a reduction in the money stock, which shifts the *LM* curve toward the left, as shown in Figure 13.3. The rise in the interest rate to i' reduces *AD* by reducing consumption and investment, causing real income to fall to Q'. This can only occur, of course, if employment falls to $L_d < L_f$ as shown. At the initial price level, nominal wage, and hence real wage, w_f, this means that employment is at point x in the third quadrant of the graph.

Figure 13.3 Money Stock Decline in the Flexible-Price *IS–LM*.

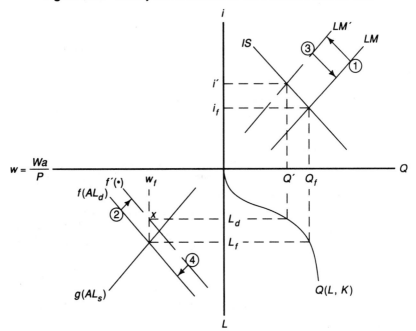

One interpretation of point x is that it is a point off the labor demand curve $f(AL_d)$, because neither the price level nor the aggregate wage have yet fallen, hence the real wage and the value of the marginal product ($P \cdot$ MPL) are unchanged.[3] A common sense reinterpretation of the demand curve, however, in which the VMP is interpreted not as referring to the value of the actual physical addition to output, but to that portion of the physical addition which can be sold, would indicate that the demand for labor has indeed fallen to $f'(AL_d)$, as shown. By this interpretation an excess supply of labor (i.e., unemployment in excess of the natural rate) clearly exists.

In the commodity market excess supply exists in the form of excess plant capacity at the given capital stock. Also, although it appears that no excess supply of output exists because (Q', i') is a point on the *IS* curve, such that real $AD = Q'$ and current production is equal to current sales, firms are holding excess inventories built up during the contraction phase, so in the relevant sense excess supplies of consumer goods do exist. For all of these reasons both prices and wage rates will be pressured to fall, and point (Q', i) is not a stable equilibrium.

If we assume for simplicity that P and Wa fall together and proportionately the real wage does not change. The fall in the price level increases the real money stock, however, shifting the *LM* curve back toward the right and reducing the interest rate in the process. The fall in the interest rate increases consumption and investment, raising real AD along the *IS* curve. The rise in aggregate demand and sales also raises the demand for labor as output expands. Real income and employment are eventually restored at Q_f and L_f because as long as they are less than those values, prices and wage rates will keep falling, shifting the *LM* further toward the right and reducing the interest rate. This is the basic sequence of events shown by the numbered arrows in Figure 13.3.

Now suppose as a second case that, beginning from the same initial equilibrium, a disturbance occurs either in the form of a decline in desired real investment or a decline in government expenditure that reduces aggregate demand, shifting the *IS* curve toward the left and reducing the interest rate. The resulting effects are illustrated in Figure 13.4, which differs somewhat from Figure 13.3 in that the labor market and the aggregate production function are not shown, so that a modified Keynesian cross diagram can be added. This allows the initial disturbance and certain later effects to be made apparent. The second quadrant of Figure 13.4 is also employed to show the demand for and supply of real money balances, the initial values of which are $L(Q_f)$ and M_s/P.

The fall in aggregate demand (interpreted here as *real* quantities demanded in the aggregate, rather than as nominal expenditure) from

Figure 13.4 *AD Decline in the Flexible-Price IS–LM.*

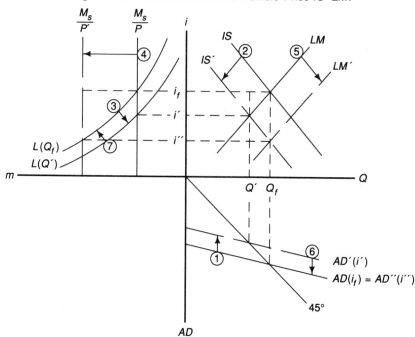

$AD(i_f)$ to $AD'(i')$ shifts the IS curve leftward. Income and the interest rate both fall.[4] The fall in the interest rate would create an excess demand for money, *ceteris paribus*, but the fall in income to Q', where the commodity market clears, reduces the demand for real money balances to $L(Q')$, so that the money market also clears.

As argued in the previous case (the monetary disturbance), although the real aggregate quantity demanded is equal to real income and output per time period at Q', net excess supplies of both goods (in the form of inventory overhang) and labor (unemployment) exist, and hence prices and wage rates will be pressured to fall. The fall in the price level increases the real money stock to M_s/P', as shown in the second quadrant. This shifts the LM curve toward the right and reduces the interest rate further, raising real aggregate demand to $AD''(i'')$. The rise in AD restores income and full employment at Q_f.

Note that the rise in income shifts the demand for real balances back to $L(Q_f)$, so that both the money and commodity markets are clearing. This is the sequence of events shown by the numbered arrows in Figure 13.4. The main lessons here, as in the previous example, are that a point such as (Q', i') is not, in fact, an aggregate equilibrium point (despite being on both the IS and LM), and that if prices are free to adjust in accordance with excess demands, they will act to equilibrate the system. Both of the examples given here run in terms of contractionary pressures because expansionary disturbances are discussed later.

Real Balance Effects in the Flexible-Price Model ———

One characteristically Keynesian feature retained in the flexible-price *IS–LM* model as it has been developed to this point is that all effects of changes in the real money stock on aggregate economic activity occur through interest rate changes. Put another way, real balance effects, in which deviations of the real money stock from real balances demanded directly alter desired purchases of both consumer and producer goods (real consumption and investment), are assumed to be absent from the model. In Chapters 5 and 9 these effects provided a vital explanation of the interconnections among markets, and macroeconomists are increasingly realizing both their theoretical and empirical importance.

Real balance effects can be included in the model by writing in the real money stock as an additional positive shift variable for both consumption and investment. In terms of the savings–investment equality describing the *IS* curve, the equations would then be written as

$$S = S\left(Q, i, \frac{M_s}{P}\right)$$

and

$$I = I\left(Q, i, \frac{M_s}{P}\right),$$

where $\Delta S/\Delta m_s < 0$ and $\Delta I/\Delta m_s > 0$ and $m_s = M_s/P$ as before. This still leaves the model determinate, because no new variables have been introduced that were not previously included and either endogenously or exogenously determined. The theoretical nature of the model is now changed, however, because the *IS* curve shifts positively with the real money stock.

Including the real balance mechanism in the model in this fashion provides answers to two arguments that were used for some time by Keynes and his followers to deny that price level adjustments would stabilize the macroeconomy. The first involved the possible existence of a **liquidity trap**, or infinitely interest-elastic demand for money, which Keynesians thought to be a possible feature of a deep recession. Graphically, a liquidity trap would be shown as a section almost horizontal to the demand for money function, as illustrated in the left-hand side of Figure 13.5.

Since the demand for money is infinitely interest-elastic over a range, the *LM* curve also has a horizontal section, as shown in the right-hand side of the graph. Beginning with a recessionary condition in which the real money stock is M_s/P and the *IS* and *LM* cross at point (Q', i), where $Q' < Q_f$, if real desired consumption and investment are functions only of income and the interest rate, even flexible prices cannot move the economy toward full employment income. True, prices and wage rates will fall, increasing the real money stock and shifting the *LM* toward the right as shown, but because the liquidity trap prevents the interest rate from falling, no increase in aggregate demand occurs and the economy stays at Q'.

This argument impressed many economists, despite repeated empirical failures to find evidence of the real-world existence of liquidity traps. The argument fails, however, if changes in the real money stock affect consumption and investment directly, so that the aggregate demand function can be written as $AD(i, m_s)$ as in Figure 13.6. In this

Figure 13.5 Liquidity Trap in the *IS–LM*.

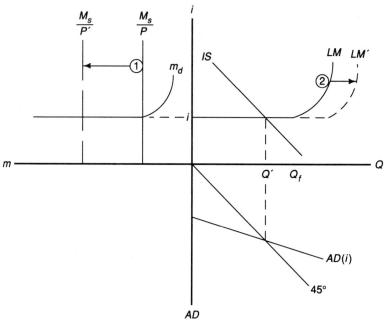

Figure 13.6 *IS–LM* with Liquidity Trap and Real Balance Effect in Consumption.

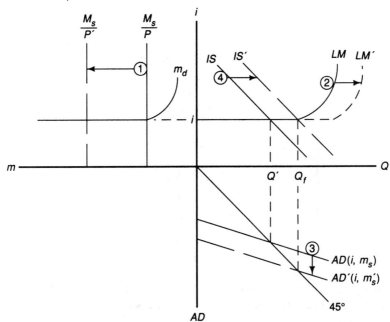

case, the fall in prices precipitated by the recession shifts the real money stock and *LM* curves outward as before and, as before, the interest rate is unaffected. The inclusion of real balance effects on consumption and investment, however, means that the increase in the real money stock shifts the *IS* curve shifts outward with the *LM* curve, and aggregate demand rises to $AD'(m_s')$, restoring the economy to equilibrium at Q_f.

The second argument often employed to deny the stabilizing properties of price level adjustments involved the possible existence of an interest-inelastic *IS* schedule. If the demand for credit for investment purposes is rather insensitive to changes in the interest rate and saving does not respond significantly to interest rate changes, as some empirical studies seem to show, then the *IS* schedule could indeed be rather interest-inelastic.

Figure 13.7 shows an initial situation in which an increasingly interest-inelastic *IS* schedule intersects a normal *LM* schedule at a level of real output and income Q' that is less than Q_f. As before, we need not inquire into the nature of the original disturbance that created this recessionary situation. Again prices and wage rates will fall, increasing

Figure 13.7   Flexible-Price *IS–LM* with Interest-Inelastic *IS*.

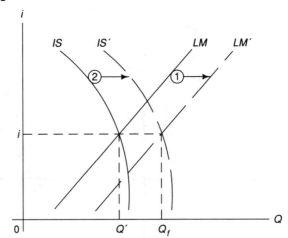

the real value of the money stock (not shown in this case), and shifting the *LM* curve toward the right.

Given the interest-inelastic *IS* curve and the fact that the nominal rate of interest cannot become negative, no such *LM* shift by itself can raise *AD* enough to restore income, output and employment at Q_f. As in the liquidity trap case, however, this result depends on the assumption that the rise in m_s affects *AD* only through the interest rate effect on consumption and investment, which in this case is too small. If the increase in the real money stock raises demand for producer and consumer goods through direct substitution from cash balances, however, so that the *IS* curve shifts rightward to *IS'* as the *LM* shifts, Q_f is restored and prices stop falling.[5]

Dynamic Instability and the Real Balance Effect _____

The claim that the real balance effect (in combination with flexible relative price adjustments) constitutes a reliable macroeconomic stabilization mechanism has not gone unopposed. Indeed, Don Patinkin, the economist most responsible for elaborating real balance effects, stated the central objection himself: falling prices will increase the real money stock, *ceteris paribus*, but might also raise real balances *demanded* just as much, so that equilibrium would not be restored.[6] (In terms of the *IS–LM*, neither the *LM* nor the *IS* would shift toward the right and restore Q_f.)

At a superficial level the argument is that if people came to expect prices to continue falling they might postpone purchases to take advantage of lower future prices. Hence falling prices might cause real aggregate demand to fall, or at least to not rise. This superficial argument, often termed the **expectation effect**, deserves a response. It is difficult to believe that, in a recession, people would starve or otherwise deprive themselves indefinitely of things they need in hopes of attaining future bargains. And only indefinite postponement of additional purchases would prevent the real balance effect from operating.

At a more sophisticated level the argument rests on the observation repeatedly stressed in this book that the expected rate of change in the price level ($\Delta P^*/P = \alpha^*$) affects the perceived costs or benefits of holding real cash balances. In the case of deflation ($\alpha < 0$), money held in cash balances is gaining purchasing power. An expectation that such a rate of deflation will persist may cause an increase in desired real cash balances.

Such an increase in real balances demanded at a given expectation α^* would be a discrete shift, however, from one level to another. It would not be a continuous increase. During the shift, it is true, an existing recession might worsen, and the rate of deflation would temporarily increase. Once the demand shift was complete, however, the deflation (and consequent rise in the real money stock) would rapidly eliminate the excess demand for money and stabilize the economy, assuming that prices and wage rates were both flexible, so that real wage distortion did not occur; see Chapter 9.

Theoretically, however, stabilization would not occur if the temporary acceleration of deflation was widely misinterpreted as being permanent, so that the perceived benefits of holding money increased yet again, real balances demanded shifted outward more (ahead of the rising real money stock), and the deflation rate again accelerated in a self-reinforcing cycle. This form of the argument, in which a movement of the value of money toward equilibrium causes the equilibrium point itself to move away at an accelerating rate, is termed the **dynamic instability of the demand for money**. Taken literally, it implies that, *ceteris paribus*, every rise in the price level accelerates into hyperinflation as the demand for real balances falls toward zero, and every decline in the price level accelerates into hyperdeflation as the demand for real balances rises toward infinity.

It goes almost without saying that there is very little evidence for such dynamically unstable money demand. Hyperinflations have occured, of course, such as those in post-World War I Germany, Austria, and Poland. A study of such inflations by Phillip Cagan, however, found the demand for real money balances to be remarkably stable in each case.[7] Also, there have been significant deflations, the longest in the United States extending from the end of the Civil War in 1865 to the end of the 19th century.

The post-Civil War deflation is instructive for several reasons. First, there is no evidence that the demand for money in this period was dynamically unstable. Second, although intermittent recessions (and one depression) occured, and there was significant social discord centered in the agrarian sector, this was a period of extremely rapid overall economic growth. Indeed, real output and income, both gross and per capita, rose more rapidly in this period than in any other period of similar length in U.S. history.[8]

Some economists claim that dynamic instability (or the *expectation effect*) operated during the Great Depression of 1929 to 1940. Certainly, real money balances increased (although nominal balances fell) for some years as prices declined without restoring full employment and real GNP. Given the observable contractionary policy of the Fed, however, and its failure to act to prevent the banking collapse from further reducing the money stock (see Chapter 10), it is not hard to understand why ongoing deflation was expected and money demand increased.

Also, given the repeated contractionary shocks and relative price (particularly real wage) distortions administered to the economy by the Hoover and Roosevelt administrations, it is little wonder that market equilibration mechanisms were unable to cope. In other recessions, and in the 1893 depression, during which such policy mistakes (beyond those initiating the contraction) were not made, these equilibrating market mechanisms operated with reasonable dispatch; see Chapter 9.

Expected Inflation and the *IS–LM*

As indicated previously, it is time to alter the assumption that the expected rate of inflation (α^*) is zero. So far, price changes discussed have been understood by transactors to involve discrete adjustments from one price level to another and not continuous upward or downward movements. Given recent historical experience, an ongoing change in the price level certainly is a possibility, however. One of the nice properties of the flexible-price *IS–LM* is that it allows examination of inflation and some of its associated phenomena, particularly some interest rate effects of monetary policy, which cannot be analyzed in the fixed-price version.

As shown in Chapter 8, ex post real rate of interest is the difference between the nominal rate and the rate of inflation. That is, looking back over a period of investment or a credit contract, $r = i - \alpha$.

Because a rate of inflation that is not correctly anticipated will redistribute wealth between creditors and debtors, both parties have an incentive to anticipate inflation correctly. Therefore, the ex ante nominal rate settled on in credit transactions will have two components: the desired real interest rate, $\bar{r}$, plus a component designed to compensate for expected inflation. That is, ex ante, $i = \bar{r} + \alpha^*$.

This argument implies that an increase in the expected rate of inflation would shift the saving and investment demand functions in such a way that $S = I$ at a higher nominal interest rate (sufficient that, after inflation, the desired real rate will be attained), as shown in Figure 8.7. In terms of the $IS-LM$ model, however, this event must be illustrated as causing an outward and upward shift of the IS curve, as shown in Figure 13.8, where expected inflation has risen from $\alpha^* = 0$ to some $\alpha^{*\prime} > 0$.

Because output is fixed at Q_f by the labor market and the production function in the flexible-price version of the $IS-LM$ employed here, the interest rate rises to $i' = \bar{r} + \alpha^{*\prime}$, and the LM must shift leftward to pass through that coordinate so that both markets are clearing. What shifts the LM toward the left is the rising prices, which must exceed the rate of nominal money growth generating the inflation by enough to reduce the real value of the money stock to equality with the lower real balances demanded at the higher rates of interest and expected inflation.

With this background all three of the interest rate effects of monetary policy that are examined in the monetary model of Chapter 8 can also be explained in terms of the flexible-price $IS-LM$. Figure 13.9 begins with an initial noninflationary equilibrium at point (Q_f, i) as before. If

Figure 13.8 The Fisher Effect in the Flexible-Price $IS-LM$.

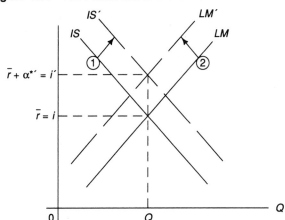

Figure 13.9 Combined Interest Rate Effects in the Flexible-Price *IS–LM*.

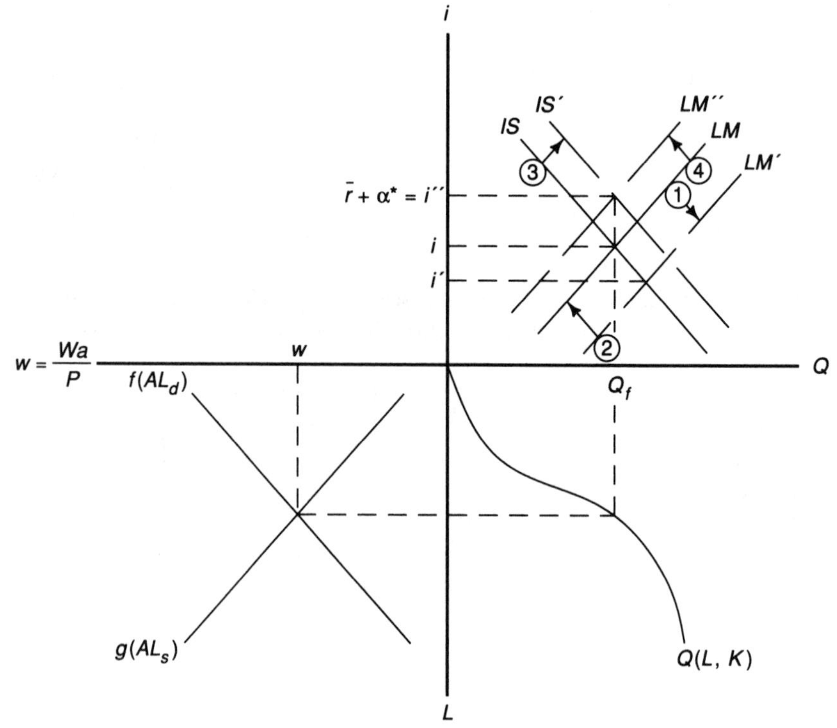

the Federal Reserve now undertakes open market purchases that increase the nominal money stock, before prices rise, the initial effect is to shift the *LM* toward the right to *LM'*, reducing the interest rate to i' to clear all markets. This is the **liquidity effect** of the monetary expansion. As before, it is an inverse relation between M_s and i.

The increase in aggregate demand resulting from the reduction in interest rates (let us ignore the real balance effect on C_0 and I) may actually raise real income to some $Q' > Q_f$, although it may be assumed here for simplicity that this involves additional sales out of inventories and not increased production. Still, it represents excess demand in the relevant sense in commodity markets, and prices begin to rise.

Because the labor market is not subject to money illusion, wage rates rise proportionately with prices, so no change in the real wage, employment or production occurs. Because output does not change, the price level increase is proportional to the initial increase in the money stock, and the real money stock is hence reduced to its original magnitude. Graphically, this means that the *LM* shifts back leftward to its initial position and the interest rate is restored to its original value. This is the **income effect** of the monetary change on the interest rate (the rise in P, Q_f given, means that $Y = P \cdot Q_f$ has risen).

If the Fed increased the nominal stock again, perhaps because it wished to peg the interest rate at i', the same event would occur again. Prices would rise and reduce M_s/P back to its initial value, restoring the interest rate to i. Indeed, if the Fed engaged in continuous money growth in an effort to peg the interest rate at i', they would cause, after an interval, continuous inflation of $\alpha = \Delta M_s/M_s$, and the *LM* would not even move. This would eventually cause expectations to center on that rate, however, such that $\alpha^* = \alpha$, and the Fisher effect would shift the *IS* curve upward, as discussed previously, raising the interest rate to $i'' = \bar{r} + \alpha^*$.

The reduction in real money balances demanded because of the rise in both the interest rate and the expected rate of inflation would cause a temporary acceleration in the inflation rate to some $\alpha' = \Delta P/P > \Delta M_s/M_s$, reducing the real money stock and shifting the *LM* leftward to *LM''*, after which the inflation rate would fall backward to equality with the growth rate of the nominal money stock, and the *LM* would stop shifting. This is the sequence of events shown by the numbered arrows in Figure 13.9. Work out for yourself the sequence of events occuring if the Fed were then to reduce the money growth rate, and hence, after an interval, the inflation rate.

This is the third time, now, that the interest rate effects of monetary policy have been discussed in this book. There is much confusion on the matter, partly caused by past Keynesian teaching that the rate of money growth and the interest rate were inversely related (liquidity effects dominate the others). Figure 13.10 shows the empirical Fisher effect observed in the United States from 1965 to 1980, which was a period of accelerating inflation. Because the expected inflation rate is unobservable, actual inflation rates are plotted against the prime interest rate (i.e., the rate that banks charge their best corporate customers). If we assume that expectations have some accuracy, however, the theorized direct relationship (with a positive intercept, because the interest rate is positive, even with zero inflation) should be observed, and it is.[9]

Ending this chapter with a discussion of inflation sets the stage for Chapters 14 and 15, because they will deal extensively with the economics and political economy of that particular social problem. Chapter 14 will deal in detail with the transformation of the opinions of economists on the neutrality of money in recent years as the theory of expectations adjustment developed. Chapter 15 will deal more generally with the causes and nature of the inflationary process, as well as with possible cures for the problem.

Figure 13.10 The Empirical Fisher Effect, 1965–1980; i = Prime Interest Rate.

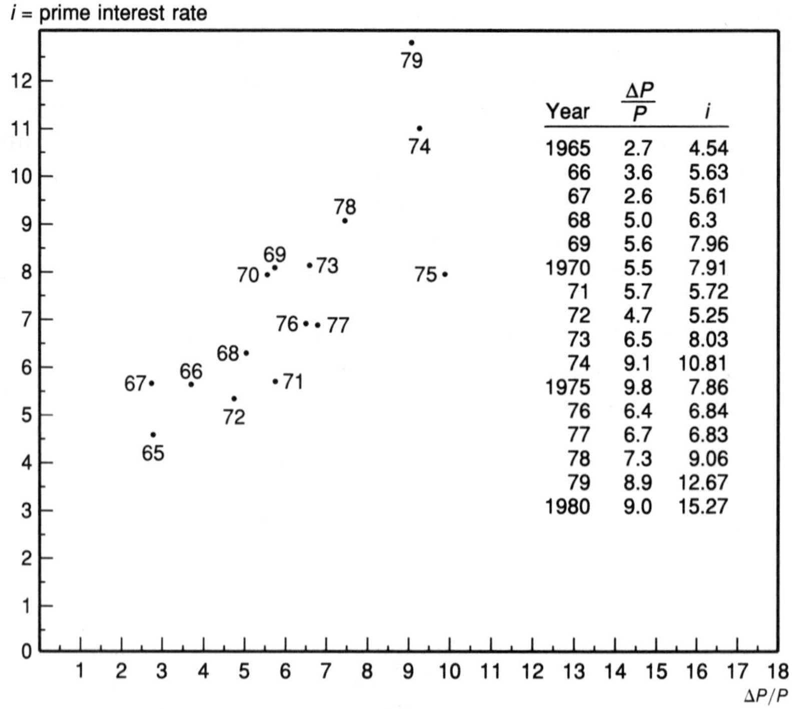

Year	$\dfrac{\Delta P}{P}$	i
1965	2.7	4.54
66	3.6	5.63
67	2.6	5.61
68	5.0	6.3
69	5.6	7.96
1970	5.5	7.91
71	5.7	5.72
72	4.7	5.25
73	6.5	8.03
74	9.1	10.81
1975	9.8	7.86
76	6.4	6.84
77	6.7	6.83
78	7.3	9.06
79	8.9	12.67
1980	9.0	15.27

Source: The Economic Report of the President, 1989: 385 and 390

Summary

The primary arguments of this chapter include the following.

1. Assuming price flexibility in the *IS–LM* amounts to changing the price level from a predetermined constant to a variable. Real saving and investment (and hence the *IS* curve) are then expressed as functions of real income and the nominal interest rate and are neutral to price level changes.

2. Admitting the price level as a variable results in money demand being interpreted in real terms as a function of real income and the interest rate. The money stock is also interpreted explicitly in real terms, and the *LM* curve equilibrium requires that $L(Y/P, i) = M_s/P$.

3. Given this real balance interpretation, a change in P has no effect on the demand for money. It does affect the real money *stock*, however, shifting the *LM* toward the left (if P rises, reducing m_s) or toward the right (if P falls, raising m_s).

4. Including a price-level variable, however, makes the two equation *IS–LM* indeterminate, because there are three variables (i, Q, and P) to be determined by only two equations.

5. The model can be made determinate by adding a labor market equation in which supply and demand are functions of the real wage. The resulting model is recursive (i.e., causal), neutral, and tends automatically toward full employment.

6. Assuming that price-level adjustment is not instantaneous, the model can be employed to examine the process of adjustment to macroeconomic shocks. Contractionary *IS* or *LM* shocks generate unemployment and excess output, which cause the price level to fall. The fall in the price level increases the real money stock, shifting the *LM* rightward, lowering the interest rate and raising *AD* until full employment is restored.

7. The model can be further modified without affecting its determinate character by including the real money stock as a shift variable in both the saving and investment functions, so that $\Delta S/\Delta m_s < 0$ and $\Delta I/\Delta m_s > 0$. This introduces real balance effects into the *IS* curve, making $\Delta IS/\Delta m_s > 0$.

8. Adding real balance effects to the *IS* curve answers certain Keynesian objections (based on the liquidity trap and interest-inelastic saving and investment functions) to the claimed equilibrating tendency of price-level adjustments.

9. Dynamic instability of the demand for money would prevent the real balance effect from working, but evidence for such instability is thin.

10. An important further advantage of the flexible-price *IS–LM* model is that it can be employed to examine inflation and to illustrate the liquidity, income, and Fisher effects of monetary policy on the nominal interest rate.

Notes

1. See Milton Friedman, "A Theoretical Framework for Monetary Analysis," in R.J. Gordon, ed., *Milton Friedman's Monetary Framework* (Fourth printing. Chicago: University of Chicago Press, 1974): 29–40.

2. Mathematically, this is seen as follows: in equilibrium

$$M_s = P \cdot L(Q_f, i_f)$$

so

$$dM_s = P \cdot dL(\cdot) + L(\cdot) \cdot dP$$
$$= L(\cdot) \cdot dP$$

because $dL(\cdot) = 0$. And taking the growth rate,

$$\frac{dM_s}{M_s} = \frac{dP \cdot L(\cdot)}{P \cdot L(\cdot)} = \frac{dP}{P}.$$

3. See Baird, *Macroeconomics: Monetary, Search and Income Theories:* 223–225.

4. The effect of the fall in the interest rate is to raise AD, partly offsetting the initial decline; see Chapter 12. For simplicity, only the net decline from $AD(i_f)$ to $AD'(i')$ remaining after this partial offset occurs is shown here.

5. Anyone who thinks that the liquidity trap and the interest-elastic IS schedule are not contemporary Keynesian arguments for ineffectiveness of monetary expansion should see Robert J. Gordon, *Macroeconomics* (4th ed., Boston: Scott, Foresman and Co., 1987): 115–117. It is worth stressing that the argument of this section also applies to the fixed-price IS–LM (i.e., the context that Gordon employs), because a change in the real money stock generates a real balance effect, whether it occurs because of a change in P with M_s given or because of a change in M_s with P given.

6. See Don Patinkin, "Price Flexibility and Full Employment," *American Economic Review* 38 (September 1948): 543–564, particularly section II on dynamic analysis and policy.

7. Phillip Cagan, "The Monetary Dynamics of Hyperinflation," in Milton Friedman, ed., *Studies in the Quantity Theory of Money* (Chicago: University of Chicago Press, 1956): 25–117.

8. An excellent discussion of this period is contained in Douglas North, et al., *Growth and Welfare in the American Past: A New Economic History* (3rd ed., Englewood Cliffs, N.J.: Prentice–Hall, 1983): Chapter XI.

9. Keynes was aware that nominal interest rates always rose during inflations and fell during deflations. He found this puzzling, however, because it contradicted his view. See John Maynard Keynes, *The General Theory of Employment, Interest, and Money* (New York: Harcourt, Brace, 1936): 141–144.

Student Self-Test ⎯⎯⎯⎯⎯⎯⎯⎯⎯⎯⎯⎯⎯⎯⎯⎯⎯⎯⎯⎯

I. True–False

T F 1. The existence of a Keynesian unemployment equilibrium appears likely even if wages and prices are flexible and adjust to disequilibrium conditions with reasonable rapidity.

T F 2. Whether in the fixed- or flexible-price IS–LM, a point on the IS curve such that $Q < Q_f$ involves excess supplies of commodities.

T F 3. It is reasonable to add a labor market equation to the IS–LM model and to specify supply and demand as functions of the real wage on an assumption that workers, at least in the long run, lack money illusion.

T F 4. If saving and investment are highly interest-inelastic, it is clear, even in the flexible-price IS–LM, that falling prices and wage rates cannot eliminate a recessionary gap.

T F 5. In the flexible-price IS–LM, a change in the expected rate of inflation shifts the IS curve inversely (a rise in α^* shifts it leftward; a fall in α^* shifts it rightward).

II. Short Answer (150 words or less each)

1. Briefly explain the determination of all variables in the flexible-price *IS–LM* in five steps, employing appropriate algebraic expressions.
2. Explain how, in the absence of real balance effects in the commodity market, a liquidity trap would prevent a flexible price level from being macroeconomically stabilizing in the case of a recessionary gap.
3. Why might an assumption of *instantly* correct expectations and *perfect* price flexibility make the flexible-price *IS–LM* rather uninteresting?
4. Why does the flexible-price *IS–LM* seem to have a great deal in common with the quantity theory?
5. How does the treatment of inflationary expectations in the flexible-price *IS–LM* relate to your answer to the previous question?

III. Completion Problems

1. Suppose that Congress sets the minimum wage at $20 per hour and indexes it to the price level, effectively pegging the real wage at a value significantly above w_f.

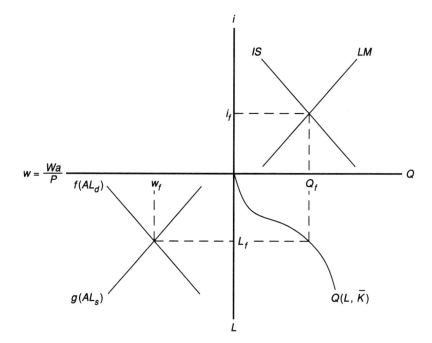

A. On the above flexible-price *IS–LM* graph, or on a copy, show all of the changes in the curves and variables on the axes that would result, indicating their sequence with numbered arrows.
B. Write a brief five-step explanation of the determination of the variables in the system, beginning with the pegging of the real wage by Congress.

2. Dynamic instability: Circle the correct answer.
   A. *Ceteris paribus*, if prices fell and increased the real money stock, but the demand for money increased at the same rate as a result, then the *IS* and *LM* curves would both
      i. Shift out toward the right.
      ii. Shift back toward the left.
      iii. Remain unchanged.
   B. *Ceteris paribus*, if prices increased and reduced the real money stock, but the demand for money fell at the same rate as a result, then the *IS* and *LM* curves would both
      i. Shift out toward the right.
      ii. Shift back toward the left.
      iii. Remain unchanged.

PART IV

Modern Macroeconomics: Revolutions and Evolution

CHAPTER 14

The Phillips Curve and Expectations Adjustment

The Keynesian revolution of the 1930s and 1940s massively transformed both theoretical and policy analysis in economics. Economics itself was dichotomized into microeconomics and macroeconomics, and the theoretical connections between the two were rather weak at first. For about three decades the teaching of macroeconomics consisted almost solely of exposition of the Keynesian cross and the Hicksian fixed-price *IS–LM* model. Keynesian economists did not begin to dominate government policy positions, however, until 1960.

When they gained power, Keynesian policies initially seemed to be successful. A tax reduction engineered by the Kennedy administration in 1962 (see Chapter 16) had the desired effect of increasing the growth of output and employment. The results of later Keynesian policies under the Johnson, Nixon, and Carter administrations, in the form of chronic deficits, rising inflation rates, and simultaneously rising unemployment rates, were less desirable.

In combination with certain theoretical developments these events gave rise to a second revolution in macroeconomics, which has partly reversed the Keynesian theoretical revolution. The first phase of this revolution is sometimes termed the **monetarist counterrevolution**, involving the emergence of the modern quantity theory as an important paradigm with many adherents.[1] The second and more recent phase involved the emergence from the monetarist camp—with some Keynesian defections also—of a small group of influential theorists known as **new classical economists**. The purpose of this chapter is to discuss this revolution and the events generating it.

The Early Phillips Curve _____

Both theoretical and empirical cracks in the Keynesian foundation began to appear as early as the 1940s. The first theoretical chink was Patinkin's demonstration of the real balance effect as an alternate (or perhaps complementary) mechanism to interest rate changes as a channel through which monetary policy could affect the real sector. Empirical evidence contradicting the Keynesian model appeared in the immediate post-war period when Federal Reserve attempts to peg bond interest rates at low levels through expansionary monetary policy were unsuccessful, resulting in the abandonment of such efforts in 1953.[2]

Perhaps a more nagging sense of discontent was generated by the inflation of the 1950s. Inflation had fallen from its high wartime levels but had not disappeared. Instead, prices continued rising steadily at a 2 to 3 percent rate throughout the decade. The Keynesian model is essentially a depression model, and it began to occur to many economists that in an inflationary period a model that assumed (without explaining) the price level to be given and consistently lacks explanatory power and must soon be either amended or replaced. This would be particularly likely if it appeared that policies of the type implied by such a model had anything to do with generating the inflation.[3]

For economists who thought highly of the Keynesian model (clearly, the vast majority at the time), an apparent solution known as the **Phillips curve** appeared in 1958. In that year a New Zealand economist, named A. W. Phillips, published an important empirical study of unemployment and wage changes in Great Britain covering several decades.[4] Phillips's data showed a clear inverse relationship between unemployment and the rate of wage inflation. That is, in periods of tight labor markets (i.e., low rates of unemployment) wage rates increased rapidly, and in periods of slack labor markets (i.e., high unemployment) wage-rate increases were slower.

Keynesian economists in the United States quickly began replicating Phillips's study with U.S. data. They made an important change in its interpretation however. By assuming that firms generally set prices at a fixed percentage markup over prime unit labor costs, the Phillips curve was transformed into an inverse relationship between the unemployment rate and the rate of price inflation.[5] In general, where Ω = the unemployment rate and $\alpha = \Delta P/P$ as before, the Phillips curve equation is

$$\alpha = f(\Omega), \frac{\Delta \alpha}{\Delta \Omega} < 0.$$

Such a Phillips curve for the years 1954 to 1969 is shown in Figure 14.1, which plots and dates the inflation and unemployment rate combinations for each year in that interval listed in Table 14.1.

In this form the Phillips curve rapidly gained wide acceptance, for at least three reasons. First, most studies conducted in the 1950s and early

Figure 14.1 The Early Phillips Curve.

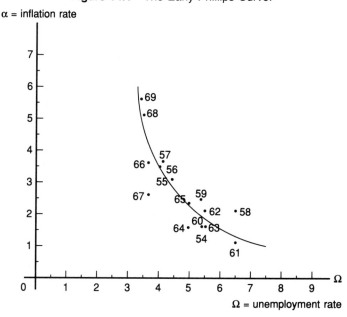

TABLE 14.1

Date	Unemployment rate	Inflation rate
1954	5.4	1.6
1955	4.3	3.2
1956	4.0	3.4
1957	4.2	3.6
1958	6.6	2.1
1959	5.3	2.4
1960	5.4	1.6
1961	6.5	1.0
1962	5.4	2.2
1963	5.5	1.6
1964	5.0	1.5
1965	4.4	2.2
1966	3.7	3.6
1967	3.7	2.6
1968	3.5	5.0
1969	3.4	5.6

Source: Economic Report of the President, 1987: 249 and 285

1960s confirmed the relationship. Second, the relationship seemed to provide at least a tenuous microeconomic basis for a theory of price level adjustment congenial to the Keynesian viewpoint. Third, economists are used to thinking in terms of hard choices involving opportunity costs, a notion clearly implied in the Phillips curve. This particularly appealed to Keynesian economists, who could now justify inflation generated by expansionary governmental policies on the basis that increases in the inflation rate were associated with reductions in the unemployment rate.

The rapid acceptance of the Phillips curve was based on an assumption that it described a stable relationship between the two variables. Only a stable relationship could be exploited for policy purposes by choosing the "socially optimal" combination of inflation and unemployment from among the many points on the curve. From the beginning, however, there were disquieting indications from many studies that the relationship might not be stable. Like a demand or supply curve, there might be variables which, by taking on different values, could cause the Phillips curve to shift inward or outward.

Such shifts would, of course, render the Phillips curve useless for policy purposes if they were unpredictable, and so efforts began to be made to identify the primary shift variables and estimate their effects on the curve. Variables employed included such things as measures of profits, union strength, productivity, dispersion of the labor force across labor markets, and so on. Where Z = such a variable (or perhaps even a *vector* of such variables), the equation of the Phillips curve became

$$\alpha = Z + f(\Omega).$$

Clearly, a change in the value of Z would shift the vertical intercept of the Phillips curve in the same direction.

The Natural Rate Hypothesis

In the late 1960s and early 1970s a set of related events occurred that caused macromonetary economists to rethink the theory of the Phillips curve. The first of these came in 1967 when Milton Friedman was elected president of the American Economic Association. The newly elected president always addresses the AEA Convention, and the remarks are later published in the Association's Journal.[6] Friedman's article has become a classic, and among its several contributions was the development of what is termed the **natural rate hypothesis** (NRH).

Friedman's discussion dealt with what he thought could and could not be accomplished with monetary policy. First he argued that monetary policy could not be employed to peg the interest rate permanently at a value different than its natural equilibrium rate. His reasoning (see Chapters 5, 8, and 13): the short-run (liquidity) effect of monetary growth on the interest rate is indeed an inverse relation, but any attempt to use it to peg the interest rate at a high or low value will set the long-run (income and Fisher) direct effects into operation, eventually restoring the natural rate, contrary to the claims of the fixed-price Keynesian model.

In the same manner of reasoning Friedman then went on to argue that monetary policy could not be employed to peg the unemployment rate. In so doing he developed the concept of the natural rate of unemployment; see Chapter 4. The concept is highly analogous to that of the natural rate of interest. According to Friedman, there is a natural, general equilibrium unemployment rate that is consistent with the degree of dynamism in the economy (i.e., the frictional factor, resulting in normal turnover and job search) and the particular structural characteristics of the labor market. He explicitly listed such structural factors as market imperfections (e.g., labor monopolies and minimum-wage laws), stochastic variability of demands and supplies, search costs, and so on.

In order to be perfectly clear, Friedman pointed out that his intention in employing the term *natural rate of unemployment* was not to imply that it was immutable and unchangeable—many of the structural and frictional factors could obviously be affected by legislation of various sorts—but only to distinguish between real and monetary forces. Attempts to reduce unemployment to some target value below the natural rate through monetary policy, however, could only be temporarily rise more rapidly than wage rates, so that the real wage rate this result could succeed in the short run by causing product prices to temporarily rise more rapidly than wage rates, so that the real wage rate fell. Firms, experiencing increased profits, would increase their employment, reducing unemployment below the natural rate. This would occur if workers did not anticipate the higher price inflation.

Sooner or later, however, workers would observe and adjust their expectations to the higher inflation rate and bring pressure for rates of wage rate increase sufficient to restore the real wage rate. As this occurred, the unemployment rate would increase until it once again approached the natural rate. By this reasoning there is no permanent (but only a temporary) tradeoff between inflation and unemployment. The Phillips curve is, in other words, a transitory and rather illusory phenomenon. As a rough empirical estimate Friedman offered two to five years as the time period such an adjustment to a new rate of inflation might require.[7]

The Adaptive Expectations Mechanism _____

Friedman's NRH was the first factor motivating economists to rethink the factors shifting the Phillips curve, because it made clear that expectations adjustment would have that effect. The second factor that caused such rethinking was an innovation in the modeling of expectations adjustment, known as the **adaptive expectations model**. This model of expectations adjustment is essentially that employed by Friedman in his permanent income hypothesis, developed in the 1950s; see Chapter 3.[8] In 1967, however, an adaptive expectations model was employed in a highly technical paper on the Phillips curve by Edmund Phelps, which reached conclusions essentially identical to those of Friedman's presidential address.[9]

According to the adaptive expectations or error learning model, people form their expectation of the rate of inflation by observing past inflation, and they adjust their expectation upward or downward in each period by some fraction of the difference between current observed and expected inflation. That is, where t = some increment of time, and $0 < \beta \leq 1$,

$$\frac{\Delta \alpha^*}{\Delta t} = \beta(\alpha - \alpha^*), \qquad \Delta t = 1.$$

From this formulation the expected rate of inflation will rise if current inflation is higher than anticipated, that is, if $\alpha > \alpha^*$ so that $\beta(\alpha - \alpha^*) > 0$. On the other hand, α^* will fall whenever current inflation is less than expected, that is, when $\alpha < \alpha^*$ so that $\beta(\alpha - \alpha^*) < 0$. If $\alpha = \alpha^*$, however, it follows that $\Delta \alpha^*/\Delta t = 0$.

Such an adjustment is easy to illustrate with a little arithmetic. Suppose that $\beta = .8$, $\alpha = .10$, and $\alpha^* = .05$. Then

$$\frac{\Delta \alpha^*}{\Delta t} = .8(.10 - .05)$$

$$= .8(.05)$$

$$= .04$$

and

$$\alpha^{*'} = \alpha^* + \Delta \alpha^*$$

$$= .05 + .04$$

$$= .09.$$

If the parameter β had been equal to one, the expectation would have adjusted fully in a single time period. Clearly, the mechanism would work the same way for negative inflation rate surprises. The reader can easily construct an example.

It is useful also to illustrate the adaptive expectations mechanism graphically. This is done in Figure 14.2, which measures actual inflation rates on the vertical axis and expected rates on the horizontal axis. If identical scales are assumed the 45° line shown connects points of long-run equilibrium at which $\alpha = \alpha^*$, so that $\Delta\alpha^*/\Delta t = 0$. All points between the 45° line and the vertical axis, such as point $A = (\alpha_a^*, \alpha)$, involve combinations of α and α^*, so that $\alpha > \alpha^*$ and $\Delta\alpha^*/\Delta t > 0$, causing α^* to increase over time until the 45° line is reached. All points between the 45° line and the horizontal axis, however, such as point $B = (\alpha_b^*, \alpha)$, involve combinations of α and α^*, so that $\alpha < \alpha^*$ and $\Delta\alpha^*/\Delta t < 0$, causing α^* to decrease toward the 45° line.

Although, as theoretical innovations, the natural rate hypothesis and adaptive expectations were impressive, by themselves they may not have revolutionized macromonetary economics. The straw that broke the back of Keynesian thinking was an empirical event. In the years immediately following these innovations, money growth and the inflation-rate accelerated and the primary predictions of the Friedman–Phelps hypothesis were borne out. As Friedman had predicted, the higher money growth was associated with higher, not lower, interest rates and more important, the unemployment rate increased rather than decreased.[10] This is shown in Figure 14.3, which duplicates Figure 14.1 except that it adds unemployment and inflation combinations from 1970 to 1980, which are listed in Table 14.2. These magnitudes are

Figure 14.2 The Adaptive Expectations Mechanism.

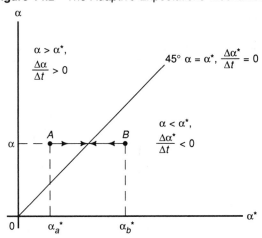

Figure 14.3 Shift in the Empirical Phillips Curve.

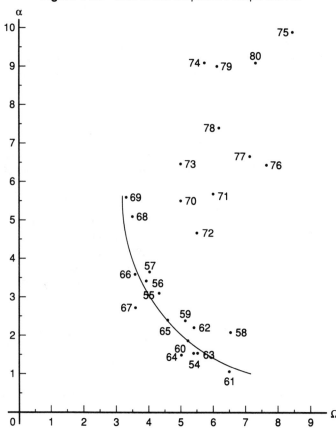

TABLE 14.2

Date	Unemployment rate	Inflation rate
1970	4.8	5.5
1971	5.8	5.7
1972	5.5	4.7
1973	4.8	6.5
1974	5.5	9.1
1975	8.3	9.8
1976	7.6	6.4
1977	6.9	6.7
1978	6.0	7.3
1979	5.8	8.9
1980	7.0	9.0

Source: Economic Report of the President, 1987: 249 and 285

clearly off the predicted values of the earlier curve, indicating that the curve itself had undergone a large outward shift. This stagflation (i.e., simultaneously rising unemployment and inflation) could not be easily explained in terms of the Keynesian model and tended to discredit the notion of the Phillips curve as a stable relationship that could be exploited for policy purposes.

The Expectations-Adjusted Phillips Curve _____

The events discussed previously shocked macromonetary economists into realizing, first, that the effects of monetary policy on real economic activity largely stem from relative price distortions and, second, that such effects themselves tend to set in motion expectations adjustments that act to correct the relative price distortions. As a result, new respect was gained for the notion of the long-run neutrality of money. These matters are easily illustrated by modeling the expected rate of inflation as the primary shift variable in the Phillips curve in the Friedman–Phelps manner to derive the **short-run expectations-adjusted Phillips curve**. Upon defining $Z = \lambda\alpha^*$, the equation of this curve becomes

$$\alpha = \lambda\alpha^* + f(\Omega),$$

where $0 < \lambda \leq 1$. If $f(\Omega)$ is assumed for simplicity to have a linear form, the equation is

$$\alpha = \lambda\alpha^* + a - b \cdot \Omega,$$

where $\Delta\alpha/\Delta\Omega = -b$ is its slope.

Given this expression, the position of the short-run Phillips curve depends on the expected rate of inflation. The curve shifts outward away from the origin as α^* rises and back toward the origin as α^* falls. Figure 14.4 shows several different possible positions of the Phillips curve associated with different possible values of α^*. A horizontal line drawn at an arbitrarily chosen actual inflation rate intersects each of the possible curves, and the associated rate of unemployment is different in each case, varying directly with α^*.

One more feature of the graph needs to be clearly understood. The Phillips curve associated with $\alpha^* = 0$ must intersect the horizontal axis at Ωn, the natural rate of unemployment, because $\alpha = 0$ also at that point. In fact, assuming a complete lack of money illusion, such that $\lambda = 1$ and that the different expectations are fully incorporated in each case in the positions of the curve, the value of α^* associated with any

Figure 14.4 The Short-Run Expectations-Adjusted Phillips Curve.

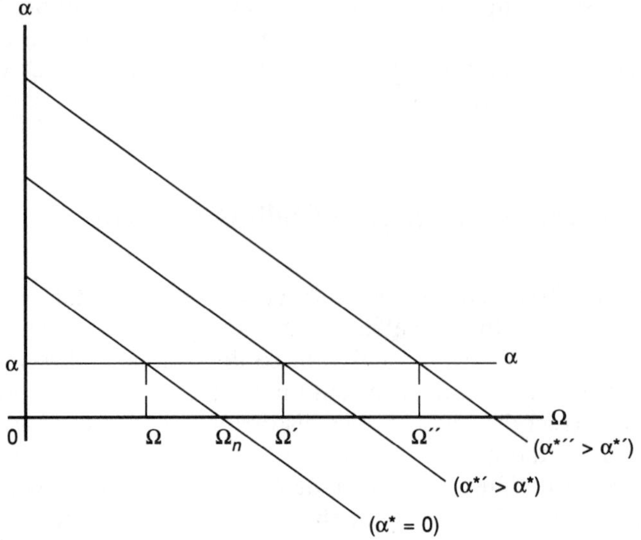

given position can be found at the point on the curve lying vertically above Ωn by reading the associated inflation rate off the vertical axis.

Now assuming adaptive expectations, such that $\alpha^* = \alpha$ and $\Delta\alpha^*/\Delta t = 0$ in long-run equilibrium, the equation of the long-run Phillips curve can be derived from that of the short-run curve. Where

$$\alpha = \lambda\alpha^* + a - b \cdot \Omega,$$

then

$$\alpha - \lambda\alpha^* = a - b \cdot \Omega,$$

and if $\alpha^* = \alpha$,

$$\alpha(1 - \lambda) = a - b \cdot \Omega$$

and

$$\alpha = \frac{a - b\Omega}{1 - \lambda}$$

is the equation of the long-run Phillips curve. Note that the slope of this curve is $\Delta\alpha/\Delta\Omega = -b/(1 - \lambda)$, which is greater than $-b$, the slope of the short-run curve. In fact, as λ approaches unity (i.e., as money illusion approaches zero), the long-run Phillips curve tends to become vertical.

The long-run Phillips curve describes the adjustment path of the short-run curve as the expected rate of inflation approaches the actual rate. To illustrate such an adjustment, suppose that initially $\alpha^* = \alpha = 0$ and $\Omega = \Omega n = 5$ percent, as shown in Figure 14.5, which combines Figures 14.2 and 14.4. Now suppose that the monetary authorities, acting on a belief that the Phillips curve is stable and that unemployment is too high, employ monetary expansion to raise the inflation rate to 4 percent and reduce the unemployment rate to 3 percent along the initial Phillips curve.

Raising α to 4 percent makes $\alpha > \alpha^*$, however, causing expectations to adjust upward, as shown in the left-hand quadrant of Figure 14.5. As α^* adjusts upward toward 4 percent, the short-run Phillips curve shifts outward in the right-hand quadrant, causing Ω to approach Ωn. A line connecting points of final equilibrium in which expectations have fully adjusted will be vertical at Ωn if $\lambda = 1$. If some money illusion persists, such that $\lambda < 1$, the line connecting the points of final equilibrium will be negatively sloped (because the short-run curve will shift only part of the way out), although steeper than the short-run curve, as shown.

Note that this adjustment process would also work in reverse, as contractionary policies were employed to reduce the rate of inflation below people's existing expectation. In that case unemployment would

Figure 14.5 Long-Run Adjustment of the Phillips Curve.

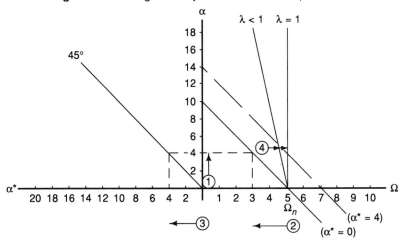

initially rise above Ωn but then approach Ωn as expectations adjusted downward, *ceteris paribus*, shifting the short-run Phillips curve toward the left. Again, the long-run curve would be vertical at Ωn if $\lambda = 1$ and negatively sloped if $\lambda < 1$.

In the years following the appearance of the Friedman–Phelps hypothesis numerous studies were undertaken to estimate the value of the parameter on the inflation expectation. The bulk of these studies were unable to reject the hypothesis that its value was unity.[11] Casual inspection of the values of inflation and unemployment from 1970 to 1980 plotted in Figure 14.3 may suffice to convince the reader of a lack of an inverse relation between the two over that period.[12]

The Accelerationist Hypothesis _____

In the example given above, the government acts on an assumption that the Phillips curve is of the form and magnitude

$$\alpha = a - b \cdot \Omega$$
$$= .10 - 2 \cdot \Omega$$

so that an inflation rate of 4 percent would reduce the unemployment rate to 3 percent. The Phillips curve has the form and magnitude

$$\alpha = \lambda \alpha^* + a - b \cdot \Omega$$
$$= \lambda \alpha^* + .10 - 2 \cdot \Omega$$

however, which is equivalent to their estimated equation only because expected inflation is initially zero. Ex post the government finds its policy frustrated, however, because an inflation rate of 4 percent causes people's expectation to rise to that magnitude, shifting the Phillips curve outward, and where $\lambda = 1$ the solution to the equation $.04 = \lambda(.04) + .10 - 2 \cdot \Omega$ is only the natural rate of unemployment, $\Omega n = 5$ percent.

Friedman, Phelps, and their followers pointed out, however, that in such cases there is a simple solution available to the government and monetary authorities if they are determined to keep unemployment below Ωn. Continuing the example, if the rise in the expected rate of inflation to 4 percent makes the equation of the Phillips curve $\alpha = .04 + .10 - 2 \cdot \Omega$, the government can work on this new curve, keeping the unemployment rate at 3 percent by raising the inflation rate to 8 percent (the solution of the equation for α if $\Omega = .03$, as can also be seen from Figure 14.5). Of course, that will cause the expected rate of inflation to adapt upward toward 8 percent over time, shifting the Phillips curve outward again, but the government need only raise the inflation rate by the required amount as that occurs.

This argument that the government can keep $\Omega < \Omega n$ permanently by causing the rate of inflation to accelerate continuously is known as the **accelerationist hypothesis**. This hypothesis gained great influence among macromonetary economists in the early 1970s, because the inflation rate was accelerating at that time, and the hypothesis seemed to explain what the monetary authorities were trying to do.[13] It should be understood, however, that the accelerationists were not saying that government should act in this manner, but only that the option to do so was available. In fact, the monetarist argument seems to have been that because there is no tradeoff between inflation and unemployment, but only between the acceleration of inflation and unemployment, the costs of such a policy would be too high.

A second important point is that accelerationism is an inherent property of the Friedman–Phelps argument because of the adaptive expectations mechanism assumed in that argument. As discussed earlier, this model assumes people's expectation of the inflation rate adjusts partially in each time period in the direction of an inflation rate that is different than the current expectation. This amounts to an assumption that the expectation is formed purely by observation of past inflation rates as a weighted average of such rates with higher weights given to more recent observations. The problem with this mechanism, however, is that it will always underestimate accelerating inflation.

Here again the point can be illustrated with a little algebra. Suppose that prices have been rising steadily at 10 percent per year for some time, so that $\alpha^* = 10$ percent also, but that the inflation rate starts rising by one percentage point per year. Assume also that $\beta = .8$ as before. Expectations begin adjusting over time as follows:

$$\frac{\Delta \alpha^*}{\Delta t} = \beta(\alpha - \alpha^*) \qquad \text{(where } \Delta t = 1 \text{ year)},$$

$$= .8(.11 - .10)$$

$$= .008$$

and

$$\alpha^{*\prime} = \alpha^* + \Delta \alpha^*$$

$$= .108 \text{ (or 10.8 percent)}.$$

But inflation has simultaneously risen to $\alpha' = 12$ percent, so

$$\frac{\Delta\alpha^*}{\Delta t} = \beta(.12 - .108)$$
$$= .8(.012)$$
$$= .0096$$

and

$$\alpha^{*\prime\prime} = \alpha^{*\prime} + \Delta\alpha^*$$
$$= .108 + .0096$$
$$= .1175 \quad \text{(i.e., 11.75 percent)}$$

which is less than α'. Also, the inflation rate has already risen to $\alpha'' = 13$ percent while the expectation was adjusting to 11.75 percent, so the expectation is not only not closing on the actual inflation rate, but it is also getting further behind. Indeed, it will always be behind as long as inflation is accelerating, even if the value of the parameter β is unity.

It is important to note that, even to the monetarists themselves, this was a disturbing property of the model. Adaptive expectations was a great step forward in modeling people as conscious beings who made rational supply and demand decisions on the basis of real relationships rather than on purely nominal magnitudes. It seemed to embody irrationality at a higher level, however. Although people could not be permanently fooled by raising prices continuously at a given rate, the government could permanently fool them into irrational supply and demand decisions through accelerating inflation.

This disturbing property of the model became even more disturbing as the inflation and unemployment experience of the 1970s unfolded. By the middle of the decade many economists had begun to realize that the same stagflationary combination of rising inflation rates and increasing unemployment rates that was clearly refuting the Keynesian view of the Phillips curve was also casting doubt on accelerationism. That is, even accelerating inflation did not result in low or falling unemployment rates.

It should be recognized that the evidence is not as clear as has sometimes been claimed. Reality is always complex, with different events affecting a variable, such as unemployment occurring simultaneously (rather than on a *ceteris paribus* basis), making it difficult to sort out the effects of each. Demographic changes may have been raising the natural rate of unemployment itself in this period, for example; see Chapter 8. Also, because of actions of the OPEC cartel, there was a major supply shock in 1973 (and another, smaller one in

1979), which had the effect of simultaneously raising the price level and causing a recession; see Chapter 9.

Nevertheless, the experience of this period not only cast severe doubt on the Keynesian notion that people can be permanently fooled by government *AD* policy generating a given rate of inflation, but it also provided little reason for believing that even accelerating inflation would permanently fool people into making incorrect supply or demand decisions. In this sense policy induced changes in the growth rate of the money stock seemed to be more neutral than orthodox monetarists claimed. It was such observations that gave rise to the second phase of the modern revolution in macromonetary theory.

Rational Expectations and Policy Ineffectiveness _____

Because accelerationism is an implication of adaptive expectations, doubts about accelerationism resulted in doubts about the adaptive expectations mechanism. The partial adjustment of expectations in this mechanism toward a new inflation rate in each time period results in the expectation being systematically incorrect (i.e., above or below the true value of inflation for an enduring period), resulting in enduring errors in supply and demand decisions. In statistical jargon this is referred to as **serial correlation of the forecast error**. (A variable is said to be *serially correlated* when, for an enduring period, it is persistently above or persistently below its trend value).

The problem with a model that implies serial correlation of forecast errors is that it appears to be incompatible with the standard economic assumption that individuals are rational maximizers. This is because such systematic forecast errors lead people to make supply and demand decisions that they later regret. Because information that their forecast errors are serially correlated is provided to people both costlessly (i.e., without the necessity of devoting resources to information search) and forcibly by their market activities, rational maximizing agents would quickly revise any decision rule that resulted in systematic errors.

It would be particularly irrational to continue employing an expectations formation rule that generated systematic errors in part as a consequence of relying solely for a data source on past observations of the variable in question while ignoring other available sources of relevant information. Instead, rational agents will settle on an expectations formation rule that employs all sources of relevant information available at reasonable cost on the factors determining the magnitude of the variable, including (in the case of the expected inflation rate) current and past monetary policy.

Individual forecast errors generated by such a rule will tend to be serially uncorrelated; that is, while the individual might occasionally make errors (even large ones), they would be randomly distributed around the correct value of the variable being anticipated. Aggregating over such rational individuals, however, the mean of agent's forecasts will center on the correct value of the variable being predicted, so long as the magnitude of that variable is being determined by a systematic, observable process. This theory is known as the **rational expectations hypothesis** (REH).

The primary implication of this theory is that as long as prices and wage rates are flexible, no systematic government demand management policy can affect real variables such as output or employment, even temporarily. In terms of the AD–AS model of Chapter 9, no systematic monetary or fiscal policy that succeeded at shifting the AD curve toward the right would raise output or employment beyond Q_f. All agents, including workers would forsee the ultimate price change resulting and adjust accordingly. The SRAS curve would shift toward the left as the price level increased, and nothing real would change, as shown in Figure 9.13. In terms of the Phillips curve, there would be no tradeoff between inflation and unemployment even in the short run, so long as that inflation was generated by systematic policy, and even accelerating inflation resulting from such policy would not reduce unemployment below the natural rate.

It follows from the proposition that rational agents will always anticipate and offset any systematic demand management policy (which is known as the **policy ineffectiveness proposition**) that only random, unsystematic monetary changes can affect real variables. By definition, such changes cannot be anticipated and hence will induce errors in expectations that will be common to rational agents in the aggregate. An unanticipated positive monetary shock will cause people to underestimate the price level or the inflation rate, such that unemployment will be below the natural rate (and output will be above Q_f). A random negative monetary shock will cause agents to overestimate the price level or the inflation rate, such that unemployment exceeds the natural rate.[14]

Because the control of the monetary authorities over the money stock is imperfect, given monetary changes usually contain both anticipated and unanticipated components. The unanticipated component will be small if control is tight and policy systematic. If we assume that only the unanticipated portion can affect real variables, however, it is natural to wonder whether the monetary authorities might want to raise the magnitude of that component. Indeed, many analysts have noted that the FOMC carries out its policy decisions in extreme secrecy, as if it wished to surprise people. Of course, such secrecy alone would not suffice to yield policy effectiveness if policy is systematic, because rational agents can observe the whole past pattern of monetary response and behavior and infer future monetary actions.

The Fed often changes its operating procedures and intermediate targets, however, as analysts have also noted. By assuming that rational agents must observe some serial correlation of errors before revising their decision rule to correctly anticipate the new behavior pattern of the monetary authorities, policy may have some effectiveness during the learning period. The frequent changes in operating procedures necessary to make policy actions continuously effective, however, would amount essentially to a policy of random monetary changes.

A policy of random changes in the money stock or its growth rate is, almost by definition, no policy at all. Certainly, from a social perspective, if not from that of the monetary authorities, such policy is undesirable. The primary policy conclusion rational expectations theorists derive, therefore, is that the random element in monetary policy should be reduced as much as possible and that the best way to do this is through imposition of some form of money growth rule. Advocacy of such a rule, and the tendency to identify aggregate demand shocks with unanticipated changes in the level or growth rate of the money supply, indicate the monetarist origins and orientation of most rational expectations theorists.

Criticisms of Rational Expectations

As with adaptive expectations, the theory of rational expectations was developed some years before it was prominently employed in monetary analysis. Its modern incarnation began with a paper by John Muth in 1961.[15] In the early 1970s, however, economists like Robert E. Lucas, Thomas Sargent, and Neil Wallace began applying the model in criticism of Phillips curve reasoning and adaptive expectations.[16] Since then, the REH has become perhaps the most important, influential, and hotly debated of recent ideas in macromonetary economics.

Criticisms of the REH abound and most have some merit. Keynesian advocates of the Phillips curve, who have to find some short-run tradeoff to justify discretionary policy, are split in their defense. One group, led by Janet Yellin and George Akerloff, insists that transactors are not completely rational; that they use rules of thumb in forming expectations and can be fooled for enduring periods. In this view, such Keynesians are perhaps uncomfortably allied with a subset of monetarists that continues to accept the smaller degree of irrationality inherent in the adaptive expectations model. Rational expectations theorists denigrate such rules as ad hoc because they are not derived from a theory of maximizing behavior. Ad hoc rules may be useful to agents although they generate some serial correlation of errors, however, as long as the cost of the information required to arrive at the correct rule exceeds the costs associated with the expectations errors at the margin.

The traditional Keynesian view that the costs of unemployment are extremely large (and hence probably sufficient to swamp any information costs necessary for agents to arrive at the correct expectations formation rule) has led a larger faction of modern Keynesians to adopt another defense: This group argues that rational expectations can be accepted as a modeling technique without accepting the policy ineffectiveness proposition because wages and prices are observably inflexible (particularly downward), and such inflexibility is itself sufficient to generate non-neutrality.

It was shown in Chapter 9 that with a downwardly sticky wage rate a negative monetary shock would have real effects, reducing output and employment, even if no money illusion existed and expectations were correct. Scope then exists for aggregate demand policy to restore full employment, and this would be true even if such policy were systematic. In Chapters 4 and 9 it was also argued that observable price and wage rigidity has both natural and artificial components. Keynesians focus on the natural factors, particularly long-term contracting in labor markets, as the central element behind price wage stickiness.

Applying the argument to an inflationary period, Keynesians claim that long-term contracting can generate Phillip curve phenomena. If overlapping multiyear labor contracts specify annual wage increases (as they often do), in essence locking in a rate of wage inflation, an enduring positive monetary shock raising the inflation rate above that value will reduce unemployment below the natural rate, at least until enough contracts terminate and are renegotiated. Also an enduring decline in the money growth rate that reduces the inflation rate below the rate of wage inflation locked in to present contracts will raise the unemployment rate above the natural rate, generating a recession that will last until a sufficient number of contracts terminate.

Both rational expectations theorists and orthodox monetarists are dubious about this Keynesian argument. For one thing, as previously pointed out, only a portion of workers are covered by explicit contracts. Second, contracting is itself a result of a rational bargaining process in which expectations are crucial to the terms agreed upon. If long-term contracting at fixed wage rates (or fixed rates of wage increase) is generating large costs for transactors as the inflation rate varies, as Keynesian theory implies, one would expect both the terms and lengths of contracts to be adjusted in order to eliminate, or at least to reduce, such costs. Contract lengths would shorten and terms would be agreed upon that would make hourly compensation more flexible, as in Japan, for example.

Remarkably, Robert Barro has pointed out that contracts could be written to allow efficient (i.e., market clearing) use of quantities (e.g., labor) even if the prices and wage rates were kept rigid by agreement. The contract could specify, for example, that workers will supply more labor when demand is higher and less when demand is lower.[17] The point in all this is that the ability to contract does not seem to explain (although contracts may embody) either existing wage and price stickiness or the tendency for firms to respond to monetary shocks by altering quantities employed for a protracted period instead of altering wage rates. Some other explanation is needed

Certainly, some degree of wage and price stickiness seems observable, not only to Keynesians but also to orthodox monetarists (although some rational expectations theorists deny this), with resulting temporary non-neutrality to monetary shocks, even when such monetary changes are anticipated. The recession of 1982 may be a good example. There is no doubt that it resulted from a systematic contractionary monetary policy undertaken to reduce an inflation rate that had become excessive. Both the existence of the contractionary policy and its probable effects were well-understood by this and other observers at the time

This is an important point. Even if the Phillips curve tradeoff has disappeared, giving credence to the effectiveness of expectations adjustment in neutralizing monetary policy, the business cycle has not. Even rational expectations theorists admit this. Unemployment and output are serially correlated for significant periods of time, and if serial correlation of forecast errors caused by adaptive expectations in the face of monetary shocks is to be denied as an explanation, then some other is needed.

One possible argument is that it may be consistent with rational expectations for wage rates and prices to take time adjusting to market clearing values following a monetary shock even in the absence (and certainly in the presence) of artificial impediments to such adjustments. Even if the monetary change is anticipated and the mean of transactors expectations centers on the true required price adjustment, any single transactor will know that he is probably in error, and all price adjustments are made by individuals.

A related point is critical here. The real world is seldom characterized by the *ceteris paribus* condition. The presence of general contractionary or expansionary monetary impulse does not mean that normal, ongoing relative supply and demand shifts are suspended. The presence of such shifts with the general impulse introduces additional uncertainty about the exact price adjustment required in particular micromarkets. For both reasons, then, such adjustments will probably be made in small experimental increments in the required direction over time in order to avoid overshooting.

Also, in deflationary cases, you-go-first considerations (see Chapter 4) will act rationally to slow wage and price reductions and motivate firms to engage in layoffs. Indeed, because incentives are the opposite in an inflationary situation (i.e., everyone wishes to go first in raising their nominal price to make gains from relative price increases during a condition of general excess demand) you-go-first reasoning, which does not depend on irrational expectations, explains a macroeconomic dichotomy: prices and wage rates are more flexible upward than downward. Some rational expectations theorists, however, reject all notions of price stickiness.

New Classical Business Cycle Theory —————————

An important subset of rational expectations theorists known as **new classical economists** has responded to the challenge to explain the serial correlation of output and employment (the business cycle) under rational expectations. The name "new classical," by the way, stems from the propensity of Lord Keynes to denigrate all economists who preceded him as "classical" economists, thereby lumping together not only the British classical school, but pre-Keynesian marginalists and quantity theorists.

Keynes's followers then developed a caricature of pre-Keynesian macroeconomic beliefs combining naive quantity theory reasoning with an assumption that prices and wages are perfectly flexible and adjust instantaneously to supply and demand shifts, such that all markets clear continuously. This caricature has been termed the **classical model**.[18] What distinguishes new classical economists is an attempt to explain the business cycle while maintaining the notions of efficient (i.e., rational) use of available information and continuous market clearing. This is a tall order, but they are oddly successful.

New classical economists assume that random money supply shocks constitute the primary source of disturbances to the macroeconomy. Because they reject both wage and price stickiness and irrational expectations, they must use some other method to explain the serial correlation of unemployment and output that follows such shocks. To do this, they assume that agents are subject to informational restrictions.[19] Firms learn about price changes in their own industry before they learn about price changes in other industries. Workers obtain information about wages and prices in their own industry before they learn about prices elsewhere.

As information about price changes elsewhere in the economy comes to agents, it does not come all at once; information on different groups of prices comes with delays of different lengths of time. At any given time agents are processing the available information efficiently and expectations are rational. Nevertheless, the serial correlation of information itself on the macroeconomic effects of a monetary shock generates serial correlation of forecast errors across economic agents.

In particular, firms experiencing price increases in their own industry, but being initially unaware that such price increases are general (and gaining such information only slowly) will mistake them for relative price increases and increase their employment and output as a result. Workers, who are offered higher wage rates as the demand for labor rises and who do not yet have the information that the price rise is not confined to their own industry, mistake the increase in their nominal wage for a real wage increase and willingly increase the quantity of labor they supply. Both output and labor markets are continuously equilibrated. Frictional search unemployment declines, and with it, the natural rate itself.

In the opposite case, a negative monetary shock that starts prices falling is initially mistaken by firms in each industry as a relative price reduction, because each has initial information only on its own industry. As a consequence they reduce output and labor demand. Workers, unaware that prices in other industries are also falling, mistake the reduced nominal wage offers for real wage reductions, and voluntarily reduce the quantity of labor they supply. Prices and wage rates adjust smoothly to equilibrate markets. Search unemployment rises, however, raising the natural rate of unemployment.

In both cases, as the serially correlated information accumulates, agents come to regret their mistakes. In the case of the expansionary monetary shock, as agents finally realize that prices in general have risen, the increases in the quantities of labor and output supplied are reversed by decreases in the supply functions, restoring the initial levels of output and employment (and also, the original natural rate). The resulting additional price-level increase will also reduce the real money stock to its pre-shock value through the real balance effect, *ceteris paribus*.

The contractionary case is the opposite. Realization that absolute and not relative prices have fallen will cause agents to reverse the decreases in the quantities of output and labor supplied by increasing their supply functions, restoring initial levels of output and employment and the initial natural rate of unemployment. The additional price reduction resulting will then raise the real money stock back to its pre-shock value through the real balance effect, *ceteris paribus*.

This theory is a remarkable intellectual exercise in that it succeeds in explaining many of the phenomena of the business cycle while maintaining its assumptions of continuous market clearing and rational expectations. Many economists question whether it is anything more than an interesting theoretical exercise, however. One could point out, for example, that while serial correlation of information is almost a definition of learning, and learning certainly takes time, the particular informational restrictions assumed in these models are not well specified or justified. In particular it is difficult to believe, in an age of television in which general business conditions, monetary, and price-level behavior are almost continuously reported, that agents could have as little information about conditions outside their own market as the theory assumes.

Keynesian economists find particularly repugnant the notion that all unemployment generated by contractionary aggregate demand shocks is voluntary, as implied by the notion of continuous market clearing. They frequently point out that the unemployment generated by contractionary conditions is primarily characterized by layoffs, rather than resignations. This claim may have merit, although it does not follow that unemployment is involuntary. If jobs are available at lower wage rates or could be made available through bidding wage rates down, and if those laid off are unwilling to accept those jobs, then their continued unemployment is voluntary.

Most monetarists also find it difficult to believe that prices and wage rates are perfectly flexible, so that all markets clear continuously. Accepting the existence of some wage and price stickiness, however, does not mean that one has to admit the degree of rigidity claimed by Keynesians, or that most such rigidity is natural, or that all (or even most) unemployment is involuntary.

Neither does one have to accept the necessity or usefulness of discretionary Keynesian demand management policy. First, as the analysis of this chapter demonstrates, if such policy works it does so by fooling people, and a policy that rests on deceit is morally suspect. Second, all of the criticisms of such policy made previously (from the observation that most such actions are destabilizing to the difficulty of dealing with lags and measuring gaps, to the likelihood that officials have goals other than macroeconomic stabilization) still apply. Indeed, in considering the nature of and reasons for chronic inflation, such considerations once again become central; see Chapter 15.

Summary

Among the important points of this chapter, the following are central.

1. Keynesian fears about the nascent obsolescence of their fixed-price model because of inflation in the 1950s were alleviated by the appearance of the Phillips curve in 1958. Originally this was an empirical inverse relation between the rate of wage inflation and the unemployment rate in Britain discovered by A. W. Phillips.

2. Keynesians in the United States added an assumption of fixed mark-up pricing over unit labor costs and transformed the curve into a relationship between the rate of final price inflation and the unemployment rate. Recognizing the possibility that other variables might affect the relationship, they also added a shift parameter and tested such variables.

3. In this form the Phillips curve was interpreted as a stable relationship that could be exploited for policy purposes, picking the optimal inflation and unemployment rates through Keynesian aggregate demand management.

4. Milton Friedman objected to the Phillips curve in 1967, arguing that there was a natural, equilibrium rate of unemployment conditioned by real factors and that any inverse relation between the rates of inflation and unemployment must be a temporary consequence of real wage distortion, which would disappear once workers accurately anticipated inflation.

5. Friedman's theoretical reasoning was buttressed by an innovation in the modeling of expectations adjustment, known as adaptive expectations. According to this theory people form their expectation of the inflation rate by observing past rates. The expectation is a weighted average of such rates and is adjusted upward or downward in each period by some fraction of the difference between the current observed rate and the prior expectation. Using this model, Edmund Phelps developed the expectations-adjusted Phillips curve, which showed the long-run Phillips curve to be vertical.

6. As inflation increased in the following years, unemployment rates were much higher than predicted by naive Phillips curve models. This evidence strongly supported the expectations-adjusted Phillips curve.

7. The accelerationist hypothesis argued that if expectations adjusted adaptively the government could still peg unemployment below the natural rate if it was willing to make the inflation rate accelerate continuously.

8. The accelerationist argument rested on adaptive expectations, however, and appeared to be falsified by the failure of accelerating inflation to keep the unemployment rate low during this period. Consequently, several important macromonetary theorists rejected the adaptive-expectations model in favor of one termed *rational expectations*.

9. The rational expectations hypothesis says that people use all relevant information sources in forming an expectation and quickly reject any estimation rule that yields serial correlation of the forecast errors. Consequently, the mean of people's expectations, individually and collectively, will center on the correct value of any variable being determined by an observable, systematic process.

10. The logical implication of rational expectations is that no systematic monetary policy will be capable of affecting real variables such as output and employment; only random, unpredictable fluctuations in money growth will do so. Most rational-expectations theorists conclude that policy should be based on stable, predictable rules imposed on the authorities, rather than on discretionary fiat.

11. New classical business cycle theory attempts to explain the serial correlation of output and employment that follows random monetary shocks in a way consistent with rational expectations. This theory assumes serial correlation of information to economic agents, which can generate serial correlation of forecast errors even if all of the available information is being processed efficiently at any given time. In this theory markets clear continuously and all unemployment is voluntary, as the natural rate itself changes over the business cycle.

NOTES

1. The cash-balance version of the quantity theory had been the dominant monetary perspective before the Keynesian revolution and, although eclipsed by the Keynesian view for some decades, never entirely disappeared. In particular, it was maintained by the Austrian school, led by Ludwig von Mises and F. A. Hayek. Academic representation of Austrians was almost nil, however, and the modern revival of the quantity theory began at the University of Chicago, led by Milton Friedman (although Don Patinkin's previously cited work was also vital). For the classic modern statement of the quantity theory, see Friedman, "The Quantity Theory of Money—A Restatement," in Milton Friedman, ed., *Studies in the Quantity Theory of Money* (Chicago: University of Chicago Press, 1956).

2. This is the famous accord between the Treasury and the Federal Reserve. See Milton Friedman and Anna Jacobson Schwartz, *A Monetary History of the United States, 1867–1960* (National Bureau of Economic Research Study, Princeton: Princeton University Press, 1963): 620–627.

3. Although it is true that self-identified Keynesian economists did not begin to dominate policy positions in the federal government until 1960, it should be recognized that policies of the sort explicit and implicit in Keynesian economics had been practiced intermittently for several decades prior to 1960. Indeed, some critics have attributed much of the popularity of Keynesian economics to the rationale that doctrine offers for policies that governmental officials and monetary authorities naturally wish to pursue.

4. A. W. Phillips, "The Relation Between Unemployment and the Rate of Change of Money Wage Rates in the United Kingdom, 1861–1957," *Economica* 25 (November 1958): 283–299.

5. See Paul Samuelson and Robert Solow, "Analytical Aspects of Anti-Inflation Policy," *American Economic Review* 50 (May 1960): 177–194.

6. Milton Friedman, "The Role of Monetary Policy," *American Economic Review* 58 (March 1968): 7–11.

7. Ibid, pp. 8–13.

8. Perhaps the earliest formal model of adaptive expectations is Phillip Cagan, "The Monetary Dynamics of Hyperinflation," in *Studies in the Quantity Theory of Money*: 25–117.

9. Edmund Phelps, "Phillips Curves, Expectations of Inflation, and Optimal Unemployment Over Time," *Economica* 34 (August 1967): 254–281.

10. Perhaps the most amazing aspect of the Friedman–Phelps hypothesis is the timing of its publication and exposition, coming, as it did, just as expectations were adjusting and the short-run Phillips Curve was, in fact, shifting after a significant period of relative stability.

11. See Anthony Santomero and John J. Seater, "The Inflation–Unemployment Trade-Off: A Critique of the Literature," *Journal of Economic Literature* 16 (June 1978): 499–544.

12. Robert E. Lucas, "Some International Evidence on the Output-Inflation Tradeoff, *American Economic Review* 63 (June 1973): 326–334 finds evidence for the expectations view of the Phillips curve for 18 countries.

13. See, for example, David Laidler, "Expectations and the Phillips Trade Off: A Commentary," *Scottish Journal of Political Economy* 23 (February 1976).

14. The term *negative* as employed here is easily misinterpreted. If the economy is normally growing, and the money stock with it, then a negative monetary shock may consist simply of an unanticipated decline in the growth rate of the nominal money stock, rather than an actual decline in M_s itself.

15. John F. Muth, "Rational Expectations and the Theory of Price Movements," *Econometrica* 29 (July 1961): 315–335.

16. See, for example, Thomas Sargent and Neil Wallace, "Rational Expectations, The Optimal Monetary Instrument, and the Optimal Money Supply Rule," *Journal of Political Economy* 83 (April 1975): 241–254, which contains a relatively simple explanation of the reasoning behind rational expectations, the policy ineffectiveness hypothesis, and the Friedman rule.

17. Robert Barro, "Long Term Contracting, Sticky Prices and Monetary Policy," *Journal of Monetary Economics* 3 (July 1977): 305–316.

18. Construction of this caricature probably began with Everett E. Hagen, "The Classical Theory of the Level of Output and Employment" (1949) in M. G. Mueller, ed., *Readings in Macroeconomics* (2nd ed., Hinsdale IL: the Dryden Press, 1971): 3–15. Versions of this "classical model" can be found in most current text books.

19. See, for example, Robert E. Lucas, "Understanding Business Cycles," *Carnegie-Rochester Conference Series on Public Policy* 5 (1976): 7–29. The discussion here is designed merely to capture the flavor of new classical business cycle theories, of which there are several versions.

Student Self-Test _____

I. True–False

T F **1.** The original Phillips curve posited a functional relationship between unemployment and commodity price inflation.

T F **2.** The short-run Phillips curve is vertical, according to the theory of adaptive expectations.

T F 3. According to the accelerationist hypothesis the government could keep unemployment below the natural rate if inflation rate expectations were formed rationally.

T F 4. Individuals whose expectations are rational are always right.

T F 5. Even if expectations are rational, the mere existence of overlapping multiyear labor contracts will generate Phillips curve phenomena and justify discretionary monetary policy.

II. Short Answer (150 words or less each)

1. Explain your answer to true–false question number 5.
2. Why might it be consistent with rational expectations for wage rates and prices to take time adjusting downward toward market clearing values following a deflationary monetary shock, even in the absence of long-term contracts and legal obstructions?
3. What are the essential differences between the adaptive expectations hypothesis and the new classical theories of how monetary shocks affect the real economy?
4. Assuming that monetary shocks have non-neutral effects, at least temporarily, due to adaptive expectations or wage and price rigidities, does it necessarily follow that Keynesian demand management policies are justified? Explain.
5. Why might the Fed have an incentive to increase the unanticipated component of monetary changes, and what evidence indicates that they might attempt to do so?

III. Completion Problems

1. Assume that $\Delta\alpha^*/\Delta t = \beta(\alpha - \alpha^*)$, where $\Delta t = 1$ year, $\beta = .75$, and $\alpha = \alpha^* = 10$ percent (or .1). Now suppose that the inflation rate drops for four years at a declining rate of four percentage points the first year and one-half the amount of the previous year for each of the next three years.
   A. At the end of the second year $\alpha =$ _____ percent and $\alpha^* =$ _____ percent.
   B. At the end of the third year $\alpha =$ _____ percent and $\alpha^* =$ _____ percent.
   C. At the end of the fourth year $\alpha =$ _____ percent and $\alpha^* =$ _____ percent.
   D. At the end of the fifth year $\alpha =$ _____ percent and $\alpha^* =$ _____ percent.

2. Assume that the Phillips curve has the form and magnitude

$$\alpha = \lambda\alpha^* + a - b\Omega$$
$$= \lambda\alpha^* + .18 - 3\Omega,$$

where $\lambda = 1$. Assume also that, initially, $\alpha = \alpha^* = .04$.
   A. $\Omega n =$ _____ percent.

B. If, given $\alpha^* = .04$, the government raises α to $\alpha' = .10$, before expectations adjust $\Omega =$ _____ percent.

C. Assuming that $\Delta\alpha^*/\Delta t = \beta(\alpha - \alpha^*)$ and that $\beta = 1$, after one year of the 10 percent inflation rate $\alpha^* =$ _____ percent and $\Omega =$ _____ percent.

D. If the government wished to keep $\Omega =$ the rate found in B even though α^* has risen to the rate just found in C above, it must set the inflation rate at $\alpha =$ _____ percent.

CHAPTER 15

Economics and Political Economy of Inflation

We live in an inflationary time. As pointed out in Chapter 1, however (see, especially, Figure 1.2), chronic inflation in this country is a recent phenomenon, unique to the post-war period. Various aspects of this phenomenon have been dealt with previously in this book. Chapters 5 to 8 developed the primary theoretical elements—the concepts of the supply of and demand for money—for understanding the determinants of the value of money. Chapter 8 stated the basic condition for inflation in terms of ongoing excess money stock growth.

Seen in those terms, inflation is the process by which, in a period of chronic excess nominal money stock growth, the public reduces the real money stock to and maintains it at the level they are willing to hold. Chapters 8, 9, 13, and 14 all dealt in whole or in part with the relative price distortions, wealth redistributions, and consequent output effects resulting from unexpected changes in the money stock or its growth rate and with the neutralizing effects of resulting expectations adjustments.

The purpose of this chapter is to pull all of these elements together and to provide needed additional analysis and data to accomplish three things. The first is to provide a more complete description of the post-war inflation phenomenon and its effects. The second is to attempt to provide a satisfactory explanation for this modern malaise, contrasting alternate theories in the process and stressing that the phenomenon is not just economic in nature but also has political roots—although they also are economic in their own way. The third aim of this chapter is to examine alternate policy proposals for dealing with the problem of inflation.

The Inflation Experience

As shown in Chapter 14, after falling from high wartime levels, inflation during the 1950s and early 1960s was persistent but steady at about 3 percent, showing no tendency to accelerate. This is probably because the growth rate of the money stock also had no tendency to accelerate. This is not to say that either magnitude was perfectly steady. Both money growth and the inflation rate varied around their mean values, so that at intervals the real money stock deviated significantly from real balances demanded and temporary recessions or expansions occurred.

In the mid-1960s this imperfect but relatively happy condition deteriorated. Money growth rates and inflation both began accelerating. Money growth continued accelerating into the late 1970s then apparently stopped rising. As a result either of the lag in effects or of a failure of expectations to adjust rapidly, the rate of price increase kept rising (making $M_s/P < M_d/P$) until stopped by the large recession of 1981 to 1982. A combination of temporarily higher money growth and sharply lower inflation raised real balances enough to end the recession in 1983. After that the inflation rate drifted downward almost to 1950s levels, with only a slight resurgence in 1987 to 1989 attributable to extremely rapid money growth during 1985 and 1986.

Figure 15.1 plots annual M1 growth rates and inflation rates as measured by the GNP deflator from 1965 to 1987. The general rising trend of both variables is obscured somewhat by their variability around those trends. This variability clearly indicates a stop–go monetary policy, with intermittent attempts to reduce the inflation rate through slower money growth followed by reinflation when the resulting unemployment became painful. Note, however, that both the peaks and troughs in the cycle of money growth are successively higher, indicating a rising trend (accelerating money growth) through the 1974 cyclic trough. The 1978 cyclic peak is lower than that of 1972, however.

Money growth seems to have stopped accelerating after 1978. Succeeding cyclic peaks (1983 and 1986) are higher, but succeeding troughs (1981, 1984, and 1987) are lower, so that money growth essentially stabilized at about 7 to 8 percent (although, unfortunately, the variability of growth around that nonaccelerating value has increased). As with money growth, the acceleration of inflation can be observed in the progressively higher peaks and troughs in the inflation-rate cycle through the trough of 1976. The cyclic inflation peak of 1981 is virtually identical to that of 1975, and the inflation rate has been much lower since then.

Figure 15.1 Money Growth and Inflation Since 1965.

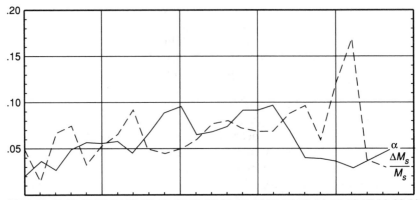

Source: *Economic Report of the President, 1989:* 313 and 385, and Federal Reserve Bank of St. Louis, *U.S. Financial Data* (7 January, 1989).

The fact that the inflation rate kept falling through 1986 even though money growth accelerated rapidly in 1982 and 1983 and accelerated even more rapidly in 1984 to 1986 seems odd at first. Two points seem pertinent. First, these periods of rapid monetary growth still seem merely to be upside deviations with nearly matching downside deviations around a basically nonaccelerating money growth rate of about 7 to 8 percent. Stabilization of money growth in that sense very likely will reduce expectations of future inflation. That it did so is indicated by the fact that nominal interest rates began declining in the recession of 1981 to 1982 and tended downward for several years, as the Fisher effect (apparently) operated.

Second, as discussed in Chapter 7, the velocity of money declined in this period (i.e., M_d increased), which is also a natural consequence of a lower α^*. With trend growth rate of real output in the 3 to 4 percent range and a long-run trend rate of velocity growth near zero, nonaccelerating money growth of about 7 to 8 percent should quite rationally be expected to result in inflation in the 3 to 4 percent range. The allegedly mysterious decline in velocity, which helped the slower money growth trend reduce α to precisely that range and to keep it there despite temporary reaccelerations of money growth, should be seen in that light.

Another phenomenon, not shown in the graph but documented and discussed more fully in Chapter 16, is that the growth rate of real output in the United States fell below its historic trend during most of the 1970s and through the early 1980s. There were probably several reasons for this, not all of which are known. One important factor, however, may have been the tendency for accelerating inflation to raise the tax burden on citizens. As will be shown, monetary changes cannot be neutral when tax brackets and depreciation allowances are stipulated in nominal terms. The importance of this factor may be indicated by the fact that real output and income growth has recovered somewhat since the 1981 Reagan tax reform. Certainly the coincidence of historically low output and employment growth with the period of accelerating inflation must be counted as striking evidence against any proposition that inflation has beneficial effects on those variables.

Yet another important phenomenon of the period concerns the change in the debt burden. The rising federal deficit and debt were discussed in Chapter 11, but that is only part of the story. For various reasons, the interaction of inflation with the tax code may reduce real interest rates.[1] This was also the effect of Federal Reserve regulation Q, which fixed interest rate ceilings on time deposits. By preventing banks from raising interest rates, this not only frustrated the operation of the Fisher effect, to the extent that real interest rates actually became negative on such deposits as inflation increased, but caused a great deal of **disintermediation**—loss of funds by the banking system as they were shifted into other (uncontrolled) financial assets. Logically and empirically, this reduced the real yields on those assets also.

As shown in Figure 15.2, nominal rates increased during the 1970s but real rates declined, and not until 1980 and 1981 did the Fisher effect raise nominal interest rates enough to restore the real interest rate to historic levels. That the effect of accelerating money growth on real interest rates was finally neutralized was probably because the Depository Institutions Deregulation and Monetary Control Act of 1980 removed the interest rate ceilings on time deposits.

The rapid money growth and low real interest rates of the 1970s involved a great deal of credit expansion. Much of this took the form of multibillion-dollar loans by large U.S. banks to governments of third-world countries, largely for capital investment in nationalized firms.[2] The farm debt problem of the 1980s in the United States is part of the same phenomenon. Investment in urban or agricultural property is one of the better hedges in an inflationary period, as expectations of higher future prices are rapidly capitalized into the present value of land. Rising inflation expectations and low real interest rates naturally resulted in farmers investing heavily in agricultural property during the 1970s.

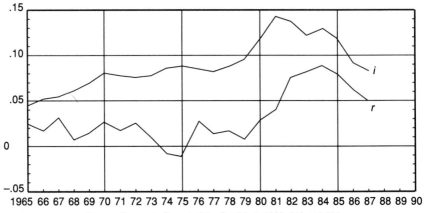

Figure 15.2 Real and Nominal Interest Rates, Aaa Bonds.

Source: *Economic Report of the President, 1989*: 313 and 390

When inflation began rapidly declining after 1981, however, the Fisher effect again operated slowly, reducing nominal interest rates only over time. This is probably because so many previous governmental efforts at disinflation were quickly reversed, so transactors were (for good reason) difficult to convince. As a consequence of this slow operation of the Fisher effect and other factors, such as increased federal borrowing as the recession raised the deficit, real interest rates rose to extremely high levels (see Figure 15.2), and all of these debt burdens increased enormously in real terms.

Many U.S. farmers were faced with bankruptcy, and debtor countries in the third world faced similar difficulty in making their loan payments. The latter problem was actually large enough to pose a threat to the solvency of large U.S. banks.[3] Indeed, although these problems moderated some as interest rates fell after 1984, much of the savings and loan industry went bankrupt, causing a large federal bailout that began in 1987. The potential exists for an even more serious crisis if monetary contraction and another recession were to raise real interest rates again.

Alternate Theories of Inflation

The monetary explanation of inflation developed in this book has become the dominant explanation among economic researchers in recent decades, but its acceptance is not universal. Among noneconomists there are probably few who clearly understand the effect of excess money growth on the value of money, and many fragmentary explanations are held to account for continuously rising prices. Even among economists competing theories exist. Indeed, opponents of the quantity theory in the economics profession seem to have been more successful as popularizers of their doctrines, which may in part account for the confusion of the public.

Most alternate explanations of inflation constitute one variation or another of what may be termed the **cost-push doctrine**. In contrast with inflation caused by pure excess money growth, which may be termed **demand-pull inflation**, cost push doctrines locate the source of price increases in the restriction of supplies through the exercise of market power by large firms or labor monopolies. The theory that firms are responsible has been very popular with neo-institutionalist economists such as John Kenneth Galbraith and with Marxists who argue that

> Giant firms increase their prices rapidly during prosperity, causing inflation by pushing profits up through the use of monopoly power over the market. Since the 1950s they have even had the power to continue raising prices during recessions (although more slowly than during expansions).[4]

Although microeconomics teaches that firms that are large relative to their markets have downward sloping demand curves and can raise market price by reducing their output, it is difficult to take a pure profit-push doctrine of this type seriously as an explanation for inflation. In the first place, even monopolists do not reduce output and raise prices continuously, but only to the point that marginal revenue equals marginal cost and profits are maximized. At worst, if a large portion of American industry were suddenly cartelized, the result would be a discrete jump in the price level. Yet inflation involves continuously rising prices. To duplicate the inflation experience of the last two decades through pure profit push would have required an accelerating concentration of industry which has manifestly not occurred.

It is worth noting that profit-push theorists postulate but do not explain market power. The normal tendency, when price and profits rise in any industry relative to others, is for firms to enter that market. Such entry adds to supply, causing price and profits to decline and, in the process, reduces the market shares of the formerly dominant firms. The implication is that few such firms would raise prices above competitive levels unless such entry could be prevented, and the advocates of the profit-push doctrine must explain the nature of the barriers employed.

Recent empirical evidence suggests that most dominant firms gain their large market shares by finding more efficient methods of production, which allow them to sell at lower, not higher prices, or by innovating new and better products.[5] This explanation is consistent with the observable fact that almost all industries that are dominated by a few large firms also contain many small competitive firms. The presence of such small firms already in an industry makes talk about entry barriers superfluous and makes the notion that the dominant firms can set prices above the competitive level appear rather silly.

By far the most persuasive example of profit push is the OPEC actions of 1973 and 1979; see Chapter 9, particularly Figure 9.16. As an organization of major oil exporting governments (which could therefore limit entry and control production within their own boundaries) OPEC was able to take advantage of the supply disruptions associated with the Yom Kippur War and the Iranian Revolution to raise world oil prices. It is certainly true that the inflation rates increased in oil-importing countries—including the United States—following these oil price increases. In both cases, however, money growth and inflation were already accelerating. By raising oil and gasoline prices directly and other costs indirectly (because oil is an input in many production processes and almost all goods are transported before being sold) the discrete oil price increases basically caused a discrete rise in the price level, temporarily accelerating price increases that were already taking place for other reasons.

Even the discrete price level jump that is attributable to OPEC actions seems to have been temporary as a consequence of competitive forces. OPEC was not able to prevent the entry of oil from the North Sea, the North Slope, and Mexico into world markets as a direct result of the high industry profits. In combination with the recession of 1980 and 1981 this entry produced large excess supplies, resulting in a collapse of OPEC control of the world market and a reduction of oil prices by about two-thirds. This reduced gasoline prices directly and other costs indirectly and certainly aided the apparent rapid reduction of inflation through 1984. Since then both the price level and inflation rate have probably been little different than they would have been, had the OPEC restrictions never occurred.

Another popular cost-push doctrine with a long history is known as the **wage-price spiral**.[6] According to this theory labor monopoly supply restrictions and legal minimum wage increases initiate the problem by pushing up the production costs of firms. This reduces profits and motivates the firms to pass the higher costs on by raising product prices. If it is then argued that unions and Congress respond by raising wage rates again, an apparent rationale for ongoing price increases is given.

This doctrine is superficially appealing. Certainly depression-era labor legislation has limited competitive entry pressures on union labor, and legal minimum wage rates cannot be undercut. Still, the argument has problems. Unless product demand curves are perfectly inelastic, labor cost increases cannot be fully passed on in higher prices.

Ceteris paribus, even with the price increases real wage rates would rise, profits and output would decline, and unemployment would increase as a result of such a wage push, generating pressures for the excessive nominal wage rates to be reduced. If the unions resisted, unemployed workers would shift over time to nonunion employers, bidding wage rates down in those sectors in order to obtain jobs.

In the case of the minimum wage law, workers priced out of employment in covered fields of unskilled labor tend to shift over time to fields that Congress has conveniently left uncovered by the law, again reducing wage rates in those fields to obtain employment.[7] In both cases, then, wage increases in some sectors causing price increases in the associated output markets would eventually cause wage (and consequently, price) decreases in other sectors.

Ceteris paribus, it follows that the wage push assumed by the theory would cause a discrete rise in the price level in the short run, but that in the long run would alter relative prices, the allocation of resources, and the composition of output. The rise in the price level would only be permanent if the coverage of the minimum wage law was universal and/or all labor was unionized so that no employment substitution could occur.

The reasoning of the last few paragraphs is microeconomic but is easily expressed macroeconomically as in Figure 15.3. Any kind of wage cost push (step 1 in the graph) shifts the SRAS curve upward and toward the left (step 2). The price level rises, but not by as much as wage rates increased (shown by the vertical shift in the SRAS curve), because the reduction in real money balances reduces the aggregate quantity of output demanded as people attempt to add to their nominal money stocks. At the new equilibrium price level (P') the real wage is therefore excessive, and unemployment (in excess of the natural rate) appears. At some point increasing unemployment must prevent any further wage increase, *ceteris paribus*. As a consequence, any such wage and price increase must be self-limiting, and no such process, by itself, can explain ongoing inflation.

Ceteris paribus, unemployment in excess of the natural rate must eventually cause wage rates to fall back to the competitive level, restoring the initial magnitudes shown in Figure 15.3. The only way that a cost-push-induced price and wage level increase could be sustained would be if it were followed by an increase in the nominal money stock that was large enough to reduce the real wage back to the competitive level and restore the initial real money stock, as shown by the shift from AD to AD' in Figure 15.3. This is sometimes referred to as *validating* the wage increase. Any subsequent cost push could then be validated by an additional increase in the money stock, and so on, as the authorities attempt in each case to avoid the recessionary effects.

Figure 15.3 Cost–Push and Monetary Validation.

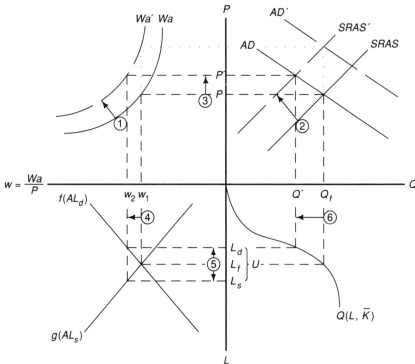

Such a sequence could account for ongoing inflation, and it will be argued that wage push is an important initiating element. Of course, with wage, price, and money stock increases following in a repeated chicken–egg sequence, to the point that inflation becomes expected and the competition is for relative rates of increase, it becomes difficult to distinguish this from the demand-pull case. The important point, however, is that an ongoing expansion of the money stock relative to the demand for money is not only a sufficient explanation for inflation but is also a necessary element of any other explanation.

There is a reasonably good historical case by which to judge these arguments. As pointed out in Chapter 10, President Franklin Roosevelt cartelized major portions of American industry under provisions of the National Industrial Recovery Act of 1933. Millions of American workers were then forced into labor monopolies as a result of the Norris–La Guardia (1932) and Wagner (1935) Acts. Conditions were never better for pure cost-push inflation. The consequence of the labor and output restrictions that followed, however, was not inflation, but a worsening of depression conditions in each case.[8]

Taxation, Inflation, and Neutrality _____

Government is a necessary institution even in a market society, and in order for government to provide and maintain the institutional framework of law, order, and protection of property rights within which a market system can function, operating revenue must be obtained. Although other methods are imaginable, a tax system is usually employed.[9] Tax rates are usually specified as percentages of certain nominal dollar incomes. In a period of inflation such as the United States has recently experienced, in which such nominal incomes are rising, real tax rates and burdens might be increased, altering the allocation of resources between the private and public sectors in a way that is not socially optimal. In other words, the tax system might cause excess money growth to be not only non-neutral but also socially harmful.

As an example of the way in which inflation might raise tax rates, consider a progressive income tax that taxes all income up to $20,000 at a 10 percent rate, all additional income up to $30,000 at a 20 percent rate, and all income earned over $30,000 at a 30 percent rate. For a typical family with a single income of $30,000, the tax will be

$$
\begin{aligned}
T = t(Y) &= .1(Y \leq \$20,000) + .2(\$20,000 < Y \leq \$30,000) \\
&= .1(\$20,000) + .2(\$10,000) \\
&= \$2000 + \$2000 \\
&= \$4000.
\end{aligned}
$$

This family's disposable income is

$$
\begin{aligned}
Y^d &= Y - T \\
&= \$30,000 - \$4000 \\
&= \$26,000.
\end{aligned}
$$

Now suppose that the inflation rate is $\alpha = .1$ so that this typical household's income rises the next year to $Y' = \$33,000$. The tax becomes

$$
\begin{aligned}
T' &= t(Y') \\
&= .1(\$20,000) + .2(\$10,000) + .3(\$3000) \\
&= \$2000 + \$2000 + \$900 \\
&= \$4900.
\end{aligned}
$$

After-tax income becomes

$$Y^{d'} = Y' - T'$$
$$= \$33,000 - \$4900$$
$$= \$28,100.$$

This looks like a net improvement until it is remembered that each dollar is worth 10 percent less in the second year. Both taxes paid and after tax income must be deflated for comparison with the first year values. Doing so gives us real taxes paid of $\$4900/1.1 = \$4454.54$, which is greater than the \$4000 first year tax, and real disposable income of $\$28,100/1.1 = \$25,545$, which is less than the first year's disposable income of \$26,000.

From this example it should be clear that a progressive tax code with brackets specified in nominal dollar terms results in rising real tax rates and shifts real income and resources from the private to the public sector in a period of inflation. The tendency for inflation to raise nominal incomes into higher tax brackets is known as **bracket creep**.[10] Although Congress partly offset bracket creep through periodic tax-rate reductions, it is clear that the process operated to increase real income tax burdens in the United States throughout the post-war period of accelerating inflation.

A virtually identical problem exists with business taxes. One of the primary expenses associated with the use of a business asset is deprecia-tion. The law recognizes this by allowing depreciation as a deduction before taxes are paid. Depreciation allowances are written into the law as a portion of the original nominal cost of the equipment however. This results in inadequate depreciation over the life of an asset during an inflationary period, in which the replacement cost is rising.

Consider a decision by a firm to invest in a \$50,000 item of equip-ment that is expected to last ten years and add enough to the produc-tion of the firm to increase its net revenue by \$10,000 per year after subtracting the additional operating expenses incurred.[11] Assume that annual legal tax depreciation is \$5000 per year over the machine's life (i.e., \$50,000/10), and also that the difference between the net revenue and the depreciation deduction is taxed at a 50 percent rate.

Table 15.1 shows the effects of four different inflation rates (in-cluding zero) on nominal cash flow, nominal taxes paid, real (infla-tion-adjusted) cash flow, and real taxes paid. Nominal cash flow is disposable net revenue, calculated as the difference between net rev-enue and taxes paid. Real cash flow and real taxes are calculated by dividing the nominal magnitudes by one plus the inflation rate in each case. The firm is assumed to be typical in that its net revenue rises by the inflation rate.

TABLE 15.1

Item	Inflation rate			
	0%	5%	10%	50%
Net revenue	$10,000	$10,500	$11,000	$15,000
Depreciation	5,000	5,000	5,000	5,000
Nominal tax	2,500	2,750	3,000	5,000
Nominal cash flow	7,500	7,750	8,000	10,000
Real tax	2,500	2,619	2,727	3,333
Real cash flow	7,500	7,381	7,273	6,667

Note in the last two rows of the table that as the inflation rate increases, the real cash flow, or real after-tax net revenue available to the firm, decreases, while the real tax paid by the firm increases. This is a consequence of the fact that the depreciation allowance shown in the second row is the same in each column, because, as pointed out above, the tax law does not permit it to rise with inflation, even though the cost of replacing the equipment increases along with the prices of everything else. If the depreciation allowance increased by the rate of inflation, no change in real cash flow or real tax paid would occur.

The implication of the argument here is that given the tax treatment of capital, inflation reduces the after-tax real rate of return on investment in production. The medicine required to alleviate excess taxation of both corporate and individual incomes in an inflationary period is to *index* tax brackets and corporate depreciation allowances—that is, to tie them to a price index—so that they automatically rise along with prices and nominal incomes. In fact, after a long and difficult political struggle, income tax brackets were indexed by a section of President Reagan's 1981 Economic Recovery Tax Act, effective in 1985, and bracket creep has been essentially eliminated since. Depreciation allowances have not yet been indexed. Even that would not entirely eliminate the problem, however, as there is yet another subtle tax effect of inflation in operation.

The Tax on Cash Balances

The quantity theory approach to inflation developed in this book assumes that there is a stable demand function for real money balances into which the expected rate of inflation enters as an independent variable.[12] Where $M_d/P = m_d$, this demand function (from Chapter 5) can be written as

$$m_d = f(Q^*, i, \alpha^*).$$

Quantity theorists also assume, despite Keynesian objections, that the money stock is essentially an exogenous variable under the control of the government and monetary authorities. The inflation rate is then determined by the rate of "excess" money growth, such that

$$\frac{\Delta M_s}{M_s} - \frac{\Delta m_d}{m_d} \approx \frac{\Delta P}{P}$$

$$= \alpha,$$

which will be positive whenever $\Delta M_s / M_s > \Delta m_d / m_d$ for an enduring period.

The relationship between the expected rate of inflation and the real money stock demanded and held can be illustrated as in Figure 15.4. Actual and expected inflation are measured on the vertical axis where, by assumption, $\alpha = \alpha^*$ (expectations are correct). The real money stock is measured on the horizontal axis. Line D-D' shows that the quantity of real balances demanded declines (that is, velocity rises) as the inflation rate rises, say from α to α'; see Chapter 6, particularly Figures 6.10 and 6.11.

Now assume that the existing inflation rate is a result of the federal government's financing deficits through debt monetization. Assume also, for simplicity and clarity of analysis, that trend $\Delta Q / Q = 0$. Be-

Figure 15.4 The Demand for Real Balances As a Function of Expected Inflation.

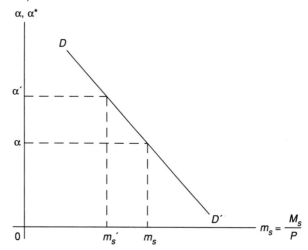

cause the inflation is fully anticipated, it has no effect on output or output growth. It follows that the goods and services purchased by the government with the money it creates would otherwise have been purchased by the public. Obviously, then, the monetary expansion literally transfers both purchasing power and real resources from the private to the public sector.

The reader may have heard it said that inflation is a hidden tax. Few people who say this, however, fully recognize just how true that statement is. As first user of the new money the government is able to purchase resources it could not otherwise. This makes prices and nominal incomes rise for the public. If everyone's expenditures increased at the same rate as their nominal incomes (which would be necessary in order to purchase the same quantity of real goods at the higher prices), no one's cash balances would rise proportionately with their income. In order to add enough to their nominal balances to maintain the desired level of real balances relative to income at the higher prices, people must spend less than their income for some time. Doing so releases real resources equivalent in value to those acquired by the government. Inflation is therefore a literal tax on cash balances held by the public.

As long as the public is willing to hold a particular positive quantity of real money balances at any given inflation rate, it is subject to the tax, even if real balances demanded decline as inflation rises. The tax rate is the rate of inflation (i.e., the rate at which money held loses value), and the tax base is the quantity of real balances held. The total revenue obtained by the government from any tax (T), is the product of the rate and the base. So for the tax on cash balances,

$$T_\alpha = \alpha \cdot m_s.$$

Because real money balances held will decline, reducing the tax base as the inflation rate rises, it is not obvious that higher inflation rates will always result in increased revenue. It is natural to ask, then, what rate of inflation the government would pick if it wished to obtain the maximum revenue. The answer can be seen in Figure 15.5, which duplicates and adds to Figure 15.4. Assuming that the demand curve $D–D'$ is linear, and remembering that a demand curve is an average revenue curve, there must be a marginal revenue curve associated with it (e.g., line MR_α) which is also linear and which cuts the horizontal axis at one-half the distance from zero to the horizontal intercept of the demand curve.

Because $T_\alpha = \alpha \cdot m_s$, revenue must be zero at either intercept of $D–D'$, where $\alpha = 0$ (the horizontal intercept) or $m_s = 0$ (the vertical intercept). It follows that as the government raises α above zero, T_α first rises, then falls. Total revenue is maximized when the marginal tax

Figure 15.5. The Tax on Cash Balances

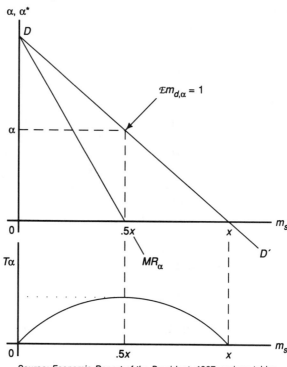

Source: *Economic Report of the President, 1987:* various tables.

revenue resulting from an incremental increase in α is zero. If the government wishes to obtain the maximum revenue from the tax on cash balances, it will choose that rate of inflation.

At the associated point on the demand curve D–D' the **elasticity of demand for real balances with respect to the rate of inflation**, defined as $\mathcal{E}m_{d,\alpha} = \%\,\Delta m_d / \%\,\Delta \alpha$, is unitary. At that rate of inflation, assuming the costs of money creation to be trivial and that the government ignores the social costs, it will also maximize its net revenue, or profits, from the tax.

The three left-hand columns of Table 15.2 show the real money stock (calculated as $m_s = $ M1/GNP deflator), inflation rate, and revenue from the tax on cash balances (in billions of 1982 dollars) for each year in the period 1965 to 1986. The relationships shown among these variables in the table are more complex than in the previous simple model because real output growth, although below trend, was still positive during this period, which tended to partly offset the tendency for rising inflation to reduce real balances demanded (in

TABLE 15.2

Year	m_s	α	T_α	$Q = \dfrac{GNP}{P}$	$\dfrac{m_s}{Q}$	$\dfrac{T_\alpha}{Q}$
1965	$501.5	.027	$13.5	2087.6	.24	.006
1966	496.3	.036	17.8	2208.3	.225	.008
1967	515.6	.026	13.4	2271.4	.227	.006
1968	528.9	.05	26.4	2365.6	.224	.012
1969	517.1	.056	28.9	2423.3	.213	.012
1970	515.7	.055	28.3	2416.2	.213	.012
1971	519.8	.057	29.6	2484.8	.209	.012
1972	541.9	.047	25.5	2605.5	.208	.009
1973	537.2	.065	34.9	2744.1	.195	.013
1974	513.8	.091	46.8	2729.3	.188	.017
1975	490.1	.098	48.0	2695.0	.182	.018
1976	491.9	.064	31.5	2826.7	.174	.011
1977	498.2	.067	33.0	2958.6	.187	0.11
1978	502.8	.073	36.7	3115.2	.161	.012
1979	494.5	.089	44.0	3192.4	.155	.014
1980	483.3	.09	43.5	3187.1	.152	.014
1981	469.2	.097	45.5	3248.8	.144	.014
1982	479.9	.064	30.7	3166.0	.152	.010
1983	511.7	.039	20.0	3279.1	.156	.006
1984	517.6	.038	19.7	3489.9	.148	.006
1985	562.0	.033	18.5	3585.2	.157	.005
1986	637.9	.027	17.2	3676.5	.174	.005

Source: Economic Report of the President, 1987: various tables

Figure 15.5 this could be shown by a rightward shift in line $D-D'$ as output rises). As a consequence the real money stock generally increased over the period despite the accelerating inflation (although absolute declines occurred in 1966, 1969 to 1970, 1973 to 1975, and 1979 to 1981, the last three of which resulted in recessions).

In order to show that the inverse relationship postulated in Figures 15.4 and 15.5 between real balances demanded and the rate of inflation actually existed during this period, it helps to express the real money stock as a proportion of real GNP, m_s/Q, and to observe the relationship between those numbers and the inflation rates shown. Clearly, real money balances held declined relative to GNP (velocity rose) as the inflation rate accelerated over this period (and have recently begun rising as α has declined), as previously discussed.

The reader may also note a strong positive correlation between the inflation rate and the tax revenue in Table 15.2. Although the government never quite raised the inflation rate into the region of diminishing returns, annual revenue seems to have approached its maximum at about $50 billion in 1982 dollars at an inflation rate close to 10 percent.

Increases in α in the years 1979 to 1981 reduced the tax base (m_s) so much that revenue hardly rose at all and higher inflation rates probably would have made it decline.

If the real tax revenue is expressed as a proportion of real GNP, as in the right-hand column of the table, the same result is observed. This ratio also rises and falls with the inflation rate over the period, finally nearing its maximum at about $\alpha = .1$. Increases in the inflation rate in 1980 and 1981 failed to increase revenue relative to GNP. The questions of why and how inflation was then reduced, just after the government seemed to have approached its maximum revenue, is part of the general question of the motives for inflation that can now be addressed.

The Political Economy of Inflation

The most nagging question raised by the monetary theory of inflation is this: If inflation is a simple consequence of growth rates of the money stock that chronically exceed the long-run trend growth of the demand for real money balances, and if the government (through the Federal Reserve) controls the money stock, why is that excess money growth not eliminated? Or rather, why has inflation endured and accelerated for so long in the post-war period, and what happened in the early 1980s that allowed it to be reduced but not eliminated?

In the broadest sense, the answer to this question must be that excess money growth and inflation has been an outcome of the incentives inherent in the post-war democratic institutions and monetary systems within which monetary and political authorities make their decisions. The universal adoption in this century of fiat money systems under discretionary control of central banks is a central element of such an explanation. The switch from the gold standard to fiat money during the depression essentially reduced the cost of creating base money to zero, and as pointed out in Chapter 8, the Federal Reserve (and any similar central bank) has a profit motive for excess money growth and inflation because all of its salaries, expenses, and perquisites are paid for with interest earned on loans made and securities purchased with base money it creates. That is, the Fed is a major recipient of revenue from the tax on cash balances (although it passes the bulk on to the Treasury).

Inflation is not only a tax that generates revenue for and transfers resources to the federal government, but is also a means of raising other taxes. Of course these methods are of dubious legitimacy. The U.S. Constitution mandates specific methods of taxing and raising taxes for the federal government, which do not include the tax on cash balances or bracket creep. Their use cannot have been entirely accidental, as their natures have long been known, and their effects could have been offset by indexation and other methods long ago. So why have they been employed for so long?

A theoretical explanation can be provided by the same sort of analysis applied to the political economy of deficits in Chapter 11. Politicians in democratic states must compete with each other by offering alternative programs of expenditure and finance aimed at satisfying diverse constituencies and interest groups in such a way as to maximize votes obtained. Since the Johnson administration in the mid-1960s, competition on the expenditure side has increasingly involved targeted income transfers, the recipients of which have organized to support the continuance and expansion of such payments.

An important point here is that the vast bulk of transfer payments are received by members of the middle class, rather than by the poor (who vote in very small numbers), and that the bulk of tax revenue is also extracted from the middle class. Because no gain is made by one whose taxes to provide such transfers equal the individual's subsidy, the recipients have an incentive to resist the taxation (through votes, witholding and granting of campaign contributions, letters to congressmen, etc.) in order to insure that they are net beneficiaries. Those who are not recipients, and who may even oppose such expenditures, have an even stronger incentive to resist the taxation required to fund such programs.

As a consequence of the strong, organized, and expanding political demand for such income transfer payments and the persistent opposition to the explicit taxation required to fund them, the incentive faced by political agents is to offer and vote for the expenditures, but not to vote for explicit tax increases. Instead, the revenue required to cover the expenditures is acquired in part through deficit finance (deferring the necessary taxation forward in time) and in part by taxing in the present by means that are not understood by the public as constituting a tax (the tax on cash balances) and by raising taxes in the present by means that cannot be attributed by the electorate to specific politicians (e.g., bracket creep and understated depreciation).[13] This surreptitious means of taxing and raising taxes solves many problems for political agents.

The connection between transfer payments and inflation can be seen in Figure 15.6, which shows transfer payments as a percentage of federal expenditures (TP/E, read from the right-hand vertical scale) and inflation rates (from Figure 15.1, read from the left-hand scale) over the period 1965 to 1986. TP/E increased from 25 percent in 1966 to 42 percent in 1976, after which it stopped rising and began falling slightly in 1984. The period of proportionately rising transfer payments

Figure 15.6 Transfer Payments and Inflation.

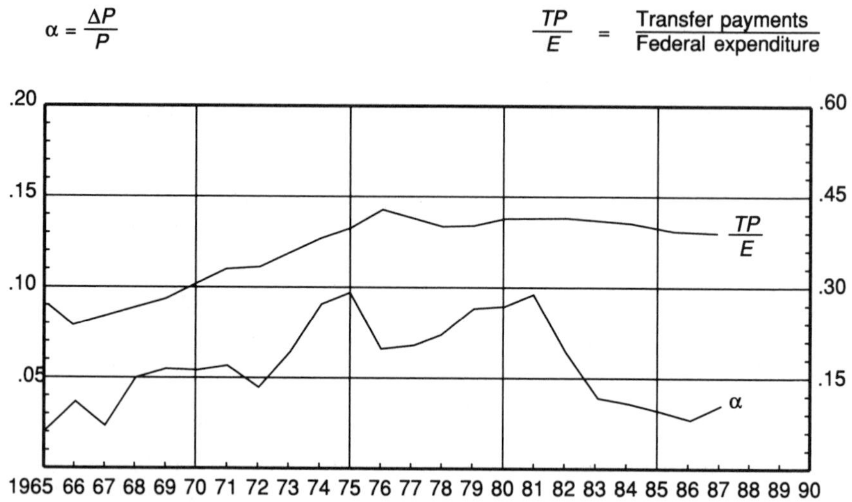

$$\alpha = \frac{\Delta P}{P}$$

$$\frac{TP}{E} = \frac{\text{Transfer payments}}{\text{Federal expenditure}}$$

1965 66 67 68 69 70 71 72 73 74 75 76 77 78 79 80 81 82 83 84 85 86 87 88 89 90

Source: Economic Report of the President, 1989: 313 and 403

corresponds well with the period of clearly accelerating inflation. Also, the peak and post-peak period of TP/E roughly overlaps the period during which inflation stopped accelerating and began declining. Correlation does not prove causation, of course, but in this case it certainly fails to contradict the hypothesis developed above, to say the least.[14]

A closely related incentive for the political authorities to engage in an inflationary policy relates to the alternate means available to the government for deficit finance. The government can sell its bonds to private parties, including individuals and commercial banks, rather than monetizing the debt by selling them to the Federal Reserve. In a period of rising deficits, however, the resulting increased competition for a limited supply of savings may raise interest rates, crowding out private sector investment and hurting the housing and capital goods industries; see Chapter 11. This results in political pressures that political decisionmakers would like to avoid.

Monetizing a portion of the deficit directly reduces the pressure of deficit finance on interest rates. The bonds can not only be sold to the Fed for high prices, but because the Fed returns a large portion of its earnings to the Treasury, the effective interest rate on such loans is extremely low. The excess money growth and inflation resulting, in part, from such debt monetization, also reduces the real interest rate on the debt, to the extent that expectations lag behind the inflation rate, or the operation of the Fisher effect is impeded by interest rate ceilings and/or taxes on interest income. As shown above, these effects actually dominated during the period of accelerating inflation, so that real interest rates were reduced despite rising deficits. The fact that the federal government was thus able to effectively repudiate much of its debt through inflation made debt monetization an attractive and frequent method of finance.

It is also worth remembering at this point that the public prefers low interest rates to high ones, and to the extent that people have been led to believe that the Fed controls the interest rate, this may result in indirect political pressures on the monetary authorities to employ interest-rate targeting and to set the targets at low values. Following such a strategy in the 1970s, the Fed may actually have lost control of the money stock as the Wicksell effect operated; see Chapter 8. The point here is that all these incentives for the political and monetary authorities to engage in inflationary low-interest-rate policies are mutually reinforcing.

A third and crucial motive for government tó follow an inflationary policy relates to the cost-push phenomena. Not all political competition involves targeted income transfers. Some programs aim at affecting market outcomes by other means. Because of certain widespread public attitudes concerning the difficulties that low-skilled workers have in "getting ahead," and the supposedly superior bargaining power of firms, many political agents have found that large campaign contributions and bloc votes can be obtained by supporting pro-union and minimum-wage legislation. Such legislation aims, it should be noted, at redistributing incomes directly rather than through taxes and subsidies.

The effect of the deterioration in the structural conditions of the labor market and the associated cost pushes resulting from such legislation has not been to redistribute income from capital to labor but to increase the natural rate of unemployment.[15] This in itself led to increased demand for such programs as unemployment compensation and welfare to alleviate the distress generated. Given this situation, monetary expansion and inflation not only helped solve the finance problem for such programs but also could be employed to reduce unemployment directly by reducing the real wage back to the full employment level.

At this point we have our answer to the initial question: the chronic inflation of the post-war period has essentially been the outcome of the demand for and supply of income transfers through the democratic political system. The incentives inherent in that political system are the central element in this explanation, but attitudes are also important. Public attitudes affect demand for transfers. Demand for transfers began to increase during the depression, and accelerated during the 1960s, as people began to accept the notion that government should insure citizens against virtually every possible detrimental contingency.

Attitude changes also affected supply. Keynesian economics, for example, removed the attitudinal constraints against the unbalanced budgets and monetary expansion needed to fund such transfers. What is more, with its emphasis on total expenditure as the prime determinant of employment and output in the context of a model in which the price level was assumed to be predetermined and constant, Keynesian economics led both politicians and economists to believe that unemployment could be essentially eliminated without producing inflation. These attitudes weakened when chronic inflation appeared, but Phillips-curve reasoning provided sufficient rationale for continuing monetary expansion.

In the 1960s and 1970s, the propagation of monetarist doctrines such as the natural rate hypothesis, adaptive expectations, and the tax on cash balances further weakened support for inflationary policies by demonstrating both their monetary nature and that their success depends on the public being deceived in various ways. The effect of this revelation was also limited, however. Many political authorities seem to have viewed the deception as morally justified. The notion that people must often be forced to do what is "in their own best interest" inheres in the welfare state philosophy (it is *always* employed in defence of compulsory social security, for example), and easily justifies deception in the finance of such programs. Also, the egalitarian aspects of that philosophy easily justify the covert expropriation of lenders, who are often perceived (incorrectly, in many cases) as being wealthy.

The Inflation Reduction of the 1980s _____

The political economy theory not only explains why an inflationary policy has been pursued in the post-war period, but seems to at least partly explain the success in reducing the inflation rate during the Reagan administration. In part this may have been due to the anti-inflationary attitudes of that administration, but the roots seem to lie earlier, in a change in the structure of incentives faced by politicians relying on a policy based on deception when people stopped being deceived.

Inflation could only be used to reduce unemployment by reducing real wage rates as long as workers were subject to money illusion or, at least, had expectations that lagged behind the inflation rate. This stopped being the case in the late 1960s. Authorities faced with the neutralization of their policy appear to have responded by causing money growth and inflation to accelerate, but it appears that workers were able to correctly anticipate even accelerating inflation, as argued in Chapter 14. Thus the 1970s were characterized by accelerating inflation and high unemployment rates, contrary to both the Keynesian beliefs and the experience of earlier decades.

The story with debt repudiation by inflation is basically the same. Real interest rates could only be reduced by inflation as long as expectations lagged and transactors continued to suffer interest rate ceilings and confiscatory taxation. All the illusions necessary to allow these conditions began to disappear in the late 1970s as the source of these problems came to be understood in financial markets. Expectations adjusted, and financial innovations designed to allow escape from interest rate ceilings brought political pressures for their removal. By 1980 to 1981 the effects of inflation on real interest rates had been largely neutralized as nominal rates reached very high levels. As discussed previously, this raised all debt burdens, including that on the national debt, to crushing levels.

The use of inflation to tax and raise taxes also began reaching its limits. As will be discussed in detail in Chapter 16, tax rates may get high enough to cause declining revenues by discouraging economic activity and encouraging tax avoidance. The revenue curve from the tax on cash balances is a clear example of such a *Laffer curve*. Although neither U.S. tax rates in general nor the tax on cash balances in particular seem to have passed the point of diminishing returns, the declining rates of saving, productivity, and output growth in the decade of the 1970s seem to represent this process in operation, and bracket creep has been a prime (but not the only) suspect.

Although taxing and raising taxes by inflation prevents citizens from attaching blame to specific politicians, it can eventually result in a "throw them all out" voter mentality. As a consequence, by the end of the Carter administration taxation through inflation exceeded its political if not its economic limits and began generating strong political pressures for tax reduction. These pressures not only resulted in the election of Ronald Reagan as President in 1980, but also in a slight Republican majority in the Senate for the first time since 1956.

For all these reasons the inflation policy became unprofitable. In essence, those relying on the policy found the political costs rising at the same time as the benefits began falling. Consequently, it became politically feasible for serious efforts to be made to reduce inflation, and the growth rate of the money stock stopped accelerating. In combination with this, the Reagan administration instituted a policy of tax reductions and reforms (including indexation of brackets) designed to spur output. The withdrawal symptoms resulting from this policy, as expectations apparently lagged the inflation rate on the high side, were painful. The social benefits, however, in terms of the greatly reduced inflation and recovery in the growth rates of productivity, output, and employment that characterized the long expansion following the recession of 1981 to 1982, clearly exceeded the costs.

Policies to Eliminate Inflation

Because the degree to which inflation is employed as a matter of policy depends on the costs and benefits faced by political agents and the monetary authorities, it is not obvious that inflation will not begin accelerating again in the future. Some factors seem to reduce that possibility. Indexation of the income tax brackets, which removes a large source of benefit to the federal government from inflationary policy, is not likely to be rescinded soon. The tax on cash balances can still be employed, but the maximum revenue from that tax seems too small a portion of federal revenue to constitute a significant temptation by itself. Also, without the interest rate ceilings on time deposits or some similar instrument, accelerating inflation could not be used quite as successfully to covertly repudiate federal debt.

Other factors may be more favorable. For one, business depreciation allowances are still not indexed. More important, if expectations are formed adaptively, a prolonged period of relatively low inflation such as that experienced during the Reagan administration, by reducing α^*, recreates the central condition for the successful application of inflationary policy. Although the point is arguable, expectations seem to have significantly lagged the inflation rate on the high side since α began declining in 1981 and have not been fully rational (in the technical sense).

If the government soon decides to resume inflationary policy, given that the experience of the 1970s is still fresh, it is likely that α^* will probably adjust upward more rapidly than before, inflation will accelerate sooner and more rapidly, and the period of non-neutrality in which the government can successfully manipulate real variables will be shorter. In that case the marginal political benefits of such a policy will fall quickly below the marginal costs, motivating another monetary contraction and recession like that of 1981, or worse.

In order to avoid such a sequence of events it would be best to find a permanent solution. If one thing is clear from the analysis of the preceding section it is that such a solution must consist of an institutional reform eliminating the incentives for political and monetary authorities to generate excess money growth. Probably the simplest such reform to institute, and the one most likely to find legislative support if proposed by a major political candidate, would be a simple Friedman (money growth) rule, preferably at a constitutionally mandated rate. Merely asking the Fed to stabilize the money growth rate or to report target intervals (as occurred in the 1970s) will not do; see Chapter 8.

A second option that has recently come under serious discussion is the reinstitution of some form of the gold standard. Either the government could be required to redeem its currency in gold at a specified rate of exchange, or the federal gold stock could be sold and private banks could be required to undertake conversions on demand at the parity rate. If this were done the money supply would grow over time at about the rate of world gold production, which is regulated by the same market forces as the production of other goods and services. Past experience indicates that a great deal of long-run price stability would result, although other problems might appear; see Chapter 17 for a detailed discussion of the operation and problems of the gold standard.

Perhaps the most exciting and utopian new idea is to divest government of any money-creation function and to institute a competitive private monetary system, or at least to allow people to transact, contract, and denominate in foreign currencies. Several economists (including the 1974 Nobel prize winner, F. A. Hayek) have argued that if people were able to substitute freely between distinct, privately provided currencies at market-determined rates of exchange, those currencies that were falling in value because of excessive growth rates would be eliminated from the market by such substitution, and only currencies of stable value would remain.[16]

It may be that more than monetary reform is necessary, because monetary reform alone would not solve the problems that excess money growth was employed to alleviate. Recognizing that wage push has been a prime motive for such excess money growth, Keynesian economist have often advocated what is known as an **incomes policy**. This involves the use of mandatory price and wage controls or voluntary guidelines to prevent wage rate increases that exceed the growth in productivity and result in cost push. Some Keynesians have advocated a **tax-based incomes policy**, in which firms granting excessive wage-rate increases would be penalized by higher tax rates.[17]

Incomes policies have, in fact, been tried several times. Aside from the mandatory price controls applied during World War II, voluntary guidelines were applied during the Kennedy and Johnson administrations between 1962 and 1966, and by the Carter administration. Mandatory wage-price controls were applied to different degrees between 1971 and 1974 by the Nixon administration. The results were not encouraging. Neither voluntary guideline program restrained inflation. The Nixon wage-price freeze may have exercised some restraint, but prices increased faster when the controls were lifted.[18]

The most important problem with wage-price controls, even in the tax incentive form, is that they prevent necessary relative price adjustments. Relative supply and demand shifts are always occurring, both in output and labor markets and in both inflationary and noninflationary periods, resulting in relative price and wage-rate changes that signal necessary resource reallocations. Not every wage-rate increase in excess of the average productivity growth in the economy constitutes an unjustified cost push, and not every price increase is inflationary.

By preventing or penalizing such necessary adjustments, price controls produce distortions, resource misallocations, and lost output. These effects became significant during the Nixon wage–price freeze. A far more logical and sensible method of eliminating wage push pressures, that Keynesians have never been willing to consider, would be to create more competition in labor markets by altering the laws that have generated excess labor monopoly. The result of such legislation would not only be a reduction in cost push pressures, but also a more (rather than less) efficient allocation of labor resources, a lower natural rate of unemployment, and an increase in associated output.

Mere monetary reform would also leave unsolved, or perhaps worsen, the problem of financing transfer payments that citizens want but do not wish to pay for. One of the most notable features of the Reagan period was that the decline in inflation was not associated with decline in the deficit. Lost revenue from the tax on cash balances and automatic tax increases was replaced by additional federal borrowing from private parties. In combination with the 1981 recession and increased military expenditures, this raised the deficit. Transfer payments continued increasing in real and nominal dollar magnitudes and decreased as a proportion of expenditure only slightly; see Figure 15.6.

Here again some institutional reform is needed. A balanced budget amendment to the constitution would prevent deception in the finance of expenditures through temporal displacement of taxation.[19] It would also help to constitutionally require that every expenditure proposal be accompanied in the same bill by a proposal of finance through open taxation, so that the public is informed of the costs as well as the benefits. Of course, changing institutional incentives in this manner seems difficult, but changes in the Constitution have been made in the past, and our national ability to eliminate inflation may depend ultimately on our willingness to engage in appropriate Constitutional innovations.

Summary

The essential points of this chapter can be summarized as follows.

1. Accelerating money growth caused inflation to rise above 1950s levels in the mid-1960s and to accelerate through 1981, although the money growth rate essentially stopped rising after 1978. Real interest rates, productivity growth, and real output growth all slowed during this period.

2. Although money growth became more variable, the elimination of its accelerating trend caused the inflation rate to fall back to the 3 to 4 percent levels sustainable by the rate of excess money growth after 1981. Productivity and real output growth recovered somewhat, although the real interest rate rose and increased real federal, private, and foreign debt burdens.

3. Some theorists explain inflation in terms of profit or cost pushes from the supply side, attributable to market power. Such explanations for continuously rising prices are inadequate on their own terms. As an explanation of political pressures for excess money growth to cure the unemployment generated, however, cost–push phenomena may have some explanatory power.

4. Because the U.S. tax code specified both income tax brackets and depreciation allowances in nominal terms before 1985, the period of accelerating inflation increased real tax burdens, creating significant investment and production disincentives and an excessive resource shift from the private to the public sector.

5. Although income tax bracket creep was eliminated by ERTA, depreciation allowances are still not indexed to the inflation rate.

6. Inflation is a tax on cash balances held by the public, which shifts resources from the private to the public sector. The tax rate is the rate of inflation and the base is the quantity of real balances held.

7. If we assume that the government (through the Federal Reserve) controls the money stock, chronic excess money growth and inflation must be explained in terms of the incentives faced by political and monetary authorities in the post-war democratic institutions and monetary systems.

8. The governmental use of excess growth as a means of taxing cash balances, raising other tax rates and, repudiating federal debt surreptitiously, can be explained in terms of increasing post-war political competition centered on targeted income transfers, combined with public resistance to the open taxation required to fund such transfers.

9. The Reagan period disinflation appears to have been made possible by a decline in the benefits and rise in the costs of inflationary policy to political authorities. This occurred as the public's rising inflation expectations acted to neutralize that policy, and tax resistance stiffened.

10. Although governmental incentives have been reduced, conditions could motivate use of the inflation policy in the future. Precluding this requires institutional reform to reduce or eliminate the remaining incentives.

11. Alternate institutional innovations for the monetary system include a Friedman (fixed money growth) rule or some other objective monetary response legislation, restoration of the gold standard, or creation of a private, competitive monetary system.

12. More than monetary reform may be necessary to eliminate underlying pressures for excess money growth, such as wage–cost pushes and the desire of the public for income transfers it does not wish to pay for. Keynesians have advocated incomes policies to limit wage and price increases. It seems preferable to legislate a reduction of monopoly power in labor markets and pass a balanced budget amendment.

Notes

1. See below, and see also Steven Holland, "Real Interest Rates: What Accounts for Their Recent Rise?" in James A. Wilcox and Frederic S. Mishkin, eds., *Current Readings on Money, Banking and Financial Markets* (Boston: Little, Brown and Co., 1987): 67–78.

2. Michael Mussa, "U.S. Macroeconomic Policy and Third World Debt," *Cato Journal* 4 (Spring/Summer 1984): 81–95 is an excellent readable discussion of the third-world debt problem. There are also several other excellent papers on the subject in the same issue of *The Cato Journal*.

3. Anna Schwartz, in her comment in *Constructive Approaches to the Foreign Debt Dilemma* (Washington, D.C.: Taxpayers Foundation, 1983): 12–16, points out that even if the banks involved had to admit default on these loans and this resulted in some bank failures, it need not lead to a collapse of the financial and monetary system. The government can guarantee that deposits can be converted into currency at will.

4. E. K. Hunt and Howard Sherman, *Economics: An Introduction to Traditional and Radical Views* (New York: Harper and Row, 1975): 265.

5. See Michael Smirlock, et al., "Tobin's Q and the Structure-Performance Relationship," *American Economic Review* 74 (December 1984): 1051–1060, Sam Peltzman, "The Gains and Losses from Industrial Concentration," *Journal of Law and Economics* 20 (October 1977): 229–263, and Harold Demsetz, *The Market Concentration Doctrine* (Washington, D.C.: The American Enterprise Institute, 1973): 19–25.

6. See Thomas Humphrey, "On Cost-Push Theories of Inflation in the Pre-War Monetary Literature," in Humphrey, ed., *Essays on Inflation* (Richmond: Federal Reserve Bank of Richmond, 1980): 19–25.

7. The classic paper on this matter is Yale Brozen, "Minimum Wage Rates and Household Workers," *Journal of Law and Economics* 5 (October 1962): 103–110.

8. Benjamin M. Anderson, *Economics and the Public Welfare: A Financial and Economic History of the United States, 1914–1946* (1949) (Indianapolis: Liberty Press Edition, 1979): 325–327, and 425–438.

9. Alternative methods might include user fees, voluntary contributions, or endowment of the government.

10. The intuition that the term must refer to the individual who wrote the tax code is therefore incorrect.

11. The forms of the illustrations in this section are borrowed from Baird and Casuto, *Macroeconomics: Monetary, Search and Income Theories:* Chapter 12. Imitation is the sincerest form of flattery.

12. The best essay on the tax on cash balances for the intermediate level student is in Harry Johnson, *Essays in Monetary Economics* (London: Allen and Unwin, 1967): 122–126. The seminal essay, however, is Martin J. Bailey, "The Welfare Cost of Inflationary Finance," *Journal of Political Economy* 64 (April 1956): 93–110.

13. Indeed, to the extent that the public does not understand the source of inflation, the tax increases may not be blamed on government at all. Even so, at some point tax increases through inflation should result in political pressures for offsetting rate reductions and even for indexation, which is precisely what happened in the late 1970s.

14. It casts doubt on another hypothesis, however. During this period military expenditures as a proportion of total federal expenditure moved in the opposite direction as did transfer payments, with other expenditures retaining a relatively constant proportion. Contrary to the widely accepted Marxist and institutionalist hypothesis, proportional military expenditure is *inversely* correlated with inflation. This is most striking for the Reagan years in particular.

15. Phillip Cagan, *Persistent Inflation* (New York: Columbia University Press, 1979), estimated that unions and minimum-wage laws each accounted for about one-half of a percentage point out of the natural unemployment rate, or about 16 percent of total unemployment.

16. For an introduction to and discussion of this literature see James Rolph Edwards, "Monopoly and Competition in Money," *Journal of Libertarian Studies* 4 (Winter 1980): 107–117.

17. See Henry Wallich and Sidney Weintraub, "A Tax-Based Incomes Policy," *Journal of Economic Issues* 5 (June 1971): 1–19.

18. Robert J. Gordon, The Impact of Aggregate Demand on Prices," *Brookings Papers on Economic Activity* No. 3 (1975): 613-662.

19. See Richard E. Wagner, et. al., *Balanced Budgets, Fiscal Responsibility and the Constitution* (Washington, D.C.: The Cato Institute, 1982).

Student Self-Test _____

I. True–False

T   F   **1.** The accelerating inflation of the 1970s was associated with rising growth rates of real output and employment.

T   F   **2.** The farm debt problem of the 1980s was the result of Reagan administration reductions in agricultural price supports.

T   F   **3.** The cost-push theory that wage increases cause price rises which motivate additional wage increases, and so on is a logically sufficient explanation for inflation.

T   F   **4.** The failure of Congress to index business depreciation allowances results in undertaxation of business.

T   F   **5.** Inflation literally transfers both purchasing power and real resources from the private sector to the government and monetary authorities.

T   F   **6.** Revenue from the tax on cash balances is a linear positive function of the inflation rate.

T   F   **7.** The bulk of tax revenue budgeted for transfer payments is not received by the poor.

II. Short Answer *(150 words or less each)*

1. Why should the rise in the velocity of money after 1984 and the decline in velocity after 1981 have been predictable?

2. In what sense does the wage-price spiral explain inflation and—in part, at least—excess money growth? What happened in the 1930s when such cost-pushes occurred without being accompanied by rapid money growth?
3. Does the structure of incentives inherent in democratic political institutions motivate political agents to offer open taxation matching all proposed additions to expenditure? Explain.
4. What central fact explains the observable pattern of income transfers in the United States?
5. Why was the United States able to reduce the inflation rate in the 1980s?
6. What does the growth of taxes and transfers have to do with inflation during the 1970s? Explain.
7. Would an incomes policy be a good solution to inflation by itself or as part of a more comprehensive program? Explain.

III. Completion Problems

1. Assume an income tax of the form

$$T = t(Y)$$
$$= 0(Y \le \$20,000) + .15(\$20,000 < Y \le \$25,000)$$
$$+ .25(\$25,000 < Y \le \$30,000) + .5(Y > \$30,000).$$

Now consider a family with a single taxable income of $29,000.
A. In the initial year this family's tax payment is $T = \$$_____.
B. The family's disposable income is $Y^d = \$$_____.
C. If the annual inflation rate is 8 percent and the family's income rises at that rate, the next year it will be $Y' = \$$_____.
D. If the tax rates are not indexed, the family's tax bill in that second year will be $T' = \$$_____.
E. Its disposable income that year will be $Y^{d'} = \$$_____.
F. *Real* taxes paid in the second year will be $\$$_____ and real disposable income will be $\$$_____.
2. Line *dd* in the top graph of the figure on p. 395 shows a smooth, continuous, and linear functional relationship between real money balances demanded and the rate of inflation on the assumption that other variables affecting m_d are held constant. The equation describing the line is $m_d = 1800 - 15,000\alpha$.
A. Draw the marginal revenue curve on the top graph, or on a copy, in its appropriate location.
B. If $\alpha = .03$, then revenue from the tax on cash balances is $T_\alpha = \$$_____ billion constant dollars.
C. If $\alpha = .05$, $T_\alpha = \$$_____ billion.
D. If $\alpha = .07$, $T_\alpha = \$$_____ billion.
E. If $\alpha = .09$, $T_\alpha = \$$_____ billion.
F. Plot the revenue answers on the lower graph, or on a copy.

G. If the federal government wishes to maximize revenue from the tax it
will set $\alpha =$ _____ .

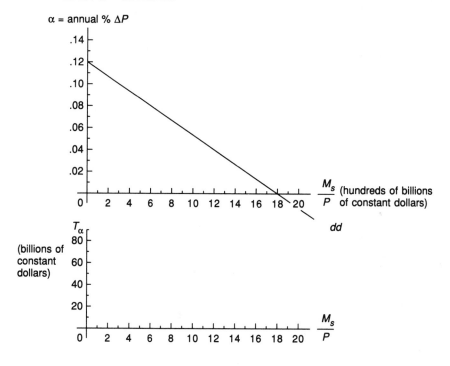

CHAPTER 16

Supply-Side Economics

The central lesson learned from both theoretical developments in macromonetary economics and economic events of recent decades is the inability of government to permanently affect real variables such as output and employment in a beneficial fashion through manipulation of a purely nominal magnitude, the money stock. Tied up with this lesson are several subsidiary lessons, such as the limitations of demand management policy imposed by lags, lack of information, the political economy of democratic states, and so on.

These observations gave impetus to the monetarist counterrevolution and rational expectations theory. As the decade of the 1970s progressed, however, it also became recognized increasingly that the underlying problem was not that fluctuations in money growth caused fluctuations in output and employment around the trend of Q_f, but that Q_f and its trend growth rate were too low. Keynesian objections aside, this cannot be corrected by raising aggregate demand. AD was obviously already excessive during this period. To correct such a decline in trend requires a policy that affects the underlying real determinants of the level and growth of Q_f—primarily the capital stock and relative prices. This realization gave rise to a school of macroeconomic theory and policy known as **supply-side economics**.

The Supply-Side Viewpoint _____

Supply-side economics rests on two observations. The first concerns Say's law (a primitive ancestor of Say's principle and Walras's law), which says that goods and services are ultimately paid for by other goods and services, with money acting primarily as the medium of exchange. According to this argument human wants are essentially unlimited, and because goods and services constitute the ultimate source of effective demands for each other, the problem of satisfying human needs and desires does not consist of stimulating sufficient demand, but of providing the necessary outputs. The economic problem lies on the *supply* side of the market, in production.[1]

The second insight is that taxes alter relative prices. In so doing they alter the incentives people face to use resources productively, causing substitutions that alter output and employment. The higher tax rates are, the greater these effects are. It seems to follow that the levels and growth rates of output and employment can be raised by lowering tax rates. It is important here to distinguish between the **average tax rate** (ATR) = T/Y) the ratio of total tax to total income—or total *taxable* income, as the analyst prefers—and the **marginal tax rate** on each additional dollar earned, $t = \Delta T/\Delta Y$; see Chapters 11 and 15. Supply siders argue that changes in the latter are crucial, because human decisions to use or not to use additional resources productively depend centrally on the marginal after-tax income expected.

Of course, supply-side economists are not anarchists. They recognize that government is necessary and beneficial, even to production, on net, to a point. Some rate of taxation is seen as necessary to divert resources from the private to the public sector so that the governmental benefits can be obtained. The problem is in finding that point at which the marginal addition to real output and income generated by provision of additional governmental services equals the marginal real output and income lost through resource extraction by taxation. For reasons that should be clear from Chapter 15, however, there is a tendency for government to expand into the region where the marginal costs exceed the marginal benefits. The essence of the supply-side viewpoint is that this has been the case in recent decades, and hence gains can be made in terms of increased levels and growth of real output and income by reducing marginal tax rates.

It should be noted that in its essence there is nothing new or radical about this viewpoint. Supply-side economics is a microeconomic approach to macroeconomic policy that focuses on three substitution effects of tax-rate changes: between legal and illegal economic activities, between saving and present consumption, and between work and leisure. The existence of the substitution effects postulated is non-controversial within the economics profession, although there is controversy, as will be shown, over their empirical magnitude, particularly relative to other, possibly offsetting, effects.

Substitution Between Legal and Illegal Economic Activities

There are costs and benefits to both legal and illegal economic activity. People in illegal activities pay no (or less) taxes but run the risk of imprisonment. Those who operate legally pay taxes but run little risk of imprisonment. *Ceteris paribus*, raising tax rates increases the costs relative to the benefits of operating legally and causes marginal shifts into the "underground economy." This not only involves increases in criminal activity (e.g., prostitution or drug peddling, very little of the income from which is reported) but also in numerous quasi-legal or unethical activities designed to reduce the tax burdens and maintain the disposable income of those involved.[2]

Perhaps the single most important such shift is toward cash transactions. As income tax rates rise millions of small businesses and self-employed professionals, including electricians, plumbers, painters, cab drivers, contractors, and even doctors and lawyers increasingly request payment in cash from regular customers, sometimes offering discounts for such payment. A large portion of this income is not reported for tax purposes.

A closely related practice is to employ workers "off the books." Because a large portion of hourly compensation goes to cover payroll taxes, every increase in such tax rates raises the incentive for firms to strike bargains with workers for unofficial employment in which such taxes are not paid. By dividing Uncle Sam's share between them, workers can obtain a higher hourly compensation and firms can obtain employees at a lower hourly cost. Perhaps the largest and most conspicuous group employed in this fashion consists of illegal Mexican immigrants, but millions of indigenous American workers are also employed part- or full-time off the books.

The use of tax shelters and other means of tax avoidance also increases as tax rates rise. All of the resources employed in creating and finding loopholes and tax shelters are wasted from the social perspective and represent lost real output and income from their alternate uses. Other underground activities distort the economic statistics. As pointed out in Chapter 2, the employment of millions of Americans in unreported activities in the underground economy causes measured employment to be too low and measured unemployment to be too high, *ceteris paribus*. Because underground economic activity is unreported, measured real GNP is also below its actual magnitude, perhaps as much as 10 or 15 percent, by some estimates.[3]

By its very nature evidence on the magnitude of the underground economy in the United States is difficult to come by. Because so much of it operates on cash transactions, Peter Gutman has pointed to the steady rise in the ratio of currency to demand deposits held from .219 in 1941 to .344 in 1976. By his estimate underground economic activity equals 14 percent of measured GNP.[4] Worse, it appears that underground economic activity grew as much as 2.5 times faster than measured GNP as bracket creep raised marginal tax rates during the 1970s.[5]

The underground economy not only causes real output to be lost, the magnitude of the economy to be misestimated, and resources to be misallocated, but it also erodes the tax base, putting an unfair burden on those who continue to pay the legal rates. Perhaps the worst consequence of the underground economy, however, is what it does to the respect for law and order as many individuals try to cheat the government in one way or another to protect themselves from what they consider confiscatory tax rates.

Substitution of Present Consumption for Future Consumption

One of the most important choices that people make concerns the use of current income they may have which exceeds that required to cover current necessities. Such income can be spent on consumption of (comparative) luxury items in the present or saved and invested in order to increase future income and consumption. This decision is not only microeconomically important for the individual or family involved, but also macroeconomically crucial, because such saving provides the funds for the net capital investment (both human and physical) and research and development that raise national productivity and real output.

This decision is made on the basis of the after-tax rate of return on investment. Logically, the higher that rate of return is, the larger the percentage of current income (S/Y) will be that is saved and invested. Conversely, increases in marginal tax rates that reduce the after-tax rate of return on investment seem likely to motivate people to substitute current consumption for future consumption at the margin. If continued, the growth rates of investment, productivity, and output might all fall.

Inflationary tax increases (perhaps in combination with other factors) seemed to cause many of these phenomena to appear in the late 1960s. Figure 16.1 shows the annual growth in per capital real GNP, $\% \Delta(Q/N)$, over the period from 1965, when inflation began accelerating, through 1987. Over much of this period, say from the prosperous year of 1965 to the cycle peak of 1981, the trend in per capita real GNP

Figure 16.1   Annual Growth in per-Capita Real Output, Q/N.

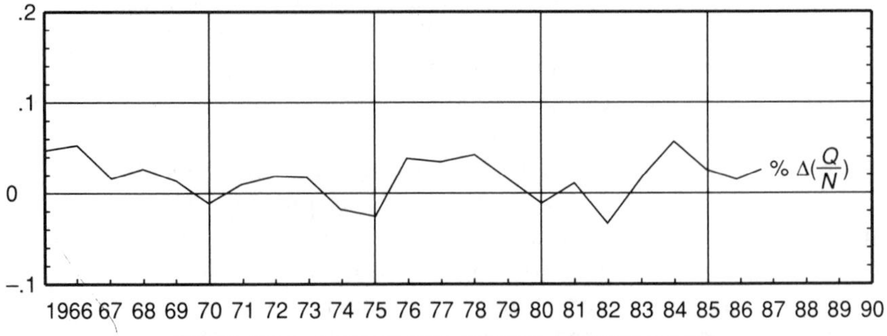

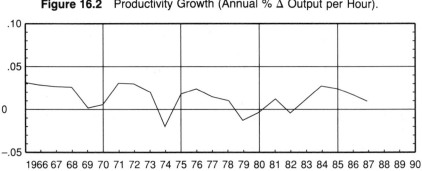

Source: Economic Report of the President, 1989: 311 and 343

growth seems to have been downward, although growth was reasonably high during the accelerating inflation of the Carter years.

Figure 16.2 plots annual productivity growth over the same period. The declining trend observable in the graph through the late 1970s has attracted a lot of attention from economists and a great deal of justified worry on the part of policymakers. Prominent explanations for the decline in productivity growth include the rise in labor force participation rates, which logically tended to reduce the marginal and average product of labor, *ceteris paribus*, and absorption of a large portion of business investment funds by costly environmental and safety regulations (EPA and OSHA) instituted early in this period. There is little doubt, however, that penalty tax rates due to bracket creep and understated depreciation as inflation accelerated also acted to reduce investment and hence also both productivity and output growth over the period.

Figure 16.2   Productivity Growth (Annual % Δ Output per Hour).

Source: Economic Report of the President, 1989: 361

The Substitution Between Labor and Leisure ————

The third substitution effect involves the labor supply decision. As explained in Chapter 4, individual choices about the allocation of scarce time between labor and leisure activities are made on the basis of anticipated costs and benefits. Assuming that workers do not supply their services with the express intent of generating revenue for the government, the chief benefit of labor to such workers is after-tax income. In Chapter 4 taxes were assumed away, so all income earned was disposable income. Under those circumstances, for a worker with a normal utility function $U = U(Y, L)$, and no nonwage income, $Y = W \cdot L$, and $\Delta Y/\Delta L = W$.

To analyze the effect of taxation and tax rate changes on labor supply, let us begin by assuming the existence of a single flat marginal rate income tax, $T = t(Y)$. The individual's disposable income is now $Y^d = W(1 - t) \cdot L$, and $\Delta Y^d/\Delta L = W(1 - t)$ defines the rate of exchange between labor and leisure, as shown in Figure 16.3. The worker maximizes utility at the initial wage and tax rates by supplying a quantity of labor L per time period at the tangency of line $W(1 - t)$ with the highest indifference curve reached.

A reduction in the tax rate to $t' < t$ pivots the constraint line upward to $W(1 - t')$. To illustrate with numbers, suppose that $W = \$10$ per hour and the flat marginal tax rate is 20 percent, or $t = .2$. In that case, the initial after-tax wage rate is $\$10(1 - .2) = \$8$. If $t' = .1$, then

Figure 16.3 Individual Labor-Leisure Substitution from Tax Rate Change.

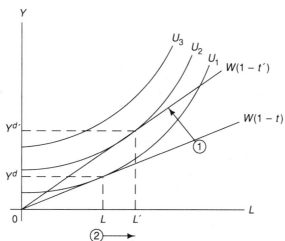

immediately after the tax-rate reduction the after-tax wage rate is $10(1 − .1) = $9 per hour. Supply-side economists argue that by increasing the cost of leisure, this would motivate the individual to offer more labor, as shown, whatever the initial wage rate was. Workers responding this way in the aggregate would shift the aggregate labor supply curve outward (rightward) at all wage rates. An increase in the tax rate, on the other hand, would decrease individual and aggregate labor supply.

Empirical evidence on the labor supply effects of taxation seems no less clear than it is for the other two substitutions. Careful experiments such as the New Jersey–Pennsylvania experiment and the Seattle–Denver income maintenance experiment, both of which faced control groups with high de facto marginal tax rates, found rather large reductions in labor supply on the part of husbands, wives, and female heads of households.[6] Jerry Hausman estimated that progressive taxation was reducing the labor supply of husbands by about 8 percent, and that of wives by 30 percent.[7]

Real-world events are always complex, however, and the period of rising marginal tax rates during the 1970s also saw a massive increase in the labor force participation rates of women and teenagers (see Chapter 8), with only a slight decline in that of white males. Whether this large scale influx occurred for other reasons or was a perverse response to the rising tax rates is as yet a matter of debate.

The Supply-Side Argument in an AD–AS Framework _____

If a reduction in marginal tax rates motivates more work, increased saving and investment, and a shift from illegal to legal activities as supply-side economists claim, then the consequences can be (imperfectly) illustrated by employing an *AD–AS* model such as Figure 16.4. The equilibrium magnitudes before the tax reduction are Q_f, Wa, and L. Expectations are assumed to adjust quickly, so the SRAS curve is deleted and only the LRAS curve is shown.

The simplest case involves a static, no-growth economy in which inflation is zero. The increase in investment as tax rates fall causes the capital stock to increase, raising the marginal product of labor. This is shown by the outward shift in the aggregate production function in the fourth quadrant of Figure 16.4. The increase in labor supply is shown in the third quadrant. Although the labor supply shift would probably occur first (even large increases in investment take time to cause significant accretions to the capital stock), because these are indepen-

Figure 16.4 Supply-Side Effects of Tax Reduction in an *AD–AS* Model.

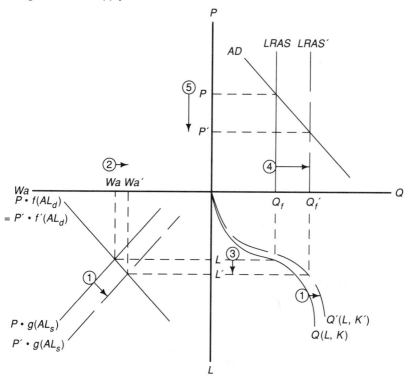

dent consequences of the tax reduction they are both labeled as event number 1.

Note that the *AD* curve and the aggregate labor demand curve do not shift in the graph. By Keynesian reasoning, a tax reduction should, by raising disposable income and hence consumption expenditure, cause the *AD* curve to shift outward. Supply-side economists deny the existence of such demand-side effects, however, due to crowding out.[8] Of course private investment cannot both increase (due to tax reduction) and decrease (due to crowding out) simultaneously, but if the tax rate reduction motivates not only more investment, but increased saving to provide the funds, total expenditure does not rise.

Because the tax reduction does not cause *AD* to shift outward, the increased employment and output, shifting the LRAS curve outward, causes the price level to fall from *P* to *P'* (steps 2 to 5). This explains why labor demand is not shown as changing. Although the rise in the marginal product of labor shown by the shift in the aggregate production function tends to raise the demand for labor in the third quadrant (by raising $VMP_L = P \cdot MPL$), the fall in the price level tends to reduce it. It is assumed for graphic simplicity that these effects roughly cancel, so that $P \cdot f(AL_d) \approx P' \cdot f'(AL_d)$.

Of course the decline in the price level, by raising the real wage, also causes the labor supply curve to increase (assuming that expectations adjust quickly), and the outward shift shown from $P \cdot g(AL_s)$ to $P' \cdot g(AL_s)$ is assumed for simplicity to be the total shift attributable to both the tax rate and price level reductions. The crucial result of the entire sequence of events is that the tax reduction produces greater employment, higher gross and per capita real output, and a lower price level.

This representation of the supply-side argument in terms of the *AD–AS* framework is somewhat imperfect in that those arguments are usually applied to an economy suffering from inflation and low but positive growth, which is hard to represent in static graphic terms. In such an economy it is argued that the tax reductions will raise the rates of growth of both employment and output and reduce the inflation rate. That is, where $\Delta M_s/M_s - \Delta m_d/m_d = \Delta P/P$, if a tax reduction raises $\Delta m_d/m_d$ by raising real output growth, the inflation rate will decline. For this reason supply siders argued that tax reduction is both a pro-growth and anti-inflation policy.

It is not hard to find a fair amount of evidence sustaining these arguments. Historically, tax reductions have often been associated with economic prosperity. For example, the individual income tax, made possible by the 16th Amendment, was instituted at the beginning of World War I and the rates were raised during the War. Andrew Mellon, Secretary of the Treasury under Presidents Harding and Coolidge, engineered a series of tax-rate reductions beginning in late 1921. Supply siders point out that the economic expansion that followed was one of the longest and most rapid in this century.[9]

One major factor accounting for the depth and length of the great depression is that the Roosevelt administration raised tax rates repeatedly, more than tripling the top marginal rate by 1936. Although the economy eventually recovered, depression-level tax rates went essentially unchanged until the Kennedy administration. Acting on the recommendation of his Keynesian advisers, who saw it as a way of spurring the economy by raising aggregate demand, and with the backing of Congress, President John F. Kennedy proposed an across-the-board reduction in income tax rates, which Congress passed in 1964.

An unusually rapid expansion followed this tax reduction. Although it is true that *AD* was rising as money growth rates increased and Keynesians see this episode as a victory for Keynesian policy, modern supply-siders argue that, abstracting from the monetary effects, the supply-side effects of the tax reductions dominated the demand-side effects. For example, investment increased rapidly following the tax reductions, while consumption as a proportion of income declined.[10]

A different sort of evidence was reported recently in a careful study by Keith Marsden of the World Bank. Marsden looked at 20 nations, which he paired by basic cultural and economic similarities, particularly per capita income, but which had significantly different tax burdens. He then compared their performance over the period from 1970 to 1979. In every case it turned out that the country in the pair that had the lowest tax burden, measured as the ratio of tax revenue to Gross Domestic Product (i.e., a measurement similar to GNP), T/GDP, had the highest average growth rate in real output and income over the period.[11]

Marsden also found that, as a group, the low-tax countries had higher growth in private consumption, employment, investment, exports, and life expectancy. And contrary to the fears of many commentators that lower tax rates favor the rich, he found no evidence that the income distributions were less equitable in the low-tax countries. Marsden's basic results are reproduced in Table 16.1. His study could, of course, be criticized on the basis that it focuses on average tax rates rather than on marginal tax rates. It seems likely, however, that there is a strong positive international correlation between ex ante marginal tax rates and the sort of ex post average tax burdens employed in Marsden's study.

First Keynesian Objection: Income Effects

Supply-side economics began to displace Keynesian reasoning as the basis of Congressional policy in the late 1970s as the declining growth rates of investment, productivity, and output became apparent. In 1979 the Joint Economic Committee, with a Democratic majority, endorsed the supply-side view. This change in attitude—however tenuous and temporary—did not occur without significant theoretical, political, and ideological struggle.[12] Numerous objections to the supply-side theory have been and continue to be raised by their Keynesian opponents. Two such objections seem of primary importance.

The first of these is that relative price changes, including those resulting from changes in tax rates, have both substitution and income effects. Keynesians charge that in focusing exclusively on the former, supply-side economics ignores the latter. Income effects may act to offset the substitutions postulated by supply-side theorists. As applied to saving and investment, the argument is that transactors may have a target level of after-tax investment income which they wish to maintain. The reduction in income per dollar invested as tax rates rise may

TABLE 16.1 Comparative Performance of Selected Countries

Country	Total tax revenue[1] as a percentage of GDP	Average annual percentage growth, 1970 to 1979						Gross domestic investment as a percentage of GDP	
		GDP	Consumption		Gross domestic investment	Exports	Labor force	1960	1979
			Public	Private					
Malawi (low tax)	11.8	6.3	6.1	5.7	2.3	4.6	2.2	10	29
Zair (high tax)	21.5	−0.7	−2.2	−1.8	−5.0	−1.1	2.1	12	9
Cameroon (low tax)	15.1	5.4	5.4	5.3	7.9	0.5	1.3	—	25
Liberia (high tax)	21.2	1.8	2.3	4.3	5.2	2.3	2.6	28	27
Thailand (low tax)	11.7	7.7	9.1	6.9	7.7	12.0	2.7	16	28
Zambia (high tax)	22.7	1.5	1.8	−2.2	−5.6	−0.7	2.4	25	21
Paraguay (low tax)	10.3	8.3	4.8	7.4	18.7	8.4	3.1	17	29
Peru (high tax)	14.4	3.1	6.5	2.9	2.7	1.7	3.0	25	14
Mauritius (low tax)	18.6	8.2	13.5	9.8	16.1	—	—	30	38
Jamaica (high tax)	23.8	−0.9	8.0	−0.6	−9.6	−6.8	2.2	30	18
Korea (low tax)	14.2	10.3	8.7	8.0	14.9	25.7	2.8	11	35
Chile (high tax)	22.4	1.9	−0.5	1.9	−2.0	10.7	1.9	17	16
Brazil (low tax)	17.1	8.7	8.6	9.1	10.1	7.0	2.2	22	23
Uruguay (high tax)	20.0	2.5	1.5	(·)[3]	7.5	4.3	0.1	18	17
Singapore (low)	16.2	3.1	6.5	2.9	2.7	1.7	3.0	25	14
New Zealand (high)	27.5	2.4	—	—	—	3.4	2.1	24	22
Spain (low tax)	19.1	4.4	5.6	4.4	2.5	10.8	1.1	19	20
U.K. (high tax)	30.4	2.1	2.8	1.7	0.8	8.2	0.3	19	20
Japan (low tax)	10.6[2]	5.2	5.0	5.3	3.2	9.1	1.3	34	33
Sweden (high tax)	30.9	2.0	3.2	2.0	−1.1	2.6	0.3	25	20

Sources: World Bank, 1981 World Bank Atlas; *World Development Report, 1981*; and *Accelerated Development in Sub-Saharan Africa* (Washington DC, 1981). IMF, *International Financial Statistics Yearbook, 1981* and *Government Finance Statistics Yearbook*, Vol. V (Washington DC, 1981). International Labor Office, *ILO Yearbook of Labor Statistics, 1980*.

— Indicates data are not available.   [2] includes nontax revenue but excludes social security contributions.   [3] (·) Indicates that figure is less than 0.005.
[1] Central government tax revenues only.

in that case motivate people to save and invest more, not less. Conversely, because a tax-rate reduction raises income earned per dollar invested, such that the target can be maintained with fewer dollars invested, saving and investment may fall.

Whatever the theoretical merit of this argument, the empirical case seems weak. The decline in the national saving rate and in business fixed investment relative to GNP, which occurred during the period of rising marginal tax rates in the 1970s, is difficult to explain away in such terms. The rapid growth in the underground economy during this period, unless it is illusory, also seems to be immune to any argument based on income effects.

As applied to the substitution between labor and leisure, the Keynesian argument initially seems more pursuasive. Figure 16.5 separates the income effect from the substitution effect of an income tax reduction in order to obtain the pure substitution effect. This is done by first reducing the marginal income tax rate from t to t' and thus shifting the after-tax wage from $W(1 - t)$ to $W(1 - t')$ as in Figure 16.3. This raises the cost of leisure but also increases the income earned from each hour of work. Both effects act to change desired labor supply.

The income increase from this hypothetical income tax rate reduction can be eliminated in utility terms by imagining that a lump-sum tax is simultaneously imposed, of a magnitude sufficient to shift the vertical intercept of the new tradeoff line downward as shown until the line just comes tangent to the initial indifference curve. The tax system thus changes from $T = t(Y)$ to $T' = \bar{T} + t'(Y)$, where $\bar{T}$ is the dollar magnitude of the lump sum. The intersection of this new tradeoff line

Figure 16.5 The Pure Substitution Effect.

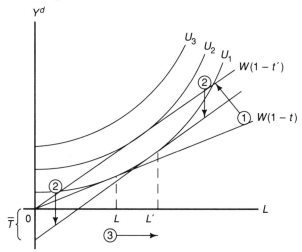

with the horizontal axis shows the amount of time the individual would have to work to earn income just sufficient to pay the lump-sum tax.

The tangency of that line with the indifference curve yields the individual's desired labor time, which is now L'. Clearly, the pure substitution effect of the tax-rate change (which can always be found by rotating the constraint line along the initial indifference curve) is inverse: reducing the marginal tax rate and thus raising the cost of leisure (without changing income) motivates the individual to offer more work. Reducing the cost of leisure by raising the tax rate (without changing income), on the other hand, motivates the individual to offer *less* work.

In order to see the income effect of a tax change in its purity, it is necessary to abstract from the substitution effect. Employing the same general form of the tax system, $T = \bar{T} + t(Y)$ in Figure 16.6, where the individual's initial desired work time is L, makes this easy. Reducing the lump sum tax to $\bar{T}' < \bar{T}$ raises the individual's income at all work levels, shifting the constraint upward, without changing the slope of the constraint line embodying the relative cost of leisure. The individual's desired labor supply falls to L'.

The pure income effect on desired labor supply (which can be found by shifting the intercept of the constraint line without changing its slope) is positive: reducing taxes to raise disposable income (without changing the relative cost of leisure) reduces desired labor supply. Leisure time is, after all, a normal good that people would like to have more of as their income rises, like other normal goods. It also follows

Figure 16.6 The Pure Income Effect.

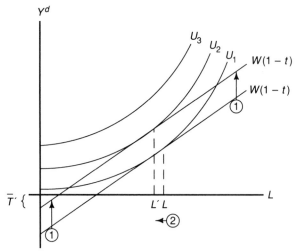

that raising taxes and hence reducing income (without changing the relative cost of leisure) increases desired labor supply for the individual.

Because a change in a marginal tax rate involves both an income and a substitution effect, and the two have opposite effects on an individual's desired labor supply, whether a given worker will offer more or less labor as a result depends on which effect is strongest. Figure 16.7 illustrates a case in which the positive income effect exceeds the negative substitution effect, such that a reduction in the marginal income tax rate from t to t' motivates an individual to offer less employment at the initial wage rate. This result is to be compared with that in Figure 16.3, in which the substitution effect is clearly greater.

The Keynesian argument is that if, at the initial wage structure, the income effect is stronger than the substitution effect for most workers, a reduction in marginal tax rates would cause aggregate labor supply to decline, rather than rise as supply siders claim (and as shown in Figure 16.4). A tax increase, it follows, would cause labor supply to increase as workers tried to maintain their after-tax income. And in any real-world case, according to this argument, it is impossible to predict *a priori* whether the substitution or income effect will dominate, so the case for supply side tax reductions to increase incentives to work is not made.[13]

Figure 16.7 Perverse Tax Effect on Individual Labor Supply.

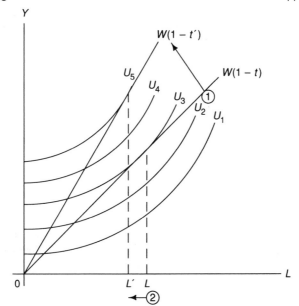

Supply-side economists have objected strenuously to this argument. They point out that it is one thing to argue that an autonomous increase in the aggregate production function that raises real aggregate income may result in workers taking part of the increase in increased leisure, reducing labor supply. That can occur. It is quite another thing to argue that a simple tax reduction can reduce aggregate labor supply. As Sir John Hicks pointed out in his classic masterpiece, *Value and Capital*, the income effects of a relative price change tend to cancel in the general equilibrium (because price increase that raises the income of the seller reduces that of the buyer, and a price decrease that reduces the income of the seller raises that of the buyer), while the substitution effects aggregate.[14]

A mere tax-rate decrease does not per se increase society's production possibilities and raise aggregate income, and hence can generate no initial aggregate income effect. Real output and income can only rise if the substitutions occur, raising investment and work. In the aggregate, therefore, the substitution effects have to dominate. Workers could not possibly respond to a tax-rate reduction by reducing labor supply in the aggregate, *ceteris paribus*, because that would make real output and income fall, destroying the very effect (i.e., rising income) that would supposedly be making labor supply decline.[15]

Another perspective on the issue stressed by some supply-side economists involves consideration of the uses of the tax revenue, not only the sources. Consider a tax, the revenue from which is employed to finance transfer payments to a subset of the population. The transfer payment is in essence a lump-sum subsidy, which has the effect of shifting the labor–leisure tradeoff constraint of the recipient vertically upward by the amount of the subsidy (Tr) as shown in Figure 16.8. This is because the individual's income, without any employment, is equal to the amount of the subsidy.

Such a person's optimal employment will not be zero, however, but the amount L', shown by the tangency of the post-subsidy constraint $W(1 - t)$ with the highest indifference curve reached, if the subsidy is not reduced as additional income is earned. It is unambiguous that the increase in the recipient's income generated by such a subsidy tends to reduce desired labor supply. If the effect of the tax on taxpayers, who find their income reduced by the tax, is to motivate less work, then desired labor supply falls for both taxpayers and subsidy recipients.

In order for the tax to cause a net increase in aggregate labor supply, the income effect would not only have to exceed the substitution effect for taxpayers, but also exceed it by enough to swamp the income effect on subsidy recipients. This is extremely unlikely, and it follows that a tax and subsidy reduction would almost certainly increase aggregate

Figure 16.8 Effect of Transfer Payment on Individual Labor Supply.

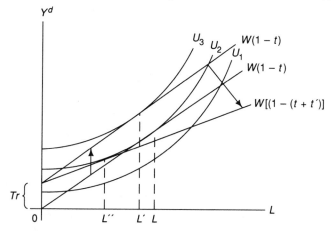

labor supply. It is probable that the very worst case resulting from a change in tax rates in either direction would be no net change in labor supply at all, and even that is unlikely.

The likelihood that the substitution effects will dominate can also be seen by modifying the subsidy case just discussed. Because many transfer payments, such as Aid to Families with Dependent Children (AFDC), are aimed at benefitting the poor, they are reduced as the recipient earns additional income in the labor market. Supposing for simplicity that the subsidy is reduced by an amount equal to a constant proportion t' of each additional dollar earned, and that subsidy recipients pay income taxes also, the effective marginal tax rate faced by such an individual is $t + t'$. This reduces the person's after-tax wage to $W[1 - (t + t')]$, as shown in Figure 16.8, further reducing desired labor supply to L'' through the substitution effect. Actually, the graph may understate the work disincentive resulting. In some states the effective marginal tax rate faced by welfare recipients equals or exceeds 100 percent, and in all states it is very high.[16]

Although consideration of the tax and transfer system makes clear the tendency of tax changes to cause opposite income changes for net taxpayers and subsidy receivers so that the income effects largely cancel, leaving the substitution effects, it is certainly true that some tax revenue is employed for uses that directly benefit taxpayers also. It is obvious, however, that those expenditures also tend to cause canceling income changes (tax increases reducing citizen income, while additional government services provided raise it, and vice versa for tax-rate and expenditure reductions), such that any net (utility) income change would be unlikely to offset the substitution effects.[17] It seems hard to deny, then, that tax-rate increases would reduce aggregate labor supply, and reductions increase it, *ceteris paribus*.

Second Keynesian Objection: Deficits and Crowding Out

The second major Keynesian objection to a policy of tax reductions based on supply-side reasoning is that such reductions will increase the deficit by reducing tax revenues. If the deficit is then financed by borrowing, private investment will be crowded out, which will offset any beneficial effects of tax rate reductions on output growth and employment.[18] It should perhaps be remarked how out of character this argument is for Keynesian economists, because crowding out is an argument that had long been employed against their own view that deficits improve the economy by stimulating aggregate demand, and because they had never, before the advent of supply-side economics, shown concern about reductions in private investment caused by government borrowing. Nevertheless, it is a serious argument.

The response of supply-side economists was to point out that there is a distinction between tax rates and tax revenue, and whether (or the extent to which) a reduction in tax rates reduces revenues and creates (or enlarges) a deficit depends on how high rates were initially. The revenue from a tax is the product of the rate (t), and the base, β. That is,

$$T = t \cdot \beta.$$

In the case of a property tax or an income tax, for example, the revenue collected would be the product of the tax rate and the dollar value of the property or income on which the tax was levied. But as the tax rate changes, the substitution effects discussed previously cause such a tax base to change in the opposite direction. In percentage terms,

$$\frac{\Delta T}{T} \approx \frac{\Delta t}{t} + \frac{\Delta \beta}{\beta}.$$

In the simple static growth case, Δt and $\Delta \beta$ have opposite signs, so a reduction in tax rates ($\Delta t/t < 0$) will only cause revenue to fall if $\Delta t/t > \Delta \beta/\beta$. If tax rates fall 10 percent, for example, and the tax base increases by 6 percent because of increased investment and work and because shifts out of the underground economy cause more income to be reported, tax revenue would only fall by about 4 percent. If the substitutions resulting from a 10 percent tax reduction caused the tax base to increase by, say, 12 percent, revenue would actually rise by about 2 percent.

The revenue curve can be argued to have a logical shape, being zero both when $t = 0$ and at some penalty rate $\bar{t} \leq 100$ percent. As the tax rate rises above zero and increases toward inhibitive levels, the revenue resulting must first rise to some maximum and then fall, as shown in Figure 16.9. The curve, which is termed the **Laffer curve** after economist Arthur Laffer, can be interpreted in terms of a particular tax on a particular base or as expressing the general relationship between the level of marginal taxation and the value of all income and assets taxed in the economy.[19] In either case, marginal tax rates (e.g., t) in the declining region of the curve are obviously too high, because they are discouraging a great deal of economic activity, and the same revenue can be obtained by a lower rate (e.g., t') in the rising region of the curve.

It is not hard to find illustrations of the Laffer curve. In fact, tax revenue almost never changes in proportion with changes in tax rates. A 30 percent reduction in the tax rate on capital gains in 1979, for example, caused enough increased reporting of such gains that revenue fell only $1 billion that year, which was less than one-half of the decline predicted by static revenue considerations. In a more extreme example, the tax on state bank notes included in the National Bank Act of 1863 (actually, an 1864 amendment) produced no revenue for the government, because although the rate was only ten percent it was high

Figure 16.9 The Laffer Curve.

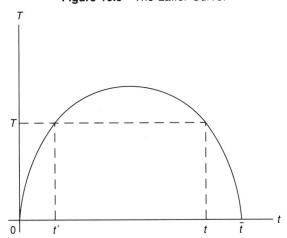

enough to destroy profitibility from issuing such notes, and all such issuance ceased.

As the prominent Keynesian Alan Blinder has pointed out, however, that it is one thing to prove the existence of a Laffer curve and quite another to prove that existing tax rates (in the aggregate) are on its downhill side.[20] Some radical popularizers of supply-side economics seem to have claimed this to be the case, arguing that a general tax-rate reduction would be self-financing, so that revenue might rise, making greater government expenditure possible. In fact, this argument may have been of some importance in breaking down Congressional resistance to the Reagan tax reductions.

Prominent supply-side economists such as Laffer and Paul Craig Roberts, however, have been careful never to claim that U.S. marginal tax rates as a whole were in the declining region of the curve. In their view the validity of supply-side tax policy did not rest on such a claim. Tax rates can be excessive even in the rising portion of the curve. The maximum revenue is not necessarily the optimum. Tax reductions in the rising range will involve less than proportional losses in revenue as the substitution effects increase economic activity, wealth, and welfare, raising the tax base. Resulting increases in the deficit may therefore not be large, and crowding out of private investment by government borrowing will not be significant if the tax reductions increase the saving rate.

Some economists and policy-makers with supply-side leanings argued from the first that the attainment of the benefits from tax reductions could best be assured by reducing government expenditure simultaneously, so that no increase in the deficit would appear. As Milton Friedman has pointed out many times, the best indicator of the burden of government on the economy is its level of expenditure. Staunch supply-side revolutionaries resisted this reasoning, however, on the basis that expenditure reductions were politically unfeasible, and if coupled with the proposed tax reductions would ensure the defeat of the tax program in Congress. As the supply-side program found expression in the Reagan administration, both of these viewpoints were represented, but the latter dominated events.

Supply-Side Economics in the Reagan Era: Myth and History

The poor economic (and foreign policy) performance in the late 1970s resulted in Ronald Reagan being elected President on an explicitly supply-side economic platform and in control of the Senate passing to the Republicans for the first time since 1956. As a result, President Reagan's supply-side program found expression in the **Economic Recovery Tax Act** (ERTA) which became law late in 1981, although this was modified by the **Tax Equity and Fiscal Responsibility Act** (TEFRA) of 1982. In 1986 the administration obtained passage of a more general **Tax Reform Act** (TRA). It is far too early to evaluate the tax-reform act, but events following the passage of ERTA and TEFRA have already been used to evaluate the supply-side effects of the tax-rate changes involved.

The centerpiece of ERTA was a three-stage phased reduction in marginal tax rates: by 5 percent in 1982 (reduced from an originally proposed 10 percent), 10 percent in 1983, and 10 percent again in 1984. ERTA also provided accelerated depreciation of business assets for tax purposes, allowing faster recovery of invested capital by the firm than is provided by linear depreciation, in order to reduce the impact of inflation; see the discussion of depreciation allowances in Chapter 15. A third crucial feature of the Act was indexation of income-tax brackets beginning in 1985. TEFRA primarily modified some of the accelerated cost depreciation features of ERTA that were considered too generous.

It was certainly bad luck that the first major economic event following passage of ERTA was the recession of 1982 to 1983, the largest in the post-war period. Because it was clearly the result of deliberate contractionary monetary policy already in progress to fight the rapidly accelerating inflation, responsible critics of the Reagan administration have been careful not to attribute the recession to ERTA. The recession was followed, however, by the longest expansion in post-war history and a series of very large deficits in the federal budget, both of which have been the subject of important claims by both advocates and opponents of supply-side tax cuts.

Considering the deficits first, we see that Figure 16.10 partly duplicates and partly extends Figure 11.7 by showing the federal deficit as a percentage of GNP from 1970 to 1988. Deficits have indeed increased by this measure, and Reagan-era deficits are the largest in this interval. It should be noted, however, that there is no sharp break in the trend of growth in the deficit relative to the economy in the Reagan period. In other words, if Ronald Reagan had never been elected President, but the ratio of the deficit to GNP had kept growing at the previous rate, the deficits experienced in the early- to mid-1980s would have been little different from those actually experienced. The deficit growth appears therefore to be a structural problem (as explained in Chapter 11) which preceded the Reagan administration, and which first-term

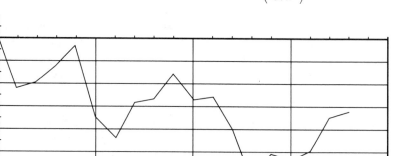

Figure 16.10 Budget Balance/GNP $\left(\dfrac{T-G}{GNP}\right)$.

Source: Economic Report of the President, 1989: 308 and 397, and Survey of Current Business (March 1989): 3

Reagan policies, including tax reductions, did not significantly affect (although the deficit/GNP ratio declined rather steadily in his second term).

Deficits rise when the growth of federal revenue is less than the growth of expenditures. Accordingly, critics have generally attributed the large deficits of the 1980s to two features of the Reagan program: an increase in military expenditures and the ERTA tax reductions. On the first issue, John Tatom has shown that the rise in military expenditures actually accounts for a much smaller portion of the increase in federal expenditure in this period than does the increase in transfer payments, particularly for social security, which occurred in the same period.[21]

Another factor that Tatom points to, which affects both the expenditure and revenue sides, is the recession of 1982 to 1983. By both increasing unemployment and poverty and reducing income, a recession causes increased government expenditures while simultaneously reducing the growth (and perhaps even the level) of tax collections, raising the deficit. Although revenue and expenditure may then approach normal growth rates during the following expansion, larger-than-normal deficits may persist for some time. It appears that this phenomenon, and not the ERTA tax reductions, was primarily responsible for the large Reagan-era deficits.

The primary justification for this claim lies in the fact that a combination of bracket creep and increases in social security taxes, which had been passed late in the Carter administration and were being phased in over time, almost completely offset the ERTA tax reductions, so that little or no net reduction in marginal or average tax rates actually occurred. This is shown in Table 16.2, which is duplicated from another study by Tatom, in which he compared the tax burdens in 1980 (before ERTA) and 1984 for families with the 1980 median income, one-half the 1980 median income and twice the 1980 median income.[22] The 1984 incomes were adjusted upward above inflation by 8 percent because that was the aggregate growth in real output and income over the period. The high income-tax burden was computed for both one-wage-earner and two-wage-earner families.

If we look only at the personal income tax rates, it would appear that even after bracket creep, by 1984 ERTA had reduced marginal tax rates significantly in every income category, although average tax rates fell only for the higher-income families and actually increased for low-income families and for those with incomes near the median who pay the bulk of taxes. Adding in employee-paid social security taxes, we find that the marginal tax-rate reductions are smaller in every category except one-wage-earner families with twice the median income (who are exempt from social security taxes), and the average tax-rate reductions disappear for the high-income groups.

When employer-paid contributions to social security are considered also, the 1984 average tax rates are higher yet for every income category, and only the single wage earner with twice the median income retains a significant marginal tax-rate reduction. For the median-income category most closely representing the bulk of taxpayers the reduction in marginal tax rates is a trivial 1.7 percent. It makes no sense to attribute a decline in revenue and resulting deficit to a tax reduction that does not occur.

A case that the tax reductions bear at least partial responsibility for the deficit might be made if a decline in revenue could be traced to the higher-income groups which, because they are exempt from social security taxes, actually experienced significant marginal tax-rate reductions from ERTA. In fact, however, that is not what happened. ERTA reduced the marginal tax rate on all unearned (i.e., investment) income above $100,000 from 70 percent to 50 percent in 1982, a 29 percent reduction that was not phased-in over three years as were those on other income categories. The immediate result was, however, that revenue collected from all such taxpayers increased by 13 percent that year, although income-tax revenue as a whole fell by 2 percent and the economy was in the midst of a large recession.

Aside from contradicting the claim that ERTA caused the deficit increase, it appears clear that the tax rates on the upper income brackets were in the declining region of the Laffer curve. Defining β to

TABLE 16.2 1980 to 1984 Changes in Tax Burdens for Selected Incomes: Real Income Gain of 8 Percent

	One-half median income			1980 median income			Twice 1980 median income					
							One wage earner			Two wage earners		
	1980	1984¹	Percentage change	1980	1984¹	Percentage change	1980	1984¹	Percentage change	1980	1984	Percentage change
Personal income tax rates												
T/Y	4.3%	6.0%	39.5%	11.9%	12.1%	1.7%	22.3%	22.0%	-1.3%	22.3%	22.0%	-1.3%
$\Delta T/\Delta Y$	16.0	14.0	-12.5	24.0	22.0²	-8.3	43.0	38.0	-11.6	43.0	38.0	-11.6
Personal income tax plus employee-paid social security tax												
T/Y	10.5	12.7	21.0	18.1	18.8	3.9	26.1	26.4	1.1	28.4	28.7	1.1
$\Delta T/\Delta Y$	22.1	20.7	-6.3	30.1	28.7²	-4.7	43.0	38.0	-11.6	49.1	44.7	-9.0
Total tax rate (including employer social security contribution)												
T/Y	16.6	19.7	18.7	24.2	25.8	6.6	29.9	31.0	3.7	34.6	35.7	3.2
$\Delta T/\Delta Y$	28.3	27.7	-2.1	36.3	35.7%	-1.7	43.0	38.0	-11.6	55.3	51.7	-6.5

¹ Excludes deduction for a married couple when both work.
² Income is $23 below next tax bracket, where the marginal tax rate rises 3 percentage points.

refer to those in that income category, where $T = t \cdot \beta$ and

$$\frac{\Delta T}{T} \approx \frac{\Delta t}{t} + \frac{\Delta \beta}{\beta}$$

so that

$$\frac{\Delta T}{T} + \frac{\Delta t}{t} \approx \frac{\Delta \beta}{\beta}$$

and by substitution,

$$.13 + .29 \approx \frac{\Delta \beta}{\beta}$$

$$.42 \approx \frac{\Delta \beta}{\beta}$$

and the tax reduction caused an approximately 42 percent increase in reported incomes in excess of $100,000 that year. This sort of massive increase in the reporting of high incomes was not a transient effect of the tax reductions either, but continued in succeeding years.[23]

The same general argument applies to other issues in supply-side economics. Because ERTA only succeeded in providing small net tax relief to the bulk of taxpayers, only small supply-side effects should be observed, and strong claims either for or against supply-side economics on the basis of events in this period are not justified. Relatively small effects seem to be what we have, in fact, observed. The expansion following the 1982 recession has been the longest in post-War history, but not the most rapid. The data presented in Figures 16.1 and 16.2 seem to indicate that output growth and productivity growth have begun to improve since passage of ERTA, but in each case the gain does not appear to be large and may simply be a transient upside deviation around the declining trend.

There are good theoretical reasons for believing that supply-side tax reductions, particularly if combined with federal expenditure reductions, might be a powerful tool for improving the performance of the macroeconomy, although some economists doubt this. Indeed, some empirical evidence does seem to indicate clear benefits have accrued from the Reagan tax reductions. Figure 16.11 plots real purchases of new plants and equipment (calculated by deflating nominal investments of this kind by the GNP deflator for producers' durable equipment) as a percentage of real GNP over the period 1965 to 1987. The four highest observations of this measure of relative investment in the entire series

Figure 16.11 Real Business Expenditures on New Plant and Equipment As a Percentage of Real GNP, 1965–1987.

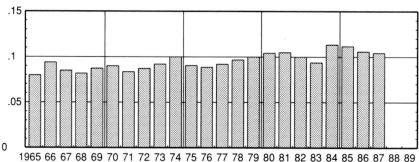

Source: *Economic Report of the President, 1989:* 310, 312 and 369

(.113, .114, .106, and .105) occur during the Reagan administration in 1984, 1985, 1986, and 1987.

On the other hand, saving has performed poorly in this period by most measures. Quite aside from the dissaving represented by the large federal budget deficits, the private saving rate has been very low, contrary to the hopes of supply siders. The result of this disparity between domestic saving and investment has been that much of the funds have been supplied by foreigners; see Chapter 18. Although the low saving rate may be attributable to the rise in the real value of social security payments in the 1980s (one of the primary motives for saving is to provide for retirement), it appears that ERTA has not provided a clear case by which to make an empirical judgement for or against supply side economics.

The Reagan period will still provide additional evidence, because the tax-reform Act produced significant marginal tax-rate reductions. Here again, however, there were offsets that will probably confuse the issue. TRA was deliberately designed to be revenue-neutral, with increases in business taxes offsetting personal tax reductions. A clear modern experiment with supply-side economics may have to await the emergence of another Andrew Mellon.

Summary

Here are the major arguments of this chapter in summary form.

1. Given the inability of monetary policy to permanently affect real variables in a socially beneficial fashion, the slow output and productivity growth of the 1970s made it clear that a new policy was needed that would operate directly on the underlying determinants of such variables.

2. Supply-side economics aims at stimulating growth by increasing the incentives people have to use resources productively. It is argued that this can be accomplished through reductions in marginal tax rates.

3. Taxes alter relative prices, causing substitutions between legal and illegal economic activities, between present and future consumption, and between leisure and work. Marginal tax-rate reductions arguably motivate increased legal activity, increased saving and investment, and increased work, generating higher real output and income.

4. The existence of such substitution effects is noncontroversial within the economics profession, and a good deal of evidence in the historical record supports this view. The empirical magnitude of such effects is a matter of dispute, however.

5. One major Keynesian objection to supply-side tax reductions is that the relative price changes resulting have income effects that may arguably offset the substitution effects. The argument seems weak on the macroeconomic level, however, for at least two reasons: First, as J. R. Hicks pointed out, the substitution effects of relative price changes tend to aggregate in the general equilibrium, whereas income effects tend to cancel. Second, perverse income effects on aggregate labor supply would tend to eliminate the very income changes supposedly generating them.

6. A second major Keynesian objection to supply-side tax reductions is that deficits would be generated or increased, producing crowding out effects that would offset any beneficial effects of the tax reductions on production.

7. Supply-side economists counter by distinguishing between tax revenue and tax rates and arguing that tax-rate reductions, by increasing the tax base through the substitution effects, would cause tax revenue to fall by less than the tax rates and might even produce increased revenue. Given that most such substitution effects take time to operate, however, the Keynesian objection seems valid. To insure effectiveness of a tax-rate reduction policy, it seems necessary to simultaneously reduce federal expenditure in order to avoid an increase in the deficit.

8. Supply-side tax reductions became a major explicit element of Reagan administration policy, embodied in the Economic Recovery Tax Act (ERTA) of 1981 and the Tax Reform Act (TRA) of 1986. However, the tax rate reductions of ERTA were essentially offset by social security tax increases, bracket creep (before 1985), and the administration's own Tax Equity and Fiscal Responsibility Act (TEFRA) of 1982. Consequently, strong claims for or against supply-side economics are hard to justify on the basis of Reagan-period evidence as yet.

Notes

1. The discussions in Bruce Bartlett, *Reaganomics: Supply Side Economics in Action* (Westport Connecticut: Arlington House, 1981): 1–3, and George Gilder, *Wealth and Poverty* (New York: Basic Books, 1981): 23, 31–35, and 38–40 are typical.

2. See "The Undergound Economy's Hidden Force," in Annual Editions *Economics 84/85* (Guilford, Connecticut: The Dushkin Publishing Group, 1984): 46–51, originally published in *Business Week* (April 5, 1982).

3. Ibid., p. 47.

4. See Peter Gutman, "The Subterranean Economy," *Financial Analysts Journal* 33 (November/December 1977): 26–27, and "The Grand Unemployment Illusion," *Journal of the Institute for Socioeconomic Studies* 4 (Summer 1979): 20–29.

5. According to Edgar Feige of the University of Wisconsin and Robert McGee of Florida State University, as quoted in "The Underground Economy's Hidden Force": 48.

6. Congress of the United States, *Materials Related to Welfare Research and Experimentation: Assembled by the Staff of the Committee on Finance for the Use of the Subcommittee on Public Assistance, Committee on Finance, United States Senate,* Committee Print, 95th Congress, 2nd Session (Washington: U.S. Government Printing Office, 1978): 114–118. See also John F. Cogan, *Negative Income Taxation and Labor Supply: New Evidence from the New Jersey–Pennsylvania Experiment* (Santa Monica, California: The Rand Corporation, 1978), for evidence of the effect on the labor supply of white males in particular.

7. Jerry Hausman, "The Effects of Taxes on Labor Supply," in Henry Aaron and Joseph Pechman, eds., *How Taxes Affect Economic Behavior* (Washington: Brookings Institution, 1981).

8. See, for example, Norman B. Ture, "Supply Side Analysis and Public Policy," in David G. Raboy, ed., *Essays in Supply Side Economics* (Washington D.C.: The Institute for Research on the Economics of Taxation, 1982): 7–28.

9. Bartlett, *Reaganomics:* Chapter 8, details this history.

10. Paul Craig Roberts, *The Supply-Side Revolution in Economics* (Cambridge, Massachusetts: Harvard University Press, 1984): 76–81.

11. Keith Marsden, "Taxes and Growth," *Finance and Development* 20 (September 1983): 40–43.

12. See Roberts, *The Supply-Side Revolution in Economics:* Passim. As an economic adviser to Congressman Jack Kemp, then to the minority staff on the House Budget Committee, and later as a Treasury official under the Reagan administration, Roberts was an important participant in the debates over fiscal policy during this period, and his book is both a fascinating account of these political struggles and an illuminating introduction to supply-side economic theory.

13. See, for example, James Barth, "The Reagan Program for Economic Recovery: Economic Rationale," Federal Reserve Bank of Atlanta *Economic Review* (September 1981): 4–14, particularly p.5.

14. J. R. Hicks,*Value and Capital* (London: Oxford University Press, 1946): 31–37.

15. Roberts, *The Supply-Side Revolution in Economics:* 41. This argument forgets the possibility of real income gains in the form of increased utility if private goods substituted for public goods at the margin are more highly valued, however. See also note 17.

16. It should be clearly understood that the tendency to substitute leisure for labor by individuals in such circumstances has nothing to do with laziness per se, but is simply a rational response to the structure of incentives faced.

17. James Gwartney and Richard Stroup, "Labor Supply and Tax Rates: A Correction of the Record," *American Economic Review* 73(June 1983): 446–451 develop this analysis in detail.

18. See Roberts, *The Supply-Side Revolution in Economics:* 26–27.

19. Descriptions of the Laffer curve long preceded Arthur Laffer. Andrew Mellon understood the concept and argued that tax reductions for the rich in particular would be self-financing, a prediction that turned out to be correct. Mellon even wrote a supply-side book on tax theory and policy entitled *Taxation: The People's Business* (New York: Macmillan, 1924). The great French predecessor of modern marginalist economics, Jules Dupuit, wrote in 1844 that, "If a tax is gradually increased from zero up to the point where it becomes prohibitive, its yield is at first nil, then increase by small stages until it reaches a maximum, after which it gradually declines until it becomes zero again," as quoted in A. B. Atkinson and N. H. Stern, "Taxation and Incentives in the U.K.: A Comment," *Lloyds Bank Review* (April 1980). Other statements of the idea occurred even earlier that this, although few were quite as clear.

20. Alan Blinder, "Thoughts on the Laffer Curve," in *The Supply Side Effects of Economic Policy* (St. Louis: Center For the Study of American Business, Washington University, and the Federal Reserve Bank of St. Louis, 1981): 81–92.

21. John A. Tatom, "A Perspective on the Federal Deficit Problem," *Federal Reserve Bank of St. Louis Review* (June/July 1984): 5–14.

22. John A. Tatom, "The 1981 Personal Income Tax Cuts: A Retrospective Look at Their Effects on the Federal Tax Burden," *Federal Reserve Bank of St. Louis Review* (December 1984): 4–17.

23. As a consequence, the proportion of total income tax revenue collected that is collected from the rich has increased significantly during the Reagan administration. This is in striking contrast to the belief that has guided the progressive tax structure, as Warren Brooks has repeatedly pointed out. See Brooks, "Defusing Reagan's Fairness Issue: The Rich Pay More in U.S. Taxes," *The Detroit News* (March 26,1984): editorial page.

Student Self-Test

I. True–False

T F 1. The notion that human wants are unlimited and that goods and services purchase each other, hence the economic problem consists of stimulating production, not demand, is known as Say's principle.

T F 2. Enduring reductions in marginal tax rates should reduce underground economic activity at the margin, *ceteris paribus*.

T F 3. The pure substitution effect of marginal tax rate changes on the amount of labor that workers willingly supply is inverse.

T F 4. The pure income effect of marginal tax rate changes on the amount of labor that workers willingly supply is direct.

T F 5. According to Sir John Hicks, the fact that a rise in a relative price raises the income of the seller but lowers that of the buyer means that substitution effects tend to cancel in the aggregate.

T   F   6. Net marginal tax rate reductions for most taxpayers resulting from the Economic Recovery Tax Act of 1981 were large enough to provide valid empirical evidence on the aggregate economic effects of such tax reductions.

II. Short Answer *(150 words or less each)*

1. Explain the two basic insights of supply-side economics. Comment briefly if you disagree.
2. The Reagan supply-side program seemed to combine restraint on money growth—or at least on the acceleration of money growth—with tax-rate reductions. Keynesian opponents of this policy often complained that it was a self-contradictory combination of an expansionary fiscal policy with a contractionary monetary policy. Do you agree or disagree? Explain.
3. Is it possible or likely for workers to respond in the aggregate to a tax-rate reduction by reducing the amount of labor they willingly supply? Explain.
4. Can it legitimately be argued that the poor face the highest marginal tax rates of any group in our society? What does this do to their incentive to work? Explain.
5. It is widely believed that a progressive income-tax structure is necessary in order to make the rich pay their fair proportionate share of tax revenue. Does the experience of the Reagan administration confirm this view? Explain.

III. Completion Problems

1. Consider a hypothetical country with $3000 billion (3 trillion) in aggregate taxable income that collects $1200 billion in revenue from a single flat rate income tax.
   A. The tax rate must be $t =$ _____ percent.
   B. If the government raises the tax rate by 12 percent and the tax base declines by 9 percent as a result, revenue _____ (rises/falls) by about _____ percent.
   C. If the 12 percent increase in t results in a 16 percent decline in taxable income reported, revenue collected would _____ (rise/fall) by about _____ percent.
   D. Suppose that the tax rate is reduced by 20 percent and that the tax base rises by 16 percent. Revenue would _____ (rise/fall) by about _____ percent.
2. For simplicity of analysis, consider a static, no-growth economy in which inflation is zero and in which the government significantly increases the income tax rate, *ceteris paribus*.
   A. Show on the graph or on a copy, all of the shifts in the curves and the variable changes that would result. Keep things fairly simple.
   B. Illustrate the sequence of the curve shifts and variable changes with numbered arrows.
   C. Write a brief description explaining this sequence of events.

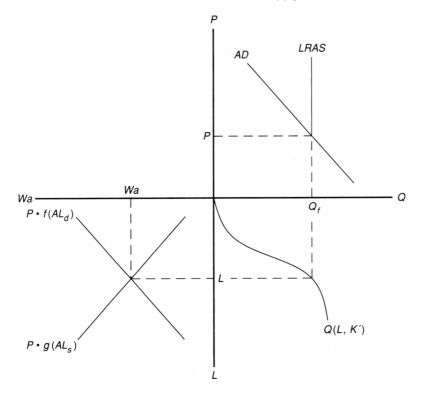

3. Tax policy in history:
   A. The long expansion of the roaring 1920s may have resulted from a series of tax rate _____ (increases/reductions) engineered by a Treasury Secretary named _____ .
   B. Under the administration of Franklin Roosevelt tax rates were _____ (raised/reduced) several times. A large tax reduction was passed in the 1960s by the _____ administration, after which output and employment growth _____ (increased/fell).
   C. The phased tax reduction passed by the Reagan administration in 1981 was termed the _____ . This was followed by the _____ of 1982. The third and last major tax act of the Reagan era was termed the _____ .

CHAPTER 17

The International Monetary System: The Balance of Payments and the Gold Standard

Thus far the analysis of this book has focused only intermittently on international transactions. The importance of international transactions should be apparent, however, not only from the increasing relative magnitude of such transactions over time, but also from the intensity of recent debate on international trade and finance issues. The purpose of this chapter and Chapter 18 is to focus on the international economy, particularly on the nature and genesis of the current international monetary system.

The Economic and Accounting Balance of Payments

The factors motivating people on different sides of international boundaries to engage in exchange are the same as those motivating people in the same country to do so. People with different tastes, resource endowments, and knowledge have different comparative advantages in production, and there are utility and productivity gains that will result from specializing and engaging in exchange.

Virtually all governments attempt to keep track of transactions between domestic and foreign citizens (including governmental transactions). The statistical record of such transactions kept by the U.S. government is known as the **balance of payments account**. In accordance with the nature of double-entry bookkeeping, the balance of payments is *made* to balance by procedures similar to those of a firm that adds a net worth entry to the liability side of its balance sheet to account for the discrepancy between its assets and liabilities. In the case of the balance of payments accounts, the balance reflects the equality between the value of items bought from or sold to foreigners and the payments made in those transactions.

In the case of a sale by a U.S. citizen to a foreigner, an **export**, whether the item sold is a physical commodity of some sort, an immaterial service, or a financial asset such as a stock or bond, the value of the item sold is registered in our accounts as a **credit**. That is, it is registered with a positive sign (+) on its dollar magnitude. The payment for the item, on the other hand, is registered as a **debit**, with a minus sign (−) on its dollar magnitude. The dollar magnitudes of credit and debit items for exports are thus equal and sum to zero.

The story is similar for purchases by U.S. citizens from foreigners (i.e., **imports**), whether of goods, services, or financial assets, although the signs are reversed. The value of an item imported is recorded as a debit in our BOP Accounts, and the payment is registered as a credit. For imports also, then, the dollar magnitudes of credit and debit entries are equal and sum to zero.

Because the dollar magnitudes of credit and debit entries are equal and sum to zero both for exports and imports, the overall balance of payments account always sums to zero, as assets and liabilities plus net worth sum to zero on a firm's balance sheet. Note, however, that this does not imply any equality of exports and imports. To illustrate, U.S. exports worth $500 billion would be matched in the accounts by debit entries of −$500 billion representing the foreign payments for those exports. But U.S. imports could be −$650 billion, with matching credit entries totaling $650 billion representing the payments made to foreigners.

Subtracting the absolute value of imports from that of exports (both broadly defined) leaves $EX - IM = \$500$ billion $- \$650$ billion $= -\$150$ billion. Such a negative magnitude would be termed a **balance of payments deficit**. Note that such a surplus of non money imports over exports implies a matching export or outflow of 150 billion U.S. dollars to foreigners. The basic reason such an outflow of dollars might occur is explained in Chapter 5 and explained more fully here. It would result if there were an excess domestic stock of real and nominal money balances and would cease when stock equilibrium between the demand for and supply of money was restored.

The same reasoning applies to the opposite case. An excess of domestic exports of all nonmoney items (goods, services, and financial assets) over domestic imports, so that $EX - IM > 0$ and a matching import of dollars occurred, would be the result of an excess domestic demand for real and nominal dollars and would cease when the flow through the balance of payments restored the stock monetary equilibrium.

As pointed out in Chapter 5, this mechanism operates whenever different countries use the same money or when exchange rates between monetary units in different countries are fixed. When exchange rates between different national currencies are market-determined, monetary disequilibria cause changes in those rates that act to equate exports and imports without a balance of payments flow. All of this is clarified later in this chapter and in Chapter 18, but the basic point is that there are natural economic processes (e.g., temporary Balance of Payments flows or exchange-rate changes) tending to equalize aggregate nonmoney exports and imports, making the *economic* BOP = 0.

Categorical Division of U.S. Balance of Payments _____

For various reasons—most relating to past criticisms of its methods—the U.S. Department of Commerce, which measures the balance of payments, does not give it much rigorous categorical structure. Economists have therefore had to develop a more complete analytical division of the accounts. One major category that Commerce reports in the accounts is the **trade account**, which lists the values of transactions (both imports and exports) in physical commodities of all sorts, whether consumer goods, capital goods, or raw materials. A balance is shown on this account, termed the **balance on merchandise trade**. Exports need not equal imports in this subaccount, hence the balance of trade can show a deficit or a surplus.

Historically, the United States has often run a slight deficit in the trade account balance. The trade account is a subcategory of a larger subset of the overall balance of payments. The larger subset is termed the **current account** and includes international transactions in immaterial services and income from foreign and domestic investments abroad in addition to the trade account entries. (Certain unilateral transfers, such as gifts and donations, are included also.) International service transactions include such things as travel, transportation, and lodging expenses for U.S. and foreign tourists, shipping services for U.S. and foreign companies on each other's air or shiplines, insurance or management consulting services traded internationally, and so on.

Adding such service transactions and overseas investment income flows in with trade account transactions yields the **balance on current account**, which is also reported in the balance of payments account. Historically, the United States has usually run a slight surplus in international service transactions, largely offsetting its traditional trade account deficit, so that the current account balance has netted out not too far from zero. Figures 17.1 and 17.2 show the trade account and

Figure 17.1 Balance of Merchandise Trade (Exports–Imports), in Billions of Current Dollars □ and Constant (1967) Dollars ■.

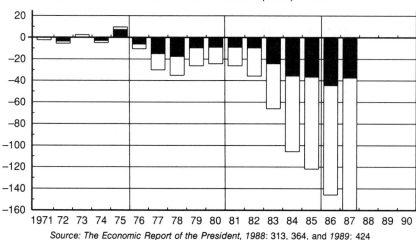

Source: The Economic Report of the President, 1988: 313, 364, and 1989: 424

current account balances from 1971 to 1987 in billions of current and constant dollars. Negative magnitudes represent deficits in these sub-accounts and positive magnitudes indicate surpluses.

Notice that both the current and trade account deficits reached large magnitudes in the 1980s. Of course, the picture given by the

Figure 17.2 Balance on Current Account (Exports–Imports), in Billions of Current Dollars □ and Constant (1967) Dollars ■.

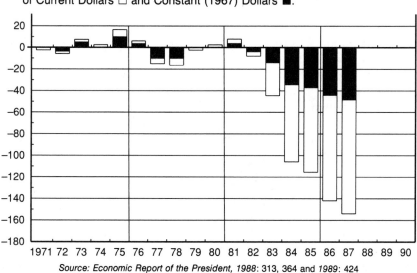

Source: Economic Report of the President, 1988: 313, 364 and 1989: 424

purely nominal magnitudes is rather misleading because the value of money has declined enormously over this period, but even deflated to constant-dollar magnitudes, these deficits became very large. Why this occurred will be one of the significant stories of Chapter 18.

The remaining transactions in the balance of payments are of two types. The largest category consists of international transactions in financial assets, such as stocks, and securities of various maturities, including corporate and governmental bonds of all types. Sales of U.S. stocks and bonds to foreigners constitute exports of financial capital, and purchases of foreign securities by Americans constitute imports of such capital. For analytical purposes economists term the balance on such transactions the **capital account balance**, although the Commerce Department reports no such balance in the balance of payments accounts. Here also, the dollar values of U.S. exports and imports may not be equal, and the capital account balance may show a surplus or deficit.

The last type of transactions in the balance of payments accounts consists of transfers of international reserve assets between the Federal Reserve and foreign central banks. This can be termed the **official reserves account**. Because the U.S. dollar is itself the primary form of international reserves, this balance essentially expresses the net dollar outflow or inflow associated with differences between U.S. exports of all nonmonetary items and our imports of all such items. Today such flows result when central banks act to fix the exchange rates between domestic and foreign currency (i.e., keep them from changing) at a time of monetary disequilibrium or when they create such disequilibria by changing exchange rates away from the market levels; see Chapter 18.

If the official reserves account balance were zero, so that no net export or import of dollars was occurring, the value of exports of all other items would have to equal the value of imports of such items. A current account deficit of −$116 billion such as the one Americans experienced in 1985 would have to be matched by a $116 billion capital account *surplus* once all statistical discrepancies were accounted for. Also, a current account surplus (i.e., exports of goods and services over imports of $18 billion such as that in 1975 would have to be matched by an $18 billion deficit (i.e., imports of financial assets in excess of exports) in the capital account.

A simple way of expressing the argument just made is that the sum of the three balances must equal zero. That is, the current account balance (CAB) + the capital account balance (KAB) + the official reserves account balance (ORB) = 0. The accounting balance of payments always balances. The economic balance of payments, however, can be read from the official reserves account balance, which will have the same magnitude but opposite sign. That is, where

$$CAB + KAB + ORB = 0$$
$$ORB = -CAB - KAB$$
$$= -(CAB + KAB).$$

If the ORB = \$5 billion, then the sum of the current account and capital account balances would be +\$5 billion. U.S. citizens would be selling goods, services, and financial assets abroad worth \$5 billion more than they were purchasing abroad, causing a net dollar inflow of \$5 billion through the balance of payments.

At this point it is difficult to further illuminate such transactions without more information about the nature of the international monetary system. It will be useful to begin with a more detailed discussion of the gold standard than was undertaken in Chapter 5 and to trace its evolution (or devolution) into the current system.

The Gold Coin Standard

The simplest and purest form of gold standard, in which currency does not exist and all major trading nations use gold coins for money, was discussed briefly in Chapter 5. Some embellishment is useful here, however. Consider a two-country world, consisting of country A and country B, whose citizens engage in trade with each other. The initial demands for real and nominal money balances and initial gold stocks in the two countries are shown in the first and third quadrants of Figure 17.3. The real value of gold in each country is $R = 1/P$, because prices of all other goods in both countries are stated in ounces or in fractions of an ounce of gold, and the nominal (gold) price of gold is $P_g = 1$.

The fourth quadrant shows the entire world monetary gold stock as a 45° line running from the vertical to the horizontal axis, on the assumption that the units in which the money stocks are measured in each country are the same. The intercept on each axis shows what the (gold) money stock in each country would be if it had the entire world gold stock. The initial national money stocks shown in the first and third quadrants (M_{sa} and M_{sb}) show the portions of the world gold stock initially possessed by their citizens.

At all times the money stocks in countries A and B sum to the world monetary gold stock. Indeed, they could be so added and shown as a single (vertical) stock for the world economy. Also, the demands for money in the two countries could be summed horizontally into a total world demand for money, and the two functions could then be shown determining the world real value of gold (R) and hence the world price level. In Figure 17.3 the initial situation is that the real values of gold (and hence the price levels) are equal to each other, making $R_a = R_b = R$.

Now imagine the following disturbance, *ceteris paribus*: the demand for money falls in country A to M'_{da} and, simultaneously, the demand for money rises in country B to M'_{db}, so that the total world demand for money does not change (hence $\Delta R = 0$). There are two ways of interpreting what follows. By the first interpretation, the real value of gold falls in country A (i.e., the price level rises) to some R'_a determined at the intersection of M'_{da} with the initial money stock, M_{sa}. Simultaneously, the real value of gold *rises* in country B (the price level *falls*) to some R'_b determined at the intersection of M'_{db} with M_{sb}.

Figure 17.3 Offsetting Demand Shifts in a Two-Country Gold Coin Standard Model.

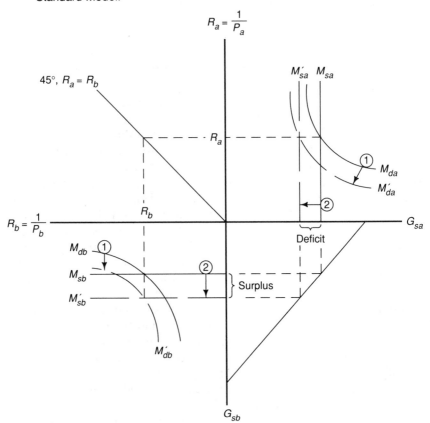

Because prices for equivalent goods, services, and financial assets are now lower in country B than in country A, country A will begin running a balance of payments deficit as exports by its citizens to country B fall and their imports from country B rise. Country B, in contrast, will run an equivalent BOP surplus as exports by its citizens rise and their imports fall. The country A deficit (and country B surplus) means, however, that country A is making net payments to country B in gold (i.e., A is exporting gold) equal in value to the excess of its imports over its exports.

The resulting decrease in the money stock in country A to M'_{sa} and increase in country B money stock to M'_{sb} raises the real value of gold (reduces the price level) in country A and reduces the real value of gold in country B (raises the price level) until, once again, the real values of gold and the price levels are equivalent in the two countries. At that point stock monetary equilibrium is restored and the BOP goes to zero in both countries.

This interpretation is termed the **price–specie flow mechanism**. The argument is that divergent national price levels cause specie flows through the balance of payments in each country that reallocate the world gold stock until its value per unit is everywhere the same (hence the price-level divergence is eliminated). This interpretation is attributable to David Hume, the great British classical economist and philosopher.[1] It was the dominant interpretation of the operation of the international monetary mechanism among economists from the middle of the 19th century until about 1970.

Unfortunately, the interpretation of the mechanism in terms of divergent price levels results from a superficial reading of Hume.[2] Immediately following his description of the price–specie flow, Hume explained that the specie flows should best be thought of as acting to prevent significant divergences between national price levels. In this interpretation, which is central to the modern **monetary approach to international adjustment**, the monetary flows occur rapidly. Prices of goods and services, in contrast, adjust too slowly to move much before the monetary flows are complete. A clear explanation of how such flows can occur at initial prices, as people adjust expenditures and sales in an effort to adjust their cash balances to desired levels, is given in Chapter 5.

Evidence on which of these theoretical mechanisms best describes the actual operation of an international gold standard has been developed by Donald McCloskey and Richard Zecher.[3] The price–specie flow mechanism implies that, for periods of a year or so, price levels in trading nations will move inversely. The monetary approach mechanism implies that such price levels should be positively related even over such short periods; see Figure 17.4. Both theories imply parallel price level movements over longer periods.

The matrix of simple correlations between annual changes in retail prices of trading nations under the classical gold standard calculated by McCloskey and Zecher is shown in Table 17.1, which duplicates their Table 16.1. Note that all of the correlations are positive. Some are small, perhaps because retail price indices include many nontraded goods.

Just how rapidly such flows actually operate is an important issue. Consider the previous case. If the flows operate rather slowly, price adjustments are slow, and expectations are adaptive, a nation in the position of country A could experience a rather prolonged inflationary expansion because of the decline in M_{da}. On the other hand, given the same conditions, a country in the position of country B could experience a rather prolonged contraction of income, output, and employment until sufficient money was supplied through the international payments mechanism.

The record of the U.S. economy under the gold standard seems to be that such shocks were relatively brief, and quickly corrected, but also relatively frequent. This seems in accordance with the basic monetary approach perspective, but not with extreme interpretations of that approach in which gold flows and national money stocks adjust so rapidly in accordance with changes in relative money demands that excess demands never appear.

Because it is somewhat unrealistic to suppose that precisely offsetting demand shifts occur (in a two-country world; in a many-country world such shifts are likely to be offsetting by the law of large numbers), consider Figure 17.4 in which the demand for money declines only in country A. Here again there will be a balance of payments flow. Country A will run a BOP deficit, as before, as its citizens attempt to reduce their excess money holdings (essentially by importing more and exporting less). The flow itself will not be sufficient to restore stock equilibrium, however, because the world demand for money has fallen

TABLE 17.1 Simple Correlation Between Annual Changes in Retail Prices, 1880 to 1912

	United States	Britain	Germany	France	Sweden
United States	1.00	0.57	0.28	0.24	0.38
Britain		1.00	0.53	0.42	0.57
Germany			1.00	0.45	0.62
France				1.00	0.32
Sweden					1.00

Figure 17.4 Demand Decline in a Two-Country Gold Coin Standard Model.

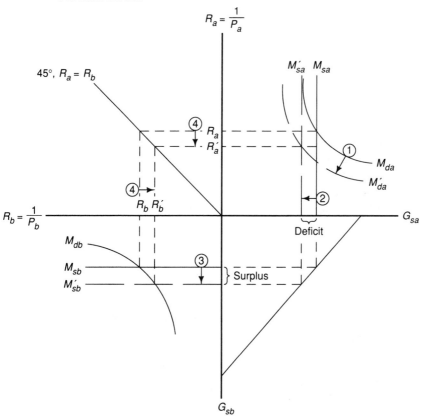

on net. A worldwide real balance effect will also be required. Prices will rise and reduce the real value of gold to equality with real money balances demanded in both countries.

How far do R_a and R_b fall, and what magnitude of BOP flow is involved? The real value of gold will fall in both countries until the excess demand for money that *would be* generated in country B if money did *not* flow in (which describes country B's BOP surplus) is equal to the remaining excess nominal money stock in country A (which describes its BOP deficit). This point is shown by Cartesian coordinate (R_b', R_a') on the 45° line in the second quadrant of Figure 17.4.

There are other illustrations that could be performed with this graphic mechanism. An increase in the world gold stock, for example, would be shown by an outward shift of the 45° line in the fourth quadrant, and it would be educational to consider what would happen if all of this accretion occurred initially in a single country, as in the case of the California gold discovery of 1849. This exercise is left to the reader, however. The basic lessons of the model are already clear.

First, there is an equilibrium international allocation of the world money stock which is determined by the relative demands for money in each country. This concept is termed the **natural distribution of specie hypothesis** and is also attributable to Hume.[4] It follows that governmental monetary authorities, even if they hold a monopoly over the minting of coins, cannot control the money stocks in any country. Attempts to do so (perhaps by withholding coins paid in taxation from circulation, or disgorging previously accumulated gold stocks through increased minting and expenditure) would cause offsetting balance of payments flows. Such an offset would be virtually total in a world with many countries on the gold standard, such that changes in the money stock in one country had small effect on the world gold stock. And last, once the equilibrium allocation is reached, the value of money is everywhere the same.

The Short-Run Classical Gold Standard

The pure gold coin standard is not a modern monetary system. As explained previously, paper money was introduced in the 16th century, and deposit money came into wide use late in the 19th century. Gold coins circulated widely through much of this period, but gold increasingly performed a reserve, monetary-base function. As long as most if not all trading nations defined their different national monetary units in terms of gold, however, exchange rates between those currencies were fixed, and it was still true that the world monetary system employed a single money. This was the situation in the period of the classical gold standard, which covered approximately the last quarter of the 19th century to World War I. It is useful for the purposes of this chapter to model such a system.

Under a classical gold standard the monetary authorities and/or commercial depository institutions hold stocks of gold and are legally committed to convert gold into currency (and perhaps into deposits) or currency into gold on demand at a fixed rate that is known as the **parity** or *par*. In the United States the parity was $21.50 per ounce. For simplicity it will be assumed here that all such conversion is undertaken by a monetary authority known as the Treasury.

The real value of gold was described previously as $R = 1/P$, on the assumption that all money consisted of gold coins, hence prices of other goods and services were expressed in terms of gold, and the nominal price of gold was $P_g = 1$. Strictly speaking, however, the real value of gold should be expressed (as should any other relative price), as the ratio of its nominal price to the price level. That is, $R = P_g/P$. Arithmetically, if $P_g = \$20/\text{ounce}$ and $P = 100$ (the base-year value of the index), then $R = \$20/100$. If government maintains the committed parity so that $P_g = \text{par}$, then

$$R = \frac{\text{par}}{P}$$

$$R = \text{par} \cdot \left(\frac{1}{P}\right).$$

Now consider a country that is just one among many in the world economy. In the short run the real value of gold is determined exogenously on the world market by the world gold stock and the world stock demand for gold. If the domestic government maintains the parity, then in the equation $R = \text{par} \cdot (1/P)$ the only remaining unknown is the domestic price level, and its value is determined.[5] To illustrate, if $R = .2$ and par $= \$20$, then

$$R = \text{par} \cdot \left(\frac{1}{P}\right)$$

$$.2 = \$20 \left(\frac{1}{P}\right)$$

$$.2/20 = \frac{1}{P}$$

$$20/.2 = P$$

$$100 = P.$$

The implication here is that, with the parity fixed, the real value of gold exogenously determined, and an existing domestic demand for real money balances, the domestic money stock must simply take on the value required to make the equation balance.

This mechanism operates primarily through the balance of payments, as does the gold coin standard. Basically, any domestic excess demand for money results in a domestic BOP surplus and an inflow of gold from other countries in payment. The gold is either accepted directly by the domestic exporters as payment and then taken to the Treasury and exchanged for dollars, or the foreigners themselves take it to the Treasury and exchange it for dollars to use in payment. In either case, the gold inflow continues, and the Treasury continues to issue gold certificate currency at the parity rate until the domestic money stock has expanded enough to eliminate the domestic excess demand at the world price level.

Gold acquired by the Treasury in the process would increase the Treasury's assets, and the currency issued in the process of purchasing the gold would constitute an addition to its liabilities, as shown in the T account, Table 17.2. The table presumes a $10 million net inflow of gold. It is also worth noting that if the banking system issues additional notes or deposits against these gold certificates on a fractional reserve basis, the money stock may rise by a multiple of the value of the gold inflow.[6]

In the opposite case, a net excess domestic money supply would cause a BOP deficit and net outflow of gold to foreign countries in payment. Domestic citizens would obtain the gold with which to make the payments primarily by purchasing it from the Treasury at the parity price, decreasing its assets by the amount of the outflow. The currency used in this manner would be removed from circulation (thereby decreasing the Treasury's liabilities outstanding), and the domestic money stock would contract to equality with the quantity demanded at the world price level, at which point the BOP flow would cease.

This mechanism is illustrated in Figure 17.5, where the first quadrant shows the domestic demand for money and three alternate possible domestic money stocks. The third quadrant shows the world gold stock and demand for gold, which interact to determine the real value of gold, read from the horizontal axis to the left of the vertical axis. The ray from the origin in the second quadrant does not show equality between the internal values of money in a pair of nations, as in Figures 17.3 and 17.4. Instead, its slope represents the domestic parity, or par value of gold in terms of the domestic currency unit. That is, the equation $R = \text{par} \cdot (1/P)$ can be recognized as a linear equation with a zero intercept and a slope given by $\Delta R / \Delta(1/P) = \text{par}$, and the line is so labeled. A higher parity price would be represented by a steeper line (closer to the R axis) and vice versa for a lower official gold price.

Because the world real value of gold (R) is determined in the third quadrant, assuming that the Treasury maintains its commitment to convert at par on demand, the domestic price level initially or even-

TABLE 17.2 Treasury

Assets	Liabilities
Gold	Gold certificates
+$10 million	+$10 million
(500 thousand ounces at $20/ounce)	

Figure 17.5 Domestic Money Stock Determination Under a Classical Gold Standard.

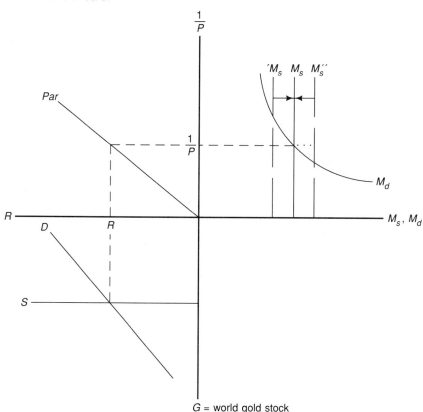

G = world gold stock

tually must be determined at P and the value of money at $1/P$. If the domestic money stock was $'M_s$ such that an excesss demand for money existed (matched by excess supplies in other countries by Walras's law, given that world monetary equilibrium obtains), a domestic balance of payments surplus and gold import would increase the internal money stock to M_s as shown.

If the money stock was initially M''_s, such that a domestic excess money stock existed (matched by net excess demands for money abroad by Walras's law, given the world monetary equilibrium and integrated world markets), the home country would run a balance of payments deficit and export gold until the money stock declined to M_s. In either case, the domestic money stock is the dependent variable. P determines M_s domestically, rather than M_s determining P, and the quantity theory holds only at the world level.

Under this system all of the same results obtained for the gold coin standard hold. There is a natural distribution of the world money stock in accordance with the relative demands for money in different countries, which is obtained through the balance of payments mechanism, and in equilibrium the value of money (except, perhaps, for minor differences attributable to the cost of shipping gold) is everywhere the same. The only complicating factor is that the use of different currency names and denominations in different countries means that international price level comparisons must be made by looking through currency exchange rates.

Here again, it makes no sense for a government to attempt to alter the money stock, as any such attempt will cause an offsetting balance of payments flow and may result in worse effects. A good example occurred in the United States after the Civil War. During the war the government suspended specie convertibility and printed greenbacks to aid wartime finance, causing a large inflation. Afterward attempts were made to reduce the money stock and deflate, so that convertibility could be restored at the pre-war parity. Significant money stock reduction did not actually occur, but this was a period of rapid industrialization and real output growth, which increased the demand for money, so prices fell.[7]

A coalition of silver mining and agricultural interests who thought that deflation was hurting them brought political pressures that resulted in passage of the Bland–Allison Act over the veto of President Hayes in 1878.[8] Under this act the government monetized silver at a high price by purchasing it with silver certificates. The intent was to increase the profits of the mining interests (which it did) and to reverse the deflation by increasing the money stock relative to the demand for money.

In 1879, however, the government resumed gold convertibility. Because gold certificates and silver certificates were both forms of dollar-denominated currency, the effect of the silver purchases was offset over time by balance of payments deficits, which caused gold certificates to leave circulation as gold was shipped to other countries. The domestic money stock increased little, if at all, relative to demand.[9] In frustration, Congress passed the Sherman Silver Purchase Act in 1890 and increased the rate of silver purchases. The result was that prices began rising in 1892, but the decline in the monetary gold stock accelerated.

By 1893 the U.S. gold stock was so small that serious doubts existed about the government's ability to maintain gold convertibility. This resulted in a banking panic. The run on the banks caused a severe monetary contraction (and suspension of convertibility), which produced a depression. Too late, Congress repealed the Sherman Silver Purchase Act that year. Downward price and wage adjustments acted by raising real balances and reversing the gold outflow to end the crisis by 1897, although this depression rivaled the Great Depression of the 1930s in its depth.

The Long-Run Operation of the Gold Standard _____

It is important to distinguish the long-run operation of the gold standard from its short-run operation. The central fact is that gold is primarily produced by private, profit-seeking firms, employing resources that have alternate uses and hence opportunity costs. In the long run, therefore, the world stock of gold is an endogenous economic function of its real unit value (R) which is ultimately determined by the world demand for gold and the opportunity cost of production at R_e, where gold producers are just earning a "normal" rate of return.[10]

It is certainly possible for world demand and supply changes to cause the real value of gold to deviate from its opportunity cost in the short run.

Consider Figure 17.6, for example, in which real output growth not matched by additional gold production shifts both world gold demand and the demand for money in a typical country outward relative to the world gold stock and domestic money stock; see event 1 in the graph. Because excess demands for money appear in all countries, balance of payments flows are not generated. Instead, prices everywhere fall, raising the value of money in each country to equate real balances supplied and demanded. Because $R = \text{par}/P$ the fall in national price levels also raises R and equilibrates the world gold stock and quantity demanded; see event 2 in the graph.

However, R is now above the opportunity cost of production, represented by R_e, generating economic profits for gold producers. This results in existing mines increasing production, old mines with thin lodes (and high unit costs) reopening, and additional resources being invested in prospecting. Eventually, new sources are found and the gold stock shifts out relative to demand (step 3), increasing national money stocks in the process. Prices rise, the value of money declines, and the real value of gold falls back to equality with R_e as the economic profits in gold mining are competed away. Consequently, the long-run supply curve of gold is essentially horizontal at R_e, as shown in Figure 17.6, and the value of money is secularly stable.

The opposite story is easily told. If, beginning from R_e, random new lode discoveries caused the world gold stock to increase relative to demand (and hence caused national money stocks to do the same as the gold was monetized), reducing the real value of currencies and gold, R would fall below R_e, causing gold producers to suffer economic losses.

Figure 17.6 Long-Run Supply and the Price Level Under the Classical Gold Standard.

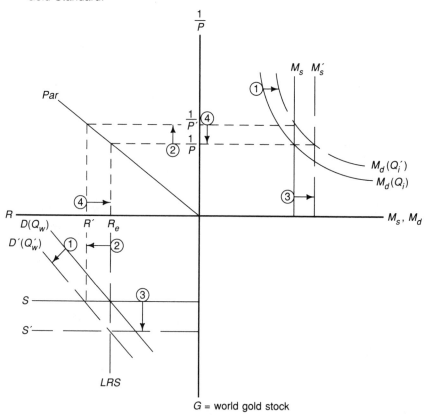

G = world gold stock

Additional gold production would be discouraged until real economic growth raised the demands for gold and money enough to restore R_e. Historically, production based on such profit and loss considerations caused the world stock of gold to grow over time at a rate roughly equal to the growth in world demand, which is essentially determined by the rate of growth of real GNP, so that the real value of gold and the price level were secularly stable.[11]

Criticisms and the Demise of the Gold Standard _____

No monetary system is perfect, of course, and the gold standard has had many critics. No one denies that it produced a great deal of long-run stability in the price level, as shown in Figure 17.7 (which

Figure 17.7   Wholesale Prices Since 1800.

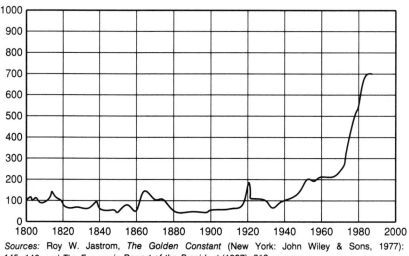

Sources: Roy W. Jastrom, *The Golden Constant* (New York: John Wiley & Sons, 1977): 145–146, and *The Economic Report of the President* (1987): 313.

duplicates Figure 1.2). The contrast with the price-level performance in the fiat money period after 1930 is striking. Also, no one denies that the gold standard period was a period of remarkable real economic growth. However, comparing the classical gold standard period with the post World War II period, Michael Bordo found that annual money stock variability, price-level variability, and output variability were all higher under the gold standard.[12]

Theoretically, this is not hard to explain, because the operation of the short-run gold standard mechanism rapidly transmits monetary shocks between countries. A good example occurred in 1907, when a combination of rising demand for money in the United States and deflationary actions undertaken by the Bank of England to stem the resulting gold flow from England to the United States administered a deflationary shock to the American economy.[13] In part, however, Bordo's data may simply reflect the greater instability of a largely agricultural economy dependent on the vagaries of weather rather than on any defect of the gold standard itself.

A closely related criticism with a longer history is that the gold standard is subject to random shocks on the monetary metal. Any shift of the world monetary gold stock due to new discoveries of rich loads, technical innovations in production, depletion, and rising production costs, and so on would produce domestic inflation or deflation. Output and employment would also be temporarily affected. Shifts in the demand for nonmonetary gold would have the same effects. Hence, so the argument goes, it would be far better to have a fiat money system in which rational and altruistic monetary authorities would act to prevent such arbitrary fluctuations in the money stock.

This argument was and is persuasive because it rests on a set of at least partially correct observations about historical events and the working of the gold standard. The Australian, South African, and Klondike gold discoveries produced inflation at the turn of the century, for example, although it was extremely mild by modern standards. But Hugh Rockoff presents persuasive evidence that the majority of such discoveries were not random, exogenous events occurring at equilibrium and tending to destabilize the value of gold and money. Instead they were endogenous responses to deviations of R from its long-run trend, which tended to restore that value and hence were stabilizing in their effect.[14]

Certainly, it must be admitted that there were some events that occurred during the classical gold standard period that are best described as random, exogenous disturbances. Political events, wars, and the actions of foreign monetary authorities come under this heading. The gold drain to Britain in 1907 mentioned previously is a good example. Still, the gold standard preserved the value of money for an amazing period, and no inflation or deflation that occurred under that system approached in magnitude those that occurred when convertibility was suspended.

The conclusions reached by the random shock argument may therefore be invalid, at least where it is used to justify a fiat money system in which the level and growth rate of the money stock are determined at the discretion of the monetary authorities. It can be argued that random supply and demand shocks under a gold standard are not nearly so arbitrary and capricious as the decisions of such men, who, being self-interested beings like everyone else but lacking the competitive constraints of the market, may often fail to act in the rational and altruistic basis supposed.

When restoration of the gold standard began to be discussed seriously in the early 1980s, some critics responded that supply conditions made it impractical. Instead of being competitive, the bulk of world gold production occurs in the USSR and the Union of South Africa. If the monetary system of the free world depended on gold, according to these critics, one of those states might be inclined to manipulate the world gold stock for geopolitical purposes.

The chief danger here would be from withholding of production in order to generate world deflation and recession. The ability of such states to add to the world monetary gold base and cause inflation would be limited, because that could reduce R to below real production costs and cause large losses in the producing states themselves. In recent years it has become clear, however, that withholding of gold production by these states would be unlikely. For economic reasons both the USSR and South Africa badly need all the foreign exchange they can earn from gold sales. Also, their share in world production has been declining recently as Brazilian and other production has expanded. Supply is becoming more competitive over time.

Perhaps the most famous criticism of the gold standard is that of Milton Friedman, who argued that the opportunity cost, in terms of the value of goods and services forgone due to the use of resources for mining, storage, guarding, and so on, is excessive. He estimated that these costs amounted to 1.5 percent of GNP.[15] Garrison recently countered that such costs are not avoided by the adoption of a paper standard, because gold continues to be mined, stored, and guarded.[16] Friedman has since essentially accepted this argument and pointed out that the resource costs associated with the use of fiat money are significant.[17]

Monetarists have been the source of many recent criticisms of the gold standard, preferring a fixed money growth rule as a method of stabilizing the price level and the economy. Indeed, in combination with a flexible exchange rate system, such a rule would probably insulate the domestic economy from many exogenous shocks a gold standard would be subject to; see Chapter 18. On the other hand, a fixed money-growth rule has no method of handling unpredictable short-run shifts in the demand for money. Such shifts, if they endured, would generate economic expansions and contractions that would be eliminated only through real balance effects over time.

In contrast, the short-run mechanism of the gold standard will quickly cause the money stock to adjust through the Balance of Payments in the direction of the money demand shift, dampening and eventually eliminating any output and employment effects. This would occur faster than could be attained through a real balance effect resulting from a price-level adjustment. Belief in the efficacy of a constant growth rate Friedman rule requires faith that in the absence of money growth fluctuations, the demand for money is rather stable around its long-run growth path. Such faith may be justified, but some doubts remain.

In recent years one of the most frequently stated objections to the gold standard concerns the difficulty of restoring gold convertibility, particularly in terms of picking the right parity. That this objection may reflect ideological and political motives more than rational analysis seems implicit in the simple historical observation that many nations have successfully restored convertibility in the past. Obviously, it cannot be that hard. Nations on commodity standards frequently suspended convertibility during wartime, in order to aid war finance through monetary expansion. Britain restored convertibility in 1821, following the Napoleonic wars, and the United States did so after the Civil War.

This is not to say that there is no difficulty involved in restoring convertibility. Britain ultimately failed in its post-World War I attempt. The reason for its failure is well known, however: the British attempted to restore the pre-war parity after a significant inflation, which (before suspension occurred) had caused the export of much of its gold stock. Given the low value of British money, the excess demand for gold at the pre-war parity was too large for the depleted reserves. The attempt would have been successful if Britain had either deflated further before restoring convertibility or set an appropriately higher parity.

Whether as a consequence of belief in such alleged problems or because the gold standard acted to prevent governmental authorities from manipulating national money stocks as they wished (see Chapter 15), all major nations suspended gold convertibility by their citizens in the 1930s. The current international fiat money system, in which central banks generate distinct forms of base money at essentially zero cost (to themselves), then emerged, although the role of gold in the international monetary system did not end entirely until 1972, as shown in Chapter 18. To say the least, experience with this system has been less than satisfactory, and proposals for reform have proliferated in recent years. Considering such alternate reforms, Robert Barro has observed:

> In this context the choice among different monetary constitutions—such as the gold standard, a commodity-reserve standard, or a fiat standard with fixed rules for setting the quantity of money (possibly in relation to stabilizing a specified price index)—may be less important than the decision to adopt *some* monetary constitution. On the other hand, the gold standard actually prevailed for a substantial period (even if from an "historical accident," rather than a constitutional choice process), whereas the world has yet to see a fiat currency system that has obvious "stability" properties.[18]

Summary

Here, in summary form, are the major arguments of this chapter.

1. In considering the balance of payments in transactions between domestic and foreign citizens, it is important to distinguish between the *accounting* balance of payments (or Balance of Payments Account), and the *economic* balance of payments.

2. The balance of payments account is a government statistical record of known international transactions involving American citizens. In that account each export or import results in two entries of identical magnitude and opposite sign—one for the value of the item and the other for the value of the payment. Hence the account always sums to zero.

3. This does not mean that exports of all nonmoney items must equal imports of such items. In any given period U.S. exports can be (and have been) greater than, equal to, or less than our imports. The existing relationship between domestic exports and imports, and the net monetary flow associated, constitutes the economic balance of payments.

4. A condition in which the value of domestic exports of all nonmoney items exceeds that of domestic imports (a balance of payments surplus) implies a net inflow of money in payment equal to the difference. The opposite is true for a domestic balance of payments deficit.

5. Balance of payments monetary flows stem from stock monetary disequilibria, and tend to be self-eliminating. In equilibrium the economic balance of payments will be zero. That is, the values of domestic exports and imports of nonmoney items will be equal, as will the values of monetary payments.

6. The balance of payments account can be analytically decomposed into three categorical divisions: the current account (listing transactions in physical goods and immaterial services), the capital account (for trade in financial assets), and the official reserves account, (showing the net monetary flow—the economic deficit or surplus).

7. The balances on all three accounts must sum to zero. It follows that whenever the ORB = 0, the capital and current account balances must be of opposite sign and identical magnitude.

8. A basic international equilibration mechanism is easily illustrated with a simple two-country gold coin standard model. Monetary disequilibrium originating in either country generates a balance of payments flow (and in some cases a real balance effect), which reallocates the world gold stock until monetary equilibrium is restored in both nations and the value of money is everywhere the same.

9. While it used to be thought that this mechanism operated from divergent price levels (the price–specie flow mechanism), it is now understood that the specie flows act to prevent significant divergences.

10. In a classical gold standard different countries employ distinct fractional reserve currencies that are convertible into gold at legally fixed parity rates. With some complications the same mechanism described in the gold coin model also operates in this system.

11. Under such a gold standard the real value of gold (R) is determined by the world supply of and demand for gold. Given R and a domestic parity, the domestic price level is determined at a value consistent with prices elsewhere. The nominal money stock then adjusts through the balance of payments to satisfy nominal balances demanded at that price level.

12. Historically, this system severely limited governmental control over domestic money stocks. Efforts to exercise such control (except where employed to hasten removal of disequilibria; see Note 5) tended to cause offsetting balance of payments flows and, in some cases, worse effects.

13. In the long run, profits and losses in gold production caused supply adjustments that tended to match growth in the world gold and money stocks to growth in the world demands for gold and money, preserving the secular stability of the value of money.

14. Although the gold standard had many beneficial properties, it also had imperfections and was eventually eliminated. It is not obvious, however, that the current discretionary fiat money system is an improvement or that the gold standard was eliminated primarily because of its faults.

Notes

1. See David Hume, "Of the Balance of Trade," reprinted in Eugene Rotwein, ed., *Writings on Economics* (Freeport, N.Y.: Books for Libraries Press, 1955).

2. See Robert E. Keleher, "Of Money and Prices: Some Historical Perspectives, in Bluford H. Putnam and D. Sykes Wilford, eds., *The Monetary Approach to International Adjustment* (New York: Praeger Publishers, 1978): 22–24.

3. Donald N. McCloskey and J. Richard Zecher, "How the Gold Standard Worked, 1880–1913," in Jacob A. Frenkel and Harry G. Johnson, eds., *The Monetary Approach to the Balance of Payments* (Toronto and Buffalo: The University of Toronto Press, 1976): 357–385. Aside from the correlations of price movements presented below, McCloskey and Zecher developed a great deal of other evidence supporting the monetary interpretation. For example, they were able to predict the British and U.S. Balance of Payments flows with surprising accuracy as residuals from the predicted demands for money and actual domestic money supplies.

4. Hume, op. cit. These concepts all underwent extensive development at the hands of David Ricardo and the British classical Economists who followed him. Hume and other members of the classical school—with the exception of Nassau Senior—had a flow concept of the demand for money, however. Indeed, even some economists such as Alfred Marshal, who had begun to think of the demand for money in stock terms, continued to rely on the flow analysis in their international monetary analysis. The first economist to correctly state the *stock* demand expenditure *flow* distinction in the hypothesis of the Natural Distribution of Specie was probably Ludwig von Mises, in his *Theorie des Geldes und der Umlaufsmittel* (Munich and Leipzig: Dunker & Humblot, 1912): 206–207. A revised 1924 edition of this classic was translated into English and published as *The Theory of Money and Credit* (London: Jonathan Cape, Ltd., 1934).

5. The model here is essentially that developed in Lance Girton and Don Roper, "J. Laurence Laughlin and the Quantity Theory of Money," *Journal of Political Economy* 86 (August 1978): 599–625.

6. Fractional reserve banking gives rise to limited scope for manipulation of national money stocks under the gold standard. For example, because its notes were held as convertible reserves by the country banks, the Bank of England could alter the reserve ratio—and hence the money stock in Britain—by altering its discount rate. It is sometimes claimed that the gold standard was managed by the Bank of England by following the "rules of the game". These rules supposedly specified that the central bank of a nation should raise the discount rate and deflate when gold was flowing out, and reduce the discount rate and expand the money stock when gold was flowing in. By this procedure the Bank of England in particular was able to limit gold flows—because monetary disequilibria were removed more quickly—and thus England managed to operate on very small gold reserves.

This argument amounts to using monetary manipulation to justify monetary manipulation, however. The only reason England had such small reserves (relative to the money stock) in the first place was because of past inflationary actions of the Bank that had reduced the reserve ratio and raised ϕ. All any nation had to do for the gold standard to work was fulfill its commitment to convert on demand at par.

7. See Milton Friedman, *Monetary History of the United States: 1867–1960* (Princeton, N.J.: Princeton University Press, 1963): 29–44.

8. The price of silver certainly was low. The silver interests blamed this on the "crime of 1873," in which silver was demonetized. There seems to be little evidence, however, that the relative prices of agricultural output had fallen during the deflation. In fact, Jeffrey G. Williamson, "Greasing the Wheels of Sputtering Export Engines: Midwestern Grains and American Export Growth," *Journal of Economic History* 17 (July 1980), finds that real agricultural prices improved in this period. Of course it could be that deflation caused the real interest rate to be high, raising the debt burden on farmers. According to Robert Higgs, "Patterns of Farm Rental in the George Cotton Belt, 1880–1900," *Journal of Economic History* 37 (June 1974), however, nominal interest rates actually fell as rapidly or more rapidly than prices in this period.

9. The restoration of gold convertibility reduced the expected rate of inflation and caused the demand for money to rise rapidly from 1879 to 1882. This produced a Balance of Payments surplus and associated inflow of gold, rapidly increasing the money stock during that period. Only after that did the silver purchases begin to produce intermittent offsetting deficits and a gold outflow.

10. At equilibrium in a no-growth world, gold production during any period would be just sufficient to replace depreciation in the world gold stock as some was lost, some decayed, and some was used up in production processes.

11. This is not to say that R_e itself cannot change. If, for example, gold is a resource that tends to deplete more rapidly than other raw materials, or technological change in gold mining did not keep pace with that in others, R_e would tend to rise over time. Graphically, the long-run supply curve would have a slight upward slope. In this case, as some economists believe, the world economy would experience a mild secular deflation over time. Expectations would easily adjust to such a deflation, however, and it is difficult to believe it would have any real effects if it occurred.

12. Michael D. Bordo, "The Classical Gold Standard: Some Lessons for Today," *Federal Reserve Bank of St. Louis Review* (May 1981): 2–16, and Bordo, "The Gold Standard: Myths and Realities," in Barry N. Siegel, ed., *Money in Crisis: The Federal Reserve, the Economy, and Monetary Reform* (Cambridge, Massachusetts: Ballinger Publishing Co., 1984): 197–237.

13. Friedman, *Monetary History*: 152–167.

14. See Hugh Rockoff, "Some Evidence on the Real Price of Gold, its Cost of Production, and Commodity Prices," in Michael D. Bordo and Anna J. Schwartz, eds., *A Retrospective on the Classical Gold Standard* (Chicago: The University of Chicago Press, 1984).

15. Milton Friedman, "Commodity Reserve Currency," in Friedman, *Essays in Positive Economics* (Chicago: University of Chicago Press, 1953).

16. Roger W. Garrison, "Gold, a Standard and an Institution," *The Cato Journal* 3 (Spring 1983): 223–238.

17. Milton Friedman, "Has Government any Role in Money?" *Journal of Monetary Economics* 17 (1986): 37–62.

18. Robert J. Barro, "Money and the Price Level Under the Gold Standard," *The Economic Journal* 89 (March 1979): 31.

Student Self-Test

I. True–False

T F **1.** The economic balance of payments is always zero.

T F **2.** The U.S. balance of payments accounts can have a positive, negative, or zero sum.

T F **3.** If the United States acquires $10 billion on net in international reserves in a given year, and the current account is in surplus by $12 billion, then the United States must have run a $2 billion deficit in its capital account that year.

T F **4.** Under the gold standard it is logically necessary for price levels in different countries to diverge for a redistribution of the world gold stock to occur through the balance of payments mechanism.

T F **5.** It is conceivable that a large increase in the nonmonetary demand for gold could administer a deflationary shock to an economy.

T F **6.** The mild inflation that began after 1895 was a successful result of the monetization of silver under the Bland–Allison Act of 1878 and the Sherman Silver Purchase Act of 1890.

II. Short Answer (150 words or less each)

1. Explain the difference between the price–specie flow mechanism and the monetary approach to international adjustment as ways in which national monetary disequilibria are corrected under the gold standard.

2. What does it mean to say that the domestic money stock is an endogenously determined variable for a small country under the classical gold standard? What role do the monetary authorities have in the attainment of monetary equilibrium for such a country?

3. Explain: a) why the long-run price level was stable under the classical gold standard and b) how maintenance of the parity and the operation of the specie flow mechanism limited governmental control over national money stocks.

III. Completion Problems

1. Where the U.S. balance of payments account is assumed to have three categorical divisions—the current account, the capital account, and the official reserves account—answer the following questions.

   A. If U.S. import of goods and services exceed exports by $60 billion, and the U.S. imports net official international reserves are worth $5 billion, our capital account must be in _____ (deficit/surplus) by $_____ billion.

   B. If citizens of other countries buy $40 billion more U.S. financial securities than U.S. citizens purchase from citizens and governments of other countries, and the foreign exchange markets are clearing, then the U.S. current account must be in _____ (deficit/surplus) by $_____ billion.

2. The graph below shows a two-country gold coin standard world. The world monetary gold stock consists of 8 billion ounces. The base-year gold price indices in each country are assumed to be unity ($P_a = 1$ and $P_b = 1$ in each nation's base year). Real balances demanded are 4 billion in country A and 2.4 billion in country B.

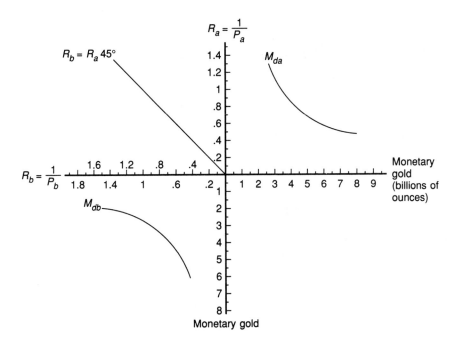

   A. Draw a line in the third quadrant in the correct location and shape to represent the existing world monetary gold stock.

   B. In equilibrium, the monetary gold stock in country A will be $M_{sa} =$ _____ billion ounces. Illustrate this with a vertical line labeled M_{sa} in the first quadrant.

    C. Country B will have a monetary gold stock of M_{sb} = _____ billion
    ounces in equilibrium. Illustrate this by a horizontal line parallel to the
    R_b axis and labeled M_{sb} in the third quadrant.
    D. In equilibrium the price level in country A will be P_a = _____.
    E. In equilibrium the price level in country B will be P_b = _____.
3. The first quadrant in the graph below shows the demand for money in the
    small country of Utopia, which is one of many countries on a classical gold
    standard, and which calls its currency the Utopian dollar ($). The third
    quadrant shows the world gold stock and stock demand for gold, which
    determine its real value (R). Assume that the Utopian government sets and
    maintains the parity price of gold at $12.50.

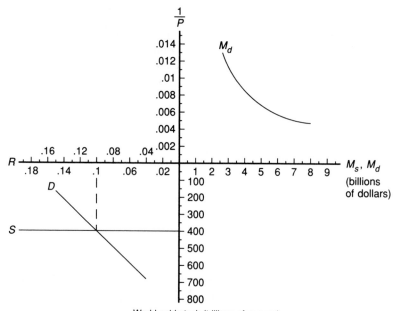

World gold stock (trillions of ounces)

    A. Draw a straight line in the second quadrant that accurately represents
    that par value, and label it *par*.
    B. Given R and par, the price level in Utopia will be P = _____.
    C. In equilibrium the money stock will be M_s = $_____ billion.

CHAPTER 18

International Monetary System: Modern Exchange Rate Regimes and the Balance of Payments

An important property of the gold standard was that the exchange rates between different national monetary units were definitionally determined. If the U.S. government maintained the dollar price of gold at, say $21/ounce, and the French government maintained the franc price of gold at, say Fr 50/ounce, then obviously, $21 was worth Fr 50, and $1 was worth Fr $50/21 \approx$ Fr 2.38. Actual exchange rates varied around such definitional magnitudes only within narrow margins determined by the cost of shipping gold, which was decreasing over time because of technological advances in transportation.

With the demise of the gold standard and the emergence of fiat money systems in Western nations, political agents and monetary authorities were faced with the issue of how to determine exchange rates between their respective monetary units. The basic options were, first, to fix exchange rates through central bank actions at some values determined through international agreement, or second, to allow free market determination of the rates. For much of the post-World War II period the first method was employed, although since 1972 major nations have employed the second. The purpose of this chapter is to develop models to illuminate the nature and operation of foreign exchange markets, both in the abstract and as they have actually worked in the post-War period.

International Trade and the Exchange Rate _____

In order for trade to occur between citizens of different nations that use their own distinct forms of fiat money, there must be markets in which people can exchange and acquire each other's currencies. An American who purchases a Toyota pays in dollars, but Toyota Corporation ultimately wants to get paid in yen, because that is the money in which it pays its wages, salaries, and dividends. For this to occur, some American citizens—usually financial institutions or currency dealers—must be able to acquire yen from some Japanese, who acquire dollars in exchange. Broadly speaking, such markets are termed **foreign exchange markets**.

Because currencies are exchanged for each other in such markets, the prices established can always be thought of in two ways. In the market in which Americans and Britons exchange dollars and pound sterling, for example, the exchange rate (E) could be expressed as the dollar price per unit of sterling ($\$/£$) or it could be expressed as the sterling price per dollar ($£/\$$). For purposes of this book, however, an exchange rate will always be defined as the dollar price per unit of the foreign currency.

As with any other price, an exchange rate must be explained in supply and demand terms. There is a demand for pound sterling, for example, by U.S. citizens who wish to purchase (import) British goods, services, or financial assets. Where sterling demanded and supplied in this market is measured on the horizontal axis of a graph such as Figure 18.1, the dollar demand for sterling can be argued to be a downward sloping (inverse, that is) function of the exchange rate, $E = \$/£$, because a fall in the dollar price of sterling makes British

Figure 18.1 Supply and Demand in the Dollar-Sterling Exchange Market.

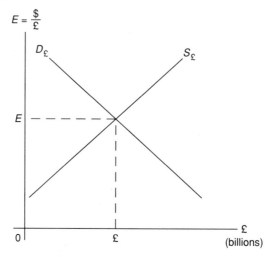

goods, services, and financial assets cheaper to Americans, whereas a rise in E makes them more expensive.

To illustrate this point, note that if $E = \$/£$, it follows that $E \cdot £ = \$$. Therefore the dollar value equivalent (net of transportation cost) of the sterling price of any British good, service, or asset can be computed by the formula

$$E \cdot £price = \$price$$

and will vary positively with the exchange rate. For example, an insurance policy from Lloyds of London with a monthly premium of £200 will cost an American $280 per month if $E \cdot \$1.40$, but this rises to $300 per month if $E = \$1.50$ and to $320 if $E = \$1.60$.

On the supply side, British citizens willingly offer various amounts of sterling in exchange for dollars so that they can use the dollars to purchase American goods, services, and financial assets. The supply function for sterling in this market can be modeled as a positive (i.e., rising) function of E because a rise in the dollar price of sterling reduces the sterling prices of U.S. items to British citizens, and a fall in E makes them more expensive. To see this, note that if $E = \$/£,$, then $£ = \$/E$. It follows that the sterling price of any good can be computed by the formula $£price = \$price/E$, and will vary inversely with the exchange rate. An American home computer worth $800 therefore costs a British citizen £571 if $E = \$1.40$ (because $800/1.4 = 571.43$), but £533 if $E = \$1.50$, and £500 if $E = \$1.60$.

Obviously, there must be some low E at which American goods are so expensive in comparison to similar British goods that Britons would be unwilling to offer any sterling in exchange for dollars. On the other hand, there are exchange rates high enough to make American goods very cheap relative to British equivalents, so that a great deal of sterling would be offered for dollars. Putting the supply and demand curves derived by such reasoning together, the normal excess demand mechanism yields the equilibrium exchange rate as well as an associated equilibrium quantity of sterling (and dollars) traded, as shown in Figure 18.1.

The Monetary Approach to the Exchange Rate _____

An important theoretical question concerns the ultimate determinants of the exchange rate. That is, why does E take on a certain value in equilibrium and not some other? The most influential explanation among economists is known as the **purchasing power parity** (or **PPP**) **doctrine**. By this theory E will settle at a value equal to the ratio of the price levels in the two countries. Mathematically,

$$E = \frac{P_{us}}{P_f},$$

where P_f = the foreign price level and P_{us} is the American price level (designated as P previously, when only prices of American goods were being considered). If $P_{us} = 100$ and $P_f = 400$, for example, E should settled at $0.25.

This is termed **absolute purchasing power parity.** Multiplying both sides by P_f, it follows that

$$E \cdot P_f = P_{us}.$$

Continuing the example, we find that at PPP $0.25 = 100/400$ and $0.25 \times 400 = 100$. In other words, the exchange rate settles at a value such that, translating through that rate, the price levels (and hence the values of money) in the two countries are the same.

This doctrine is illustrated for the gold coin standard in Figures 17.2 and 17.3 (see Chapter 17), where the purchasing power of gold was equalized in each country by reallocation of the world specie stock through the balance of payments. The argument here is that the market excess demand mechanism will, if allowed, adjust exchange rates between fiat currencies to produce the same result in equilibrium. This should occur because if $E > P_{us}/P_f$ such that $E \cdot P_f > P_{us}$ there should be an excess supply of the foreign currency offered for dollars with which to buy the comparatively cheap U.S. goods, forcing the exchange rate down. On the other hand, if $E < P_{us}/P_f$ such that $E \cdot P_f < P_{us}$ there would be an excess demand by Americans for the foreign currency (to buy the cheap foreign goods and services with), forcing E to rise.

If $E = P_{us}/P_f$ in equilibrium, an even deeper understanding of the ultimate determinants of the exchange rate can be obtained by remembering what determines national price levels. From Chapter 7, the domestic demand for real money balances is

$$\frac{M_d}{P} = k \cdot Q.$$

The price level is determined where

$$\frac{M_d}{P} = \frac{M_s}{P}$$

or where (by substitution)

$$\frac{M_s}{P} = k \cdot Q,$$

such that

$$\frac{P}{M_s} = \frac{1}{k \cdot Q}$$

and therefore

$$P = \frac{M_s}{k \cdot Q}.$$

The same is true of the foreign country. If $M_{df}/P_f = k_f \cdot Q_f$, the foreign price level is determined where $M_{df}/P_f = M_{sf}/P_f$, or (by substitution)

$$\frac{M_{sf}}{P_f} = k_f \cdot Q_f$$

such that

$$P_f = \frac{M_{sf}}{k_f \cdot Q_f}.$$

From this it follows that, if $E \cdot P_{us}/P_f$, then by substitution

$$E = \frac{M_s/(k \cdot Q)}{M_{sf}/(k_f \cdot Q_f)}.$$

Or, more simply,

$$E = \frac{M_s/m_d}{M_{sf}/m_{df}}.$$

In other words, the exchange rate is determined by the relative supplies of and demands for money in the two countries. This theory is known as the **monetary approach to the exchange rate**, and it is part of the broader monetary approach to international adjustment (MAIA) mentioned in Chapter 17.[1] In this view all factors affecting the exchange rate act through nominal money stocks and the demands for real balances in the two countries.

Clearly, $\Delta E/\Delta M_s > 0$. That is, a rise in the domestic money stock will increase the dollar prices of foreign exchange, *ceteris paribus*, making foreign goods more expensive, just as it will later raise the dollar prices of domestic goods. Such a rise in E is termed a **depreciation of the dollar** (or a **fall** in the dollar). On the other hand, *ceteris paribus*, a decline in M_s will reduce E, making foreign goods cheaper, just as it will later lower prices of domestic goods if it endures. Such a fall in E is termed an **appreciation of the dollar** (or a **rise** in the dollar) on the foreign exchange market.

The domestic demand for real balances affects the exchange rate in the opposite direction, that is, $\Delta E/\Delta m_d < 0$. Any factor, such as a rise in domestic real income that *raises* m_d, *ceteris paribus*, will reduce the exchange rate (by reducing the demand for foreign exchange), whereas a fall in domestic production that lowers m_d will increase E, *ceteris paribus*. For the foreign country these relations are reversed. That is, $\Delta E/\Delta M_{sf} < 0$ and $\Delta E/\Delta m_{df} > 0$. This makes sense if one remembers that reducing the dollar price per unit of foreign money means raising the foreign money price of the dollar and vice versa.

Relative PPP and Interest Rate Parity

There are many alleged (and some meaningful) qualifications to absolute PPP because of such factors as tariffs (i.e., taxes on imports), transportation costs, and imperfect international substitutes, all of which can result in equilibrium price differentials between domestic and foreign products. None of these qualifications deny the operation of the forces (whether balance of payments flows or changes in E) tending to produce PPP, however, because deviations from such equilibrium differentials will still cause those equilibrating forces to operate.

If $E = P_{us}/P_f$ in equilibrium, it follows that the exchange rate should adjust to maintain PPP as relative price levels change. In the case of a discrete change in one of the price levels, a discrete ΔE should result. For example, *ceteris paribus*, a jump in P_{us} should cause E to rise proportionately to maintain equilibrium. This point is illustrated in Figure 18.2 for rise in the U.S. price level from $P = 100$ to $P' = 137.5$. Note that the demand curve and the supply curve both shift up. A jump in our price level logically affects not only our willingness to buy a foreign currency but also their willingness to sell. In this context it should be easy to see how a fall in our price level or ΔP_f in either direction should affect E such that $E \cdot P_f = P_{us}$ in the new equilibrium.

Figure 18.2 Exchange Rate Adjustment to Maintain Purchasing-Power-Parity.

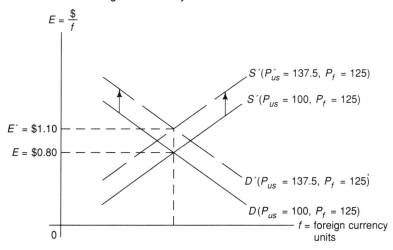

This mechanism should also operate to adjust for ongoing price level changes, that is, inflation or deflation. Mathematically, if $E \approx P_{us}/P_f$ in equilibrium, then $\% \Delta E \approx \% \Delta P_{us} - \% \Delta P_f$, and the exchange rate should rise or fall over time at a rate roughly equal to the difference between the inflation rates in the two countries. If the inflation rate in the United States is 5 percent and that in West Germany is only 2 percent, and these rates endure, then the dollar price of the deutschmark ($E = \$/DM$) should rise at about 3 percent per year. This is termed **relative purchasing power parity**.

Figure 18.3 shows an index of the trade-weighted exchange value of the dollar from 1970 to 1987. An index value of 100 represents PPP, and the base year of the index is 1973 because estimated PPP obtained in that year (almost). The trade-weighted index is a weighted average of foreign currency prices per dollar ($1/E$), with the weights based on the relative dollar values of U.S. trade with the ten nations in the index. Deviations below PPP = 100 in this index therefore indicate a high dollar price per unit of foreign currency (a low value of the dollar), and deviations above 100 indicate $E <$ PPP (a high value of the dollar).

As expected, the index tends to oscillate around PPP over time, but the deviations seem larger and more enduring than PPP theory would predict. The high value of the dollar between 1981 and 1985 is particularly interesting. This, of course, was the period of Reagan administration disinflation in the United States, and in terms of relative PPP one might expect declining U.S. inflation to make the dollar prices of foreign currencies fall. But the approximately 40 percent rise in the

Figure 18.3 Index of the Multinational Trade-Weighted Foreign Currency Value of the Dollar, 1970–1987.

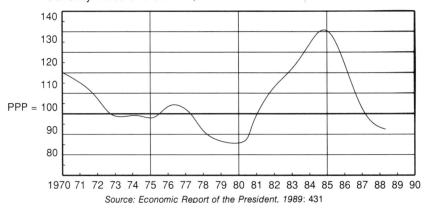

Source: Economic Report of the President, 1989: 431

trade-weighted index between 1981 and 1985 far exceeded the increase predicted by the change in measured inflation differentials.

Some portion of this and other deviations are easy to explain with an extension of the theory. Foreign exchange markets, like financial asset markets, act quickly to incorporate expectations based on new information (concerning, in particular, changes in money supply and demand relations) about likely future conditions into current exchange rates. Thought of this way, the absolute and relative PPP equations should be written as $E = P^*_{us}/P^*_f$, and $\% \Delta E \approx \alpha^*_{us} - \alpha^*_f$. Because exchange rates adjust quickly to the (expected) future relations between national price levels, long before the price levels have actually taken on the new values predicted, E will deviate for some time from actual current PPP. This is termed the **asset market view of the exchange rate**, and it is an important element of the monetary approach.

At best, however, even the asset market view explains only part of the rise of the dollar in the 1980s that was unaccounted for by actual inflation differentials at the time. Consequently, a theory known as the **interest rate parity doctrine** gained some prominence. By this theory financial markets in major trading countries are linked into a single world market. International financial capital flows resulting from and tending to limit real interest rate differentials will cause exchange rates to deviate from PPP. In particular, assuming financial market transactors have rational expectations, the theory predicts that the change in the exchange rate will deviate from the inflation rate differential by the difference between the foreign and domestic real interest rates.

Algebraically,

$$\% \Delta E = (\alpha_{us} - \alpha_f) + r_f - r_{us},$$

and if $r_f = r_{us}$, relative PPP holds. That is, if $\alpha_{us} = \alpha_f$, then % $\Delta E = 0$ as predicted. But if $r_f = 5$ percent and $r_{us} = 10$ percent while $\alpha_{us} = \alpha_f$, E should decline by 5 percent. Indeed, for any given inflation differential, a situation of $r_f = r_{us} = -5$ percent would cause E to fall five percentage points more than relative PPP would predict. The relevance of this story for the Reagan disinflation is that the real interest rate in the United States was very high during that period, as discussed in Chapter 15, due to the large federal budget deficit, the apparent slow operation of the Fisher effect, and the rise in the return on investment in real capital generated by ERTA in 1981. What is more, this caused a large flow of foreign investment funds into the United States, making exchange rates fall.[2]

It seems easy to show, however, that the apparent contradiction between PPP and interest rate parity is illusory. Because the yield on a financial asset is $i = d/p_a$ (see Chapter 3), and hence varies inversely with the price of the asset (and positively with nominal dividends, which vary positively with final goods prices), the effects of interest rate changes on exchange rates could be accounted for by defining national price levels to include financial asset prices as well as those of final goods and services.

By this reasoning, most, if not all, of the apparent deviation of exchange rates from PPP shown by indices such as Figure 18.3 are due to a failure to correctly define and measure price levels and the value of money. Including financial asset prices in the U.S. price index during the disinflation period of 1981 to 1985, for example, would result in a more accurate measure of the U.S. inflation rate. If foreign price levels were then treated the same way, a more correct measure of inflation differentials would result, and exchange rates would be much closer to measured PPP.

The Great Trade Deficit and Employment in the Reagan Years

Despite the argument just made it is sometimes useful to consider interest rate differentials by themselves, because the process by which they alter exchange rates also alters the composition of trade. Consider Figure 18.4 in which it is supposed that there are only two nations in the world, the United States and the United Kingdom. In this graph the total demand curve is decomposed into two components. Line $d\pounds$ shows the demand by U.S. citizens for sterling with which to purchase goods and services from Britain. Line $D\pounds$ shows the total demand for sterling by Americans, so the horizontal distance between the two curves at any exchange rate, read from the horizontal axis, shows the

Figure 18.4 Current and Capital Account Balances in a Two-Country World.

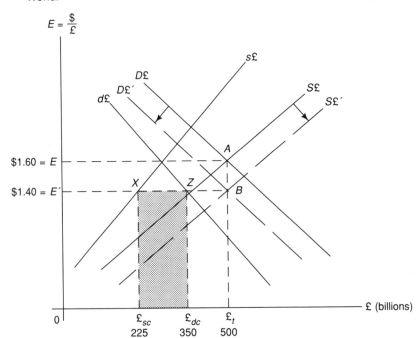

amount of sterling demanded in order to purchase British financial assets such as stocks and bonds.

The sterling supply curve is similarly decomposed. Line $s\pounds$ shows the amount of sterling offered at each exchange rate for dollars with which to purchase American goods and services. Line $S\pounds$ shows the total sterling supply, so the horizontal distance between the two curves at any exchange rate, read from the axis, shows the amount of sterling offered for dollars with which to purchase American financial assets.

In the initial situation, the market is clearing at $E = \$1.60$, at which total sterling purchased by Americans is $\pounds_t = \pounds 500$ billion. It follows that the total dollar value of American imports of all items from Britain is $IM_{us} = E \cdot \pounds_t = \$1.60 \times 500$ billion, or $\$800$ billion. But the $\$800$ billion acquired by British citizens for $\pounds 500$ billion is used to import goods, services, and financial assets from the United States, so $IM_{uk} = \$800$ billion also, and because our imports are their exports and their imports are our exports, $BOP_{us} = BOP_{uk} = 0$. Note also that in the initial situation $d\pounds$ and $s\pounds$ intersect at equilibrium E, so the current account balances are also zero for both nations, and by implication (because the exchange market is clearing), so are the capital account balances.

Now assume that the real interest rate rises in the United States (making $r_{us} > r_{uk}$), perhaps because of an increase in the federal deficit that is not monetized. This causes two things to happen: First, there will be a decrease in American demand for British financial assets, as some American investors decide to invest a large portion of their funds at home. This reduces total American demand for sterling to some $D£'$ as shown. Second, the total supply of sterling offered for dollars will shift out to some $S£'$ as British investors are motivated to invest some additional portion of their funds in the United States rather than in Britain. For simplicity these shifts are assumed proportional, so that $\Delta £_t = 0$.

The fall in the exchange rate such that $E < P_{us}/P_{uk}$ as measured by conventional indices, disturbs the current and capital account balances, although the overall BOP = 0 for both nations as long as the market clears. U.S. imports of current account items (i.e., goods and services) can be found from the $d£$ curve, and U.S. exports of current account items can be read from the $s£$ curve. U.S. current account imports (British Current Account exports) total $E' \cdot £_{dc} =$ 1.40×350 billion = \$490 billion. U.S. current account exports (British imports) total $E \cdot £_{sc} = 1.40 \times 225$ billion = \$315 billion. The U.S. current account balance (exports minus imports) is therefore \$315 billion − \$490 billion = −\$175 billion. In the graph this deficit (British surplus) is shown by the shaded rectangle $£_{sc}xz£_{dc}$.

The U.S. capital account imports (investment in Britain, or British capital exports) can be read in sterling values from the horizontal axis as the difference between total sterling acquired by Americans and that portion acquired to make current account purchases with, or $£_t − £_{dc} = £500 − £350 = £150$ billion. The dollar value is $E' \cdot (£_t − £_{dc}) = \$1.40 \times 150$ billion = \$210 billion. In Figure 18.4 this is represented by area $£_{dc}zB£_t$.

The U.S. capital account exports (British capital imports, or investment in the United States) can be read in sterling value on the horizontal axis as the difference between total sterling sold for dollars and that portion which Britons sell for dollars with which to import American current account items, or $£_t − £_{sc} = £500$ billion $− £225$ billion = £275 billion. In dollars this is $E' \cdot (£_t − £_{sc}) = \$1.40 \times 275$ billion = \$385 billion, represented by rectangle $£_{sc}xB£_t$. The U.S. capital account balance, exports minus imports, is then easily computed as \$385 billion − \$210 billion = \$175 billion, and this surplus is identical to the U.S. current account deficit.

Although the argument here is simplified, something very much like this seems to be what happened to the United States in the 1981 to 1985 period. It is harder to explain why the trade and current account deficits persisted after 1986 (although at reduced levels, both in real and nominal magnitudes), when the exchange index fell below 100 (the dollar decreased in value until $E >$ PPP as measured by conventional indices).

There is one more important point to make here. During this entire period the American television networks and popular press, focusing myopically on the effects of the great trade and current account deficits, created a climate of virtual xenophobic hysteria concerning alleged loss of employment as a result of Americans purchasing a larger dollar value of goods and services from foreigners (particularly Japanese) than we were selling abroad. In virtually none of the media stories was it recognized that the U.S. current account deficit was matched by a capital account surplus or that such increased American and foreign investment in the United States generates increased employment, output, and income, offsetting any lost through the current account. If the capital account was mentioned at all it was said that we were "selling off America," as if some (unspecified) future disaster must result from foreign investment.[3]

Figure 18.5 plots as Cartesian coordinates the current account deficit as a percentage of GNP and civilian employment as a percentage of the population for each year from 1970 to 1986; the year is shown first, with e/N and Deficit/GNP listed in parentheses. It is immediately observ-

Figure 18.5 The Current Account Deficit and Employment, 1970–1986.

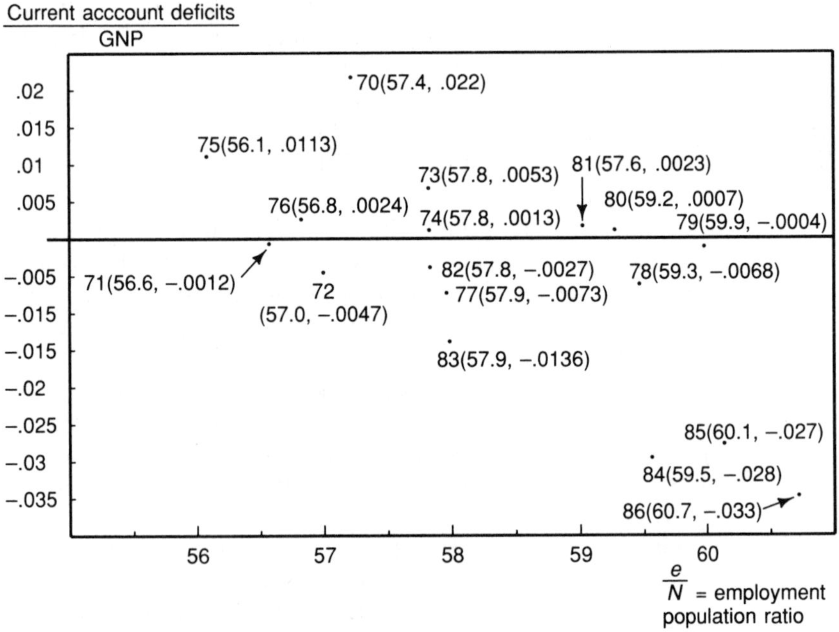

Current acccount deficits / GNP

$$\frac{e}{N} = \text{employment population ratio}$$

Source: Economic Report of the President, 1989: 308, 349, and 424

able that larger relative current account deficits are associated with higher—not lower—employment rates in this period. Indeed, the employment rate reached its highest levels in decades precisely in those years, 1984 to 1986, which had the highest relative current account deficits. Of course other factors, such as the Reagan tax reductions and the erosion of the real value of the minimum wage, were operating to raise employment in this period and might have masked a negative net employment effect of the deficit. There seems to be little evidence here, however, that any such negative net effect—of significant magnitude—existed.[4]

Exchange Market Intervention and the Balance of Payments

It has been pointed out that the economic balance of payments between a pair of countries is zero as long as the foreign exchange market clears. But what if an exchange rate is above or below equilibrium? Consider Figure 18.6, which shows the exchange market between U.S. dollars and West German deutschmarks (DM). Suppose that $P_{us} = 120$ and $P_g = 200$, so that the initial equilibrium exchange rate is $E = \$0.60$. Now suppose that, simultaneously, an excess demand for money appears in the United States (because of either a

Figure 18.6 Disequilibrium in the Dollar-Deutschmark Exchange Market.

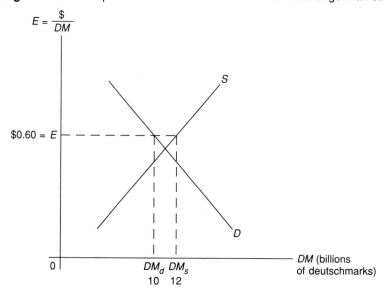

decline in M_s or a rise in m_d) and an excess money stock appears in Germany (because of either a rise in M_{sg} or a decline in m_{dg}).

Remembering the monetary approach to the exchange rate, both of these events act to reduce E. That is, the supply and demand curves shown in Figure 18.6 have both just shifted downward from an initial intersection at $E = \$0.60$, which is not shown.[5] Assuming (for expositional purposes) that the exchange rate does not decline instantly as the curves shift downward, an excess supply of marks offered for dollars appears. If neither government intervenes, the short side of the market, the quantity demanded by private American citizens, determines the quantity that transacts, and the economic BOP still equals zero for both nations.

In this particular case, where $E = \$0.60$ and the quantity of marks demanded by American citizens is $DM_d = DM\ 10$ billion, U.S. imports of all German items (goods, services, and securities) will total $IM_{us} = E \cdot DM_d = \$0.60 \times 10\ \text{billion} = \$6\ \text{billion}$. Because West Germans are only able to trade DM 10 billion for (6 billion) dollars with which to purchase American goods, services, and securities, that is the dollar value of their imports from the United States. And because our imports are their exports and their imports are our exports, $IM_{us} = EX_{us}$ and $IM_g = EX_g$.

Of course, it has been stressed in this book that foreign exchange markets are efficient and that exchange rates adjust very quickly to clear the market, if allowed. It could occur, however, that either the Bundesbank (the West German central bank) or the Federal Reserve would intervene in this market to fix the exchange rate at $E = \$0.60$ to prevent it from falling to clear the market. To do this, one of the central banks would have to enter the market as an additional demander of marks, in essence shifting total market demand out to the dotted demand curve (the sum of private plus central bank demand) shown in Figure 18.7, which intersects the mark supply function at $E = \$0.60$.

The bank would purchase the excess private supply, offering dollars in exchange. Of course, the Bundesbank could do this only if it had a previously accumulated supply of dollars, and its ability to make such purchases would be limited as that supply depleted. Because the Federal Reserve can create as many dollars with which to purchase marks as it wishes, its ability to fix the exchange rate above equilibrium is less limited, and it would therefore be more likely to do so.

One effect of such intervention is to alter the balance of payments. American private citizens are still able to acquire only DM 10 billion with which to purchase German goods, services, and securities, so U.S. imports are still $E \cdot DM_d = \$6$ billion, and this is also the value of German exports of all items to America. German citizens, however, are now able to supply an additional DM 2 billion marks for dollars

Figure 18.7 Central Bank Intervention in the Dollar-Deutschmark Exchange Market.

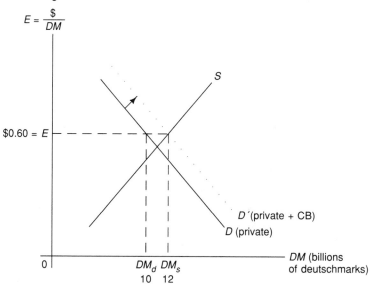

with which to purchase American items, so U.S. exports (and German imports) become $EX_{us} = E \cdot DM_s = \$0.60 \times 12$ billion $= \$7.2$ billion. The U.S. balance of payments in its transactions with West Germany is therefore in surplus by the magnitude $EX_{us} - IM_{us} = \$7.2$ billion $- \$6$ billion $= +\$1.2$ billion, and this is matched by an identical German deficit.

This is not the end of the story, however, as can be seen by considering the effects of such exchange market intervention on the books of the central banks involved, shown in Tables 18.1 and 18.2. The Federal Reserve purchased DM 2 billion, which shows up as additional assets on its books in Table 18.1. The Fed will usually not hold these marks, however, but trade them to the Bundesbank for a form of international reserve asset called **Special Drawing Rights** (SDRs). This

TABLE 18.1 Federal Reserve

Assets	Liabilities
Foreign exchange	B = C + R
+DM 2 billion	+$1.2 billion
−DM 2 billion	
Special drawing rights	
+$1.2 billion	

TABLE 18.2 Bundesbank

Assets	Liabilities
Special drawing rights −DM 2 billion	B_g −DM 2 billion

is why a negative entry for DM 2 billion is shown following the positive entry, and a +$1.2 billion entry is shown under SDRs in Table 18.1. It is this acquisition (import) of international reserve assets that is registered in our official reserves account with a minus sign, and which matches the net surplus in our current and capital accounts, so that the accounting BOP = 0.

In the process of buying marks, however, the Fed creates $1.2 billion, which constitutes an increase in the U.S. monetary base. *Ceteris paribus*, when the German citizens who traded marks for these dollars spend them, the U.S. money stock expands through the multiple deposit creation process by $\Delta M_s = \phi \cdot \Delta B$. The opposite process occurs in Germany. The Bundesbank loses international reserves (SDRs) worth DM 2 billion (which equals $£1.2 billion at $E = \$0.60$), and its monetary base declines by the same amount, as shown in Table 18.2. *Ceteris paribus*, this causes the money stock to decline in Germany by $\Delta M_s = \phi_g \cdot \Delta B_g$.

If we recall the initial disturbance that shifted the mark foreign exchange supply and demand curves down to the positions shown in Figure 18.6 (the simultaneous appearance of an excess demand for money in America and an excess supply of money in West Germany), the effect of these money stock changes is obvious. The rise in the U.S money stock eventually eliminates the excess demand there, and the decline in the German money stock eliminates the excess supply in that country. This would occur without significant change in the price level in either country. At that point the deutschmark foreign exchange supply and demand curves would have shifted back to equilibrium at $E = \$0.60$ as shown in Figure 18.8, because that is still PPP, given that $P_{us} = 120$ and $P_g = 200$.

There are two points that need to be stressed here. First, if what caused the initial excess money demand in the United States was a policy-induced decline in M_s, and what caused the initial excess money stock in West Germany was a Bundesbank action increasing M_{sg}, then the Federal Reserve action pegging the exchange rate (acceded to by the Bundesbank) offset those initial policy actions in both countries. In short, pegging exchange rates at fixed levels limits discretionary central bank control over domestic money stocks.[6]

Figure 18.8 Restoration of Exchange Market Equilibrium After Money Stock Adjustments.

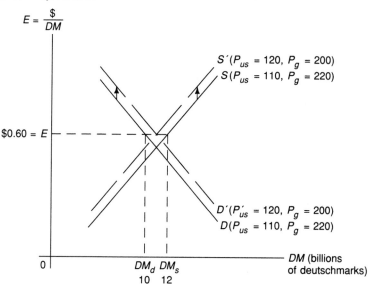

The second point is closely related to the first. Suppose that a rise in m_d caused the initial excess U.S. money demand and that a decline in m_{dg} caused the initial German excess money stock. The resulting rise in the U.S. money stock and the decline in the West German money stock (and the associated payments balances) as the Fed acted to peg E then make it clear that the stock of money is demand determined in each country. An international monetary system based on exchange rates that are fixed through central bank sales and purchases shares both of these qualities with the gold standard. Important qualifications to this general point are described in the next section.

One more example should be considered briefly here. Suppose that the demand for money rises in a single country (the "home" country), *ceteris paribus* (no offsetting excess supply of money appears elsewhere). Further suppose that this country is relatively small and trades with many others. Excess supplies would be generated in the foreign exchange markets where its citizens purchase other currencies for purposes of international trade, as in the previous case.

As its central bank purchased the excess foreign currency supplies (trading its own currency in exchange) in order to maintain the initial (i.e., internationally agreed-upon) exchange rates, the money stock of the home country would rise, eventually eliminating the domestic excess demand for money. Also, as the home country central bank traded the foreign currencies it acquired back to the central banks of its trading partners for international reserves, their money stocks would decline. In this case, however, the fall in the money stock experienced by each trading partner would be trivial and none would notice a significant decline in their price level. This is the small-country case, and it implies the large-country case, which is the next subject.

The United States in the Bretton Woods System ———

The Hawley–Smoot Tariff caused an international trade war in the 1930s, and, in combination with the demise of the gold standard, generated chaos in foreign exchange markets. After World War II the major Western nations sent representatives to a conference at Bretton Woods New Hampshire. At that conference several agreements were reached concerning the international monetary system. One was that central banks would peg their currencies to the dollar (or in some cases, to the British pound sterling) on the understanding that dollars accumulated in the process could be exchanged to the Fed for gold on demand at $35/ounce.

In essence, the dollar was to be held by other central banks as a convertible international reserve currency, sometimes called a **key currency**. Further, in recognition that the fixed exchange-rate values would often deviate from the market rates, a process was agreed upon by which members could get permission to adjust the pegged values toward market levels if disequilibrium became persistent.

At first the pegged rates were set deliberately low. The nature and effects of this process can be seen from Figure 18.9, which shows a dollar price of sterling that is below equilibrium. As before, if this were a temporary market disequilibrium with no central bank intervention, the balance of payments would be zero. The short side of the market (in this case, the quantity supplied) would determine transactions. American exports (and hence British imports) would be $EX_{us} = E \cdot \text{£}_s = \$1.40 \times 10$ billion $= \$14$ billion. U.S. imports (hence British exports) would be the same dollar magnitude, because Americans would only be able to acquire £10 billion with which to purchase British products and securities.

Suppose that $E = \$1.40$ is the rate agreed upon at Bretton Woods, however. To keep E at that value, one of the central banks must enter the market as an additional seller of sterling, supplying the excess amount demanded by Americans at that value so that, in effect, total market supply intersects demand at Cartesian coordinate $(\text{£}_d, E)$. The effect on the balance of payments between the United States and Britain is obvious. $IM_{us} = E \cdot \text{£}_d = \$1.40 \times 15$ billion $= \$21$ billion,

Figure 18.9 Pegging an Exchange Rate Below Purchasing Power Parity.

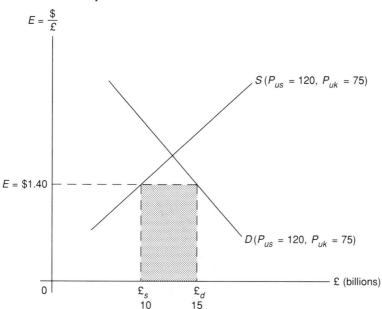

which is also the value of British exports to the United States. Because British private citizens sell only $£_s = 10$ billion to Americans for dollars, however, $EX_{us} = E \cdot £s = \$14$ billion. The American balance of payments with Britain is therefore in deficit by $EX_{us} - IM_{us} = -\$7$ billion. Graphically, this is shown by the shaded area in Figure 18.9.

Because the Federal Reserve could not sell sterling for any prolonged period, it would be the Bank of England that pegged E in this manner. The dollars acquired would enter as dollar-denominated assets on the bank's books, as shown in Table 18.3. Because the dollar was to be an international reserve asset by agreement, the acquisition of such dollars was why the rates were initially set somewhat low for all other currencies. In the case shown, the acquisition of dollars through sterling sales causes the British monetary base to increase by

TABLE 18.3 Bank of England

Assets	Liabilities
£securities	$B_£ = £C + £R$
	$+£5$ billion
$assets	
$+\$7$ billion	

£5 billion each period. The money stock in Britain would expand by $\Delta M_{s£} = \phi_{uk} \cdot \Delta B_£$.

The rise in the money stocks of countries that agreed to set dollar exchange rates low and to sell their currencies to acquire dollars for reserves soon brought equilibrium to the system. The rising British money stock, for example, would increase demand for both domestic and foreign goods by British citizens, shifting the supply curve of Sterling offered for dollars outward, as shown in Figure 18.10. In anticipation of the rise in the British price level, the American demand for sterling will decrease, and these shifts will eliminate the BOP. When P_{uk} rises (say from 75 to 86 as shown), PPP is restored at the pegged exchange rate.

There is one important difference between this case and the hypothetical case of a dollar exchange rate pegged above equilibrium. When foreign central banks pegged E below equilibrium their money stocks expanded (unless they sterilized the effects of the dollar purchases through offsetting open market sales of their domestic securities), but the American money stock usually did not contract. In most cases the dollars were held by the foreign central banks and not returned to the Fed either for gold or SDRs. Also, the dollars acquired by the foreign CBs (exported by the United States) would be registered in our official

Figure 18.10 Restoration of PPP at a Pegged Exchange Rate Through Price Level Adjustment.

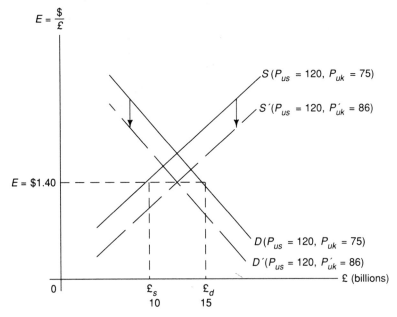

reserves account with a positive sign to match the net deficit in our current and capital accounts.

After foreign central banks acquired stocks of convertible dollar reserves and equilibrium was restored through the appropriate price-level adjustments, the international monetary system created at Bretton Woods seemed to operate well for a time. Tariff barriers were reduced through multinational negotiations, Western Europe recovered from the war, and trade expanded enormously. Few serious problems emerged until the late 1960s when U.S. monetary policy became excessively expansionary; see Chapter 15.

The effect of excess money growth in the United States was to disturb the equilibria which existed at the pegged exchange rates by both increasing the demands for foreign currencies and decreasing foreign currency supply functions as all parties anticipated higher U.S. inflation. Such upward vertical shifts in these curves generated large U.S. balance of payments deficits (and foreign surpluses) as foreign central banks acted to maintain the agreed-upon exchange rates by selling their currencies to Americans.

Foreign governments had three options to deal with the problem. The first was to import U.S. inflation by allowing the acceleration of their own money growth as they pegged E. This at least had the virtue of limiting if not eliminating the BOP by counteracting the upward vertical shifts of the exchange market supply and demand curves as their inflation rate approached ours (such that $\% \ \Delta E \approx \% \ \Delta P_{us} - \% \ \Delta P_{uk} \approx 0$).

The second option was to avoid importing U.S. inflation by a process known as **sterilization**. This means that foreign central banks that were selling their own money and purchasing dollars could simultaneously engage in open market sales of their own securities. This would offset the effects of the dollar purchases on their monetary base and prevent their money growth from accelerating. The problem with that option was that their balance of payments surpluses (and the U.S. deficit) would become permanent and would increase as U.S. inflation continued accelerating.

A third option was to periodically **revalue the foreign currency** (or **devalue the dollar**) through a discrete upward adjustment in the pegged level of E. The problem with this option was that the international monetary authorities could not keep such intentions, nor their likely time of occurrence, a secret from the financial community. When word leaked out, a crisis was generated immediately as transactors in the foreign exchange market all tried to either get into (or stay in) the appreciating (foreign) currency, shifting the supply and demand curves upward more, magnifying the disequilibrium, and forcing the revaluation. This occurred several times during the period 1968 to 1971.

None of these options were good. The overall U.S. balance of payments deficit kept rising. Eventually, foreign central bankers became tired of accumulating larger stocks of dollars that were rapidly losing value, so they began exchanging them to the Federal Reserve for gold at the agreed-upon rate. Faced with an accelerating decline in the U.S. gold stock and potential loss of control over our money stock (as the loss of gold reserves offset the open market security purchases used by the Fed to increase M_s), President Nixon "closed the gold window" (i.e., stopped converting dollars to gold) in August 1971. Other countries immediately stopped pegging exchange rates and allowed them to float to market levels. This ended the Bretton Woods system.[7]

Floating Rates and Exchange Market Stability

The emergence of the floating exchange-rate system immediately ended the balance of payments problem as exchange markets were allowed to clear at market levels. It also gave central banks more complete control over their domestic money stocks, because monetary policy actions would cause the exchange rate to adjust and no longer cause offsetting changes in international reserves. In essence, equilibrium is produced by real balance effects involving changes in both the internal and external value of the dollar, as explained in Chapter 5.

This solution, which had long been advocated by Milton Friedman and other monetarists, would have been adopted earlier had it not been for fears that market exchange rates would fluctuate widely and discourage a large amount of international trade. A good deal of such trade is conducted on a credit basis, and exchange rate fluctuations introduce an element of risk. Indeed, much of the reason for the initial pegging of exchange rates under Bretton Woods was to achieve the advantages of the gold standard—the stable exchange rates and enhanced trade—without the perceived disadvantages, the necessity for conversion of currency by citizens that limited government control over national money stocks.

As a matter of fact, exchange rates have fluctuated widely in the floating-rate period—actually rather more than Friedman and others predicted—but there seems to be little evidence that the growth of trade has been reduced by this factor.[8] It is true, however, that exchange rate fluctuations have not only been large relative to PPP considerations but have also been associated in the 1980s with large Current and (offsetting) capital account imbalances. This may be a result of the large federal budget deficits and Reagan tax reductions that raised real interest rates in the United States, as previously argued.

Some other causes of the exchange rate variability are clear. For one, having gained control over their domestic money stocks, national central banks have pursued different monetary policies with divergent, and in many cases highly variable, monetary growth rates. For another, governments have periodically intervened in the foreign exchange markets, ostensibly to limit exchange rate fluctuations, although it is arguable that such periodic interventions are hardly stabilizing, may have had other motives, and may even account for a good deal of the observed instability. As a consequence of such periodic interventions, the current system is often termed a "dirty float."

Some economists have advocated a return to a Bretton Woods type of system, perhaps based on **target zones** (or bands), within which exchange rates would be allowed to float. Central bank intervention would then occur only when exchange rates moved outside the bands.[9] It seems likely, however, that such target zones would delay and not prevent the appearance of the sort of balance of payments crises that plagued the Bretton Woods system, because they would not directly attack the divergent national monetary policies that pressure changes in exchange rates.

One proposed reform that addresses this problem and which would eliminate exchange rate instability, is to institute a (Western) world central bank with a single world currency, or at least a small number of regional central banks based on common "currency areas" comprising large groups of nations. Some movement in this direction has been stimulated lately by the agreement of the European Common Market countries to create a common European currency, the ECU, as well as a common European central bank by 1992.

Opposition to this type of solution to the problems of divergent national monetary policies and exchange rate instability is rather strong, however. It might merely substitute a worse problem. The potential inflationary hazard posed by a single central bank with discretionary control over the money stock of the entire Western world (or a large part of it) intimidates many economists. Also, national political elites hesitate to yield the power to control national money stocks for internal policy objectives, although some will certainly support such a proposal if they think that *they* might end up with significant control over the world money stock.

An alternative proposed by economists such as Robert Mundel is to restore the gold standard.[10] This might occur through international agreement. Restoring gold convertibility by citizens for national currencies would stabilize exchange rates and divest national governments of the power to manipulate money growth for internal policy objectives. For reasons discussed extensively in chapter 17, opposition to a gold standard is strong. Although gold standard advocates have been gaining support, their numbers are still small, and a reform of that type seems unlikely in the near future.

A simpler reform would be to enact legal or constitutional fixed rate money growth rules in trading countries. If the United States did this, many other nations might follow. (Such international demonstration effects have recently operated in the cases of the Reagan tax reductions and the Thatcher denationalizations). An effort could also be made to encourage other nations, by treaty or international agreement, to institute such rules. In either case, money growth and inflation rates would then be more stable and predictable, and exchange rate variability would be greatly reduced.

This type of reform also has too few advocates at present to attain institutionalization in the near future. Indeed, it is characteristic of the state of macroeconomics (and hence policy advice) at this time, that it consists of several strong schools of thought, with no concensus or established orthodoxy. In this situation of stable theoretical equilibrium it seems apparent that the present system of national discretionary control over fiat money stocks combined with floating exchange rates will continue unless another severe crisis forces a reform.

Summary

The major points of this chapter can be summarized as follows.

1. International trade requires international exchange of moneys. Domestic and foreign monetary units trade at rates of exchange determined by supplies and demands in the foreign exchange markets.

2. Where a dollar–foreign-currency exchange rate is defined as the dollar price per unit of the foreign money, or $E = \$/f$, a rise in E makes the goods and services of that country more expensive to Americans and makes our goods and services cheaper to the foreigners, *ceteris paribus*. A decline in E has the opposite effect.

3. Theoretically, the market should set the exchange rate at an equilibrium value equal to the ratio of the domestic and foreign price levels such that, comparing through the exchange rate, the price levels and the values of money are the same. This is a condition known as absolute purchasing-power parity.

4. Because the value of money is determined in each country by the nominal money stock and the demand for real balances, it is arguable that all factors affecting an exchange rate operate through relative money demands and supplies in the two nations. This theory is known as the monetary approach to the exchange rate.

5. Given absolute PPP, an exchange rate should adjust to maintain that relationship as relative national price levels change. For ongoing changes, the rate of change in the exchange rate over time should equal the difference between the domestic and foreign inflation rates. This is known as relative purchasing power parity.

6. Empirically, although absolute and relative PPP seem valid in the long run, conventional indices show significant and enduring deviations, particularly in the 1980s.

7. Some part of such deviations can be explained by recognizing that foreign exchange markets are asset markets, which rapidly adjust exchange rates in the present to values consistent with expected future price levels. This is a basic assumption of the monetary approach.

8. Another important explanation, known as interest rate parity, predicts that international capital flows will cause exchange rate movements to deviate from relative PPP, and hence from absolute PPP, over time by the difference between foreign and domestic real interest rates.

9. Such investment flows, caused by high domestic real interest rates, seem to have caused the overvaluation of the dollar in the early and mid-1980s. Common claims that the associated trade and current account deficits caused net domestic employment loss seem dubious, however.

10. Under an international fiat money system, central banks can peg exchange rates at chosen levels through purchases and sales of foreign and domestic currencies.

11. When national monetary disequilibria occur and one or more central banks intervene to prevent exchange rate change, the effect is to generate balance of payments flows and to alter national money stocks (and in some cases, price levels) in such a way as to remove the monetary disequilibrium.

12. If such a monetary disequilibrium originates in open market operations (or other monetary policy actions) in a particular country, the effect of the subsequent central bank actions maintaining the fixed exchange rate is to offset the effects of the initial monetary policy actions on that nation's money stock. Fixing exchange rates therefore limits central bank control over national money stocks.

13. When a nation is large relative to the world economy and/or when its currency is a key currency, held by other central banks as an international reserve asset, it retains control of its domestic money stock. The United States was a key-currency country under the Bretton Woods system.

14. Excessive U.S. money growth in the late 1960s and early 1970s generated chronic balance of payments disequilibria and worldwide inflation as foreign central banks bought dollars and sold their own currencies in order to maintain pegged rates at treaty values. The system ended by a U.S. decision in 1971 after increasing foreign central bank trades of dollars for gold threatened the United States not only with loss of its gold stock but also with loss of control over its money stock.

15. The subsequent movement of exchange rates to equilibrium values eliminated the balance of payments disequilibria and allowed nations to follow independent monetary policies. Exchange rate fluctuations have been large under the dirty-float system, however, and this has generated some concern and many proposals for reform.

Notes

1. For a basic, readable discussion of the MAIA see Michael Connolly, "The Monetary Approach to an Open Economy: The Fundamental Theory," in Bluford H. Putnam and D. Sykes Wilford, eds., *The Monetary Approach to International Adjustment* (New York: Praeger Publishers, 1979): 6–18.

2. Variations of this explanation for the large appreciation of the dollar in this period have been made by many economists. See, for example, Rudiger Dornbush, "The Overvalued Dollar," *Lloyds Bank Review*, No. 152 (April 1984): 1–12.

3. The closest thing to a reasonable argument being made here is that we are incurring debt that must be paid off in the future. To the extent that debt is being incurred, however, we are not "selling off America"—debt is not equity—and to the extent the investments are in equity, we are not incurring debt. And in any case, the investments are generating the real production and income from which any such dividend or interest payments will be made. Americans gain in this process as employees and as consumers, both now and in the future, because the investments are helping to regenerate and modernize the physical capital stock in the United States. See Mack Ott, "Is America Being Sold Out?" *Federal Reserve Bank of St. Louis Review* (March/April 1989): 47–64.

4. For an excellent and lucid discussion of the alleged harm from such deficits, see K. Alec Chrystal and Geoffrey E. Wood, "Are Trade Deficits a Problem?" *Federal Reserve Bank of St. Louis Review* (January/February 1988): 3–11.

5. The amount of the downward shift is determined by the new anticipated PPP. Assume that $E = \$0.60$ initially because $P_{us} = 120$ and $P_g = 200$, so that $P_{us}/P_g = 120/200 = .6$. By ignoring real interest rate distortions for simplicity, if the magnitudes of the excess money demand in the United States and excess supply in West Germany were such that it was expected to take a real balance effect through a price level reduction to 110 to eliminate the U.S. excess demand and a price level increase to 220 to eliminate the German excess money stock, then the new intersection of the curves would be at $E' = \$0.50$.

6. For a simple formal model of this general argument, see Connolly, "The Monetary Approach to an Open Economy: The Fundamental Theory".

7. Richard N. Cooper, "Is There a Need for Reform?" *The International Monetary System After Bretton Woods, Conference Series,* No. 28 (Boston: Federal Reserve Bank, 1984): 19–38 and 53–55 contains a good, readable discussion of the origin, operation, defects, and demise of the Bretton Woods system.

8. See Martin J. Bailey and George S. Tavlas, "Trade and Investment Under Floating Rates," *The Cato Journal* 8 (Fall 1988): 421–442.

9. See John Williamson, *The Exchange Rate System* (2nd ed., Washington, D.C.: Institute for International Economics, 1985).

10. See, for example, Robert A. Mundell, "International Monetary Options," *The Cato Journal* 3 (Spring 1983): 189–210.

Student Self-Test

I. True–False

T F **1.** Under a condition of purchasing power parity it should not be possible to make a gain in purchasing power simply by exchanging currencies on the foreign exchange market.

T F **2.** A nation in which the real interest rate falls below that of its international trading partners (perhaps because of balancing its governmental budget), *ceteris paribus*, should experience a depreciation in the external value of its currency, a capital account deficit, and a current account surplus.

T F **3.** Where the exchange rate is defined as it is in this chapter, and P_f is the foreign price level, a condition of $E \cdot P_f < P_{us}$ should result in an excess supply of the foreign currency, according to the absolute PPP doctrine.

T F **4.** *Ceteris paribus*, a rise in the demand for money in Britain should make $E = \$/\pounds$ fall.

T F **5.** The Bretton Woods system established an international regime in which exchange rates were freely set by the market.

II. Short Answer (150 words or less each)

1. Explain the initial effect of the appearance of an excess demand for money in this country on our economic balance of payments under a fixed exchange rate system.

2. Give one empirical and at least one theoretical reason why relative purchasing power parity has been modified by addition of a real interest rate differential to explain exchange rate movements.

3. Explain why it is that countries that had large current account surpluses in their trade with the United States during the 1980s do not appear to have experienced significant increases in their domestic employment as a result.

4. Explain why it is largely futile for a small country in a fixed exchange rate system to attempt to increase its domestic money stock at a rate exceeding that at which other countries are raising theirs.

5. Explain the nature of the mechanism eliminating monetary disequilibria under a flexible exchange rate system and why such a system gives central banks control over their domestic money stocks which they lack under a fixed exchange rate system.

III. Completion Problems

1. Where the dollar–deutschmark exchange rate is $E = \$/DM$,

   A. Fill in the equivalent dollar prices for the West German goods in the following table for the alternate possible exchange rates shown.

German good	Deutschmark price	$ price at E = $0.50	$ price at E = $0.55	$ price at E = $0.60
Mercedes-Benz	DM100,000			
Lufthansa ticket to N.Y.	DM550			
German AA Bond	DM1,880			

   B. Fill in the equivalent mark prices for the American goods in the following table for the same possible exchange rates.

American good	Dollar price	DM price at E = $0.50	DM price at E = $0.55	DM price at E = $0.60
I. H. Tractor	$60,000			
Dodge Ramcharger	$22,000			
Mcdonald's Hamburger	$0.50			

2. The following shows the amounts of British pound sterling demanded and supplied on the foreign exchange market at various values of $E = \$/£$.

E = $/£	$D_£$ (billions)	$S_£$ (billions)
$1.65	15	35
1.60	20	30
1.55	25	25
1.50	30	20
1.45	35	15

   Suppose that the Bank of England fixes the dollar price of sterling at $1.50.

   A. The dollar value of American exports to Britain would be $_____ billion.

   B. The dollar value of American imports from Britain would be $_____ billion.

   C. The sterling value of British imports from the United States would be £_____ billion.

   D. The sterling value of British exports to the United States would be £_____ billion.

   E. If the Bank of England does not sterilize and the money multiplier in the British banking system is four, the British money stock will rise by £_____ billion.

3. Purchasing power parity and interest rate parity:

   A. If $P_{us} = 250$ and $P_{uk} = 150$, absolute PPP theory predicts that the market will set $E = \$/\pounds = \$$_____ (to the nearest cent.).

   B. If $P_{uk} = 260$ and $E = \$0.75$, absolute PPP theory implies that $P_{us} =$ _____.

   C. If $\alpha_{us} = 4$ percent and $\alpha_{uk} = 6$ percent as measured by conventional price indices, relative PPP theory predicts $\% \ \Delta E \approx$ _____.

   D. If $\alpha_{us} = 5$ percent and $\alpha_{uk} = -6$ percent (Britain is experiencing deflation), relative PPP theory predicts $\% \ \Delta E \approx$ _____.

   E. If $\alpha_{us} = 3$ percent and $\alpha_{uk} = 3$ percent when the real interest rates in the two countries are $r_{uk} = 4$ percent and $r_{us} = 7$ percent, interest rate parity theory predicts that E will _____ (rise/drop) by _____ percent.

   F. If the U.S. price level rises 10 percent and the British price level rises 2 percent while $r_{uk} = 6$ percent and $r_{us} = 3$ percent, then E should _____ (rise/drop) by _____ percent.

Index